Open Source

From the Internet's infrastructure to operating systems like GNU/Linux, the open
source movement comprises some of the greatest accomplishments in computing over
the past quarter century. Its story embraces technological advances, unprecedented
global collaboration, and remarkable tools for facilitating distributed development.
The evolution of the Internet enabled an enormous expansion of open development,
allowing developers to exchange information and ideas without regard to constraints of
space, time, or national boundary. The movement has had widespread impact on
education and government, as well as historic, cultural, and commercial repercussions.
Part I discusses key open source applications, platforms, and technologies used in open
development. Part II explores social issues ranging from demographics and psychology
to legal and economic matters. Part III discusses the Free Software Foundation, open
source in the public sector (government and education), and future prospects.

FADI P. DEEK received his Ph.D. in computer and information science from the New
Jersey Institute of Technology (NJIT). He is Dean of the College of Science and
Liberal Arts and Professor of Information Systems, Information Technology, and
Mathematical Sciences at NJIT, where he began his academic career as a Teaching
Assistant in 1985. He is also a member of the Graduate Faculty – Rutgers University
Ph.D. Program in Management.

JAMES A. M. MCHUGH received his Ph.D. in applied mathematics from the Courant
Institute of Mathematical Sciences, New York University. During the course of his
career, he has been a Member of Technical Staff at Bell Telephone Laboratories (Wave
Propagation Laboratory), Director of the Ph.D. program in computer science at NJIT,
Acting Chair of the Computer and Information Science Department at NJIT, and
Director of the Program in Information Technology. He is currently a tenured Full
Professor in the Computer Science Department at NJIT.

D0107908

Open Source
Technology and Policy

FADI P. DEEK
New Jersey Institute of Technology

JAMES A. M. McHUGH
New Jersey Institute of Technology

CAMBRIDGE
UNIVERSITY PRESS

CAMBRIDGE UNIVERSITY PRESS
Cambridge, New York, Melbourne, Madrid, Cape Town, Singapore, São Paulo, Delhi

Cambridge University Press
32 Avenue of the Americas, New York, NY 10013-2473, USA

www.cambridge.org
Information on this title: www.cambridge.org/9780521881036

First published 2008

Printed in the United States of America

A catalog record for this publication is available from the British Library.

Library of Congress Cataloging in Publication Data
Deek, Fadi P.
Open source : technology and policy / Fadi P. Deek, James A. M. McHugh.
p.   cm.
Includes index.
ISBN-13: 978-0-521-88103-6 (hardback)
ISBN-10: 0-521-88103-X (hardback)
ISBN-13: 978-0-521-70741-1 (pbk.)
ISBN-10: 0-521-70741-2 (pbk.)
1. Open source software. I. McHugh, James A., 1944-   II. Title.
QA76.76.S46D44   2007
005.3–dc22   2007019230

ISBN   978-0-521-88103-6 hardback
ISBN   978-0-521-70741-1 paperback

To my children,
Matthew, Andrew, and Rebecca

Fadi P. Deek

To my parents, Anne and Peter
To my family, Alice, Pete, and Jimmy
and to my sister, Anne Marie

James A. M. McHugh

Contents

Preface

The story of free and open software is a scientific adventure, packed with extraordinary, larger-than-life characters and epic achievements. From infrastructure for the Internet to operating systems like Linux, this movement involves some of the great accomplishments in computing over the past quarter century. The story encompasses technological advances, global software collaboration on an unprecedented scale, and remarkable software tools for facilitating distributed development. It involves innovative business models, voluntary and corporate participation, and intriguing legal questions. Its achievements have had widespread impact in education and government, as well as historic cultural and commercial consequences. Some of its attainments occurred before the Internet's rise, but it was the Internet's emergence that knitted together the scientific bards of the open source community. It let them exchange their innovations and interact almost without regard to constraints of space, time, or national boundary. Our story recounts the tales of major open community projects: Web browsers that fueled and popularized the Internet, the long dominant Apache Web server, the multifarious development of Unix, the near-mythical rise of Linux, desktop environments like GNOME, fundamental systems like those provided by the Free Software Foundation's GNU project, infrastructure like the X Window System, and more. We will encounter creative, driven scientists who are often bold, colorful entrepreneurs or eloquent scientific spokesmen. The story is not without its conflicts, both internal and external to the movement. Indeed the free software movement is perceived by some as a threat to the billions in revenue generated by proprietary firms and their products, or conversely as a development methodology that is limited in its ability to adequately identify consumer needs. Much of this tale is available on the Internet because of the way the community conducts its business, making it a uniquely accessible tale. As free and open software continues to increasingly permeate our private and professional lives, we believe this story will intrigue a wide audience of computer science students and practitioners, IT managers, policy-makers in government and education, and others who want to learn about the fabled, ongoing legacy of transparent software development.

Acknowledgments

Many people helped us during the process of writing and publishing this book. Although it is impossible to know all of them by name, we offer a word of appreciation and gratitude to all who have contributed to this project. In particular, we thank the anonymous reviewers who read the proposal for the text and carefully examined the manuscript during the earlier stages of the process. They provided excellent recommendations and offered superb suggestions for improving the accuracy and completeness of the presented material.

Heather Bergman, Computer Science Editor at Cambridge University Press, deserves enormous praise for her professionalism and competence. Heather responded promptly to our initial inquiry and provided excellent insight and guidance throughout the remaining stages. Her extraordinary efforts were instrumental in getting this book into the hands of its readers.

1

Introduction

The open source movement is a worldwide attempt to promote an open style of software development more aligned with the accepted intellectual style of science than the proprietary modes of invention that have been characteristic of modern business. The idea – or vision – is to keep the scientific advances created by software development openly available for everyone to understand and improve upon. Perhaps even more so than in the conventional scientific paradigm, the very process of creation in open source is highly transparent throughout. Its products and processes can be continuously, almost instantaneously scrutinized over the Internet, even retrospectively. Its peer review process is even more open than that of traditional science. But most of all: its discoveries are not kept secret and it lets anyone, anywhere, anytime free to build on its discoveries and creations.

Open source is transparent. The source code itself is viewable and available to study and comprehend. The code can be changed and then redistributed to share the changes and improvements. It can be executed for any purpose without discrimination. Its process of development is largely open, with the evolution of free and open systems typically preserved in repositories accessible via the Internet, including archives of debates on the design and implementation of the systems and the opinions of observers about proposed changes. Open source differs vastly from proprietary code where all these transparencies are generally lacking. Proprietary code is developed largely in private, albeit its requirements are developed with its prospective constituencies. Its source code is generally not disclosed and is typically distributed under the shield of binary executables. Its use is controlled by proprietary software licensing restrictions. The right to copy the program executables is restricted and the user is generally forbidden from attempting to modify and certainly from redistributing the code or possible improvements. In most respects, the two modalities of program development

1

are polar opposites, though this is not to say there are not many areas where the commercial and open communities have cooperated.

Throughout this book, we will typically use the term *open source* in a generic sense, encompassing *free software* as referred to by the Free Software Foundation (FSF) and *open source software* as referred to by the Open Source Initiative (OSI) organization. The alternative composite terms *FLOSS* (for Free/Libre/Open Source Software) or *FOSS* are often used in a European context. The two organizations, the FSF and the OSI, represent the two streams of the free or open source movement. *Free software* is an intentionally evocative term, a rallying cry as it were, used by the FSF and intended to resonate with the values of freedom: user and developer freedom. The FSF's *General Public License* (GPL) is its gold standard for free licenses. It has the distinctive characteristic of preventing software licensed under it from being redistributed in a closed, proprietary distribution. Its motto might be considered as "share and share alike." However, the FSF *also* recognizes many other software licenses as *free* as long as they let the user run a program for any purpose, access its source code, modify the code if desired, and freely redistribute the modifications. The OSI on the other hand defines ten criteria for calling a license open source. Like the FSF's conditions for free software (though not the GPL), the OSI criteria do not require the software or modifications to be freely redistributed, allowing licenses that let changes be distributed in proprietary distributions. While the GPL is the free license preferred by the FSF, licenses like the (new) BSD or MIT license are more characteristic of the OSI approach, though the GPL is also an OSI-certified license. Much of the time we will not be concerned about the differences between the various kinds of free or open source licenses, though these differences can be very important and have major implications for users and developers (see such as Rosen, 2005). When necessary, we will make appropriate distinctions, typically referring to whether certain free software is GPL-licensed or is under a specific OSI-certified license. We will elaborate on software licenses in the chapter on legal issues. For convenience we will also refer at times to "open software" and "open development" in the same way.

We will begin our exploration by considering the rationale for open source, highlighting some of its putative or demonstrable characteristics, its advantages, and opportunities it provides. We will then overview what we will cover in the rest of the book.

1.1 Why Open Source

Before we embark on our detailed examination of open source, we will briefly explore some markers for comparing open and proprietary products. A proper comparison of their relative merits would be a massively complex, possibly infeasible undertaking. There are many perspectives that would have to be considered, as well as an immense range of products, operating in diverse settings, under different constraints, and with varied missions. Unequivocal data from unbiased sources would have to be obtained for an objective comparative evaluation, but this is hard to come by. Even for a single pair of open and proprietary products it is often difficult to come to clear conclusions about relative merits, except for the case of obviously dominant systems like Web servers (Apache). What this section modestly attempts is to set forth some of the parameters or metrics that can help structure a comparative analysis. The issues introduced here are elaborated on throughout the book.

Open source systems and applications often appear to offer significant benefits vis-à-vis proprietary systems. Consider some of the metrics they compete on. First of all, open source products are usually free of direct cost. They are often superior in terms of portability. You can modify the code because you can see it and it's allowed by the licensing requirements, though there are different licensing venues. The products may arguably be both more secure and more reliable than systems developed in a proprietary environment. Open products also often offer hardware advantages, with frequently leaner platform requirements. Newer versions can be updated to for free. The development process also exhibits potential macroeconomic advantages. These include the innately antimonopolistic character of open source development and its theoretically greater efficiency because of its arguable reduction of duplicated effort. The open source paradigm itself has obvious educational benefits for students because of the accessibility of open code and the development process' transparent exposure of high-quality software practice. The products and processes lend themselves in principle to internationalization and localization, though this is apparently not always well-achieved in practice. There are other metrics that can be considered as well, including issues of quality of vendor support, documentation, development efficiency, and so on. We will highlight some of these dimensions of comparison. A useful source of information on these issues is provided by the ongoing review at (Wheeler, 2005), a detailed discussion which, albeit avowedly sympathetic to the open source movement, makes an effort to be balanced in its analysis of the relative merits of open and proprietary software.

1.1.1 Usefulness, Cost, and Convenience

Does the open source model create useful software products in a timely fashion at a reasonable cost that are easy to learn to use? In terms of utility, consider that open source has been instrumental in transforming the use of computing in society. Most of the Internet's infrastructure and the vastly successful Linux operating system are products of open source style development. There are increasingly appealing open desktop environments like GNOME and KDE. Furthermore, many of these products like the early Web servers and browsers as well as Linux were developed quite rapidly and burst on the market. Firefox is a recent example. It is of course hard to beat the direct price of open source products since they are usually free. The zero purchase cost is especially attractive when the software product involved has already been commoditized. Commoditization occurs when one product is pretty much like another or at least good enough for the needs it serves. In such cases, it does not pay to pay more. An open source program like the Apache Web server does not even have to be best of breed to attract considerable market share; it just has to be cheap enough and good enough for the purpose it serves. Open source is also not only freely available but is free to update with new versions, which are typically available for free download on the same basis as the original. For most users, the license restrictions on open products are not a factor, though they may be relevant to software developers or major users who want to modify the products. Of course, to be useful, products have to be usable. Here the situation is evolving. Historically, many open source products have been in the category of Internet infrastructure tools or software used by system administrators. For such system applications, the canons of usability are less demanding because the users are software experts. For ordinary users, we observe that at least in the past interface, usability has not been recognized as a strong suit of open source. Open source advocate Eric Raymond observed that the design of desktops and applications is a problem of "ergonomic design and interface psychology, and hackers have historically been poor at it" (Raymond, 1999). Ease of installation is one aspect of open applications where usability is being addressed such as for the vendor-provided GNU/Linux distributions or, at a much simpler level, installers for software like the bundled AMP package (Apache, MySQL, Perl, PHP). (We use GNU/Linux here to refer to the combination of GNU utilities and the Linux kernel, though the briefer designation *Linux* is more common.) Another element in usability is user support. There is for-charge vendor-based support for many open source products just as is for proprietary products. Arguments have been made on both sides about which is better. Major proprietary software developers may have more financial resources to expend on "documentation, customer support and product training than do open source providers" (Hahn, 2002), but open source products by definition can have very wide networks of volunteer support. Furthermore, since the packages are not proprietary, the user is not locked-in to a particular vendor.

1.1.2 Performance Characteristics

Does open source provide products that are fast, secure, reliable, and portable? The overview in Wheeler (2005) modestly states that GNU/Linux is often either superior or at least competitive in performance with Windows on the same hardware environment. However, the same review emphasizes the sensitivity of performance to circumstances. Although proprietary developers benefit from financial resources that enable them to produce high quality software, the transparent character of open source is uniquely suitable to the requirements of security and reliability.

In terms of security, open source code is widely considered to be highly effective for mission-critical functions, precisely because its code can be publicly scrutinized for security defects. It allows users the opportunity to security-enhance their own systems, possibly with the help of an open source consultant, rather than being locked into a system purchased from a proprietary vendor (Cowan, 2003). In contrast, for example, Hoepman and Jacobs (2007) describe how the exposure of the code for a proprietary voting system revealed serious security flaws. Open accessibility is also necessary for government security agencies that have to audit software before using it to ensure its operation is transparent (Stoltz, 1999). Though security agencies can make special arrangements with proprietary distributors to gain access to proprietary code, this access is automatically available for open source. Open source products also have a uniquely broad peer review process that lends itself to detection of defects during development, increasing reliability. Not only are the changes to software proposed by developers scrutinized by project maintainers, but also any bystander observing the development can comment on defects, propose implementation suggestions, and critique the work of contributors. One of the most well-known aphorisms of the open source movement "Given enough eyeballs, all bugs are shallow" (Raymond, 1998) identifies an advantage that may translate into more reliable software. In open source "All the world's a stage" with open source developers very public actors on that stage. The internal exposure and review of open source occurs not just when an application is being developed and improvements are reviewed by project developers and maintainers, but for the entire life cycle of the product because its code is always open. These theoretical benefits of open source appear to be verified by data. For example, a significant empirical study described in Reasoning Inc. (2003) indicates that free MySQL had six times fewer defects than comparable proprietary databases (Tong, 2004). A legendary acknowledgment of Linux reliability was presented in the famous Microsoft Halloween documents (Valloppillil, 1998) which described Linux as having a failure rate two to five times lower than commercial Unix systems.

The open source Linux platform is the most widely ported operating system. It is dominant on servers, workstations, and supercomputers and is widely used in embedded systems like digital appliances. In fact, its portability is directly related to the design decisions that enabled the distributed open style of development under which Linux was built in the first place. Its software organization allowed architect Linus Torvalds to manage core kernel development while other distributed programmers could work independently on so-called kernel modules (Torvalds, 1999). This structure helped keep hardware-specific code like device drivers out of the core kernel, keeping the core highly portable (Torvalds, 1999). Another key reason why Linux is portable is because the GNU GCC compiler itself is ported to most "major chip architectures" (Torvalds, 1999, p. 107). Ironically, it is the open source Wine software that lets proprietary Windows applications portably run on Linux. Of course, there are open source clones of Windows products like MS Office that work on Windows platforms. A secondary consideration related to portability is software localization and the related notion of internationalization. Localization refers to the ability to represent a system using a native language. This can involve the language a system interface is expressed in, character-sets or even syntactical effects like tokenization (since different human languages are broken up differently, which can impact the identification of search tokens). It may be nontrivial for a proprietary package that is likely to have been developed by a foreign corporation to be localized, since the corporate developer may only be interested in major language groupings. It is at least more natural for open software to be localized because the source code is exposed and there may be local open developers interested in the adaptation. Internationalization is a different concept where products are designed in the first place so that they can be readily adapted, making subsequent localization easier. Internationalization should be more likely to be on the radar screen in an open source framework because the development model itself is international and predisposed to be alert to such concerns. However, Feller and Fitzgerald (2002) who are sympathetic to free software critique it with respect to internationalization and localization, contrasting what appears to be, for example, the superior acceptability of the Microsoft IIS server versus Apache on these metrics. They suggest the root of the problem is that these characteristics are harder to "achieve if they are not factored into the original design" (p. 113). Generally, open source seems to have an advantage in supporting the customization of applications over proprietary code, because its code is accessible and modification of the code is allowed by the software license.

1.1.3 Forward-looking Effects

Is open source innovative or imitative? The answer is a little of both. On the one hand, open source products are often developed by imitating the functionality of existing proprietary products, "following the taillights" as the saying goes. This is what the GNOME project does for desktop environments, just like Apple and Microsoft took off on the graphical environments developed at Xerox PARC in the early 1980s. However, open development has also been incredibly innovative in developing products for the Internet environment, from infrastructure software like code implementing the TCP/IP protocols, the Apache Web server, the early browsers at CERN and NCSA that led to the explosion of commercial interest in the Internet to hugely successful peer-to-peer file distribution software like BitTorrent. Much of the innovation in computing has traditionally emerged from academic and governmental research organizations. The open source model provides a singularly appropriate outlet for deploying these innovations: in a certain sense it keeps these works public.

In contrast, Microsoft, the preeminent proprietary developer, is claimed by many in the open community to have a limited record of innovation. A typical contention is illustrated in the claim by the FSF's Moglen that "Microsoft's strategy as a business was to find innovative ideas elsewhere in the software marketplace, buy them up and either suppress them or incorporate them in its proprietary product" (Moglen, 1999). Certainly a number of Microsoft's signature products have been reimplementations of existing software (Wheeler, 2006) or acquisitions which were possibly subsequently improved on. These include QDOS (later MS-DOS) from Seattle Computer in 1980 (Conner, 1998), FrontPage from Vermeer in 1996 (Microsoft Press Release, 1996), PowerPoint from Forethought in 1987 (Parker, 2001), and Cooper's Tripod subsequently developed at Microsoft into Visual Basic in 1988 (Cooper, 1996). In a sense, these small independent companies recognized opportunities that Microsoft subsequently appropriated. For other examples, see McMillan (2006). On the other hand, other analysts counter that a scenario where free software dominated development could seriously undermine innovation. Thus Zittrain (2004) critically observes that "no one can readily monopolize derivatives to popular free software," which is a precondition to recouping the investments needed to improve the original works; see also Carroll (2004).

Comparisons with proprietary accomplishments aside, the track record on balance suggests that the open source paradigm encourages invention. The availability of source code lets capable users play with the code, which is a return to a venerable practice in the history of invention: tinkering (Wheeler, 2005).

The public nature of Internet-based open development provides computer science students everywhere with an ever-available set of world-class examples of software practice. The communities around open source projects offer unique environments for learning. Indeed, the opportunity to learn is one of the most frequently cited motivations for participating in such development. The model demonstrably embodies a participatory worldwide engine of invention.

1.1.4 Economic Impact

Free and open software is an important and established feature of the commercial development landscape. Granted, no open source company has evolved to anything like the economic status of proprietary powerhouses like Microsoft; nonetheless, the use of open source, especially as supporting infrastructure for proprietary products, is a widely used and essential element of the business strategies of major companies from IBM to Apple and Oracle. Software companies traditionally rely at least partly on closed, proprietary code to maintain their market dominance. Open source, on the other hand, tends to undermine monopoly, the likelihood of monopolistic dominance being reduced to the extent that major software infrastructure systems and applications are open. The largest proprietary software distributors are U.S. corporations – a factor that is increasingly encouraging counterbalancing nationalistic responses abroad. For example, foreign governments are more than ever disposed to encourage a policy preference for open source platforms like Linux. The platforms' openness reduces their dependency on proprietary, foreign-produced code, helps nurture the local pool of software expertise, and prevents lock-in to proprietary distributors and a largely English-only mode where local languages may not even be supported. Software is a core component of governmental operation and infrastructure, so dependency on extranational entities is perceived as a security risk and a cession of control to foreign agency.

At the macroeconomic level, open source development arguably reduces duplication of effort. Open code is available to all and acts as a public repository of software solutions to a broad range of problems, as well as best practices in programming. It has been estimated that 75% of code is written for specific organizational tasks and not shared or publicly distributed for reuse (Stoltz, 1999). The open availability of such source code throughout the economy would reduce the need to develop applications from scratch. Just as software libraries and objects are software engineering paradigms for facilitating software reuse, at a much grander scale the open source movement proposes to preserve entire ecosystems of software, open for reuse, extension, and modification. It has traditionally been perceived that "open source software is often geared toward information technology specialists, to whom the availability of source code can be a real asset, (while) proprietary software is often aimed at less sophisticated users" (Hahn, 2002). Although this observation could be refined, generally a major appeal of open source has been that its code availability makes it easier for firms to customize the software for internal applications. Such in-house customization is completely compatible with all open source licenses and is extremely significant since most software is actually developed or custom-designed rather than packaged (Beesen, 2002). As a process, open source can also reduce the development and/or maintenance risks associated with software development even when done by private, for-profit companies. For example, consider code that has been developed internally for a company. It may often have little or no external sales value to the organization, even though it provides a useful internal service. Stallman (1999) recounts the example of a distributed print-spooler written for an in-house corporate network. There was a good chance the life cycle of the code would be longer than the longevity of its original programmers. In this case, distributing the code as open source created the possibility of establishing an open community of interest in the software. This is useful to the company that owns the code since it reduces the risk of maintenance complications when the original developers depart. With any luck, it may connect the software to a persistent pool of experts who become familiar with the software and who can keep it up to date for their own purposes. More generally, open development can utilize developers from multiple organizations in order to spread out development risks and costs, splitting the cost among the participants. In fact, while much open source code has traditionally been developed with a strong volunteer pool, there has also been extensive industrial support for open development. Linux development is a prime example. Developed initially under the leadership of Linus Torvalds using a purely volunteer model, most current Linux code contributions are done by professional developers who are employees of for-profit corporations.

References

Beesen, J. (2002). What Good is Free Software? In: Government Policy toward Open Source Software, R.W. Hahn (editor). Brookings Institution Press, Washington, DC.

Carroll, J. (2004). Open Source vs. Proprietary: Both Have Advantages. ZDNet Australia. http://opinion.zdnet.co.uk/comment/0,1000002138,39155570,00.htm. Accessed June 17, 2007.

Conner, D. (1998). Father of DOS Still Having Fun at Microsoft, Microsoft MicroNews, April 10. http://www.patersontech.com/Dos/Micronews/paterson04_10_98.htm. Accessed December 20, 2006.

Cooper, A. (1996). Why I Am Called "the Father of Visual Basic," Cooper Interaction design. http://www.cooper.com/alan/father_of_vb.html. Accessed December 20, 2006.

Cowan, C. (2003). Software security for open-source systems. *IEEE Security and Privacy*, 1, 38–45.

Feller, J. and Fitzgerald, B. (2002). Understanding Open Source Software Development. Addison-Wesley, Pearson Education Ltd., London.

Hahn, R. (2002). Government Policy toward Open Source Software: An Overview. In: Government Policy toward Open Source Software, R.W. Hahn (editor). Brookings Institution Press, Washington, DC.

Hoepman J.H. and Jacobs, B. (2007). Increased Security through Open Source, *Communications of the ACM*, 50(1), 79–83.

McMillan, A. (2006). Microsoft "Innovation." http://www.mcmillan.cx/innovation.html. Accessed December 20, 2006.

Microsoft Press Release. (1996). Microsoft Acquires Vermeer Technologies Inc., January 16th. http://www.microsoft.com/presspass/press/1996/jan96/vrmeerpr.mspx. Accessed December 20, 2006.

Moglen, E. (1999). Anarchism Triumphant: Free Software and the Death of Copyright. First Monday, 4(8). http://www.firstmonday.org/issues/issue4_8/moglen/index.html. Accessed January 5, 2007.

Parker, I. (2001). Absolute Powerpoint – Can a Software Package Edit Our Thoughts. New Yorker, May 28. http://www.physics.ohio-state.edu/w̃ilkins/group/powerpt.html. Accessed December 20, 2006.

Raymond, E. (1999). The Revenge of the Hackers. In: Open Sources: Voices from the Open Source Revolution, M. Stone, S. Ockman, and C. DiBona (editors). O'Reilly Media, Sebastopol, CA, 207–219.

Raymond, E.S. (1998). The Cathedral and the Bazaar. *First Monday*, 3(3). http://www.firstmonday.dk/issues/issue3_3/raymond/index.html. Accessed December 3, 2006.

Reasoning Inc. (2003). How Open Source and Commercial Software Compare: MySQL white paper MySQL 4.0.16. http://www.reasoning.com/downloads.html. Accessed November 29, 2006.

Rosen, L. (2005). Open Source Licensing: Software Freedom and Intellectual Property Law, Prentice Hall, Upper Saddle River, NJ.

Stallman, R. (1999). The Magic Cauldron. http://www.catb.org/esr/writings/magic-cauldron/. Accessed November 29, 2006.

Stoltz, M. (1999). The Case for Government Promotion of Open Source Software. NetAction White Paper. http://www.netaction.org/opensrc/oss-report.html. Accessed November 29, 2006.

Tong, T. (2004). Free/Open Source Software in Education. United Nations Development Programme's Asia-Pacific Information Programme, Malaysia.

Torvalds, L. (1999). The Linux Edge. In: Open Sources: Voices from the Open Source Revolution, M. Stone, S. Ockman, and C. DiBona (editors). O'Reilly Media, Sebastopol, CA, 101–112.

Valloppillil, V. (1998). Open Source Software: A (New?) Development Methodology. http://www.opensource.org/halloween/. The Halloween Documents. Accessed November 29, 2006.

Wheeler, D. (2005). Microsoft the Innovator? http://www.dwheeler.com/innovation/microsoft.html. Accessed November 29, 2006.

Wheeler, D. (2006). Why Open Source Software/Free Software (OSS/FS, FLOSS, or FOSS)? Look at the Numbers! http://www.dwheeler.com/oss_fs_why.html. Accessed November 29, 2006.

Zittrain, J. (2004). Normative Principles for Evaluating Free and Proprietary Software. University of Chicago Law Review, 71(1), 265–287.

1.2 Preview

We will view the panorama of open source development through a number of different lenses: brief descriptive studies of prominent projects, the enabling technologies of the process, its social characteristics, legal issues, its status as a movement, business venues, and its public and educational roles. These perspectives are interconnected. For example, technological issues affect how the development process works. In fact, the technological tools developed by open source projects have at the same time enabled its growth. The paradigm has been self-hosting and self-expanding, with open systems like Concurrent Versions System (CVS) and the Internet vastly extending the scale on which open development takes place. Our case studies of open projects will reveal its various social, economic, legal, and technical dimensions. We shall see how its legal matrix affects its business models, while social and psychological issues are in turn affected by the technological medium. Though we will separate out these various factors, the following chapters will also continually merge these influences. The software projects we consider are intended to familiarize the reader with the people, processes, and accomplishments of free and open development, focusing on Internet applications and free software platforms. The enabling technologies of open development include the fascinating versioning systems both centralized and distributed that make enormous open projects feasible. Such novel modes of collaboration invariably pose new questions about the social structures involved and their affect on how people interact, as well as the psychological and cognitive phenomena that arise in the new medium/modality. Open development is significantly dependent on a legal infrastructure as well as on a technological one, so we will examine basic legal concepts including issues like licensing arrangements and the challenge of software patents. Social phenomena like open development do not just happen; they depend on effective leadership to articulate and advance the movement. In the case of free and open software, we shall see how the FSF and the complementary OSI have played that role. The long-term success of a software paradigm requires that it be economically viable. This has been accomplished in free software in different ways, from businesses based purely on open source to hybrid arrangements more closely aligned with proprietary strategies. Beyond the private sector, we consider the public sector of education and government and how they capitalize on open source or affect its social role. We will close our treatment by briefly considering likely future developments, in a world where information technology has become one of the central engines of commerce and culture.

Section One of the book covers key open source Internet applications and platforms, and surveys technologies used in distributed collaborative open development. *Section Two* addresses social issues ranging from the demographics of participants to legal issues and business/economic models. *Section Three* highlights the role of the Free Software Foundation in the movement, the relation of open source to the public sector in government and education, and future prospects. A glimpse of the topics covered by the remaining chapters follows.

Chapter 2 recounts some classic stories of open development related to the Internet, like Berners-Lee's groundbreaking work on the Web at CERN, the development of the NCSA HTTP Web server and Mosaic browser, the Apache project, and more. These case studies represent remarkable achievements in the history of business and technology. They serve to introduce the reader unfamiliar with the world of open source to some of its signature projects, ideas, processes, and people. The projects we describe have brought about a social and communications revolution that has transformed society. The story of these achievements is instructive in many ways: for learning how the open source process works, what some of its major attainments have been, who some of the pioneering figures in the field are, how projects have been managed, how people have approached development in this context, what motivations have led people to initiate and participate in such projects, and some of the models for commercialization. We consider the servers and browsers that fueled the Internet's expansion, programming languages like Perl and PHP and the MySQL database so prominent in Internet applications, newer systems like BitTorrent, Firefox, and others. We also review the Fetchmail project that became famous as an exemplar of Internet-based, collaborative, bazaar-style development because of a widely influential essay.

Chapter 3 explores the open source platform by which we mean the open operating systems and desktops that provide the infrastructure for user interaction with a computer system. The root operating system model for open source was Unix. Legal and proprietary issues associated with Unix led to the development of the fundamentally important free software GNU project, the aim of which was to create a complete and self-contained free platform that would allow anyone to do all their software development in a free software environment. The flagship Linux operating system evolved out of a port of a Unix variant to a personal computer environment and then burgeoned into the centerpiece project of the open software movement. The Linux and free Unix-like platforms in turn needed a high-quality desktop style interface and it was out of this imperative that the two major open desktops GNOME and KDE emerged, which in turn depended on the fundamental functionality provided by the X Window System. This chapter recounts these epic developments in the history of computing, describing the people, projects, and associated technical and legal issues.

Chapter 4 overviews the key technologies used to manage open source projects, with a special emphasis on CVS. The free software movement emerged in the early 1980s, at a time when the ARPANET network with its several hundred hosts was well-established and moving toward becoming the Internet. The ARPANET allowed exchanges like e-mail and FTP, technologies that significantly facilitated distributed collaboration, though the Internet was to greatly amplify this. The TCP/IP protocols that enabled the Internet became the ARPANET standard on January 1, 1983, about the same time the flagship open source GNU project was announced by free software leader and advocate Richard Stallman. By the late 1980s the NSFNet backbone network merged with the ARPANET to form the emerging worldwide Internet. The exponential spread of the Internet catalyzed further proliferation of open development. The specific communications technologies used in open source projects have historically tended to be relatively lean: e-mail, mailing lists, newsgroups, and later on Web sites, Internet Relay Chat, and forums. Major open source projects like Linux in the early 1990s still began operation with e-mail, newsgroups, and FTP downloads to communicate. Newsgroups provided a means to broadcast ideas to targeted interest groups whose members might like to participate in a development project. Usenet categories acted like electronic bulletin boards which allowed newsgroup participants to post e-mail-like messages, like the famous comp.os.minix newsgroup on Usenet used by Linus Torvalds to initiate the development of Linux. A powerful collaborative development tool was developed during the late 1980s and early 1990s that greatly facilitated managing distributed software development: the versioning system. Versioning systems are software tools that allow multiple developers to work on projects concurrently and keep track of changes made to the code. This chapter describes in some detail how CVS works. To appreciate what it does it is necessary to have a sense of its commands, their syntax, and outputs or effects and so we examine these closely. We also consider newer versioning tools like the decentralized system *BitKeeper* that played a significant role in the Linux project for a period of time, its free successor *Git*, and the *Subversion* system. Other means that have facilitated open source development have been the software hosting facilities that help distributed collaborators manage their open source projects and provide source code repositories for projects. We describe some of the services they provide and the major Web sites.

There are many demographic, social, psychological, cognitive, process, and media characteristics that affect open source development. Chapter 5 overviews some of these. It also introduces a variety of concepts from the social sciences that can be brought to bear on the open source phenomenon to help provide a framework for understanding this new style of human, scientific, and commercial interaction. We first of all consider the basic demographics of the phenomenon, such as the number and scale of projects under development, the kinds of software that tend to be addressed, population characteristics and motivations for developers and community participants, how participants interact. We survey relevant concepts from social psychology, including the notions of norms and roles, the factors that affect group interactions like compliance, internalization, and identification, normative influences, the impact of power relationships, and group cohesion. Ideas like these from the field of social psychology help provide conceptual tools for understanding open development. Other useful abstractions come from cognitive psychology, like the well-recognized cognitive biases that affect group interactions and problem solving. Social psychology also provides models for understanding the productivity of collaborative groups in terms of what are called process losses and gains, as well as organizational effects that affect productivity. The impact of the collaborative medium on group interactions is worth understanding, so we briefly describe some of the classic research on the effect of the communications medium on interaction. Like the field of social psychology, media research offers a rich array of concepts and a point of departure for understanding and analyzing distributed collaboration. Potentially useful concepts range from the effect of so-called common ground, coupling, and incentive structures, to the use of social cues in communication, the richness of informational exchanges, and temporal effects in collaboration. We introduce the basic concepts and illustrate their relevance to open collaboration.

The open source movement is critically affected by legal issues related to intellectual property. Intellectual property includes creations like copyrighted works, patented inventions, and proprietary software. The objective of Chapter 6 is to survey the related legal issues in a way that is informative for understanding their impact on free and open development. In addition to copyright and patent, we will touch on topics like software patents, licenses and contracts, trademarks, reverse engineering, the notion of reciprocity in licensing, and derivative works in software. The legal and business mechanisms to protect intellectual property are intended to address what is usually considered to be its core problem: how to protect creations in order to provide incentives for innovators. Traditionally such protection has been accomplished through exclusion. For example, you cannot distribute a copyrighted work for your own profit without the authorization of the copyright owner. The FSF's GPL that lies at the heart of the free software movement takes a very different attitude to copyright, focusing not on how to invoke copyright to exclude others from using your work, but on how to apply it to preserve the free and open distribution of your work, particularly when modified. We describe the GPL and the rationales for its conditions. We also consider the OSI and the motivations for its licensing criteria. The OSI, cofounded by Eric Raymond and Bruce Perens in 1998, was established to represent what was believed to be a more pragmatic approach to open development than that championed by the FSF. The OSI reflected the experience of the stream of the free software movement that preferred licenses like the BSD and MIT licenses which appeared more attractive for commercial applications. It reflected the attitude of developers like McKusick of the BSD project and Gettys of the X Window System. We describe some of the OSI-certified software licenses including the increasingly important Mozilla Public License. We also briefly address license enforcement and international issues, and the status and conditions of the next version of the GPL: GPLv3.

Chapter 7 examines economic concepts relevant to open source development, the basic business models for open products, the impact of software commoditization, and economic models for why individuals participate in open development. Some of the relevant economic concepts include vendor lock-in, network effects (or externalities), the total cost of use of software, the impact of licensing on business models, complementary products, and the potential for customizability of open versus proprietary products. The basic open business models we describe include dual licensing, consultation on open source products, provision of open source software distributions and related services, and the important hybrid models like the use of open source for in-house development or horizontally in synergistic combination with proprietary products, such as in IBM's involvement with Apache and Linux. We also examine software commoditization, a key economic phenomenon that concerns the extent to which a product's function has become commoditized (routine or standard) over time. Commoditization deeply affects the competitive landscape for proprietary products. We will present some of the explanations that have been put forth to understand the role of this factor in open development and its implications for the future. Finally, observers of the open source scene have long been intrigued by whether developers participate for psychological, social, or other reasons. We will consider some of the economic models that have been offered to explain why developers are motivated to work on these projects. One model, based on empirical data from the Apache project, uses an effect called signaling to explain why individuals find it economically useful to volunteer for open source projects. Another model proposes that international differences in economic conditions alter the opportunity cost of developer participation, which in turn explains the relative participation rates for different geographic regions.

The chapter on legal issues recounted the establishment and motivation for the OSI in 1998 and Chris Peterson's coinage of the *open source* designation as an alternative to what was thought to be the more ideologically weighted phrase *free software*. The OSI represents one main stream of the open software movement. Of course, the stream of the movement represented by the FSF and the GNU project had already been formally active since the mid-1980s. The FSF and its principals, particularly Richard Stallman, initiated the free software concept, defined its terms, vigorously and boldly publicized its motivations and objectives, established the core GNU project, and led advocacy for the free software movement. They have been instrumental in its burgeoning success. Chapter 8 goes into some detail to describe the origin and technical objectives of the GNU project, which represents one of the major technical triumphs of the free software movement. It also elaborates on the philosophical principles espoused by the FSF, as well as some of the roles and services the FSF provides.

Chapter 9 considers the role of open source in the public sector which, in the form of government and education, has been critical to the creation, development, funding, deployment, and promotion/advocacy of open software. The public sector continues to offer well-suited opportunities for using and encouraging open source, in domains ranging from technological infrastructure to national security, educational use, administrative systems, and so on, both domestically and internationally. Open source has characteristics that naturally suit many of these areas. Consider merely the role of the public sector in supporting the maintenance and evolution of technological infrastructure for society, an area in which open software has proven extremely successful. The government has also historically played an extensive role in promoting innovation in science and technology. For example, the federal government was the leader in funding the development of the Internet with its myriad of underlying open software components. Thus public investment in open development has paid off dramatically in the past and can be expected to continue to do so in the future. The transparency of open source makes it especially interesting in national security applications. Indeed, this is an increasingly recognized asset in international use where proprietary software may be considered, legitimately or not, as suspect. Not only do governmental agencies benefit as users of open source, government and educational institutions also play a role in promoting its expanded use. Governmental policy decisions, whether of a legislative or policy-driven character, can significantly affect the expansion of open software use in the government and by the public. For example, nationalistic concerns about the economic autonomy of local software industries or about national security have made open source increasingly attractive in the international arena. Lastly, we will address at some length the uses and advantages of open source in education, including its unique role in computer science education.

We conclude our book in Chapter 10 with what, we believe, are the likely scenarios for the prospective roles of open and proprietary software. Our interpretation is a balanced one. On the one hand, the open source paradigm seems likely to continue its advance toward worldwide preeminence in computer software infrastructure, not only in the network and its associated utilities, but also in operating systems, desktop environments, and standard office utilities. Significantly, the most familiar and routine applications seem likely to become commoditized and open source, resulting in pervasive public recognition of the movement. The software products whose current dominance seems likely to decline because of this transformation include significant parts of the current Microsoft environment from operating systems to office software. However, despite a dramatic expansion in the recognition and use of open source, this in no ways means that open software will be dominant in software applications. To the contrary, the various dual modalities that have already evolved are likely to persist, with robust open and proprietary sectors each growing and prevailing in different market domains. While on the one hand, some existing proprietary systems may see portions of their markets overtaken by open source replacements, on the other hand proprietary applications and hybrid modes of commercial development should continue to strengthen. Specialized proprietary killer-apps serving mega-industries are likely to continue to dominate their markets, as will distributed network services built on open infrastructures that have been vertically enhanced with proprietary functionalities. Mixed application modes like those reflected in the WAMP stack (with Windows used in place of Linux in the LAMP stack) and the strategically significant Wine project that allows Windows applications to run on Linux environments will also be important. The nondistributed, in-house commercial development that has historically represented the preponderance of software development seems likely to remain undisclosed either for competitive advantage or by default, but this software is being increasingly built using open source components – a trend that is already well-established. The hybrid models that have emerged as reflected in various industrial/community cooperative arrangements, like those involving the Apache Foundation, the X Window System, and Linux, and based on industrial support for open projects under various licensing arrangements, seem certain to strengthen even further. They represent an essential strategy for spreading the risks and costs of software development and providing an effective complementary set of platforms and utilities for proprietary products.

SECTION ONE

Open Source – Internet Applications, Platforms, and Technologies

2

Open Source Internet Application Projects

This chapter describes a number of open source applications related to the Internet that are intended to introduce the reader unfamiliar with the world of open development to some of its signature projects, ideas, processes, and people. These projects represent remarkable achievements in the history of technology and business. They brought about a social and communications revolution that transformed society, culture, commerce, technology, and even science. The story of these classic developments as well as those in the next chapter is instructive in many ways: for learning how the open source process works, what some of its major accomplishments have been, who some of the pioneering figures in the field are, how projects have been managed, how people have approached development in this context, what motivations have led people to initiate and participate in such projects, and what some of the business models are that have been used for commercializing associated products.

Web servers and Web browsers are at the heart of the Internet and free software has been prominent on both the server and browser ends. Thus the first open source project we will investigate is a server, the so-called National Center for Supercomputing Applications (NCSA) Web server developed by Rob McCool in the mid-1990s. His work had in turn been motivated by the then recent creation by Tim Berners-Lee of the basic tools and concepts for a World Wide Web (WWW), including the invention of the first Web server and browser, HTML (the Hypertext Markup Language), and the HTTP (Hypertext Transfer Protocol). For various reasons, McCool's server project subsequently forked, leading to the development of the Apache Web server. It is instructive and exciting to understand the dynamics of such projects, the contexts in which they arise, and the motivations of their developers. In particular, we will examine in some detail how the Apache project emerged, its organizational processes, and what its development was like. Complementary to Web servers, the introduction of easily used Web browsers had an extraordinary impact on Web use, and thereby a revolutionary effect on business, technology, and society at large. The Mosaic, Netscape, and more recently the Firefox browser projects that we will discuss even shared some of the same development context. The success of the Mosaic browser project was especially spectacular. In fact it was instrumental in catalyzing the historic Internet commercial revolution. Mosaic's developer Marc Andreessen later moved on to Netscape, where he created, along with a powerhouse team of developers, the Netscape browser that trumped all competition in the browser field for several years. But Netscape's stunning success proved to be temporary. After its initial triumph, a combination of Microsoft's bundling strategies for Internet Explorer (IE) and the latter's slow but steady improvement eventually won the day over Netscape. Things lay dormant in the browser area for a while until Firefox, a descendant of the Netscape Mozilla browser, came back to challenge IE, as we shall describe.

The process of computer-supported, distributed collaborative software development is relatively new. Although elements of it have been around for decades, the kind of development seen in Linux was novel. Eric Raymond wrote a famous essay on Linux-like development in which he recounted the story of his own Fetchmail project, an e-mail utility. Although Fetchmail is far less significant as an open source product than other projects that we review, it has come to have a mythical *pedagogical* status in the field because Raymond used its development – which he intentionally modeled on that of Linux – as an exemplar of how distributed open development works and why people develop software this way. Raymond's viewpoints were published in his widely influential essay (Raymond, 1998) that characterized open development as akin to a *bazaar* style of development, in contrast to the *cathedral* style of development classically described in Fred Brooks' famed *The Mythical Man Month* (twentieth anniversary edition in 1995). We will describe Fetchmail's development in some detail because of its pedagogical significance.

We conclude the chapter with a variety of other important Internet-related open applications. A number of these are free software products that have been commercialized using the so-called dual licensing model. These are worth understanding, first of all because licensing issues are important in open development, and secondly because there is an enduring need for viable business strategies that let creators commercially benefit from open software. The first of these dual licensed projects that we will consider is the MySQL database system. MySQL is prominent as the *M* in the *LAMP* Web architecture, where it defines the backend database of a three-tier environment whose other components are Linux, Apache, Perl, PHP, and Python. Linux is considered in Chapter 3. Perl and PHP are considered here. We describe the influential role of Perl and its widely used open source module collection CPAN, as well as the server-side scripting language PHP that has its own rather interesting model for commercialization. We also briefly consider Berkeley DB and Sendmail (which serves a substantial portion of all Internet sites). Both of these are dual licensed free softwares. Additional business models for free software are examined in Chapter 7. The peer-to-peer Internet utility BitTorrent is a more recent open source creation that exploits the interconnectedness of the Internet network in a novel way and is intellectually intriguing to understand. BitTorrent has, in a few short years, come to dominate the market for transferring popular, large files over the Internet. We complete the chapter with a brief look at the fundamental BIND utility that underlies the domain name system for the Internet, which makes symbolic Web names possible. The tale of BIND represents a story with an unexpected and ironic business outcome.

2.1 The WWW and the Apache Web Server

The story of the Apache Web server is a classic tale of open development. It has its roots in the fundamental ideas for the WWW conceived and preliminarily implemented by Tim Berners-Lee at a European research laboratory. Soon afterward, these applications were taken up by students at an American university, where Berners-Lee's Web browser and server were dramatically improved upon and extended as the NCSA Web server and the Mosaic browser. The NCSA server project would in turn be adopted and its design greatly revised by a new distributed development team. The resulting Apache server's entry into the marketplace was rapid and enduring.

2.1.1 WWW Development at CERN

We begin by highlighting the origins of the Web revolution. The idea for the WWW was originated by physicist Berners-Lee at the CERN physics laboratory in Switzerland when he proposed the creation of a global hypertext system in 1989. The idea for such a system had been germinating in Berners-Lee's mind for almost a decade and he had even made a personal prototype of it in the early 1980s. His proposal was to allow networked access to distributed documents, including the use of hyperlinks. As an MIT Web page on the inventor says,

> Berners-Lee's vision was to create a comprehensive collection of information in
> word, sound and image, each discretely identified by UDIs and interconnected by
> hypertext links, and to use the Internet to provide universal access to that collection
> of information (http://web.mit.edu/invent/iow/berners-lee.html).

Berners-Lee implemented the first Web server and a text-oriented Web browser and made it available on the Web in 1991 for the NeXT operating system. In fact, he not only developed the server and browser, but also invented HTTP, HTML, and the initial URI version of what would later become URLs (uniform resource locators). His HTTP protocol was designed to retrieve HTML documents over a network, especially via hyperlinks. He designed HTML for his project by creating a simplified version of an SGML DTD he used at CERN, which had been intended for designing documentation. He introduced a new hyperlink anchor tag <a> that would allow distributed access to documents and be central to the WWW paradigm (Berglund et al., 2004). Berners-Lee kept his prototype implementations simple and widely publicized his ideas on the www-talk mailing list started at CERN in 1991. He named his browser *World-WideWeb* and called his Web server *httpd* (Berners-Lee, 2006). The server ran as a Unix background process (or daemon), continually waiting for incoming HTTP requests which it would handle.

At about the same point in time, Berners-Lee became familiar with the free software movement. Indeed, the Free Software Foundation's Richard Stallman gave a talk at CERN in mid-1991. Berners-Lee recognized that the free software community offered the prospect of a plentitude of programmer volunteers who could develop his work further, so he began promoting the development of Web browser software as suitable for projects for university students (Kesan and Shah, 2002)! He had his own programmer gather the software components he had developed into a C library named *libwww*, which became the basis for future Web applications. Berners-Lee's initial inclination was to release the libwww contents under the Free Software Foundation's GPL license. However, there were concerns at the time that corporations would be hesitant to use the Web if they thought they could be subjected to licensing problems, so he decided to release it as public domain instead, which was, in any case, the usual policy at CERN. By the fall of 1992, his suggestions about useful student projects would indeed be taken up at the University of Illinois at Urbana–Champaign. In 1994, Berners-Lee founded and became director of the W3C (World Wide Web Consortium) that develops and maintain standards for the WWW. For further information, see his book on his original design and ultimate objective for the Web (Berners-Lee and Fischetti, 2000).

2.1.2 Web Development at NCSA

The NCSA was one of the hubs for U.S. research on the Internet. It produced major improvements in Berners-Lee's Web server and browser, in the form of the NCSA Web server (which spawned the later Apache Web server) and the

Mosaic Web browser. We will discuss the NCSA server project and its successor, the still preeminent Apache Web server, in this section. The subsequent section will consider the Mosaic browser and its equally famous descendants, which even include Microsoft's own IE.

Like many open source projects, the now pervasive Apache Web server originated in the creativity and drive of youthful computer science students. One of them was Rob McCool, an undergraduate computer science major at the University of Illinois and a system administrator for the NCSA. McCool and his colleague Marc Andreessen at NCSA had become fascinated by the developments at CERN. Andreessen was working on a new Web browser (the Mosaic browser) and thought the CERN server was too "large and cumbersome" (McCool et al., 1999). He asked McCool to take a look at the server code. After doing so, McCool thought he could simplify its implementation and improve its performance relying on his system administration experience. Of course, this kind of response is exactly what Web founder Berners-Lee had hoped for when he had widely advertised and promoted his work. Since Andreessen was developing the new browser, McCool concentrated on developing the server. The result was the much improved NCSA httpd server.

While McCool was developing the improved httpd daemon, Andreessen came up with a uniform way of addressing Web resources based on the URL (Andreessen, 1993). This was a critical development. Up to this point, the Web had been primarily viewed as a system for hypertext-based retrieval. With Andreessen's idea, McCool could develop a standardized way for the Web server and browser to pass data back and forth using extended HTML tags called *forms* in what was later to become the familiar Common Gateway Interface or CGI. As a consequence of this, their extended HTML and HTTP Web protocols "transcended their original conception to become the basis of general interactive, distributed, client-server information systems" (Gaines and Shaw, 1996). The client and server could now engage in a dynamic interaction, with the server interpreting the form inputs from the client and dynamically adapting its responses in a feedback cycle of client-server interactions. Gaines and Shaw (1996) nicely describe this innovation as enabling the client to "transmit structured information from the user back to an arbitrary application gatewayed through the server. The server could then process that information and generate an HTML document which it sent back as a reply. This document could itself contain forms for further interaction with the user, thus supporting a sequence of client-server transactions."

In traditional open development style, McCool kept his server project posted on a Web site and encouraged users to improve it by proposing their own modifications. At Andreessen's recommendation, the software was released under a very unrestrictive open software license (essentially public domain) that basically let developers do whatever they wanted with the source code, just like the Berners-Lee/CERN approach. The open character of this licensing decision would later significantly expedite the development or evolution of the NCSA httpd server into the Apache server (see McCool et al., 1999; Apache.pdf, 2006). For a period of time, McCool's NCSA httpd daemon was the most popular Web server on the Internet. Indeed, the Netcraft survey (netcraft.com) gave it almost 60% of the server market share by mid-1995, surpassing the market penetration of the CERN server which by then stood at only 20%. Although Netcraft surveyed fewer than 20,000 servers at the time, there were already millions of host computers on the Internet (Zakon, 1993/2006). The Apache server that developed out of the NCSA server would be even more pervasively deployed.

2.1.3 The Apache Fork

As commonly happens in open source projects, the original developers moved on, in this case to work at Netscape, creating a leadership vacuum in the NCSA httpd project. After an interim, by early 1995, an interest group of Web site administrators or "Webmasters" took over the development of the server. The Webmasters were motivated by a mix of personal and professional needs, especially doing their jobs better. Brian Behlendorf, a computer scientist recently out of Berkeley, was one of them. He was developing the HotWired site for Wired magazine for his consulting company and had to solve a practical problem: the HotWired site needed password authentication on a large scale. Behlendorf provided it by writing a patch to the httpd server to incorporate this functionality at the required scale (Leonard, 1997). By this point, there were a large number of patches for the httpd code that had been posted to its development mailing list, but which, since McCool's departure from NCSA, had gone unintegrated because there was no one at NCSA in charge of the project. Using these patches was time consuming: the patches had to be individually downloaded and manually applied to the NCSA base code, an increasingly cumbersome process. In response to this unsatisfactory situation, Behlendorf and his band established a group of eight distributed developers, including himself, Roy Fielding, Rob Hartill, Rob Thau, and several others and defined a new project mailing list: new-httpd. For a while after its inauguration, McCool participated in the new mailing list, even though he was now at Netscape working on a new proprietary Web server. Netscape did not consider the free source Apache project as competitive with its own system, so initially there appeared to be no conflict of interest. McCool was able to explain the intricacies of the httpd daemon's code to the new group, a considerable advantage to the project. However, after Apache's release, it quickly became clear from the Netcraft market share analyses that Apache would be a major competitor to the proprietary Netscape server McCool was involved with. Thus McCool once again removed himself from participation (McCool et al., 1999).

Since the NCSA httpd daemon served as the point of departure for the new project, the new server's development can be thought of as a *fork* in the development of the original httpd project. The new group added a number of fixes which it then released as "a patchy" server. Eventually, they recognized they had to revise the code into a completely rewritten software architecture that was developed by Rob Thau by mid-1995. Thau called his design *Shambhala*. Shambhala utilized a modular code structure and incorporated an extensible Application Programming Interface (API). The modular design allowed the developers to work independently on different modules, a capability critical to a distributed software development project (Apache.pdf, 2006). By the summer of 1995 the group had added a virtual hosting capability that allowed ISPs to host thousands of Web sites on a single Apache server. This innovation represented a highly important capability lacking in the competing Netscape and Microsoft Web servers. After considerable further developmental machinations, the "Apache" version 1.0 was released at the end of 1995 together with its documentation. The thesis by Osterlie (2003) provides a detailed technical history of the development based on the original e-mail archives of the project. Although the appellation *Apache* is allegedly associated with the customary open source diff-and-patch techniques used during its development, whence it could be thought of as "a patchy" Web server, the FAQ on the server's Web site says it is eponymous for the American Indian tribe of the same name, "known for their skill in warfare . . . and endurance." Within a few years the Apache server dominated the Web server market. By late 1996, according to Netcraft.com, Apache already had 40% of the market share, by 2000 it was about 65%, and by mid-2005 it was over 70%, with Microsoft's IIS lagging far behind at around 20% of market penetration for years. More recent statistics from Netcraft credit Apache with about 60% of the Web server market versus 30% for Microsoft IIS.

The review of the Apache project by McCool et al. (1999) gives an inside look at the project. Notably, the major developers were not hobbyist hackers but either computer science students, PhDs, or professional software developers. All of them had other regular jobs in addition to their voluntary Apache involvement. Their developer community had the advantage of being an enjoyable atmosphere. Since the development occurred in a geographically distributed context, it was inconvenient if not infeasible to have physical meetings. The circumstances also precluded relying on synchronous communication because members had different work schedules. The volunteers had full-time job commitments elsewhere and so could not predictably dedicate large portions of their time to the project. Consequently, not only was the workspace decentralized, the uncoordinated work schedules necessitated asynchronous communication. E-mail lists followed naturally as the obvious means for communicating. Mockus et al. (2002) observe how the Apache development "began with a conscious attempt to solve the process issues first, before development even started, because it was clear from the very beginning that a geographically distributed set of volunteers, without any traditional organizational ties, would require a unique development process in order to make decisions." Their procedures for decision making and coordinating the project had to reflect its asynchronous, distributed, volunteer, and shared leadership character, so the team "needed to determine group consensus, without using synchronous communication, and in a way that would interfere as little as possible with the project progress" (Fielding, 1999, p. 42).

The organizational model they chose was quite simple: voting on decisions was done through e-mail, decisions were made on the basis of a voting consensus, and the source code (by 1996) was administered under the Concurrent Versions System (CVS). The core developers for Apache, a relatively small group originally of less than ten members, were the votes that really counted. Any mailing list member could express an opinion but "only votes cast by the Apache Group members were considered binding" (McCool et al., 1999). In order to commit a patch to the CVS repository, there had to be at least three positive votes and *no negative votes*. For other issues, there had to be at least three positive votes, and the positive votes had to constitute a majority. A significant tactical advantage of this approach was that the process required only partial participation, enabling the project to proceed without hindrance, even though at any given point in time only a few core developers might be active. Despite such partial participation, the voting protocol ensured that development progress still reflected and required a reasonable level of peer review and approval. Because negative votes acted as vetoes in the case of repository changes, such votes were expected to be used infrequently and required an explanation. One acceptable rationale for a veto might be to reject a proposed change because it was thought that it would interfere with the system's support for a major supported platform (McCool et al., 1999). Another acceptable rationale for a veto was to keep the system simple and prevent an explosion of features. A priori, it might appear that development deadlocks would occur frequently under such a voting system, but the knowledge-base characteristics of the core developer group tended to prevent this. Each of the group members tended to represent disjoint technical perspectives and so they primarily enforced "design criteria" relevant to their own expertise (McCool et al., 1999). Of course, problems could occur when development was rapid but the availability of CVS kept the process simple and reversible. Relatively routine changes could be committed to the repository first and then retroactively confirmed, since any patch could be easily undone. Although participants outside the core group were restricted in their voting rights, McCool's review confirms the benefits derived from the feedback obtained from users via newsgroups and e-mail.

The *Apache Group* that guided the project had eight founding members and by the time of the study by Mockus et al. (2002) had grown to twenty-five members, though for most of the development period there were only half that many. Refer to http://httpd.apache.org/contributors/ for a current list of Apache contributors, their backgrounds, and technical contributions to the project. The *core developers* were not quite synonymous with this group but included those group members active at a given point in time and those about to be eligible for membership in the group, again adding up to about eight members in total. The Apache Group members could both vote on code changes and also had CVS commit access. In fact, strictly speaking, any member of the developer group could commit code to any part of the server, with the group votes primarily used for code changes that might have an impact on other developers (Mockus et al., 2002).

Apache's pragmatic organizational and process model was in the spirit of the Internet Engineering Task Force (IETF) philosophy of requiring "rough consensus and working code" (see such as Bradner (1999) and Moody (2001)). This motto was coined by Dave Clark, Chief Protocol Architect for the Internet during the 1980s and one of the leaders in the development of the Internet. In a legendary presentation in 1992, Clark had urged an assembled IETF audience to remember a central feature of the successful procedure by which the IETF established standards, namely "We reject: kings, presidents, and voting. We believe in: rough consensus and running code" (Clark, 1992). In the IETF, the expression *rough consensus* meant 80–90% agreement, reflecting a process wherein "a proposal must answer to criticisms, but need not be held up if supported by a vast majority of the group" (Russell, 2006, p. 55). The condition about *running code* meant that a party behind a proposed IETF standard was required to provide "multiple actual and interoperable implementations of a proposed standard (which) must exist and be demonstrated before the proposal can be advanced along the standards track" (Russell, 2006, p. 55). The pragmatic, informal IETF process stood in stark contrast to the laborious ISO approach to developing standards, a process that entailed having a theoretical specification prior to implementation of standards. The IETF approach and Clark's stirring phrase represented an important "bureaucratic innovation," a way of doing things that "captured the technical and political values of Internet engineers during a crucial period in the Internet's growth" (Russell, 2006, p. 48). Free software advocate Lawrence Lessig (1999, p. 4) described it as "a manifesto that will define our generation." Although its circumstances and process were not identical to Apache's, the IETF's simple pragmatism reflected the same spirit that let productive, creative work get done efficiently, with appropriate oversight, but minimal bureaucratic overhead.

By 1998, the project had been so remarkably successful that IBM asked to join the Apache Group, a choice that made corporate sense for IBM since its corporate focus had become providing services rather than marketing software. The Apache Group decided to admit the IBM developers subject to the group's normal meritocratic requirements. The group intended the relationship with IBM to serve as a model for future industrial liaisons (McCool et al., 1999). As of this writing a significant majority of the members of the Apache Software Foundation appear to be similarly industrially affiliated (over 80%) based on the member list at http://www.apache.org/foundation/members.html (accessed January 5, 2007).

Apache Development Process

Mockus et al. (2002) provide a detailed analysis of the processes, project development patterns, and statistics for the Apache project. The generic development process applied by a core developer was as follows:

- identify a problem or a desired functionality;
- attempt to involve a volunteer in the resolution of the problem;
- test a putative solution in a local CVS source copy;
- submit the tested code to the group to review; and
- on approval, commit the code to the repository (preferably as a single commit) and document the change.

New work efforts were identified in several ways: via the developer mailing list, the Apache USENET groups, and the BUGDB reporting system (Mockus et al., 2002). The developer mailing list was the most important vehicle for identifying changes. It was the key tool for discussing fixes for problems and new features and was given the highest priority by the developers, receiving "the attention of all active developers" for the simple reason that these messages were most likely to come from other active developers and so were deemed "more likely to contain sufficient information to analyze the request or contain a patch to solve the problem" (Mockus et al., 2002). Screening processes were used for the other sources. The Apache BUGDB bug-reporting tool was actually not directly used by most developers, partly because of annoying idiosyncrasies in the tool. Instead, a few developers filtered the BUGDB information and forwarded entries thought to be worthwhile to the developer mailing list. The Apache USENET groups were also used less than one might expect because they were considered "noisy." Once again, volunteers filtered the USENET information, forwarding significant problems or useful enhancements to the developer mailing list.

Once a problem was identified, the next issue was "who would do the work?" A typical practice was for the core developers associated with the code for the affected part of the system, having either developed it or spent considerable time maintaining it, to take responsibility for the change. This attitude reflects an implicit kind of *code ownership* (Mockus et al., 2002). Correlative to this cultural practice, new developers would tend to focus on developing new features (whence features that had no prior putative "owner") or to focus on parts of the server that were not actively being worked on by their previous maintainer (and so no longer had a current "owner"). These practices were deferred to by other developers. As a rule, established activity and expertise in an area were the default guidelines. In reality, the actual practice of the developers was more flexible. Indeed, the data analysis provided by Mockus et al. (2002) suggests that the Apache group's core developers had sufficient respect for the expertise of the other core developers that they contributed widely to one another's modules according to development needs. Thus the notion of code ownership was in reality "more a matter of recognition of expertise than one of strictly enforced ability to make commits to partitions of the code base" (Mockus et al., 2002).

Regarding solutions to problems, typically several alternatives were first identified. These were then forwarded by the volunteer developer, self-charged with the problem, to the developer mailing list for preliminary feedback and evaluation prior to developing the actual solution. The prototype solution selected was subsequently refined and implemented by the originating developer and then tested on his local CVS copy before being committed to the repository. The CVS commit itself could be done in two ways: using a *commit-then-review* process that was typically applied in development versions of the system, versus a *post-for-review-first* process in which the patch was posted to the developer mailing list for prior review and approval before committing it, as would normally be done if it were a stable release being modified (Mockus et al., 2002). In either case, the modifications, including both the patch and the CVS commit log, would be automatically sent to the developer mailing list. It was not only standard practice that the core developers reviewed all such changes as posted, but they were also available to be reviewed by anyone who followed the developer mailing list. The Apache Group determined when a new stable release of the product was to be distributed. An experienced core developer who volunteered to act as the release manager, would, as part of that role, identify any critical open problems and shepherd their resolution, including changes proposed from outside the core developer group. The release manager also controlled access to the repository at this stage and so any development code that was supposed to be frozen at this stage was indeed left alone.

The development group achieved effective coordination in a variety of ways. A key software architecture requirement was that the basic server functionality was intentionally kept limited in scope, with peripheral projects providing added functionality by interfacing with the core server through well-defined interfaces. Thus the software architecture itself automatically helped ensure proper coordination, without significant additional effort required by the developer group since the interface itself enforced the necessary coordination. External developers who wanted to add functionality to the core Apache server were thereby accommodated by a "stable, asymmetrically-controlled interface" (Mockus et al., 2002). The presence of this *API* has been a key feature in the success of Apache since it greatly facilitates expanding the system's functionality by the addition of new modules. On the other hand, coordination of development within the core area was handled effectively by the simple means described previously, informally supported by the small core group's intimate knowledge of the expertise of their own members. The relative absence of formal mechanisms for approval or permission to commit code made the process speedy but maintained high quality. Bug reporting and repair were also simple in terms of coordination. For example, bug reporting was done independently by volunteers. It entailed no dependencies that could lead to coordination conflicts, since these reports themselves did not change code, though they could lead to changes in code. Similarly, most bug fixes themselves were relatively independent of one another with the primary effort expended in tracking down the bug, so that once again coordination among members was not a major issue.

Statistical Profile of Apache Development

Well-informed and detailed empirical studies of projects on the scale of Apache are uncommon. Therefore, it is instructive to elaborate on the statistical analysis and interpretations provided in Mockus et al. (2002). The credibility of their analysis is bolstered by the extensive commercial software development experience of its authors and the intimate familiarity of second author Roy Fielding with Apache. The study analyzes and compares the Apache and Netscape Mozilla projects based on data derived from sources like the developer e-mail lists, CVS archives, bug-reporting systems, and extensive interviews with project participants. We will focus on the results for the Apache project. (Another worthwhile study of the structure of open projects is by Holck and Jorgensen (2005), which compares the Mozilla and FreeBSD projects. It pays special attention to how the projects handle releases and contributions as well as their internal testing environments.)

The Apache server had about 80,000 lines of source code by 2000 (Wheeler, 2000), with approximately 400 people contributing code through 2001 (the time frame examined in Mockus et al. (2002)). The Mockus study distinguishes two kinds of Apache contributions:

code fixes   made in response to reported problems
code submissions   intended to implement new system functionality

Rounded numbers are used in the following statistical summaries for clarity. The summary statistics for Apache code contributions are as follows:

- Two hundred people contributed to 700 code fixes.
- Two hundred fifty people contributed to 7,000 code submissions.

The summary error statistics are as follows:

- Three thousand people submitted 4,000 problem reports, most triggering no change to the code base, because they either lacked detail or the defect had been fixed or was insignificant.
- Four hundred fifty people submitted the 600 bug reports that led to actual changes to the code.

The 15 most productive developers made 85% of implementation changes, though for defect repair these top 15 developers made only 65% of the code fixes. A narrow pool of contributors dominated code submissions, with only 4 developers per 100 code submissions versus 25 developers per 100 code fixes. Thus "almost all new functionality is implemented and maintained by the core group" (Mockus et al., 2002, p. 322).

The Apache core developers compared favorably with those in reference commercial projects, showing considerably higher levels of productivity and handling more modification requests than commercial developers despite the part-time, voluntary nature of their participation. The problem reporting responsibilities usually handled by test and customer support teams in proprietary projects were managed in Apache by thousands of volunteers. While the 15 most productive developers submitted only 5% of the 4,000 problem reports, there were over 2,500 mostly noncore developers who each submitted at least one problem report, thus dispersing the traditional role of system tester over many participants. The response time for problem reports was striking: half the problems reported were solved in a day, 75% in a month, and 90% in 4 months, a testimony to the efficiency of the organization of the project and the talent of the volunteers. Of course, the data used in such studies is invariably subject to interpretation. For example, metrics like productivity of groups can be affected by the procedures used to attribute credit, while response rates reported could be affected by details like when bug reports were officially entered into the tracking system.

The social and motivational framework under which the developers operated was an important element in the success of the Apache project. The meritocratic process that enables candidate developers to achieve core developer status requires persistence, demonstrated responsibility to the established core team, and exceptionally high technical capability. The motivational structure also differs significantly from commercial environments, where the project worked on and component tasks are assigned by management, not freely chosen by a developer. From this viewpoint, it seems unsurprising that the passionate, voluntary interest of the project developers should be a strong factor contributing to its success. The stakeholder base for Apache is now sufficiently broad that changes to the system must be conservatively vetted, so services to end users are not disrupted. For this reason, Ye et al. (2005) characterize it as now being a service-oriented open source project.

The Mockus et al. (2002) review makes several tentative conjectures about the development characteristics of open projects based on their data for Apache and Netscape Mozilla development (prior to 2001). For example, they suggest that for projects of Apache's size (as opposed to the much larger Netscape Mozilla project), a small core of developers create most of the code and functionality and so are able to coordinate their efforts in a straightforward way even when several developers are working on overlapping parts of the code base. In contrast, in larger development projects like Netscape Mozilla, stricter practices for code ownership, work group separation, and CVS commit authority have to be enforced to balance the potential for disorder against excessive communication requirements. Another simple pattern is that the sizes of the participant categories appear to differ significantly: the number of core developers is smaller by an order of magnitude than the number of participants who submit bug fixes, which in turn is smaller by an order of magnitude than the number of participants who report problems and defects. The *defect density* for these open source projects was lower than the compared proprietary projects that had been only feature tested. However, the study urges caution in the interpretation of this result since it does not address postrelease bug density and may partly reflect the fact that the developers in such projects tend to have strong domain expertise as end users of the product being developed. The study concluded that the open projects considered exhibited "very rapid responses to customer problems" (Mockus et al., 2002).

Reusing Open Source Creations

One of the key objectives of the open source movement is to build a reusable public commons of software that is universally available and widely applicable. Brian Behlendorf of the Apache (and later Subversion) project has some valuable insights about how to apply the creations of open development to circumstances beyond those originally envisioned. He identifies some general conditions he believes are necessary for other applications to benefit from open products and libraries when they are applied not just in environments they were originally designed for but in updated versions of those environments or when they have to be integrated with other applications (Anderson, 2004). There are three key ingredients that have to come together to effectively support the reuse of open software:

1. access to the source *code*,
2. access to the *context* in which the code was developed, and
3. access to the *communities* that developed and use the code.

One might call this the *3AC model* of what open source history has taught us about software reuse. The availability of the code for a program or software library is the first essential ingredient, not just the availability of stable APIs like in a COTS (Commercial Off-the-Shelf) environment. Open source obviously provides the source code. Source code is required for effective reuse of software because any new application or infrastructure context, like a new operating system, will necessitate understanding the code because embedding software components in new contexts will "inevitably . . . trigger some defect that the original developers didn't know existed" (Anderson, 2004). However, if you are trying to improve the code, you also need access to the context of its development. In open source projects this can be obtained from a variety of sources including e-mail archives and snapshots from the development tree that provide the history of the project and its development artifacts. This way you can find out if the problems you identify or questions you have in mind have already been asked and answered. Finally, in order to understand how the software was built and why it was designed the way it was, you also need to be able to interact with the community of people who developed the product, as well as the community of other users who may also be trying to reuse it. This kind of community contact information is also available in open source that has mailing lists for developers and users, as well as project announcements that can be scavenged for information about how the project developed. That's how you get a truly universal library of reuseable software: open code, the developmental context, and the community that made the software and uses it.

References

Anderson, T. (2004). Behlendorf on Open Source. Interview with Brian Behlendorf. http://www.itwriting.com/behlendorf1.php. Accessed November 29, 2006.

Andreessen, M. (1993). NCSA Mosaic Technical Summary. NCSA, University of Illinois. Accessed via Google Scholar, November 29, 2006.

Apache.pdf. (2006). World Wide Web. http://www.governingwithcode.org. Accessed January 10, 2007.

Berglund, Y., Morrison, A., Wilson, R., and Wynne, M. (2004). An Investigation into Free eBooks. Oxford University. http://ahds.ac.uk/litlangling/ebooks/report/FreeEbooks.html. Accessed December 16, 2006.

Berners-Lee, T. (2006). Frequently Asked Questions. www.w3.org/People/Berners-Lee/FAQ.html. Accessed January 10, 2007.

Berners-Lee, T. and Fischetti, M. (2000). Weaving the Web – The Original Design and Ultimate Destiny of the World Wide Web by Its Inventor. Harper, San Francisco.

Bradner, S. (1999). The Internet Engineering Task Force. In: Open Sources: Voices from the Open Source Revolution, M. Stone, S. Ockman, and C. DiBona (editors). O'Reilly Media, Sebastopol, CA, 47–52.

Clark, D. (1992). A Cloudy Crystal Ball: Visions of the Future. Plenary presentation at 24th meeting of the Internet Engineering Task Force, Cambridge, MA, July 13–17, 1992. Slides from this presentation are available at: http://ietf20.isoc.org/videos/future_ietf_92.pdf. Accessed January 10, 2007.

Fielding, R.T. (1999). Shared leadership in the Apache Project. Communications of the ACM, 42(4), 42–43.

Gaines, B. and Shaw, M. (1996). Implementing the Learning Web. In: Proceedings of EDMEDIA '96: World Conference on Educational Multimedia and Hypermedia. Association for the Advancement of Computing in Education, Charlottesville, VA. http://pages.cpsc.ucalgary.ca/~gaines/reports/LW/EM96Tools/index.html. Accessed November 29, 2006.

Holck, J. and Jorgensen N. (2005). Do Not Check in on Red: Control Meets Anarchy in Two Open Source Projects. In: Free/Open Software Development, S. Koch (editor). Idea Group Publishing, Hershey, PA, 1–26.

Kesan, J. and Shah, R. (2002). Shaping Code. http://opensource.mit.edu/shah.pdf. Accessed November 29, 2006.

Leonard, A. (1997). Apache's Free Software Warriors. Salon Magazine. http://archive.salon.com/21st/feature/1997/11/cov_20feature.html. Accessed November 29, 2006.

Lessig, L. (1999). Code and Other Laws of Cyberspace. Basic Books, New York.

McCool, R., Fielding, R.T., and Behlendorf, B. (1999). How the Web Was Won. http://www.linux-mag.com/1999–06/apache_01.html. Accessed November 29, 2006.

Mockus, A., Fielding, R.T., and Herbsleb, J.D. (2002). Two Case Studies of Open Source Development: Apache and Mozilla. ACM Transactions on Software Engineering and Methodology, 11(3), 309–346.

Moody, G. (2001). Rebel Code. Penguin Press, New York.

Osterlie, T. (2003). The User-Developer Convergence: Innovation and Software Systems Development in the Apache Project. Master's Thesis, Norwegian University of Science and Technology.

Raymond, E.S. (1998). The Cathedral and the Bazaar. First Monday, 3(3). http://www. firstmonday.dk/issues/issue3_3/raymond/index.html. Ongoing version: http:// www.catb.org/~esr/writings/cathedral-bazaar/. Accessed December 3, 2006.

Russell, A. (2006). "Rough Consensus and Running Code" and the Internet-OSI Standards War. IEEE Annals of the History of Computing, 28(3), 48–61.

Wheeler, D. (2000). Estimating Linux's Size. http://www.dwheeler.com/sloc/redhat71-v1/redhat71sloc.html. Accessed November 29, 2006.

Ye, Y., Nakakoji, K., Yamamoto, Y., and Kishida, K. (2005). The Co-Evolution of Systems and Communities. In: Free/Open Source Software Development, S. Koch (editor). Idea Group Publishing, Hershey, PA, 59–83.

Zakon, R. (1993/2006). Hobbes' Internet Timeline v8.2. http://www.zakon.org/robert/internet/timeline/_. Accessed January 5, 2007.

2.2 The Browsers

Browsers have played a critical role in the Internet's incredibly rapid expansion. They represent the face of the Internet for most users and the key means for accessing its capabilities. Three open source browsers have been most prominent: Mosaic, Netscape Navigator, and Firefox. The proprietary Internet Explorer browser, which is based on Mosaic, coevolved and still dominates the market. The development of these browsers is an intriguing but archetypal tale of open source development. It combines elements of academic provenance, proprietary code, open source code and licenses, technological innovations, corporate battles for market share, creative software distribution and marketing, open technology standards, and open community bases of volunteer developers and users. The story starts with the revolutionary Mosaic browser at the beginning of the Internet revolution, moves through the development of Netscape's corporately sponsored browser and its browser war with Internet Explorer, and finally on to Netscape's free descendant, Firefox.

2.2.1 Mosaic

The famed *Mosaic* Web browser was instrumental in creating the Internet boom. Mosaic was developed at the NCSA starting in 1993. The University of Illinois student Marc Andreessen (who was the lead agent in the initiative) and NCSA full-time employee and brilliant programmer Eric Bina were the chief developers. Andreessen wanted to make a simple, intuitive navigational tool that would let ordinary users explore the new WWW more easily and let them *browse* through the data available on the Web. Andreessen and Bina (1994) identified three key design decisions. The tool had to be easy to use, like a word processing Graphical User Interface (GUI) application. It had to be kept simple by divorcing page editing from presentation. (The original Berners-Lee browser had included publication features that complicated its use.) The software also had to accommodate images in such a way that both text and embedded images could appear in the same HTML page or browser window. For this, Andreessen had to introduce an HTML image tag, even though the standards for such a tag had not yet been settled. Significantly, Mosaic also introduced *forms* that users could fill out. It took a short six weeks to write the original program of 9,000 lines of code (Wagner, 2002). Mosaic transcended the capabilities of previous text-oriented tools like FTP for accessing information on the Internet. Instead, it replaced them with a multimedia GUI tool for displaying content, including the appeal of clickable hyperlinks. Mosaic was initially available for Unix but was quickly ported to PCs and Mac's. It rapidly became the killer app for Web access of the mid-1990s.

Mosaic's success was not merely a technical accomplishment. Andreessen's management of the project was nurturing and attentive. He was an activist communicator and listener, one of the top participants in www-talk in 1993 (NCSAmosaic.pdf, 2006). According to Web founder Berners-Lee, Andreessen's skills in "customer relations" were decisive in the enhancement of Mosaic: "You'd send him a bug [problem] report and then two hours later he'd mail you a fix" (quoted in Gillies and Cailliau (2000, p. 240)). Mosaic's popularity had a remarkable effect: it caused an explosion in Web traffic. Each increase in traffic in turn had a feedback effect, attracting more content to the Internet, which in turn increased traffic even further. Mosaic had over 2 million downloads in its first year, and by mid-1995 it was used on over 80% of the computers that were connected to the Internet. An article in the *New York Times* by John Markoff (1993) appreciated the implications of the new software for the Internet. The article ballyhooed the killer app status of Mosaic. However, it did not allude to the software's developers by name but only to the NCSA director Larry Smarr. This slight reflected the institutional provenance of the tool and the attitude of NCSA: Mosaic was a product of NCSA, not of individuals, and the University of Illinois expected it to stay that way. We refer the interested reader to Gillies and Cailliau (2000) and NCSAmosaic.pdf (2006) for more details.

The Mosaic license was open but not GPL'd and had different provisions for commercial versus noncommercial users. Refer to http://www.socs.uts. edu.au/MosaicDocs-old/copyright.html (accessed January 10, 2007) for the full terms of the NCSA Mosaic license. The browser was free of charge for noncommercial use, which meant academic, research, or internal business purposes, with the source code provided for the Unix version. Noncommercial licensees were allowed to not only develop the software but redistribute derivative works. These redistributions were subject to a proviso: the derivative products had to be identified as different from the original Mosaic code and there was to be no charge for the derivative product. The terms for commercial licensees were different; for commercial distribution of a modified product, license terms had to be separately negotiated with NCSA. NCSA assigned all the commercial rights for Mosaic to Spyglass in late 1994 (Raggett et al., 1998). By 1995, Microsoft had licensed Mosaic as the basis for its own early browser Internet Explorer, but by that point Netscape Navigator dominated the browser market. Ironically, however, to this day the Help > About tab on the once again dominant Internet Explorer has as its first entry "based on NCSA Mosaic. NCSA Mosaic(TM); was developed at the National Center for Supercomputing Applications at the University of Illinois at Urbana–Champaign."

Beyond the revolutionary impact of its functionality on the growth of the Internet, the Mosaic browser also expedited the Web's expansion because of the public access it provided to HTML, which was essentially an open technology. Mosaic inherited the View Source capability of Tim Berners-Lee's browser. This had a significant side effect since it allowed anyone to see the HTML code for a page and imitate it. As Tim O'Reilly (2000) astutely observed, this simple capability was "absolutely key to the explosive spread of the Web. Barriers to entry for 'amateurs' were low, because anyone could look 'over the shoulder' of anyone else producing a web page."

2.2.2 Netscape

Software talent is portable. Given the uncompromising, albeit by the book, institutional arrogation of Mosaic by the University of Illinois, there was no point in Andreessen staying with NCSA. After graduating in 1993, he soon became one of the founders of the new Netscape Corporation at the invitation of the legendary Jim Clark, founder of Silicon Graphics. Netscape was Andreessen's next spectacular success.

Andreessen was now more than ever a man with a mission. At Netscape, he led a team of former students from NCSA, with the mission "to develop an independent browser better than Mosaic, i.e. Netscape Navigator." They knew that the new browser's code had to be completely independent of the original Mosaic browser in order to avoid future legal conflicts with NCSA. As it turned out, a settlement with the University of Illinois amounting to $3 million had to be made in any case (Berners-Lee, 1999). The internal code name for the first Netscape browser was *Mozilla*, a feisty pun combining the words Mosaic (the browser) and Godzilla (the movie monster) that was intended to connote an application that would kill the then dominant Mosaic browser in terms of popularity. (The page at http://sillydog.org/netscape/kb/netscapemozilla.php, accessed January 10, 2007, provides a helpful description of the sometimes confusing use of the name Mozilla.) The development team worked feverishly. As one member of the group put it, "a lot of times, people were there straight forty-eight hours, just coding. I've never seen anything like it. . . . But they were driven by this vision [of beating the original Mosaic]" (Reid, 1997). The sense of pride and victory is even more pungent in a well-known postmortem by team member Jamie Zawinski (1999) that would come later, after Netscape's unhappy browser war with Internet Explorer:

> . . . we were out to change the world. And we did that. Without us, the change probably would have happened anyway . . . But we were the ones who actually did it. When you see URLs on grocery bags, on billboards, on the sides of trucks, at the end of movie credits just after the studio logos – that was us, we did that. We put the Internet in the hands of normal people. We kick-started a new communications medium. We changed the world.

Netscape's pricing policy was based on a quest for ubiquity. Andreessen's belief was that if they dominated market share, the profits would follow from side effects. According to Reid (1997), Andreessen thought,

> That was the way to get the company jump-started, because that just gives you essentially a broad platform to build off of. It's basically a Microsoft lesson, right? If you get ubiquity, you have a lot of options, a lot of ways to benefit from that. You can get paid by the product you are ubiquitous on, but you can also get paid on products that benefit as a result. One of the fundamental lessons is that market share now equals revenue later, and if you don't have market share now, you are not going to have revenue later. Another fundamental lesson is that whoever gets the volume does win in the end. Just plain wins.

Netscape bet on the side effects of browser momentum. It basically gave the browser away. However, it sold the baseline and commercial server they developed, originally pricing them at $1,500 and $5,000, respectively. The free browser was an intentional business marketing strategy designed to make the product ubiquitous so that profits could then be made off symbiotic effects like advertising and selling servers (Reid, 1997). In principle, only academic use of the browser was free and all others were supposed to pay $39.00. But in practice, copies were just downloaded for free during an unenforced trial period. However, although the product was effectively free of charge, it was not in any sense *free* software or open source. The original Netscape software license was proprietary (http://www.sc.ucl.ac.be/misc/LICENSE.html, accessed January 10,

2007). It also explicitly prohibited disassembly, decompiling or any reverse engineering of the binary distribution, or the creation of any derivative works.

Netscape's strategy paid off handsomely and quickly. Originally posted for download on October 13, 1994, Netscape quickly dominated the browser market. This downloaded distribution of the product was itself a very important Netscape innovation and accelerated its spread. The aggressive introduction of new HTML tags by the Netscape developers was also seductive to Web designers who rapidly incorporated them into their Web pages (Raggett et al., 1998; Griffin, 2000). Since Netscape was the only browser that could read the new tags, the Web page designers would include a note on their page that it was best viewed in Netscape. They would then provide a link to where the free download could be obtained, so Netscape spread like a virus. A major technical advantage of the initial Netscape browser over Mosaic was that Netscape displayed images as they were received from embedded HTTP requests, rather than waiting for all the images referred to in a retrieved HTML page to be downloaded before the browser rendered them. It also introduced innovations like cookies and even more importantly the new scripting language Javascript, which was specifically designed for the browser environment and made pages much more dynamic (Andreessen, 1998; Eich, 1998). Thus, brash technology meshed with attractiveness, pricing, and distribution to make Netscape a juggernaut. The company went public on August 9, 1995, and Andreessen and Clark became millionaires and billionaires, respectively. By 1996 Netscape had penetrated 75% of the market. It was eventually bought by AOL for $10 billion.

Given this initial success, how did it happen that within a few years of Netscape's triumphant conquest of the browser market, Internet Explorer, the proprietary Microsoft browser, which was deeply rooted in Mosaic, became the dominant browser? It was really Microsoft's deep pockets that got the better of Netscape in the so-called *browser wars*. Indeed, Microsoft called its marketing campaigns *jihads* (Lohr, 1999). Microsoft destroyed Netscape's browser market by piggybacking on the pervasive use of its operating system on PCs. It bundled Internet Explorer for free with every copy of Windows sold, despite the fact that it had cost hundreds of millions of dollars to develop. With its huge cash reservoirs, Microsoft was able to fund development that incrementally improved IE until step by step it became equivalent in features and reliability to Netscape. As time went by, the attraction of downloading Netscape vanished, as the products became comparable. Netscape became a victim of redundancy.

Many of Microsoft's practices were viewed as monopolistic and predatory, resulting in its being prosecuted by the federal government for illegally manipulating the software market. Government prosecutor David Boies claimed that

Microsoft was trying to leverage its de facto monopoly in Windows to increase its market share for browsers and stifle competition (Lea, 1998). A settlement, which many considered as a mere slap on the wrist to Microsoft, was reached with the Justice department in late 2001 (Kollar-Kotelly, 2002). In any case, the original Netscape Navigator browser's market share had fallen steadily. From a peak of over 80% in 1996, it dropped to 70% in 1997, 50% in 1998, 20% in 1999, to a little over 10% in 2000. Microsoft's IE rose in tandem as Netscape fell, almost saturating the market by 2002, prior to Firefox's emergence.

In a last ditch effort to rebound, Netscape decided that perhaps the proprietary IE dragon could be beaten by a reformed, more open Netscape. So early in 1998 Netscape responded to Internet Explorer by going open source – sort of. The company stated that it was strongly influenced in this strategy by the ideas expressed in Raymond's famous "The Cathedral and the Bazaar" paper (1998). Refer to the e-mail from Netscape to Raymond in the latter's epilogue to his paper, updated as per its revision history in 1998 or later. Netscape thought it could recover from the marketing debacle inflicted by the newly updated releases of Internet Explorer by exploiting the benefits of open source style-collaborative development. So it decided to release the browser source code as open source.

The new release was done under the terms of the *Mozilla Public License* (MPL). The sponsor was the newly established Mozilla Organization whose mission would be to develop open source Internet software products. The intent of the MPL license and the Mozilla Organization was to promote open source as a means of encouraging innovation. Consistent with the general sense of copy-left, distributed modifications to any preexisting source code files obtained under an MPL open source license also had to be disclosed under the terms of the MPL license. However, completely new source code files, which a licensee developed, were not restricted or covered by any of the terms of the MPL. Furthermore, this remained the case even when the additions or changes were referenced by modifications made in the MPL-licensed section of the source code. In comparison with some existing open source licenses, the MPL license had "more copyleft (characteristics) than the BSD family of licenses, which have no copyleft at all, but less than the LGPL or the GPL" licenses (http://www.mozilla.org/MPL/mpl-faq.html). The Netscape browser itself (post-1998) contained both types of files, closed and open. It included proprietary (closed source) files that were not subject to the MPL conditions and were available only in binary. But the release also included MPL files from the Mozilla project, which were now open source.

Although Netscape's market share still declined, out of its ashes would come something new and vital. The versions of Netscape released after 2000 contained a new browser engine named Gecko, which was responsible for rendering and laying out the content of Web pages. This was released under the MPL license and was open source. But, the open source releases of Netscape were not very successful, partly because of a complicated distribution package. The Netscape project was finally shut down by then owner AOL in 2003. However, a small, nonprofit, independent, open source development organization called the *Mozilla Foundation*, largely self-funded through contributions, was set up by AOL to independently continue browser development. The purpose of the foundation was to provide organizational, legal, and financial support for the Mozilla open source software project. Its mission was to preserve choice and promote innovation on the Internet (mozilla.org/foundation/). Out of this matrix, the Firefox browser would rise phoenix-like and open source from the ashes of Netscape. Thus "a descendant of Netscape Navigator (was) now poised to avenge Netscape's defeat at the hands of Microsoft" (McHugh, 2005).

2.2.3 Firefox

The Mozilla Foundation development team that produced Firefox began by refocusing on the basic needs of a browser user. It scrapped the overly complex Netscape development plans and set itself the limited objective of making a simple but effective, user-oriented browser. The team took the available core code from the Netscape project and used that as a basis for a more streamlined browser they thought would be attractive. In the process they modified the original Netscape Gecko browser layout engine to create a browser that was also significantly faster. The eventual outcome was *Firefox*, a cross-platform open source browser released at the end of 2004 by the Mozilla Foundation that has proven explosively popular. Firefox is now multiply licensed under the GPL, LGPL, or MPL at the developer's choice. It also has an End User License Agreement that has some copyright and trademark restrictions for the downloaded binaries needed by ordinary users.

Firefox has been a true mass-market success. It is unique as an open source application because the number of its direct end users is potentially in the hundreds of millions. Previous successful open source applications like Linux and Apache had been intended for technically proficient users and addressed (at least initially in the case of Linux) a smaller end-user market, while desktop environments like GNOME and KDE are intended for a Linux environment. Firefox's market advantages include being portable to Windows, Linux, and Apple. This increases its potential audience vis-à-vis Internet Explorer. It also closely adheres to the W3C standards that Internet Explorer has viewed as optional. Like the original Netscape browser, Firefox burst onto the browser scene, quickly capturing tens of millions of downloads: 10 million in its first month, 25 million within 100 days of publication, and a 100 million in less than a year. Firefox 1.5 had 2 million downloads within 2 days of publication in November 2005. It rapidly gained prominence in the browser market, capturing by some estimates 25% of the market (w3schools.com/browsers/browsers_stats.asp, accessed December 6, 2006) within a year or so of its initial release, though sources like Net Applications Market Share survey show significantly lower penetration, under 15% in late 2006 (http://marketshare.hitslink.com, accessed December 6, 2006).

Microsoft's complacency with regard to the security of Internet Explorer serendipitously helped Firefox's debut. In June 2004, a Russian criminal organization distributed Internet malware called Download.ject that exploited a composite weakness jointly involving Windows IIS servers and a security vulnerability in Internet Explorer. Ironically, the exploited security shortcoming in Internet Explorer was tied precisely to its tight integration with the Windows operating system. This integration provided certain software advantages to the browser but also allowed hackers to leverage their attacks (Delio, 2004). Although the attack was countered within a few days, its occurrence highlighted IE security holes and was widely reported in the news. US CERT (the US Computer Emergency Readiness Team) advised federal agencies at the time to use browsers other than Internet Explorer in order to mitigate their security risks (Delio, 2004). The negative publicity about IE vulnerabilities occurred precisely when the first stable version of Firefox appeared. This played right into one of Firefox's purported strengths, not just in usability but also in security, thereby helping to establish Firefox's appeal.

The (Mozilla) Firefox project was started by Blake Ross. Blake had been a contractor for Netscape from age 15 and already had extensive experience in debugging the Mozilla browser. The precocious Ross had become dissatisfied with the project's direction and its feature bloat. He envisioned instead a simpler easy-to-use browser, so he initiated the Firefox project in 2002. Experienced Netscape developer Dave Hyatt partnered with Ross, bringing with him a deep knowledge of the critical Mozilla code base. Ben Goodger was engaged to participate because of his Web site's "thorough critique of the Mozilla browser" (Connor, 2006b). He subsequently became lead Firefox engineer when Ross enrolled in Stanford at age 19. Firefox was released in late 2004 under Goodger, who was also instrumental in the platform's important add-on architecture (Mook, 2004). Although its development depended on the extensive Netscape code base, it was an "extremely small team of committed programmers" who developed Firefox (Krishnamurthy, 2005a). The core project group currently has six members: the aforementioned Ross, Hyatt, and Goodger, as well as Brian Ryner, Vladmir Vukicevic, and Mike Connor.

Key factors in the success of Firefox included its user design criteria, the characteristics and policies of its development team, and its unique, open community-based marketing strategy.

The project's central design principle was "keep it simple." Ross has used family imagery to describe the design criteria for determining which features to include in the browser. They would ask the following questions about putative features (Ross, 2005b):

> Does this help mom use the web? If the answer was no, the next question was: does this help mom's teenage son use the web? If the answer was *still* no, the feature was either excised entirely or (occasionally) relegated to config file access only. Otherwise, it was often moved into an isolated realm that was outside of mom's reach but not her son's, like the preferences window.

In the same spirit, Ross describes Firefox as being about "serving users" and contends that a window of opportunity for Firefox's development had opened because Microsoft had irresponsibly abandoned Internet Explorer, leaving "for dead a browser that hundreds of millions of people rely on" (Ross, 2006).

The Firefox development team structure was intentionally lean, even elitist. The FAQ in the inaugural manifesto for the project explained why the development team was small by identifying the kinds of problems that handicapped progress on the original Mozilla project under Netscape after 2000: "Factors such as marketing teams, compatibility constraints, and multiple UI designers pulling in different directions have plagued the main Mozilla trunk development. *We feel that fewer dependencies, faster innovation, and more freedom to experiment will lead to a better end product*" (blakeross.com/firefox/README-1.1.html, accessed December 6, 2006).

The lead developers wanted to keep the development group's structure simple, not just the browser's design. According to the manifesto, CVS access was "restricted to a very small team. We'll grow as needed, based on reputation and meritorious hacks" (README-1.1.html). Thus in typical open source style, admission was meritocratic. To the question "how do I get involved," the blunt answer was "by invitation. This is a meritocracy – those who gain the respect of those in the group will be invited to join the group." As far as getting help from participants who wanted to chime in about bugs they had detected, the FAQ was equally blunt. To the question "where do I file bugs," the answer was "you don't. We are not soliciting input at this time. See Q2." Of course the project was open, so you could get a copy of the source code from the Mozilla CVS tree. Despite these restrictions, the list of credited participants in the 1.0.4 version included about 80 individuals, which is a significant base of recognized contributors. You can refer to the Help > About Firefox button in the browser for the current credits list. Subsequent documents elaborated on how to participate in the project in a more nuanced and inclusive way but without changing the underlying tough standards (Ross, 2005a).

The study by Krishnamurthy (2005a) describes the project as a "closed-door open source project," a characterization not intended to be pejorative. It analyzes the logistic and organizational motivations for and consequences of enforcing tight standards for participating in development. Overly restrictive control of entry to participation in an open project can have negative ramifications for the long-term well-being of the project. Indeed, Firefox developer Mike Connor complained vocally at one point that "in nearly three years we haven't built up a community of hackers, and now I think we're in trouble. Of the six people who can actually review in Firefox, four are AWOL, and one doesn't do a lot of reviews" (Connor, 2006a). However, a subsequent blog by Connor described the ongoing commitment of the major Firefox developers and the number of participants in Mozilla platform projects more positively, including the presence of many corporate sponsored "hackers" (Connor, 2006b).

Although the core development team was small and initially not solicitous to potential code contributors, the project made intensive effort to create an open community support base of users and boosters. The site http://www.mozila.org/ is used to support product distribution. A marketing site at www.spreadfirefox.com was set up where volunteers were organized to "spread the word" about Firefox in various ways, a key objective of the promotional campaign being used to get end users to switch from Internet Explorer. The site www.defendthefox.com was established to put "pressure on sites that were incompatible with Firefox. Users could visit it and identify web sites that did not display appropriately when Firefox was used as the browser" (Krishnamurthy, 2005b). Although Firefox was open source, the notion that large numbers of developers would be participating in its development was mistaken; the participants were primarily involved in its promotion. The combination of a complacent competitor (Internet Explorer), an energized open volunteer force organized under an effective leader, and an innovative product was instrumental in the rapid success of Firefox (Krishnamurthy, 2005b). It also benefited from strong public recognition like being named *PC World Product of the Year 2005*.

There are a number of characteristics on which Firefox has been claimed to be superior and perceptions that have helped make it popular, including having better security, the availability of many user-developed extensions, portability, compliance with Web standards, as well as accessibility and performance advantages. We will briefly examine these claims.

Open source Firefox is arguably more secure than proprietary Internet Explorer. For example, the independent computer security tracking firm Secunia's (Secunia.com) vulnerability reports for 2003–2006 identify almost 90 security advisories for IE versus slightly more than 30 for Firefox. Furthermore, about 15% of the IE advisories were rated as extremely critical versus only 3% for Firefox. Other related security statistics from Secunia note that as of June 2006, more than 20 of over 100 IE advisories were unpatched, with one or more of these listed as highly critical. In contrast, only 4 of the 33 Secunia advisories for Firefox were unpatched and were listed as less critical. It must be kept in mind that these security vulnerabilities fluctuate over time and there are details to the advisories that make the interpretation of the statistics ambiguous, but Firefox seems to have a security edge over Internet Explorer, at least at the present time. Aside from the Firefox security model, the fact that the browser is less closely bound to the operating system than Internet Explorer, its lack of support for known IE security exposures like ActiveX, and the public accessibility of an open source product like Firefox to ongoing scrutiny of its source code for bugs and vulnerabilities arguably bolster its security.

A significant feature of Firefox is that it allows so-called *extensions* to provide extra functionality. According to Firefox Help, "extensions are small add-ons to Firefox that change existing browser functionality or add new functionality." The Firefox site contains many user-developed extensions, like the NoScript extension that uses whitelist-based preemptive blocking to allow Javascript and other plug-ins "only for trusted domains of your choice" (https://addons.mozilla.org). The extensions are easy to install and uninstall. Individuals can develop their own extensions using languages like Javascript and C++. Refer to http://developer.mozilla.org/ for a tutorial on how to build an XPCOM (Cross-Platform Component Object Model) component for Firefox. This feature helps recruit talent to further develop the product. The extension model has two important advantages. Not providing such functionalities as default features helps keep the core product lean and unbloated. It also provides an excellent venue for capitalizing on the talent and creativity of the open community. Creative developers can design and implement new add-ons. Users interested in the new functionality can easily incorporate it in their own browser. This provides the advantage of feature flexibility without feature bloat and lets users custom-tailor their own set of features. Firefox also provides a variety of accessibility features that facilitate its use by the aged and visually impaired.

The relative performance of browsers in terms of speed is not easy to judge, and speed is only one aspect of performance. A fast browser compromised by serious security weaknesses is not a better browser. Useful Web sites like howtocreate.co.uk/browserSpeed.html (accessed December 6, 2006) present a mixed picture of various speed-related metrics for browsers for performance characteristics, like *time-to-cold-start* the browser, *warm-start-time* (time to restart browser after it has been closed), *caching-retrieval-speed, script speed,* and *rendering tables*, for browsers such as Firefox, Internet Explorer, and Safari. These statistics do not uniformly favor any one of the browsers.

HTML and Javascript

We conclude our discussion of browsers with some brief remarks about HTML and Javascript, tools that are central features of the Internet experience. Both HTML (a markup language) and Javascript (a client-side scripting language that acts as the API for an HTML document's Document Object Model) have accessible source code. Therefore, in this rudimentary sense, they are not "closed source." Of course, neither are they "open source" in any strict sense of the term, since, other than the visibility of the code, none of the other features of open source software come into play, from licensing characteristics, to modification and redistribution rights, to open development processes. The HTML and Javascript contents have implicit and possibly explicit copyrights and so infringement by copying may be an issue, but there are no license agreements involved in their access. Some purveyors of commercial Javascript/HTML applications do have licenses specifically for developer use, but these are not open software licenses. Despite the absence of licensing and other free software attributes, the innate visibility of the code for these components is noteworthy (see also Zittrain, 2004). O'Reilly (2004) observed, as we noted previously, that the simple "View Source" capability inherited by browsers from Berners-Lee's original browser had the effect of reducing "barriers to entry for amateurs" and was "absolutely key to the explosive spread of the Web" because one could easily imitate the code of others.

References

Andreessen, M. (1998). Innovators of the Net: Brendan Eich and Javascript. http://cgi.netscape.com/columns/techvision/innovators_be.html. Accessed January 10, 2007.
Andreessen, M. and Bina, E. (1994). NCSA Mosaic: A Global Hypermedia System. Internet Research, 4(1), 7–17.
Berners-Lee, T. (1999). Weaving the Web. Harper, San Francisco.
Connor, M. (2006a). Myths and Clarifications. March 4. http://steelgryphon.com/blog/?p=37. Accessed December 6, 2006.
Connor, M. (2006b). Myths and Clarifications. March 11. http://steelgryphon.com/blog/?p=39. Accessed December 6, 2006.
Delio, M. (2004). Mozilla Feeds on Rival's Woes. http://www.wired.com/news/infostructure/0,1377,64065,00.html. Accessed November 29, 2006.
Eich, B. (1998). Making Web Pages Come Alive. http://cgi.netscape.com/columns/techvision/innovators_be.html. Accessed January 10, 2007.
Gillies, J. and Cailliau, R. (2000). How the Web Was Born. Oxford University Press, Oxford.

Griffin, S. (2000). Internet Pioneers: Marc Andreessen. http://www.ibiblio.org/pioneers/andreesen.html. Accessed January 10, 2007.

Kollar-Kotelly, C. (2002). United States of America v. Microsoft Corporation. Civil Action No. 98–1232 (CKK). Final Judgment. http://www.usdoj.gov/atr/cases/f200400/200457.htm. Accessed January 10, 2007.

Krishnamurthy, S. (2005a). About Closed-Door Free/Libre/Open Source (FLOSS) Projects: Lessons from the Mozilla Firefox Developer Recruitment Approach. European Journal for the Informatics Professional. 6(3), 28–32. http://www.upgrade-cepis.org/issues/2005/3/up6–3Krishnamurthy.pdf. Accessed January 10, 2007.

Krishnamurthy, S. (2005b). The Launching of Mozilla Firefox – A Case Study in Community-Led Marketing. http://opensource.mit.edu/papers/sandeep2.pdf. Accessed November 29, 2006.

Lea, G. (1998). Prosecution Says Gates Led Plan to Crush Netscape. October 20. http://www.theregister.co.uk/1998/10/20/prosecution_says_gates_led_plan/. Accessed January 10, 2007.

Lohr, S. (1999). The Prosecution Almost Rests: Government Paints Microsoft as Monopolist and Bully. January 8. The NY Times on the Web. http://query.nytimes.com/gst/fullpage.html?sec=technology&res=9C03E6DD113EF93BA35752C0A96F958260&n=Top%2fReference%2fTimes%20Topics%2fSubjects%2fA%2fAntitrust%20Actions%20and%20Laws. Accessed January 10, 2007.

Markoff, J. (1993). A Free and Simple Computer Link. December 8. http://www.nytimes.com/library/tech/reference/120893markoff.html. Accessed January 10, 2007.

McHugh, J. (2005). The Firefox Explosion. Wired Magazine, Issue 13.02. http://www.wired.com/wired/archive/13.02/firefox.html. Accessed November 29, 2006.

Mook, N. (2004). Firefox Architect Talks IE, Future Plane. Interview with Blake Ross. November 29. http://www.betanews.com/article/Firefox_Architect_Talks_IE_Future_Plans/1101740041. Accessed December 6, 2006.

NCSAmosaic.pdf. (2006). World Wide Web. http://www.governingwithcode.org. Accessed January 10, 2007.

O'Reilly, T. (2000). Open Source: The Model for Collaboration in the Age of the Internet. O'Reilly Network. http://www.oreillynet.com/pub/a/network/2000/04/13/CFPkeynote.html?page=1. Accessed November 29, 2006.

Raggett, D., Lam, J., Alexander, I., and Kmiec, K. (1998). Raggett on HTML 4. Addison-Wesley Longman, Reading, MA.

Raymond, E.S. (1998). The Cathedral and the Bazaar. First Monday, 3(3). http://www.firstmonday.dk/issues/issue3_3/raymond/index.html. Ongoing version: http://www.catb.org/~esr/writings/cathedral-bazaar/. Accessed December 3, 2006.

Reid, R.H. (1997). Architects of the Web: 1,000 Days That Built the Future of Business. John Wiley & Sons, New York.

Ross, B. (2005a). Developer Recruitment in Firefox. January 25. http://blakeross.com/. Accessed December 6, 2006.

Ross, B. (2005b). The Firefox Religion. January 22. http://blakeross.com/. Accessed December 6, 2006.

Ross, B. (2006). How to Hear without Listening. June 6. http://blakeross.com/. Accessed December 6, 2006.

Wagner, D. (2002). "Marc Andreessen," Jones Telecommunications and Multimedia Encyclopedia. Jones International. See also: http://www.thocp.net/biographies/andreesen_marc.htm. Accessed January 10, 2007.

Zawinski, J. (1999). Resignation and Postmortem. http://www.jwz.org/gruntle/nomo.html. Accessed November 29, 2006.

Zittrain, J. (2004). Normative Principles for Evaluating Free and Proprietary Software. University of Chicago Law Review, 71(1), 265.

2.3 Fetchmail

Eric Raymond, a well-known open source advocate, published an essay in 1998 about open source development. The essay was called "The Cathedral and The Bazaar" (Raymond, 1998). It famously contrasted the traditional model of software development with the new paradigm introduced by Linus Torvalds for Linux. Raymond compared the Linux style of development to a Bazaar. In contrast, Brooks' classic book on software development *The Mythical Man Month* (Brooks, 1995) had compared system design to building a Cathedral, a centralized understanding of design and project management. Raymond's essay recounts the story of his own open source development project, Fetchmail, a mail utility he developed in the early 1990s. He intentionally modeled his development of the mail utility on how Linus Torvalds had handled the development of Linux. Fetchmail is now a common utility on Unix-like systems for retrieving e-mail from remote mail servers. According to the description on its project home page, it is currently a "full-featured, robust, well-documented remote-mail retrieval and forwarding utility intended to be used over on-demand TCP/IP links (such as SLIP or PPP connections). It supports every remote-mail protocol now in use on the Internet" (http://fetchmail.berlios.de/, accessed January 12, 2007.)

Although Fetchmail is a notable project, it pales in scope and significance to many other open source projects. Efforts like the X Window System are orders of magnitude larger and far more fundamental in their application but receive less coverage. However, Fetchmail had a bard in Eric Raymond and his essay has been widely influential in the open source movement. It aphoristically articulated Torvalds' development methodology at a critical point in time and took on the status of an almost mythological description of Internet-based open source development. It also introduced the term *bazaar* as an image for the open style of collaboration.

Raymond structures his tale as a series of object lessons in open source design, development, and management that he learned from the Linux process and applied to his own project. The story began in 1993 when Raymond needed a mail client that would retrieve his e-mail when he dialed up on his intermittent connection from home. Applications like this were already available and typically used a client-side application based on the POP (or POP3) Post Office Protocol. However, the first clients he tried did not handle e-mail replies properly, whence came his first Linux-derived lesson or moral: every good work of software starts by scratching a developer's personal itch. This is a now famous aphorism in the literature on the motivations of open source developers. This motivation contrasts sharply with the workaday world of most programmers who "spend their days grinding away for pay at programs they neither need nor love. But not in the Linux world – which may explain why the average quality of software originated in the Linux community is so high" (Raymond, 1998). The lessons extend on from there and are both interesting and instructive.

A defining characteristic of open source is that it lets you build on what went before. It lets you start from somewhere, not from nowhere. It is a lot easier to develop an application if you start with a development base. Linus did that with Linux. Raymond did it with his more humble application, Fetchmail. After Raymond recognized his need for an application, he did not just start off programming it ex nihilo. That would have violated what Raymond (1998) called the second lesson of open source development: "Good programmers know what to write. Great ones know what to rewrite (and reuse)." People typically think of code reuse in the context of general software engineering or object-oriented style, class/library-based implementation. But reuse is actually a quintessential characteristic and advantage of open source development. When only proprietary software is available, the source code for previous applications that a developer wants to improve or modify is, by definition, undisclosed. If the source code is not disclosed, it cannot be easily reused or modified, at least without a great deal of reverse engineering effort which may even be a violation of the software's licensing requirements. If a proprietary program has an API, it can be embedded in a larger application, on an as-is basis, but the hidden source itself could not be adapted. Exactly the opposite is the case in the open source world, where the source code is always disclosed by definition. Since there is plenty of disclosed source code around, it would be foolish not to try to reuse it as a point of departure for any related new development. Even if the modification is eventually thrown away or completely rewritten, it nonetheless provides an initial scaffolding for the application. Raymond did this for his e-mail client, exactly as Linus had done when he initiated Linux. Linus had not started with his own design. He started by reusing and modifying the existing Minix open source software developed by Tanenbaum. In Raymond's case, he "went looking for an existing POP utility that was reasonably well coded, to use as a development base" (Raymond, 1998), eventually settling on an open source e-mail client called Fetchpop. He did this intentionally, explicitly in imitation of Linus' approach to development. Following standard open source practice, Raymond modified Fetchpop and submitted his changes to the software owner who accepted them and released it as an updated version.

Another principle of development is "reuse," and then reuse and rebuild again if appropriate. Fred Brooks' had opined that a software developer should "plan to throw one away; you will anyhow" (Brooks, 1995). This is partly an unavoidable cognitive constraint. To really understand a problem, you have to try to solve the problem. After you've solved it once, then you have a better appreciation of what the actual problem was in the first place. The next time around, your solution can then be based on a more informed understanding of the issues. With this in mind, Raymond anticipated that his first solution might be only a temporary draft. So when the opportunity for improvement presented itself, he seized it. He came across another open source e-mail client by Carl Harris called Popclient. After studying it, he recognized that it was better coded than his own solution and he sent some patches to Harris for consideration. However, as it turned out, Harris was no longer interested in the project. But, he gladly ceded ownership of the software to Raymond who took on the role of maintainer for the Popclient project in mid-1996. This episode illustrated another principle in the open source code of conduct: "When you lose interest in a program, your last duty to it is to hand it off to a competent successor" (Raymond, 1998). Responsible open source fathers don't leave their children to be unattended orphans.

Open source development has not always been distributed collaborative development, which Raymond calls *bazaar* style development. He describes the Linux community as resembling "a great babbling bazaar of differing agendas and approaches ... out of which a coherent and stable system could seemingly emerge only by a succession of miracles" (Raymond, 1998). He contrasts this with one of the longest standing open source projects, the GNU project, which had developed software the old-fashioned way, using a closed management approach with a centralized team and slow software releases. With exceptions like the GNU Emacs Lisp Library, GNU was not developed along the lines of the Linux model. Indeed, consider the sluggishness of the development of the GNU GCC Compiler, done in the traditional manner, versus the rapid development that occurred when the GCC project was bifurcated into two streams: the regular GCC development mode and a parallel "bazaar" mode of development à la Linux for what was called EGCS (Experimental GNU Compiler System) beginning in 1997. The difference in the rates of progress of the two projects was striking. The new bazaar development style for EGCS dramatically out-paced the conventional mode used for the GCC project, so much so that by

1999 the original GCC project was sunset and development was placed under the EGCS project, which almost amounted to a controlled experiment on the relative effectiveness of the bazaar and conventional methods.

In the open source and Unix tradition, users tend to be simultaneously users and developers, often expert developers or hackers. As expected, Raymond's adopted Popclient project came with its own user base. So once again in conscious imitation of the Linux development model, he recognized that this community of interest was an enormous asset and that "given a bit of encouragement, your users will diagnose problems, suggest fixes, and help improve the code far more quickly than you could unaided" (Raymond, 1998). The development principle he followed was that "treating your users as co-developers is your least-hassle route to rapid code improvement and effective debugging" (Raymond, 1998). This process of successfully engaging the user-developer base was exactly what Linus had done so well with Linux.

The use of early and frequent software releases was another quintessential characteristic of the Linux development process. This kept the user base engaged and stimulated. Linus' approach ran contrary to the conventional thinking about development. Traditionally, people believed that releasing premature, buggy versions of software would turn users off. Of course, in the case of system software like Linux and a user-developer base of dedicated, skilled hackers, this logic did not apply. The Linux development principle was "Release early. Release often. And listen to your customers" (Raymond, 1998). Granted that frequent releases were characteristic in the Unix tradition, Linus went far beyond this. He "cultivated his base of co-developers and leveraged the Internet for collaboration" (Raymond, 1998) to such an extent and so effectively that he scaled up the frequent release practice by an order of magnitude over what had ever been done previously. Releases sometimes came out at the unbelievable rate of more than once a day. It was no accident that the initiation of the Linux project and the burgeoning growth of the Internet were coincident because the Internet provided both the distributed talent pool and the social interconnectivity necessary for this kind of development to happen. Raymond's Fetchmail project intentionally followed Linus' modus operandi, with releases almost always arriving at most at 10-day intervals, and sometimes even once a day à la Linux.

This community-participation-driven process unsurprisingly required a lot of people skills to manage properly. Again per Linus' practice, Raymond cultivated his own beta list of tester supporters. The total number of participants in his project increased linearly from about 100 initially to around 1,500 over a 5-year period, and with user-developers reaching a peak of about 300, eventually stabilizing at around 250. During the same period the number of lines of code grew from under 10,000 to nearly 50,000. As with many open source projects, there are excellent development statistics. For Fetchmail, see the historical and statistical overview at http://www.catb.org/~esr/fetchmail/history.html. These user-developers had to be kept engaged, just as Linus had to keep his user-developers interested. Their egos had to be stroked by being adequately recognized for their contributions, and even given rapid satisfaction via the speedy releases incorporating new patches. Raymond added anyone who contacted him about Fetchmail to his beta list. Normally *beta testing*, where a product is given exposure to real-world users outside the development organization, would be the last round of testing of a product before its commercial release. But in the Linux model, beta testing is dispersed to the user-developers over many beta style releases, prior to the release of a stable tested product for more general users. Raymond would make "chatty announcements" to the group to keep them engaged and he listened closely to his beta testers. As a result, from the onset he received high-quality bug reports and suggestions. He summarized the attitude with the observation that "if you treat your beta-testers as if they're your most valuable resource, they will respond by becoming your most valuable resource" (Raymond, 1998). This not only requires a lot of energy and commitment on the part of the project owner, it also means the leader has to have good interpersonal and communication skills. The interpersonal skills are needed to attract people to the project and keep them happy with what's happening. The communication skills are essential because communicating what is happening in the project is a large part of what goes on. Technical skill is a given, but personality or management skill is invariably a prominent element in these projects.

The user-developer base is critical to spotting and fixing bugs. Linus observed that the bug resolution process in Linux was typically twofold. Someone would find a bug. Someone else would understand how to fix it. An explanation for the rapidity of the debugging process is summarized in the famous adage: "Given enough eyeballs, all bugs are shallow" (Raymond, 1998). The bazaar development model appeared to parallelize debugging with a multitude of users stressing the behavior of the system in different ways. Given enough such beta testers and codevelopers in the open source support group, problems could be "characterized quickly and the fix (would be) obvious to someone." Furthermore, the patch "contributions (were) received not from a random sample, but from people who (were) interested enough to use the software, learn about how it works, attempt to find solutions to problems they encounter(ed), and actually produce an apparently reasonable fix. Anyone who passes all these filters is highly likely to have something useful to contribute" (Raymond, 1998). On the basis of this phenomenon, not only were recognized bugs quickly resolved in Linux development, the overall system was relatively unbuggy, as even the Halloween documents from Microsoft observed.

Debugging in an open source environment is extremely different from debugging in a proprietary environment. After discussions with open developers, Raymond analyzed in detail how the debugging process works in open source. The key characteristic is source-code awareness. Users who do not have access to source code tend to supply more superficial reports of bugs. They provide not only less background information but also less "reliable recipe(s) for reproducing the bug" (Raymond, 1998). In a closed source environment, the user-tester is on the outside of the application looking in, in contrast to the developer who is on the inside looking out and trying to understand what the bug report submitted by a user-observer means. The situation is completely different in an open source context where the "tester and developer (are able) to develop a shared representation grounded in the actual source code and to communicate effectively about it" (Raymond, 1998). He observes that "most bugs, most of the time, are easily nailed given even an incomplete but suggestive characterization of their error conditions at *source-code level* (italics added). When someone among your beta-testers can point out, 'there's a boundary problem in line nnn', or even merely 'under conditions X, Y, and Z, this variable rolls over', a quick look at the offending code often suffices to pin down the exact mode of failure and generate a fix" (Raymond, 1998).

The leader of an open source development project does not necessarily have to be a great designer himself, but he does have to be able to recognize a great design when someone else comes up with one. At least this is one of Raymond's interpretations of the Linux development process. It certainly reflects what occurred in his own project. By a certain point, he had gone through modifications of two preexisting open source applications: Fetchpop, where he had participated briefly as a contributor, and Popclient, where he had taken over as the owner and maintainer from the previous project owner. Indeed he says that the "biggest single payoff I got from consciously trying to emulate Linus' methods" happened when a "user gave me this terrific idea – all I had to do was understand the implications" (Raymond, 1998). The incident that precipitated the revelation occurred when Harry Hochheiser sent him some code for forwarding mail to the client SMTP port. The code made Raymond realize that he had been trying to solve the wrong problem and that he should completely redesign Fetchmail as what is called a Mail Transport Agent: a program that moves mail from one machine to another. The Linux lessons he was emulating at this point were twofold: the second best thing to having a good idea yourself is "recognizing good ideas from your users" and that it is often the case that "the most striking and innovative solutions come from realizing that your concept of the problem was wrong" (Raymond, 1998). The code of the redesigned software turned out to be both better and simpler than what he had before. At this point it was proper to rename the project. He called it *Fetchmail*. Fetchmail was now a tool that any Unix developer with a PPP (Point-to-Point Protocol) mail connection would need, potentially a category killer that fills a need so thoroughly that alternatives are not needed. In order to advance it to the level of a truly great tool, Raymond listened to his users again and added some more key features like what is called multidrop support (which turns out to be useful for handling mailing lists) and support for 8-bit MIME.

Raymond also elaborates cogently on the key preconditions for a bazaar style of development to be possible in the first place. These include programmatic, legal, and communication requirements. The programmatic requirements were particular to a project, and the legal and communications infrastructure were generic requirements for the entire phenomenon.

The Linux style design process does not begin in a vacuum. Programmatically, in open source development there has to be something to put on the table before you can start having participants improve, test, debug, add features, and so on to the product. Linus, for example, began Linux with a promising preliminary system which in turn had been precipitated by Tanenbaum's earlier Minix kernel. The same was true for Raymond's Fetchmail, which, like Linux, had a "strong, attractive basic design(s)" before it went public. Although the bazaar style of development works well for testing, debugging, code improving, and program design, one cannot actually originate a product in this forum. First of all, there has to be a program to put on display that runs! There cannot be just a proposal for an idea. In open source, code talks. Secondly, the running program has to have enough appeal that it can "convince potential co-developers that it can be evolved into something really neat in the foreseeable future" (Raymond, 1998). It may have bugs, lack key features, and have poor documentation, but it must run and have promise. Remember that "attention is still a nonrenewable resource" and that the interest of potential participants as well as "your reputation is on the line" (Fogel and Bar, 2003).

Another precondition for bazaar-style open development is the existence of an appropriate legal framework. The nondisclosure agreements of the proprietary Unix environment would prevent this kind of free-wielding process. Explicitly formulated and widely recognized free software principles lay the ground for a legal milieu people can understand and depend on.

Prior to free software and Linux, the open development environment was not only legally impeded but geographically handicapped as well. The field already knew from extensive experience with the multidecade effort in Unix that great software projects exploit "the attention and brainpower of entire communities" even though coding itself remains relatively solitary. So collaborative distributed development was a recognized model – and after all it was the classic way in which science had always advanced. But remote collaboration had remained clumsy, and an effective communications infrastructure that developers could work in was needed. The Internet had to emerge to transcend the geographically bound developer communities at institutions like Bell Labs, MIT, and Berkeley that did foster free interactions between individuals and groups of highly skilled, but largely collocated, codevelopers. With the WWW emerging, the collaborative approach represented by these traditional groups could be detached from its geographic matrix and could even be exponentially larger in terms of the number of people involved. At that point, one merely needed a developer who knew "how to create an open, evolutionary context in which feedback exploring the design space, code contributions, bug-spotting, and other improvements come from hundreds (perhaps thousands) of people" (Raymond, 1998).

Linux emerged when these enabling conditions were all in place. The Linux project represented a conscious decision by Torvalds to use "the entire world as its talent pool" (Raymond, 1998). Before the Internet and the WWW that would have been essentially unworkable and certainly not expeditious. Without the legal apparatus of free and open software, the culture of development would not have had a conceptual framework within which to develop its process. But once these were in place, things just happened naturally. Linux, and its intentional imitators like Fetchmail, soon followed.

Traditional project management has well-identified, legitimate concerns: how are resources required, people motivated, work checked for quality, innovation nurtured, and so on. These issues do not disappear just because the development model changes. Raymond describes how the project management concerns of the traditional managerial model of software development are addressed or obviated in the bazaar model of development. Let us assume the basic traditional project management goals are defining the project goals, making sure details are attended to, motivating people to do what may be boring, organizing people to maximize productivity, and marshaling resources for the project. How are these objectives met in open source development?

To begin with, consider human resources. In open projects like Linux the developers were, at least initially, volunteers, self-selected on the basis of their interest, though subsequently they may have been paid corporate employees. Certainly at the higher levels of participation, they had meritorious development skills, arguably typically at the 95% percentile level. Thus, these participants brought their own resources to the project, though the project leadership had to be effective enough to attract them in the first place and then retain them. The open process also appears to be able to organize people very effectively despite the distributed environment. Because participants tend to be self-selected, they come equipped with motivation, in possible contrast to corporate organizations based on paid employees who might rather be doing something else or at least working on a different project. The monitoring provided in a conventional managerial environment is implemented radically differently in an open source, where it is replaced by widespread peer and expert review by project leaders, maintainers, committers, or beta testers. In fact, in open source "decentralized peer review trumps all the conventional methods for trying to ensure that details don't get skipped" (Raymond, 1998). Finally, consider the initial definition of the project, an issue that is also directly related to the question of innovativeness. Open projects like Linux have been criticized for chasing the taillights of other extant projects. This is indeed one of the design techniques that has been used in the free software movement where part of the historical mission has to be to recreate successful platforms in free implementations (see such as Bezroukov (1999) on the Halloween-I document). However, open projects do not always imitate. For example, Scacchi (2004, p. 61) describes how in the creation of open requirements for game software, the specifications "emerge as a by-product of community discourse about what its software should or shouldn't do . . . and solidify into retrospective software requirements." On the other hand, the conventional corporate model has a questionable record of defining systems properly, it being widely believed that half to three quarters of such developments are either aborted before completion or rejected by users. Creative ideas ultimately come from individuals in any case, so what is needed is an environment that recognizes and fosters such ideas, which the open source model seems to do quite well. Furthermore, historically, universities and research organizations have often been the source of software innovation, rather than corporate environments.

We conclude with some comments about the bazaar metaphor and Linus' law. To begin with, let us note that though Raymond's seminal *bazaar* metaphor is striking; every metaphor has its limitations. The imagery resonates with the myriad of voices heard in an open development and has an appealing romantic cache. The term also probably resonates with Raymond's personal libertarian beliefs, with their eschewal of centralized control. But it lacks adequate reference to an element essential in such development: the required dynamic, competent, core leadership with its cathedral-like element. Of course, Raymond's essay clearly acknowledges this, but the bazaar metaphor does not adequately capture it. Feller and Fitzgerald (2002, p. 160) point out that many of the most important open source projects from Linux and Apache to GNOME and FreeBSD are in fact highly structured, with a cadre of proven developers with expertise acknowledged in the development community (p. 166). Raymond himself underscores that a project must begin with an attractive base design which more often than not comes from one or perhaps a few individuals. Contributions from a broader contributor pool may subsequently radically redefine the original vision or prototype, but all along there is either a single individual like Linus Torvalds or a small coherent group that adjudicates and vets these contributions, integrating them in a disciplined way and generally steering the ship (Feller and Fitzgerald, 2002, p. 171). The bazaar can also be a source of distraction. Participation by "well meaning ... (but) dangerously half clued people with opinions – not code, opinions" (Cox, 1998) may proliferate like in a bazaar, but this does not advance the ship's voyage. Such caveats aside, it is also indisputable that some of the unknown voices emanating from the bazaar may ultimately prove invaluable, even if this is not obvious at first. As Alan Cox observes, there are "plenty of people who given a little help and a bit of confidence boosting will become one with the best" (Cox, 1998). The bazaar can also provide helpful resources from unexpected sources. For example, Cox advises that "when you hear 'I'd love to help but I can't program', you hear a documenter. When they say 'But English is not my first language' you have a documenter and translator for another language" (Cox, 1998).

We next comment about the reliability achieved by open processes. Raymond's statement of Linus' law, "with enough eyeballs, all bugs are shallow," focuses on parallel oversight as one key to the reliability of open source. The implication is that bugs are detected rapidly. One might ask "are the products actually more reliable and is the reliability due to the fact that there are many overseers?" The record of performance for open source systems generally supports the thesis that open development is often remarkably effective in terms of the reliability of its products. There are also specific studies like the analysis of the comparative reliability of MySQL mentioned in Chapter 1. Even the Halloween memos from Microsoft refer to Microsoft's own internal studies on Linux that accentuate its record of reliability. The "eyeballs" effect is presumably part of the explanation for this reliability.

Research by Payne (1999, 2002), which compares security flaws in open and closed systems, suggests that other causes may be at work as well. It suggests that a mixture of practices explains reliability/security differences for the systems studied. The study examined the security performance of three Unix-like systems in an effort to understand the relation between the security characteristics of the systems, their open or closed source status, and their specific development processes. The systems considered were OpenBSD, the open source Debian GNU/Linux distribution, and the closed source Sun Solaris system. Granted the myriad uncertainties intrinsic to any such study, Payne concluded that in terms of metrics like identified security vulnerabilities, OpenBSD was the most secure of the three, followed at a considerable distance by Debian and Solaris, with a slight edge given to Debian over Solaris. The results suggest an overall security advantage for open source systems, though the relative closeness of the Debian and Solaris evaluations imply that open source status per se is not the decisive driving factor. Indeed, as it turns out, there was a major difference in the development processes for the systems that likely explains much of the outcome. Namely, the "OpenBSD source code is regularly and purposely examined with the explicit intention of finding and fixing security holes ... by programmers with the necessary background and security expertise to make a significant impact" (Payne, 2002). In other words, the factor that produced superior security may actually have been focused in auditing of the code by specialists during development, though open source status appears to be a supplemental factor.

Another perspective on the reliability or security benefits of open source is provided by Witten et al. (2001). Their analysis is guarded about the general ability of code reviews to detect security flaws regardless of the mode of development. However, they observe that the proprietary development model simply obliges users to "trust the source code and review process, the intentions and capabilities of developers to build safe systems, and the developer's compiler" and to "forfeit opportunities for improving the security of their systems" (Witten et al., 2001, p. 61). They also underscore the important role that open compilers, whose operation is itself transparent, play in instilling confidence about what a system does. Incidentally, they observe how security enhancing open compilers like Immunix Stackguard, a gcc extension (see also Cowan, 1998), can add so-called canaries to executables that can "defeat many buffer overflow attacks" (Witten et al., 2001, p. 58). From this perspective, Linus' law is about more than just parallel oversight. It is a recognition of the inherent advantages of transparency: open source code, a process of open development, the ability to change code, giving the user control of the product, open oversight by many community observers, and even the transparency and confidence provided by open compilers.

References

Bezroukov, N. (1999). A Second Look at the Cathedral and Bazaar. First Monday, 4(12). http://www.firstmonday.org/issues/issue4_12/bezroukov/. Accessed January 5, 2007.

Brooks, F.P. (1995). The Mythical Man-Month – Essays on Software Engineering, 20th Anniversary Edition, Addison-Wesley Longman, Reading, MA.

Cowan, C. (1998). Automatic Detection and Prevention of Buffer-Overflow Attacks. In: Proceedings of the 7th USENIX Security Symposium, USENIX, San Diego, 63–78.

Cox, A. (1998). Cathedrals, Bazaars and the Town Council. http://slashdot.org/features/98/10/13/1423253.shtml. Accessed December 6, 2006.

Feller, J. and Fitzgerald, B. (2002). Understanding Open Source Software Development. Addison-Wesley, Pearson Education Ltd., London.

Fogel, K. and Bar, M. (2003). Open Source Development with CVS, 3rd edition. Paraglyph Press. http://cvsbook.red-bean.com/.

Payne, C. (1999). Security through Design as a Paradigm for Systems Development. Murdoch University, Perth, Western Australia.

Payne, C. (2002). On the Security of Open Source Software. Information Systems, 12(1), 61–78.

Raymond, E.S. (1998). The Cathedral and the Bazaar. First Monday, 3(3). http://www.firstmonday.dk/issues/issue3_3/raymond/index.html. Ongoing version: http://www.catb.org/~esr/writings/cathedral-bazaar/. Accessed December 3, 2006.

Scacchi, W. (2004). Free and Open Source Development Practices in the Game Community. IEEE Software, 21(1), 59–66.

Witten, B., Landwehr, C., and Caloyannides, M. (2001). Does Open Source Improve System Security? IEEE Software, 18(5), 57–61.

2.4 The Dual License Business Model

A software product can be offered under different licenses depending, for example, on how the software is to be used. This applies to proprietary and open source products and provides a basis for a viable business model. Karels (2003) examines the different commercial models for open products. The Sendmail and MySQL products described later are representative. They have their feet planted firmly in two worlds, the commercial one and the open community one. On the one hand, the business model provides "extensions or a professional version under a commercial license" for the product (Karels, 2003). At the same time, the company that markets the product continues its management of the open version. A key distinction in the dual license model is whether the free and commercial products are identical. For the companies and products we discuss the breakout as follows:

1. Open and proprietary code *different*   Sendmail, Inc.
2. Open and proprietary code *same*   MySQL AB, Berkeley DB, Qt

But with the proper license, proprietary enhancements can be done, for example, for MySQL. Licensing duality can serve a company in a number of ways. It continues the operation of the open user-developer base. It also promotes goodwill for the company with the user-developer base. It maintains and improves acceptance for the open source base version. The continued sponsored development of the open version simultaneously helps maintain and expand the market for the commercial product. With products like Sendmail, the proprietary enhancements may include security improvements, such as e-mail virus checking. Its distributions may typically provide "configuration and management tools, higher-performance or higher-capacity versions" (Karels, 2003) to supplement the root product in order to make a more attractive, commercially viable product. The company's product can thus end up incorporating both open and commercially licensed software. From the customer's point of view, the product is now much like a traditional software product that is licensed and paid for. One ongoing challenge for the distributor is to "maintain differentiation between the free and commercial versions" since the commercial product competes with its open fork, at least when the commercial version is different. In order for the open version to retain market share, its functionality has to be maintained and upgraded. In order for the commercial version to avoid competition from evolving open variants, it has to continue to provide "sufficient additional value to induce customers to buy it and to reduce the likelihood of a free knockoff of the added components" (Karels, 2003). The commercial version also has to provide all the accoutrements associated with a conventional software provider, such as support, training, and product documentation.

Products that can be successfully marketed under a dual licensing framework tend to have what are called strong network effects; that is, the benefit or value of using a copy of the software tends to depend on how many other people also use the software. For example, e-mail is not of much value if you have no one to e-mail; conversely, its value is greater the more people you can reach. For such products, the broader the user base, the more valuable the product. In the dual license model, the free, open license serves the key role of establishing a wide user base by helping to popularize the product with users (Valimaki, 2005). This popularized base helps make the product a *branded* entity, which is extremely valuable for marketing purposes, especially for IT organizations that are converting to open applications (Moczar, 2005). These effects in turn make the proprietary license more worth buying for the relatively limited group of potential commercial developers. It also makes it more attractive for them to create a commercial derivative under the proprietary license because; for example, the product will have an established audience of users. There is another economic reason for allowing mixed license options like this: the open source version can be used to build up a coterie of independent developers, bug spotters, and so on – free contributors who can help enhance the product in one way or another, benefiting the commercial company. As we will see later when we discuss configuration management tools, Larry McVoy created a dual *faux* free license for BitKeeper, especially for use on the Linux kernel. This had the express purpose of building BitKeeper's proprietary market share and also obtaining highly useful input about bugs in the product from the Linux kernel developers who used it. This "dual licensing" business strategy worked very well until it had to be discontinued because of the open community controversies about the "free" license version.

References

Karels, M. (2003). Commercializing Open Source Software. ACM Queue, 1(5), 46–55.
Moczar, L. (2005). The Economics of Commercial Open Source. http://pascal.case.
    unibz.it/handle/2038/501. Accessed November 29, 2006.
Valimaki, M. (2005). The Rise of Open Source Licensing: A Challenge to the Use of
    Intellectual Property in the Software Industry. Turre Publishing, Helsinki, Finland.

2.4.1 Sendmail

The open source product *Sendmail* is a pervasive Internet e-mail application. However, its story is much less well known than Fetchmail's because of the unique influence of Raymond's (1998) Cathedral and Bazaar article that ensconced Fetchmail's development as a canonical story of the practices and principles of open development, even though Fetchmail is for a far more limited use than Sendmail. Sendmail is worth discussing, not only because it carries most of the world's e-mail traffic, but because it represents another major open source application that eventually morphed into dual open and commercial versions.

The Sendmail project was started as an open project at UC Berkeley in 1981 by Eric Allman, who has also maintained the project since that time as an open development. Allman had previously authored the ARPANET mail application *delivermail* in 1979 that was included with the Berkeley Software Distribution (BSD), which in turn would subsequently include Sendmail instead. Sendmail is a Mail Transfer Agent or MTA. As such, its purpose is to reliably transfer e-mail from one host to another, unlike mail user agents like Pine or Outlook that are used by end users to compose mail. The software operates on Unix-like systems, though there is also a Windows version available. The open source version of Sendmail is licensed under an OSI-approved BSD-like license (see http://directory.fsf.org for verification), as well as, since 1998, under both generic *and* custom commercial licenses. Sendmail serves a significant percentage of all Internet sites, though there appears to be a decline over time (Weiss, 2004). It represents a de facto Internet infrastructure standard like TCP/IP, Perl, and Apache.

Naturally, and healthily, the free software movement has never been about *not* making money. The time frame in which time spent, effort, and talent are fungible with compensation may be elastic, but it is finite. People eventually have to cash in on their products or their expertise in one way or another, or switch to another line of work where they can make a living. This is obviously appropriate and expected since their involvement will almost always have been long, intense, and valuable. Thus for Sendmail as with many open source projects, the project originator and leader Allman eventually took the project on a commercial route, establishing Sendmail Inc. in 1998 in order to develop a commercial version of the software (see http://www.sendmail.org/ and the complementary commercial site http://www.sendmail.com). The expanded commercialized version of the product is *different* from the open source version and offers many features not available in the open version. For example, it provides a GUI interface that *significantly* facilitates the installation and configuration of the software, in contrast to the open source version that is well known to be extremely complicated to install. The commercial product also incorporates proprietary components that are combined with the open source components. According to the Sendmail Inc. Web site, their commercial products provide "clear advantage over open source implementations" in a variety of ways, from security and technical support to enhanced features. The Sendmail Inc. and its project maintainer Allman still manage the development of the open source project, but they now use its development process to also support the continued innovation of both the open and the commercial version of the product. After the Sendmail incorporation, the licensing arrangement was updated to reflect the dual open source and commercial offerings. The original license for the pure open source application remained essentially the same, a few remarks about trademarks and such aside. For redistribution as part of a commercial product, a commercial license is required.

References

Raymond, E.S. (1998). The Cathedral and the Bazaar. First Monday, 3(3). http://www.firstmonday.dk/issues/issue3_3/raymond/index.html. Ongoing version: http://www.catb.org/~esr/writings/cathedral-bazaar/. Accessed December 3, 2006.

Weiss, A. (2004). Has Sendmail Kept Pace in the MTA Race? http://www.serverwatch.com/stypes/servers/article.php/16059_3331691. Accessed December 1, 2006.

2.4.2 MySQL – Open Source and Dual Licensing

MySQL (pronounced My S-Q-L) is the widely used open source relational database system that provides fast, multiuser database service and is capable of handling mission-critical applications with heavy loads. It is suitable for both Web server environments and embedded database applications. MySQL is famous in open source applications as the M in the LAMP software architecture. The company that owns MySQL provides a *dual licensing* model for distribution that permits both free and proprietary redistribution. One of the notable characteristics of MySQL as an open source project is that virtually all of its development is done by the company that owns the product copyright. This model helps keep its license ownership pure, ensuring that its proprietary license option remains undisturbed. (We will not consider the other major open source database PostgreSQL (pronounced postgres Q-L) which is licensed under the BSD license. The BSD's terms are so flexible that the dual licensing model we are considering does not seem to come into play unless proprietary extensions are developed or value-added services are provided.)

MySQL was initially developed by Axmark and Widenius starting in 1995 and first released in 1996. They intended it to serve their personal need for an SQL interface to a Web-accessible database. Widenius recalls that their motivation for releasing it as an open source product was "because we believed that we had created something good and thought that someone else could probably have some use for it. We became inspired and continued to work on this because of the very good feedback we got from people that tried MySQL and loved it" (Codewalkers, 2002). The trademarked product *MySQL* is now distributed by the commercial company MySQL AB founded by the original developers in 2001. The company *owns* the copyright to MySQL.

All the core developers who continue the development work on MySQL work for MySQL AB, even though they are distributed around the world. The complexity of the product is one disabling factor in allowing third-party involvement in the project (Valimaki, 2005). Independent volunteer contributors can propose patches but, if the patches prove to be acceptable, these are generally *reimplemented* by the company's core developers. This process helps ensure that the company's copyright ownership of the entire product is never clouded or diluted (Valimaki, 2005). The code revisions ensure that GPL'd code created by an external developer, who is de facto its copyright owner, is not included in the system, so that the overall system can still be licensed under an alternative or dual proprietary license that is not GPL. The business and legal model is further described later. Sometimes code contributions are accepted under a shared copyright with the contributor. Despite the strict handling of patch proposals by external contributors, a significant number of the company's employees were actually recruited through the volunteer user-developer route. Indeed, according to Hyatt (2006), of MySQL AB's 300+ full-time employees, 50 of them were originally open source community volunteers for MySQL.

MySQL was originally distributed for Unix-like environments under a *free-of-charge* and *free* open source license that allowed free redistribution under the usual copyleft restriction (according to which any modifications had to be redistributable under the same terms as the original license). On the other hand, the distribution license of MySQL in Windows environments was originally only as so-called shareware that allowed copying and redistribution of the product but did not permit modification and in fact required users to pay a license fee to use the software after an initial free trial period. This was changed to the standard GPL for all platforms after 2000 (Valimaki, 2005).

The MySQL AB distribution uses the dual licensing business model. The *same* technical product is distributed both as a free GPL-licensed package and under different licensing terms for the purpose of proprietary development. Refer to http://www.mysql.com/company/legal/licensing/ (accessed January 10, 2007) for the legal terms of the license. Some of the basic points to keep in mind follow. If you embed MySQL in a GPL'd application, then that application has to be distributed as GPL by the requirements of the GPL license. However, the MySQL proprietary license allows commercial developers or companies to modify MySQL and integrate it with their own proprietary products and sell the resulting system as a proprietary closed source system. The license to do this requires a fee ranging up to $5,000 per year for the company's high-end server (as of 2005). Thus if you purchase MySQL under this commercial license, then you do *not* have to comply with the terms of the GNU General Public License, of course only in so far as it applies to MySQL.

You cannot in any case infringe on the trademarked MySQL name in any derivative product you create, an issue that arose in the dispute between MySQL and NuSphere (MySQL News Announcement, 2001). The commercial license naturally provides product support from MySQL AB, as well as product warranties and responsibilities. These are lacking in the identical but free GPL'd copy of the product, which is offered only on an as-is basis. This proprietary form of the license is required *even if* you sell a commercial product that only merely requires the user to download a copy of MySQL, or if you include a copy of MySQL, or include MySQL drivers in a proprietary application! Most of MySQL AB's income derives from the fees for the proprietary license with additional revenues from training and consultancy services. The income from these services and fees adds up to a viable composite open source/proprietary business model. As per Valimaki (2005), most of the company's income comes from embedded commercial applications.

The preservation of copyright ownership is a key element in the continued viability of a dual license model like MySQL AB's. In particular, the licensee must have undisputed rights to the software in order to able to charge for the software, distribute it under different licenses, or modify its licensing policies (Valimaki, 2005). The generic open source development framework, where development is fully collaborative and distributed, tends to undermine or diffuse copyright ownership since there are many contributors. For example, there could be "hidden liabilities in code contributions from unknown third parties" (Valimaki, 2005). Thus, maintaining the ability to dual license with a proprietary option mandates that the developer of any new or modified code for the system must ensure that he has exclusive copyright to the work – whence the cautious behavior by MySQL AB with respect to how development contributions are handled.

MySQL AB appears to apply a rather strict interpretation of what the conditions of the GPL mean in terms of its own legal rights (Valimaki, 2005, p. 137). For example, consider a hypothetical case where someone develops a client for MySQL. The client software might not even be bound either statically or dynamically with any of the MySQL modules. The client software could just use a user-developed GUI to open a command prompt to which it could send dynamically generated commands for MySQL based on inputs and events at the user interface. The client would thus act just like an ordinary user, except that the commands it would tell MySQL to execute would be generated via the graphical interface based on user input, rather than being directly formulated and requested by the user. However, since the composite application requires the MySQL database to operate, it would, at least according to MySQL AB's interpretation of the GPL, constitute a *derivative work* of MySQL and so be subject to GPL restrictions on the distribution of derivative works if they are used for proprietary redistribution; that is, the client, even though it used no MySQL code, would be considered a derivative of MySQL according to MySQL AB. As per Valimaki (2005, p. 137), it seems that "the company regards all clients as derivative works and in order to even *use* a client with other terms than GPL the developer of the client would need to buy a proprietary license from MySQL AB" and that in general "if one needs their database in order to run the client, then one is basically also distributing MySQL database and GPL becomes binding," though this does not appear to be supported by either the standard GPL interpretation or the copyright law on derivative works (Valimaki, 2005).

Ironically, in the tangled Web of legal interactions that emerge between corporate actors, MySQL AB was itself involved in mid-2006 in potential legal uncertainties vis-à-vis the Oracle Corporation and one of its own components. The situation concerned MySQL AB's use of the open source InnoDB storage engine, a key component that was critical to MySQL's handling of transactions. The InnoDB component ensures that MySQL is ACID compliant. (Recall that the well-known *ACID* rules for database integrity mean transactions have to satisfy the following behaviors: *atomicity*: no partial transaction execution – it's all or nothing in terms of transaction execution; *consistency*: transactions must maintain data consistency – they cannot introduce contradictions among the data in the database; *isolation*: concurrent transactions cannot mutually interfere; *durability*: committed transactions cannot be lost – for example, they must be preserved by backups and transaction logs.) Oracle acquired the InnoDB storage engine and in 2006, it bought out Sleepycat which makes the Berkeley DB storage engine also used by MySQL. The InnoDB storage engine was effectively a plug-in for MySQL, so alternative substitutions would be feasible in the event that MySQL's continued use of the storage engine became problematic. Additionally, the InnoDB engine is also available under the GPL license. Nonetheless, such developments illustrate the strategic uncertainties that even carefully managed dual licensed products may be subject to (Kirk, 2005).

References

Codewalkers. (2002). Interview with Michael Widenius. http://codewalkers.com/interviews/Monty_Widenius.html. Accessed November 29, 2006.

Hyatt, J. (2006). MySQL: Workers in 25 Countries with No HQ. http://money.cnn.com/2006/05/31/magazines/fortune/mysql_greatteams_fortune/. Accessed November 29, 2006.

Kirk, J. (2005). MySQL AB to Counter Oracle Buy of Innobase. ComputerWorld, November 23. http://www.computerworld.com.au/index.php/id;1423768456. Accessed February 11, 2007.

MySQL News Announcement. (2001). FAQ on MySQL vs. NuSphere Dispute. http://www.mysql.com/news-and-events/news/article_75.html. Accessed November, 29 2006.

Valimaki, M. (2005). The Rise of Open Source Licensing: A Challenge to the Use of Intellectual Property in the Software Industry. Turre Publishing, Helsinki, Finland.

2.4.3 Sleepycat Software and TrollTech

Sleepycat Software and TrollTech are two other examples of prominent and successful companies that sell open source products using a dual licensing business model.

Berkeley DB

Sleepycat Software owns, sells, and develops a very famous database system called Berkeley DB. The software for this system was originally developed as part of the Berkeley rewrite of the AT&T proprietary code in the BSD Unix distribution, a rewrite done by programmers Keith Bostic, Margo Seltzer, and

Mike Olson. The software was first released in 1991 under the BSD license. Recall that the BSD license allows proprietary modification and redistribution of software with *no* payments required to the original copyright owners. The original software became widely used and embedded in a number of proprietary products.

Berkeley DB is not an SQL database. Queries to the Berkeley DB are done through its own specific API. The system supports many commercial and open applications, ranging from major Web sites to cell phones, and is one of the storage engines available for MySQL. The software currently has over 200 million deployments (Martens, 2005). Berkeley DB is a C library that runs in the same process as an application, considerably reducing interprocess communication delays. It stores data as key/value pairs, amazingly allowing data records and keys to be up to 4 GB in length, with tables up to 256 TB. The Sleepycat Web site describes the Berkeley DB library as "designed to run in a completely unattended fashion, so all runtime administration is programmatically controlled by the application, not by a human administrator. It has been designed to be simple, fast, small and reliable" (sleepycat.com). We refer the reader to the article by Sleepycat CTO Margo Seltzer (2005) for a commanding analysis of the opportunities and challenges in database system design that go far beyond the traditional relational model. In response to the demand for Berkeley DB and some needs for improvements in the software, its developers founded Sleepycat, further significantly developed the product, and subsequently released it under a dual licensing model in 1997 (Valimaki, 2005). The license model used by Sleepycat is like that of MySQL. Versions earlier than 2.0 were available under the BSD, but later versions are dual licensed. The noncommercial license is OSI certified. However, the commercial license requires payment for proprietary, closed source redistribution of derivatives. About 75% of the company's revenues come from such license fees. Similarly to the MySQL AB model, Berkeley DB software development is basically internal, with any external code contributions reimplemented by the company's developers. This is motivated, just as in the case of MySQL, not only by the desire to keep ownership pure but also because of the complexity of the product.

The Qt Graphics Library

Another company that has long used a dual license model is TrollTech. TrollTech develops and markets a C++ class library of GUI modules called Qt (pronounced "cute" by its designers), which was eventually adopted by and played an important role in the open source KDE project. Qt is cross-platform, supporting Unix-like, Windows, and Macintosh environments and provides programmers with an extensive collection of so-called widgets. It is an extremely widely

used open GUI development library. Qt was first publicly released in 1995, originally under a restrictive though still open source license, which prohibited the
free redistribution of modifications. The use of Qt in the GPL'd KDE desktop
environment caused a well-known licensing controversy. Eventually TrollTech
was pressured by the open source community to release its product not merely
as open source but under the GPL and despite the initial aversion of the company
founder toward the GPL because of doubts about the implications of the GPL
in a dual license context (Valimaki, 2005). As it turned out, the approach was
successful and increased the popularity of the product. The company's sales
derive largely from its licensing fees. Proprietary development of the product
requires it be purchased under a commercial license. The free version helps
maintain the open source user base. An educational version of the product that
integrates with Microsoft's Visual Studio.NET is available for Windows.

References

Martens, C. (2005). Sleepycat to Extend Paw to Asia. InfoWorld. http://infoworld.com/
    article/05/06/22/HNsleepycat_1.html. Accessed November 29, 2006.
Seltzer, M. (2005). Beyond Relational Databases. ACM Queue, 3(3), 50–58.
Valimaki, M. (2005). The Rise of Open Source Licensing: A Challenge to the Use of
    Intellectual Property in the Software Industry. Turre Publishing, Helsinki, Finland.

2.5 The P's in LAMP

The first three letters of the ubiquitous LAMP open source software stack
stand for Linux, Apache, and MySQL. The last letter P refers to the scripting
language used and encompasses the powerful programming language Perl, the
scripting language PHP, and the application language Python. These are all open
source (unlike, for example, Java whose major implementations are proprietary
even if programs written in it are open). Perl comes with an immense open
library of Perl modules called CPAN. We will focus our discussion on PHP and
Perl. Concerning Python, we only note that it is a widely ported open source
programming language invented by Guido van Rossum in 1990 and used for
both Web and applications development, such as in BitTorrent and Google, and
sometimes for scripting.

2.5.1 PHP Server-Side Scripting

PHP is a server-side scripting language embedded in HTML pages. It typically interfaces with a background database, commonly MySQL, as in LAMP

environments. Thus, it allows the creation of data-based, dynamic Web pages. The name PHP is a recursive acronym like GNU, standing for *P*HP *H*ypertext *P*reprocessor, though it originally referred to Personal Home Page tools. The Netcraft survey indicates that PHP is the most widely deployed server-side scripting language, with about one-third of all Internet sites surveyed having PHP installed by early 2004.

PHP is another instructive tale of open source development. It illustrates some of the ways in which open source projects originate, the influence of their initial developers and the impact of new developers, the degree of open source commitment, and attitudes toward commercialization. In the case of PHP, the original developer Rasmus Lerdorf was later joined by a group of other major core developers. Lerdorf has kept with the open source project but did not join in its commercialization – except in the indirect sense that he is currently involved as a development engineer in its vertical application internally within Yahoo. In fact, Lerdorf seems to believe that the greatest monetary potentials for open source lies in major vertical applications like Yahoo rather than in support companies (like Zend in the case of PHP) (Schneider, 2003). Some of the core PHP developers formed a commercial company named Zend, which sells a number of PHP products, including an encoder designed to protect the intellectual property represented by custom PHP scripts by encrypting them!

Programmers are often autodidacts: open source helps that happen. Rasmus Lerdorf in fact describes himself as a "crappy coder" who thinks coding is a "mind-numbing tedious endeavor" and "never took any programming courses at school" (Schneider, 2003). He has an engineering degree from the University of Waterloo. But despite an absence of formal credentials in computer science and the self-deprecatory characterization of his interests, he had been quite a bit of a hacker since his youth, hacking the CERN and NCSA server code soon after the latter's distribution (Schneider, 2003). He was a self-taught Unix, Xenix, and Linux fan and learned what he needed from looking at the open source code they provided. To quote from the Schneider interview (2003), "What I like is solving problems, which unfortunately often requires that I do a bit of coding. I will steal and borrow as much existing code as I can and write as little 'glue' code as possible to make it all work together. That's pretty much what PHP is."

Lerdorf started developing PHP in 1994–1995 with a simple and personal motivation in mind, the classic Raymond "scratch an itch" model. He wanted to know how many people were looking at his resume, since he had included a URL for his resume in letters he had written to prospective employers (Schneider, 2003). He used a Perl CGI script to log visits to his resume page and to collect information about the visitors. To impress the prospective employers, he let visitors see his logging information (Schneider, 2003). People who visited the page soon became interested in using the tools, so Lerdorf gave the code away in typical open source fashion, setting up a PHP mailing list to share the code, bug reports, and fixes. He officially announced the availability of the initial set of PHP tools (Version 1.0) in mid-1995, saying that "the tools are in the public domain distributed under the GNU Public License. Yes, that means they are free!" (see reference link under Schneider (2003)). Admittedly, there are a lot of ambiguities in that statement, from *public domain* to *free*, but the intent is clear. His own predisposition to open source was partly related to money. As Lerdorf observes, "I don't think I was ever really 'hooked' by a 'movement'. When you don't have the money to buy SCO Unix and you can download something that works and even find people who can help you get it up and running, how can you beat that?" (Yank, 2002). Lerdorf worked intensively on the PHP code for several years. Being the leader and originator of a popular open source project is not a lark. Like Linus he personally went through all the contributed patches during that period, usually rewriting the code before committing it. He estimates that he wrote 99% of the code at that time. Lerdorf's involvement with open source has continued in a proprietary context at Yahoo. Unlike many organizations, Yahoo has what Lerdorf describes as a "long tradition of using open source" (like FreeBSD) for use in their own extremely complex and demanding infrastructure (Schneider, 2003). Andrei Zmievski is currently listed as the PHP project administrator and owner on freshmeat.net and the principal developer of PHP since 1999. PHP 4 is licensed under the GPL. There are over 800 contributors currently involved in its development (available at http://www.php.net).

Open source developments can go through generational changes as the product or its implementation evolves in response to outside events or the insights of new participants. This happened with PHP. Computer scientists Zeev Suraski and Andi Gutmans became involved with PHP in mid-1997 as part of a Web programming project at the Technion in Israel. An odd syntax error in PHP led them to look at the source code for the language. They were surprised to see that the program used a line-by-line parsing technique, which they recognized could be dramatically improved upon. After a few months of intense development effort, they had recoded enough of the PHP source to convince Lerdorf to discontinue the earlier version of PHP and base further work on their new code. This led to a successful collaboration between Lerdorf and a new extended group of seven PHP core developers. Lerdorf has observed that "this was probably the most crucial moment during the development of PHP. The project would have died at that point if it had remained a one-man effort and it could easily have died if the newly assembled group of strangers could not figure out how to work together towards a common goal. We somehow managed to juggle our egos and other personal events and the project grew" (Lerdorf, 2004). Another major overhaul followed. At the time, PHP still used an approach in which the code was executed as it was parsed. In order to handle the much larger applications that people were using PHP for, the developers had to make yet another major change. This once again led to redesigning and reimplementing the PHP engine from scratch (Suraski, 2000). The new compilation engine, which used a compile first and then execute approach, was separable from PHP 4. It was given its own name the Zend engine (combining *Zee*v + *And*i). It is licensed under an Apache-style as-is license. The company does not dual license the Zend engine but provides support services and additional products for a fee.

Although the PHP language processor is open source and the scripting language programs are human-readable text (on the server side), its major commercial distributor Zend ironically has tools for hiding source code that is written in PHP – just like in the old-fashioned proprietary model! Gutmans and Suraski, along with another core developer Doron Gerstel, founded Zend in 1999. It is a major distributor of PHP-related products and services. From an open source point of view, a particularly interesting product is the Zend Encoder. The Zend Web site describes the encoder as "the recognized industry standard in *PHP intellectual property protection*" – italics added (http://www.zend.com/). The encoder lets companies distribute their applications written in PHP "without revealing the source code." This protects the companies against copyright infringement as well as from reverse engineering since the distributed code is "both obfuscated and encoded" (http://www.zend.com/). As the site's selling points describe it, this approach allows "Professional Service Providers (to) rely on the Zend Encoder to deliver their exclusive and commercial PHP applications to customers without revealing their valuable intellectual property. By protecting their PHP applications, these and other enterprises expand distribution and increase revenue" (http://www.zend.com/). It is important to understand that it is not the source code for the PHP compiler that is hidden, but the PHP scripts that development companies write for various applications and that are run in a PHP environment that are hidden. Furthermore, the application source code is not being hidden from the end users (browser users), since they would never have seen the code in the first place since the PHP scripts are executed on the server and only their results are sent to the client, so there's nothing to hide from the client. The code is being hidden from purchasers of the code who want to run it on their own Web servers. In any case, this model represents an interesting marriage of open source products and proprietary code. The encoding is accomplished by converting the "plain-text PHP scripts into a platform-independent binary format known as Zend Intermediate Code. These encoded binary files are the ones that are distributed (to prospective users) instead of the human-readable PHP files. The performance of the encoded PHP application is completely unaffected!" (http://www.zend.com/). None of this turns out to be open license related, since the proprietary nature of the distributions that Zend is targeting is not about the PHP environment itself which is GPL'd but about scripts written using PHP. Nonetheless, the thinking is not on the same page as traditional open source distribution where disclosure of source is viewed as beneficial.

There are striking arguments to be made about the cost-effectiveness of open tools like PHP and open platforms. Who better to hear them from than an open source star and proprietary developer like Rasmus Lerdorf? In an interview with Sharon Machlis (2002), Lerdorf did an interesting back-of-the-envelop calculation about the relative cost benefits of open applications versus proprietary tools like Microsoft's. In response to the hypothetical question of why one would choose PHP over (say) Microsoft's ASP, he estimated that (at that time) the ASP solution entailed (roughly): $4,000 for a Windows server, $6,000 for an Internet security and application server on a per CPU basis, $20,000 for an SQL Enterprise Edition Server per CPU, and about $3,000 per developer for an MSDN subscription, at a final cost of over $40,000 *per CPU*. In contrast, you could build an equivalent open source environment that did the same thing based on Linux, Apache + SSL, PHP, PostgreSQL, and the Web proxy Squid, for free. The price comparisons become even more dramatic when multiple CPUs are involved. Granted if you have an existing Microsoft shop in place, then the open source solution does have a learning curve attached to it that translates into additional costs. However, especially in the case where one is starting from scratch, the PHP and free environment is economically very attractive.

References

Lerdorf, R. (2004). Do You PHP? http://www.oracle.com/technology/pub/articles/php_experts/rasmus_php.html. Accessed November 29, 2006.

Machlis, S. (2002). PHP Creator Rasmus Lerdorf. http://www.computerworld.com/softwaretopics/software/appdev/story/0,10801,67864,00.html. Accessed November 29, 2006.

Schneider, J. (2003). Interview: PHP Founder Rasmus Lerdorf on Relinquishing Control. http://www.midwestbusiness.com/news/viewnews.asp?newsletterID=4577. Accessed November 29, 2006.

Suraski, Z. (2000). Under the Hood of PHP4. http://www.zend.com/zend/art/underphp4-hood.php. Accessed November 29, 2006.

Yank, K. (2002). Interview – PHP's Creator, Rasmus Lerdorf. http://www.sitepoint.com/article/phps-creator-rasmus-lerdorf. Accessed November 29, 2006.

2.5.2 Perl and CPAN

According to the perl.org Web site, the open source programming language Perl, together with its largely open library of supporting perl modules CPAN, is a "stable, cross-platform programming language ... used for *mission-critical* projects in the public and private sectors and ... widely used to program *web applications*" (italics added). Perl 1.0 was initially released by its designer Larry Wall about 1987, with the much revised Perl 5 version debuting in 1994. Perl is a procedural language like C. It is also implemented with a combination of C and some Perl modules. Perl has some of the characteristics of Unix shell programming and is influenced by Unix tools like awk and sed. Although Perl was originally designed for text manipulation, it has become widely used in many systems applications, particularly to *glue* systems together. It was also the original technology used to produce dynamic Web pages using CGI. Its diverse applicability has given it a reputation as a system administrator's Swiss army knife. In fact, hacker Henry Spencer comically called Perl a Swiss army chainsaw (see the *Jargon File* at http://catb.org/jargon/html/index.html), while for similar reasons others call it "the duct tape of the Internet." The Perl 5 version allowed the use of modules to extend the language. Like the Linux module approach, the Perl 5 module structure "allows continued development of the language without actually changing the core language" according to developer Wall (Richardson, 1999). This version has been under continuous development since its release. Perl is highly portable and also has binary distributions like ActivePerl, which is commonly used for Windows environments. Perl and CPAN modules are pervasive in financial applications, including long-standing early use at the Federal Reserve Board and more recently in many bioinformatics applications. Indeed a classic application of Perl as an intersystem glue was its application in integrating differently formatted data from multiple genome sequencing databases during the Human Genome Project (Stein, 1996).

The essay by Larry Wall (1999), the inimitable creator of Perl, is worth reading for a philosophical discourse on the design and purpose of Perl. Wall discourses, among other things, on why the linguistic complexity of Perl is needed in order to handle the complexity of messy real-world problems. Wall's academic background is interesting. Although he had worked full time for his college computer center, his graduate education was actually in linguistics (of the human language kind) and he intended it to be in preparation for doing biblical translations. The interview with Wall in Richardson (1999) describes what Wall calls the "postmodern" motivation behind Perl's design.

Perl is open source and GPL compatible since it can be licensed using either the GPL or the so-called *Artistic License*, an alternative combination called the *disjunctive license* for Perl. The GPL option in this disjuncture is what makes Perl GPL compatible. The Free Software Foundation considers the Artistic License option for Perl to be vague and problematic in its wording and so it recommends the GPL. On the other hand, the perl.com Web site characterized the Perl license as the Artistic license, which it describes as "a kinder and gentler version of the GNU license – one that doesn't infect your work if you care to borrow from Perl or package up pieces of it as part of a commercial product" (perl.com). This last is a very important distinction since it allows the code for Perl or Perl modules to be modified and embedded in proprietary products.

A very significant part of Perl's power comes from CPAN, which stands for *Comprehensive Perl Archive Network*, an immense library of Perl modules that is far more extensive than the Java class libraries or those available for either PHP or Python. The CPAN collection located at cpan.org was started about 1994, enabled by the module architecture provided by Perl 5. It currently lists over 5,000 authors and over 10,000 modules. The search engine at search.cpan.org helps programmers sort through the large number of modules available. The modules are human-readable Perl code, so they are naturally accessible source. However, a limited number of Perl binaries are also available, but these are not stored on the CPAN site. While the Perl language itself is distributed as GPL (or Artistic), the modules written in Perl on the CPAN site do not require any particular license. However, the CPAN FAQ does indicate that most, though not all, of the modules available are in fact licensed under either the GPL or the Artistic license. Contributors do not have to include a license but the site recommends it. With the limited exception of some shareware and commercial software for Perl IDEs, SDKs and editors as indicated on the binary ports page of the Web site, the site stipulates that it *strongly disapproves* of any software for the site that is not free software at least in the sense of free of charge.

References

Richardson, M. (1999). Larry Wall, the Guru of Perl. 1999–05–01. Linux Journal. http://www.linuxjournal.com/article/3394. Accessed November 29, 2006.

Stein, L. (1996). How Perl Saved the Human Genome Project. The Perl Journal. 2001 version archived at Dr. Dobb's Portal: www.ddj.com/dept/architect/184410424. Accessed November 29, 2006. Original article: TPJ, 1996, 1(2). Also via: http://scholar.google.com/scholar?hl=en&lr=&q=cache:vg2KokmwJNUJ:science.bard.edu/cutler/classes/bioinfo/notes/perlsave.pdf+++%22The+Perl+Journal%22+stein. Accessed November 29, 2006.

Wall, L. (1999). Diligence, Patience, and Humility. In: Open Sources: Voices from the Open Source Revolution, M. Stone, S. Ockman, and C. DiBona (editors). O'Reilly Media, Sebastopol, CA, 127–148.

2.6 BitTorrent

BitTorrent is a next-generation P2P Internet utility. It was created by Brahm Cohen in 2002 and has become extremely widely used, particularly for sharing popular multimedia files. We discuss it here for two reasons. It represents a next generation type of Internet service, called a *Web 2.0 service* by O'Reilly (2005). It also facilitates the largest peer-to-peer network according to estimates done by CacheLogic. BitTorrent works by exploiting the interconnectivity provided by the Internet, avoiding the bottlenecks that occur if every user tries to get an entire copy of a file from a single source, as is done in the client-server model of data exchange. It also differs from conventional peer-to-peer networks, where exchanges are limited to a single pair of uploaders and downloaders at any given time. Under the BitTorrent protocol, a central server called a *tracker* coordinates the file exchanges between peers. The tracker does not require knowledge of the file contents and so can work with a minimum of bandwidth, allowing it to coordinate many peers. Files are thought of as comprising disjoint pieces called *fragments*. Initially, a source or *seed server* that contains the entire file distributes the fragments to a set of peers. Each peer in a pool or so-called *swarm* of peers will at a given point have some of the fragments from the complete file but lack some others. These missing fragments are supplied by being exchanged transparently among the peers in a many-peer-to-many-peer fashion. The exchange protocol used by BitTorrent exhibits a fundamental, remarkable, and paradoxical advantage. The more people who want to have access to a file, the more readily individual users can acquire a complete copy of the file since there will be more partners to exchange fragments with. Thus BitTorrent is an example of what has been called a *Web 2.0 service*. It exhibits a new network externality principle, namely, that "the service gets better the more people use it" (O'Reilly, 2005). In contrast to earlier Internet services like Akamai, BitTorrent can be thought of as having a BYOB (Bring Your Own Bottle) approach. Once again, O'Reilly expresses it succinctly:

> ...every BitTorrent consumer brings his own resources to the party. There's an implicit "architecture of participation," a built-in ethic of cooperation, in which the service acts primarily as an intelligent broker, connecting the edges to each other and harnessing the power of the users themselves.

Developer Cohen's software also avoids the so-called *leeching* effect that occurs in P2P exchanges under which people greedily download files but selfishly refuse to share their data by uploading. The BitTorrent protocol rules require that downloaders of fragments also have to upload fragments. In Cohen's program, the more a user shares his files, the faster the torrent of fragments from other users downloads to his computer. This reflects a motto Cohen had printed on T-shirts: "Give and ye shall receive" (Thompson, 2005). It's a "share and share alike" principle. BitTorrent now carries an enormous share of world Internet traffic, currently one-third according to the estimate by CacheLogic, though some aspects of the estimate have been disputed. The BitTorrent license is a custom variation of the Jabber license. It reserves the BitTorrent™ name as a trademark, which prevents the name from drifting into generic usage. Although the BitTorrent source code is open source, it does not appear to be an OSI-certified license or a free software license, partly because of some relicensing restrictions, although the license definition seems to be GPL-like in character. The BitTorrent company is now acting as a licensed distributor for movie videos, an important, new open source business model.

References

O'Reilly, T. (2005). What is Web 2.0 Design Patterns and Business Models for the Next Generation of Software. http://www.oreillynet.com/pub/a/oreilly/tim/news/2005/09/30/what-is-web-20.html. Accessed November 29, 2006.

Thompson, C. (2005). The BitTorrent Effect. Wired.com, Issue 13.01. http://wired.com/wired/archive/13.01/bittorrent.html. Accessed November 29, 2006.

2.7 BIND

BIND is a pervasive and fundamental Internet infrastructure utility. From an open source business model point of view, BIND is instructive precisely because it led to such an unexpected business model. The model did not benefit the original developers and was not based on the software itself. Instead it was based indirectly on information services that were enabled by the software.

The acronym BIND stands for Berkeley Internet Domain Name. BIND is an Internet directory service. Its basic function is to implement domain name services by translating symbolic host domain names into numeric IP addresses, using distributed name servers. The DNS (Domain Name System) environment is an enormous operation. It relies on domain name data stored across billions of resource records distributed over millions of files called zones (Salamon, 1998/2004). The zones are kept on what are called authoritative servers, which are distributed over the Internet. Authoritative servers handle DNS name requests for zones they have data on and request information from other servers otherwise. Large name servers may have tens of thousands of zones. We will not delve further into how the system works.

The general idea of using symbolic names for network communications was originally introduced to support e-mail on the ARPANET, long before the Internet, in fact going back to the mid-1970s. As network traffic increased, the initial implementation approaches had to be completely revised (see RFC 805 from 1982, as well as RFC 881, etc.). The original version of the new BIND software was written in the early 1980s by graduate students at UC Berkeley as part of the development of Berkeley Unix under a DARPA grant. Its current version BIND 9 is much more secure than earlier BIND versions and is outsourced by the Internet Software Consortium to the Nominum Corporation for continued development and maintenance.

The business opportunity that emerged from BIND is interesting because it turned out to be neither the software itself nor the service and marketing of the software that was profitable. Instead, the profit potential lay in the service opportunity provided by the provision of the domain names. It is highly ironic that the project maintainer for BIND which is arguably "the single most mission critical program on the Internet" had "scraped by for decades on donations and consulting fees," while the business based on the registration of domain names that was in turn based on BIND thrived (O'Reilly, 2004). As O'Reilly observed,

> ... domain name registration – an information service based on the software – became a business generating hundreds of millions of dollars a year, a virtual monopoly for Network Solutions, which was handed the business on government contract before anyone realized just how valuable it would be. The ... opportunity of the DNS was not a software opportunity at all, but the service of managing the namespace used by the software. By a historical accident, the business model became separated from the software.

References

O'Reilly, T. (2004). Open Source Paradigm Shift. http://tim.oreilly.com/articles/paradigmshift_0504.html. Accessed November 29, 2006.

Salamon, A. (1998/2004). DNS Overview and General References. http://www.dns.net/dnsrd/docs/whatis.html. Accessed January 10, 2007.

3

The Open Source Platform

We use the term *open source platform* to refer to the combination of open operating systems and desktops, support environments like GNU, and underlying frameworks like the X Window System, which together provide a matrix for user interaction with a computer system. The provision of such an open infrastructure for computing has been one of the hallmark objectives of the free software movement. The GNU project sponsored by the Free Software Foundation (FSF) had as its ultimate objective the creation of a self-contained free software platform that would allow computer scientists to accomplish all their software development in a free environment uninhibited by proprietary restrictions. This chapter describes these epic achievements in the history of computing, including the people involved and technical and legal issues that affected the development. We shall also examine the important free desktop application GIMP which is intended as a free replacement for Adobe Photoshop. We shall reserve the discussion of the GNU project itself to a later chapter.

The root system that serves as the reference model for open source operating systems is Unix whose creation and evolution we shall briefly describe. Over time, legal and proprietary issues associated with Unix opened the door to Linux as the signature open source operating system, though major free versions of Unix continued under the BSD (Berkeley Software Distributions) aegis. The Linux operating system, which became the flagship open source project, evolved out of a simple port of Unix to a personal computer environment, but it burgeoned rapidly into the centerpiece project of the movement. To be competitive with proprietary platforms in the mass market, the Linux and free Unix-like platforms in turn required high-quality desktop style interfaces. It was out of this necessity that the two major open desktops GNOME and KDE emerged. Underlying the development of these desktops was the extensive, longstanding development effort represented by the X Window System, and an open source project begun in the early 1980s at MIT that provided the basic underlying windowing capabilities for Unix-like systems.

3.1 Operating Systems

This first section addresses the creation of Unix and its variants and the emergence of Linux.

3.1.1 Unix

The Unix operating system was developed at AT&T's Bell Telephone Laboratories (BTL) during the 1970s. An essential factor in the historic importance of Unix lay in the fact that it was the first operating system written in a high-level language (C), although this was not initially so. This approach had the critical advantage that it made Unix highly portable to different hardware platforms. Much of the development work on Unix involved distributed effort between the initial developers at AT&T's BTL and computer scientists at universities, especially the development group at University of California (UC) Berkeley that added extensive capabilities to the original AT&T Unix system during the 1980s. Remember that the network communications infrastructure that would greatly facilitate such distributed collaboration was at this time only in its infancy. While Unix began its life in the context of an industrial research lab, it progressed with the backing of major academic and government (DARPA) involvement.

From the viewpoint of distributed collaboration and open source development, the invention and development of Unix illustrates the substantial benefits that can accrue from open development, as well as the disadvantages for innovation that can arise from proprietary restrictions in licensing. The Unix story also illustrates how distributed collaboration was already feasible prior to the Internet communications structure, but also how it could be done more effectively once even more advanced networked communications became available (which was partly because of Unix itself).

Initially the AT&T Unix source code was freely and informally exchanged. This was a common practice at the time and significantly helped researchers in different organizations in their tinkering with the source code, fixing bugs, and adding features. Eventually, however, licensing restrictions by AT&T, considerable charges for the software to other commercial organizations, and legal conflicts between AT&T and the UC Berkeley handicapped the development of Unix as an open source system, at least temporarily during the early 1990s. The early 1990s was also precisely the time when Linux had started to emerge and quickly seize center stage as the most popular Unix-like system, offered with open source, licensed under the General Public License (GPL), and free of charge.

Necessity is the mother of invention – or at least discomfort is. The development of Unix at Bell Labs started when Ken Thompson and Dennis Ritchie wrote an operating system in assembly language for a DEC PDP-7. The project was their reaction to Bell Labs' withdrawal from the Multics time-sharing operating system project with MIT and General Electric. Even though the Multics project had problems (like system bloating), it was an important and innovative system and the two programmers had become accustomed to it. Its unavailability and replacement by an inferior, older system frustrated them (Scott, 1988). In response, they decided to design a new, simple operating system to run on their DEC machine. Interestingly, the idea was not to develop a BTL corporate product but just to design and implement a usable and simple operating system that the two developers could comfortably use. In addition to the core of the operating system, the environment they developed included a file system, a command interpreter, some utilities, a text editor, and a formatting program. Since it provided the functionality for a basic office automation system, Thompson and Ritchie persuaded the legal department at Bell Labs to be the first users and rewrote their system for a PDP-11 for the department.

In 1973, a decisive if not revolutionary development occurred: the operating system was rewritten in C. The C language was a new high-level programming language that Kernighan and Ritchie had just invented and which was, among other things, intended to be useful for writing software that would ordinarily have been written in assembly language, like operating systems. This extremely innovative approach meant that Unix could now be much more easily updated or ported to other machines. In fact, within a few years, Unix had been ported to a number of different computer platforms – something that had never been done before. The use of a higher level language for operating system implementation was a visionary development because prior to this, operating systems had always been closely tied to the assembly language of their native hardware. The high-level language implementation made the code for the operating system "much easier to understand and to modify" (Ritchie and Thompson, 1974), which was a key cognitive advantage in collaborative development. Furthermore, as Raymond (1997) observed:

> If Unix could present the same face, the same capabilities, on machines of many different types, it could serve as a common software environment for all of them. No longer would users have to pay for complete new designs of software every time a machine went obsolete. Hackers could carry around software toolkits between different machines, rather than having to re-invent the equivalents of fire and the wheel every time.

The Unix environment was also elegantly and simply designed as a toolkit of simple programs that could easily interact. Allegedly the terse character of the Unix and C commands was just an artifact of the fact that teletype machines that communicated with the PDP were quite slow: so the shorter the commands (and the error messages), the more convenient it was for the user!

The professional dissemination of their work by Ritchie and Thompson also strongly affected the rapid deployment of Unix. At the end of 1973, they gave a report on Unix at the Fourth ACM Symposium on Operating Systems, which was later published in the *Communications of the ACM* (Ritchie and Thompson, 1974). As Tom Van Vleck observed, this report still "remains one of the best and clearest pieces of writing in the computer field" (Van Vleck, 1995). The ACM symposium presentation caught the eye of a Berkeley researcher who subsequently persuaded his home department to buy a DEC on which to install the new system. This initiated Berkeley's heavy historic involvement in Unix development, an involvement that was further extended when Ken Thompson went to UC Berkeley as a visiting professor during 1976 (Berkeley was his alma mater). The article's publication precipitated further deployment.

The system was deployed widely and rapidly, particularly in universities. By 1977, there were more than 500 sites running Unix. Given the legal restrictions that the AT&T monopoly operated under, because of the so-called 1956 consent decree with the U.S. Department of Justice, AT&T appeared to be prohibited from commercially marketing and supporting computer software (Garfinkel and Spafford, 1996). Thus, de facto, software was not considered as a profit center for the company. During this time, the source code for Unix, not merely the binary code, was made available by AT&T to universities and the government, as well as to commercial firms. However, the distribution was under the terms of an AT&T license and an associated *nondisclosure agreement* that was intended to control the release of the Unix source code. Thus, although the source code was open in a certain sense, it was strictly speaking not supposed to be disclosed, except to other license recipients who already had a copy of the code. University groups could receive a tape of the complete source code for the system for about $400, which was the cost of the materials and their distribution, though the educational license itself was free.

The distribution of Unix as an operating system that was widely used in major educational environments and as part of their education by many of the top computer science students in the country had many side-benefits. For example, it meant – going forward – that there would be within a few years literally thousands of Unix-savvy users and developers emerging from the best research universities who would further contribute to the successful dispersion, development, and entrenchment of Unix. A *Unix culture* developed that was strongly dependent on having access to the C source code for the system, the code that also simultaneously served as the documentation for the system programs. This access to the source code greatly stimulated innovation. Programmers could experiment with the system, play with the code, and fix bugs, an advantage for the development of Unix that would have been nonexistent if the distributions of the Unix source and system utilities had only been available in binary form.

By 1978, the Berkeley Computer Systems Research Group, including students of Ken Thompson at Berkeley, were making add-ons for Unix and distributing them, always with both the binary executable and the C source code included, basically for the cost of shipping and materials as so-called *Berkeley Software Distributions* of Unix – but only as long as the recipient had a valid Unix source license from AT&T. The license under which the BSD application code itself was distributed was very liberal. It allowed the BSD-licensed open source code, or modifications to it, to be incorporated into closed, proprietary software whose code could then be kept undisclosed.

Legal issues invariably impact commercializable science. An important legal development occurred in 1979 when AT&T released the 7th version of Unix. By that point AT&T was in a legal position to sell software, so it decided that it was now going to commercialize Unix, no longer distributing it freely and no longer disclosing its source code. Companies, like IBM and DEC, could receive the AT&T source-code licenses for a charge and sometimes even the right to develop proprietary systems that used the trademark *Unix*, like DEC's Ultrix. Almost inevitably the companies created differentiated versions of Unix, leading eventually to a proliferation of incompatible proprietary versions. The UC Berkeley group responded to AT&T's action at the end of 1979 by making its next BSD release (3BSD) a complete operating system, forking the Unix development (Edwards, 2003). Berkeley, which was now strongly supported by DARPA especially because of the success of the virtual memory implementation 3BSD, would now come to rival Bell Labs as a center of Unix development. Indeed, it was BSD Unix that was selected by DARPA as the base system for the TCP/IP protocol that would underlie the Internet. During the early 1980s the Berkeley Computer Systems Research Group introduced improvements to Unix that increased the popularity of its distributions with universities, especially because of its improved networking capabilities.

The networking capabilities provided by BSD 4 had what might be described as a meta-effect on software development. BSD version 4.2 was released in 1983 and was much more popular with Unix vendors for several years than AT&T's commercial Unix System V version (McKusick, 1999). But version 4 didn't merely improve the capabilities of an operating system. It fundamentally altered the very way in which collaboration on software development could be done because it provided an infrastructure for digitally transmitting not only communication messages but also large amounts of source code among remotely located developers. This created a shared workspace where the actual production artifacts could be worked on in common.

However, AT&T did not stand still with its own Unix versions. The AT&T System V variants, starting with the first release in 1983 and continuing to release 4 of System V in 1989 (also designated SVR4), eventually incorporated many of the improvements to Unix that had been developed at Berkeley (Scott, 1988). Indeed, release 4 of System V had over a million installations. However, these commercial releases no longer included source code. System V was the first release that AT&T actually supported (because it was now a commercial product) and ultimately became the preferred choice for hardware vendors, partly because its operating system interfaces followed certain formal standards better (Wheeler, 2003). While the Unix license fees that AT&T charged universities were nominal, those for commercial firms had ranged as high as a quarter of a million dollars, but AT&T lowered the costs of the commercial license with the release of System V. Many private companies developed their own private variations (so-called flavors) of Unix based on SVR4 under license from AT&T. Eventually, AT&T sold its rights to Unix to Novel after release 4 of System V in the early 1990s.

BSD Unix evolved both technically and legally toward free, open source status, divorced from AT&T restrictions. Throughout the 1980s, Berkeley's Computer Science Research Group extensively redeveloped Unix, enhancing it – and rewriting or excising almost every piece of the AT&T Unix code. The BSD distributions would ultimately be open source and not constrained by the AT&T licensing restrictions. Indeed, by 1991, a BSD system (originally Net/2) that was almost free of any of the AT&T source code was released that was freely redistributed. However, in response to this action by Berkeley, AT&T, concerned that its licensing income would be undermined, sued Berkeley in 1992 for violating its licensing agreement with AT&T. Later Berkeley countersued AT&T for not giving Berkeley adequate credit for the extensive BSD code that AT&T had used in its own System V! The dispute was settled by 1994. An acceptable, free version of Unix called 4.4BSD-Lite was released soon after the settlement. *All* infringements of AT&T code had been removed from this code, even though they had been relatively minuscule in any case.

The legal entanglements for BSD Unix caused a delay that created a key window of opportunity for the fledgling Linux platform. Indeed, the timing of the legal dispute was significantly disruptive for BSD Unix because it was precisely during this several year period, during which UC Berkeley was stymied by litigation with AT&T, that Linux emerged and rapidly gained in popularity. That said, it should be noted, in the case of Linux, that half of the utilities that come packaged with Linux in reality come from the BSD distribution – and of course Linux itself in turn depends heavily on the free or open tools developed by the GNU project (McKusick, 1999).

The BSD open source versions that forked from 4.4BSD-Lite and which were essentially free/open Unix-like clones included four systems: OpenBSD, NetBSD, BSDI, and most significantly FreeBSD. These versions were all licensed under the BSD license (at least the kernel code and most new code) which unlike the GPL permits both binary and source code redistribution. It includes the right to make derivative works that can be taken proprietary, as long as credit is given for the code done by the Berkeley group. OpenBSD is the second most popular of these free operating systems, after FreeBSD. It has recognized, empirically verified, strong security performance, as we briefly elaborated on in Chapter 2. NetBSD was designed with the intention of being portable to almost any processor. BSDI was the first commercial version of Unix for the widespread Intel platform (Wheeler, 2003). FreeBSD is the most popular of all the free operating systems, after Linux. Unlike Linux, it is developed under a single Concurrent Versions System (CVS) revision tree. Additionally, FreeBSD is a "complete operating system (kernel and userland)" and has the advantage that both the "kernel and provided utilities are under the control of the same release engineering team, (so) there is less likelihood of library incompatibilities" (Lavigne, 2005). It is considered to have high-quality network and security characteristics. Its Web site describes it as providing "robust network services, even under the heaviest of loads, and uses memory efficiently to maintain good response times for hundreds, or even thousands, of simultaneous user processes" (http://www.freebsd.org/about.html, accessed January 5, 2005). Yahoo uses FreeBSD for its servers as does the server survey Web site NetCraft. It is considered an elegantly simple system that installs easily on x86 compatible PCs and a number of other architectures. FreeBSD is also considered as binary compatible with Linux in the sense that commercial applications that are distributed as binaries for Linux generally also run on FreeBSD including software like Matlab and Acrobat.

For more information on the Unix operating system and its history, we refer the interested reader to Raymond (2004) and Ritchie (1984).

Open Standards for Unix-like Operating Systems

Standards are extremely important in engineering. And, as Andrew Tanenbaum quipped: "The nice thing about standards is that there are so many of them to choose from" (Tanenbaum, 1981)! Standards can be defined as openly available and agreed upon specifications. For example, there are international standards for HTML, XML, SQL, Unicode, and many other hardware and software systems, sanctioned by a variety of standards organizations like the W3C consortium or the International Organization for Standardization (ISO). Publicly available standards are important for software development because they define criteria around which software products or services can be built. They ensure that software implementers are working toward an agreed upon shared target. They help guarantee the compatibility and interoperability of products from different manufacturers or developers.

Standards help control emergent chaos: something that was definitely happening in the development of Unix-like systems. The closed versions of Unix developed by AT&T and eventually the various Unix vendors naturally tended to diverge increasingly over time, partly because the code bases were proprietary and the individual hardware vendors' needs were specialized. Such divergences may have the advantage of allowing useful specialized versions of a system to emerge, tailored to specific hardware architectures, but they also make it increasingly difficult for software developers to develop applications programs that work in these divergent environments. It also increases the learning difficulties of users who work or migrate between the different variations. Establishing accepted, widely recognized standards is a key way of guarding against the deleterious effects of the proliferation of such mutating clones of an original root system.

Operating systems exhibit the scale of complexity that necessitates standards. In the context of operating systems, standards can help establish uniform user views of a system as well as uniform system calls for application programs. Two related standards for Unix (which have basically merged) are the *POSIX* standard and the *Single Unix Specification*, both of which were initiated in the mid-1980s as a result of the proliferation of proprietary Unix-like systems. Standards do not entail disclosing source code like in the open source model, but they do at least ensure a degree of portability for applications and users, and mitigate against the decreasing interoperability that tends to arise when closed source systems evolve, mutate, and diverge. Thus, while open source helps keep divergence under control by making system internals transparent and reproducible, open standards attempt to help control divergence by maintaining coherence in the external user and programming interfaces of systems.

POSIX refers to a set of standards, defined by the IEEE and recognized by the ISO, which is intended to standardize the Applications Program Interface for programs running on Unix-like operating systems. *POSIX* is an acronym for *Portable Operating Systems Interface*, with the post-pended X due to the Unix connection. The name was proposed (apparently humorously) by Stallman who is prominent for his role in the Free Software Foundation and movement. POSIX was an effort by a consortium of vendors to establish a single standard for Unix, making it simpler to port applications across different hardware platforms. The user interface would look the same on different platforms and programs that ran on one POSIX system would also run on another. In other words, the user interface would be portable as would the Application Programmer Interface, rather than the operating system.

The POSIX standards include a compliance suite called the *Conformance Test Suite*. Actually, the term *compliance* is weaker than the stronger term *conformance* that implies that a system supports the POSIX standards in their entirety. The POSIX standards address both user and programming software interfaces. For example, the Korn Shell is established as the standard user command-line interface, as are an extensive set of user commands and utilities like the command for listing files (ls). These standards fall under what is called POSIX.2. The standards also define the C programming interface for system calls, including those for I/O services, files, and processes, under what is called POSIX.1. The POSIX standards were later integrated into the so-called *Single Unix Specification*, which had originated about the same time as the POSIX standards. The Single Unix Specification is the legal definition of the Unix system under the Unix trademark owned by the *Open Group*. The Open Group makes the standards freely available on the Web and provides test tools and certification for the standards.

References

Edwards, K. (2003). Technological Innovation in the Software Industry: Open Source Development. Ph.D. Thesis, Technical University of Denmark.

Garfinkel, S. and Spafford, G. (1996). Practical Unix and Internet Security. O'Reilly Media, Sebastopol, CA.

Lavigne, D. (2005). FreeBSD: An Open Source Alternative to Linux. http://www.freebsd.org/doc/en_US.ISO8859-1/articles/linux-comparison/article.html. Accessed February 10, 2007.

McKusick, M. (1999). Twenty Years of Berkeley Unix: From AT&T-Owned to Freely Redistributable. In: Open Sources: Voices from the Open Source Revolution, M. Stone, S. Ockman, and C. DiBona (editors). O'Reilly Media, Sebastopol, CA, 31–46.

Raymond, E. (2004). The Art of UNIX Programming. Addison-Wesley Professional Computer Series. Pearson Education Inc. Also: Revision 1.0. September 19, 2003. http://www.faqs.org/docs/artu/. Accessed January 10, 2007.

Raymond, E.S. (1997). A Brief History of Hackerdom. http://www.catb.org/~esr/writings/cathedral-bazaar/hacker-history/. Accessed November 29, 2006.

Ritchie, D. (1984). The Evolution of the UNIX Time-Sharing System. Bell System Technical Journal, 63(8), 1–11. Also: http://cm.bell-labs.com/cm/cs/who/dmr/hist.pdf. Accessed January 10, 2007.

Ritchie, D. and Thompson, K. (1974). The UNIX Time-Sharing System. Communications of the ACM, 17(7), 365–375. Revised version of paper presented at: Fourth ACM Symposium on Operating System Principles, IBM Watson Research Center, Yorktown Heights, New York, October 15–17, 1973.

Scott, G. (1988). A Look at UNIX. U-M Computing News. University of Michigan Computing Newsletter, 3(7).

Tanenbaum, A. (1981). Computer Networks, 2nd edition. Prentice Hall, Englewood Cliffs, NJ.

Van Vleck, T. (1995). Unix and Multics. http://multicians.org/unix.html. Accessed January 10, 2007.

Wheeler, D. (2003). Secure Programming for Linux and Unix HOWTO. http://www.dwheeler.com/secure-programs. Accessed November 29, 2006.

3.1.2 Linux

Linux is the defining, triumphant mythic project of open source. It illustrates perfectly the paradigm of open development and the variegated motivations that make people initiate or participate in these projects. It led to unexpected, unprecedented, explosive system development and deployment. It represents the metamorphosis of an initially modest project, overseen by a single individual, into a global megaproject.

Linux was the realization of a youthful computer science student's dream of creating an operating system he would like and that would serve his personal purposes. It began as a response to limitations in the Minix PC implementation of Unix. As described previously, Unix had originally been freely and widely distributed at universities and research facilities, but by 1990 it had become both expensive and restricted by a proprietary AT&T license. An inexpensive, open source Unix clone named *Minix*, which could run on PCs and used no AT&T code in its kernel, compilers, or utilities, was developed by Professor Andrew Tanenbaum for use in teaching operating systems courses. In 1991, Linus Torvalds, then an undergraduate student at the University of Helsinski got a new PC, his first, based on an Intel 8086 processor. The only available operating systems for the PC were DOS, which lacked multitasking, and Minix. Linus bought a copy of Minix and tried it on his PC, but was dissatisfied with its performance. For example, it lacked important features like a terminal emulator that would let him connect to his school's computer. A *terminal emulator* is a program that runs on a PC and lets it interact with a remote, multiuser server. This is different from a command-line interpreter or shell. Terminal emulators were frequently used to let a PC user log on to a remote computer to execute programs available on the remote machine. The familiar *Telnet* program is a terminal emulator that works over a TCP/IP network and lets the PC running it interact with the remote server program (SSH would now be used). Commands entered through the Telnet prompt are transmitted over the network and executed as if they had been directly entered on the remote machine's console. Linus implemented his own terminal emulator separate from Minix and also developed additional, Minix-independent programs for saving and transferring files.

This was the beginning of the Linux operating system. The system's name is an elision of the developer's first name *Linus* and *Unix* (the operating system it is modeled on). Linux is said to be a *Unix-like* operating system in the sense that its system interfaces or system calls are the same as those of Unix, so programs that work in a Unix environment will also work in a Linux environment. It would be worthwhile for the reader to look up a table of Linux system calls and identify the function of some of the major system calls to get a sense of what is involved.

The post that would be heard round the world arrived in late August 1991. Linus posted the note on the Usenet newsgroup comp.os.minix (category: Computers > Operating Systems > Minix), a newsgroup of which Linus was a member, dedicated to discussion of the Minix operating system. He announced he was developing a free operating system for the 386(486) AT clones. These networked communications groups that had first become available in the 1980s would be key enabling infrastructures for the kind of distributed, collaborative development Linux followed. The group provided a forum for Linus to tell people what he wanted to do and to attract their interest. The posted message asked if anyone in the newsgroup had ideas to propose for additional features for his system. The original post follows:

From: torvalds@klaava.Helsinki.FI (Linus Benedict Torvalds)
Newsgroups: comp.os.minix
Subject: What would you like to see most in minix?
Summary: small poll for my new operating system
Message-ID: <1991Aug25.205708.9541@klaava.Helsinki.FI>
Date: 25 Aug 91 20:57:08 GMT
Organization: University of Helsinki

Hello everybody out there using minix –

I'm doing a (free) operating system (just a hobby, won't be big and professional like gnu) for 386(486) AT clones. This has been brewing since april, and is starting to get ready. I'd like any feedback on things people like/dislike in minix, as my OS resembles it somewhat (same physical layout of the file-system (due to practical reasons) among other things).

I've currently ported bash(1.08) and gcc(1.40), and things seem to work. This implies that I'll get something practical within a few months, and I'd like to know what features most people would want. Any suggestions are welcome, but I won't promise I'll implement them :-)

Linus (torvalds@kruuna.helsinki.fi)

PS. Yes – it's free of any minix code, and it has a multi-threaded fs. It is NOT portable (uses 386 task switching etc), and it probably never will support anything other than AT-harddisks, as that's all I have :-(.

Though Linux would become a dragon-slayer of a project, the initial post was a "modest proposal" indeed, though it does convey the sense of the development. It was motivated by personal need and interest. It was to be a Unix-like system. It was to be free with a pure pedigree. Just as Minix contained none of the proprietary AT&T Unix code, Linux too would contain none of the Minix code. Linus wanted suggestions on additional useful features and enhancements. A few basic Unix programs had already been implemented on a specific processor, but the scale was small and it was not even planned to be "ported" (adapted and implemented) on other machines. A little later, Linus posted another engaging e-mail to the Minix newsgroup:

From: torvalds@klaava.Helsinki.FI (Linus Benedict Torvalds)
Newsgroups: comp.os.minix
Subject: Free minix-like kernel sources for 386-AT
Message-ID: <1991Oct5.054106.4647@klaava.Helsinki.FI>
Date: 5 Oct 91 05:41:06 GMT
Organization: University of Helsinki

Do you pine for the nice days of minix-1.1, when men were men and wrote their own device drivers? Are you without a nice project and just dying to cut your teeth on an OS you can try to modify for your needs? Are you finding it frustrating when everything works on minix? No more all-nighters to get a nifty program working? Then this post might be just for you :-)

The rest of the post describes Linus' goal of building a stand-alone operating system independent of Minix. One has to smile at the unpretentious and enthusiastic tone of the e-mail. The interest in making a "nifty program" sort of says it all.

Linux would soon become a model of Internet-based development which itself relied on networked communication and networked file sharing. Linus encouraged interested readers to download the source code he had written and made available on an FTP server. He wanted the source to be easily available over FTP and inexpensive (Yamagata, 1997). Thus in addition to collaborators communicating with each another via the network, the networked environment provided the means for the rapid dissemination of revisions to the system. Potential contributors were asked to download the code, play with the system developed so far, tell about any corrections, and contribute code. The patch programs had already been introduced some years earlier, so the exchange of code changes was relatively simple.

Releases were to follow quickly as a matter of development strategy and Unix functionality was soon matched. Within a month of his October 1991 announcement, ten people had installed the first version on their own machines. Within two months, 30 people had contributed a few hundred error reports or contributed utilities and drivers. When the *comp.os.linux* newsgroup was subsequently established, it became one of the top five most read newsgroups (Edwards, 2003). Later in 1991, Linus distributed what he called version 0.12. It was initially distributed under a license that forbade charging for distributions. By January 1992, this was changed and Linux was distributed under the GNU GPL. This was done partly for logistic reasons (so people could charge for making disk copies available) but primarily out of Linus' appreciation for the GPL-licensed GNU tools that Torvalds grew up on and was using to create Linux. Linus gave credit to three people for their contributions in a December release. By the release of development version 0.13, most of the patches had been written by people other than himself (Moon and Sproul, 2000). From that point on, Linux developed quickly, partly as a result of Linus' *release-early, release-often* policy. Indeed, within a year-and-a-half, Linus had released 90 updated versions (!) of the original software, prior to the first user version 1.0 in 1994. By the end of 1993, Linux had developed sufficiently to serve as a replacement for Unix. Version 1.0 of the Linux kernel was released in March 1994.

Linux is just the *kernel* of an operating system. For example, the *command-line interpreter* or *shell* that runs on top of the Linux kernel was not developed by Linus but came from previously existing free software. There were of course other key free components used in the composite GNU/Linux system, like the GNU C compiler developed by the FSF in the 1980s. Successive Linux versions substantially modified the initial kernel. Linus advocated the then unconventional use of a monolithic kernel rather than a so-called microkernel. Microkernels are small kernels with hardware-related components embedded in the kernel and which use message-passing to communicate between the kernel and the separate outer layers of the operating system. This structure makes microkernel designs portable but also generally slower than monolithic kernels because of the increased interprocess communication they entail. Monolithic kernels, on the other hand, integrate the outer layers into the kernel, which makes them faster. Linux's design uses modules that can be linked to the kernel at runtime in order to achieve the advantages offered by the microkernel approach (Bovet and Cesati, 2003). A fascinating historical exchange about kernel design occurred in the heated but instructive debate between Minix's Tanenbaum and Linux's Torvalds in their controversial early 1992 newsgroup discussions. Refer to Tanenbaum's provocative "Linux is obsolete" thread in the comp.os.minix newsgroup and Linus' equally provocative response; (see also DiBona et al., 1999, Appendix A).

Bugs in operating systems can be difficult, unpredictable critters, but Linux's massive collaborative environment was almost ideally suited for these circumstances. Since operating systems are subject to temporal and real-time concurrent effects, improvements in the system implementation tend to focus on the need to remedy bugs – as well as on the need to develop new device drivers as additional peripherals are developed (Wirzenius, 2003). Typical operating system bugs might occur only rarely or intermittently or be highly context-dependent. Bugs can be time-dependent or reflect anomalies that occur only in some complicated context in a concurrent user, multitasking environment. The huge number of individuals involved in developing Linux, especially as informed users, greatly facilitated both exposing and fixing such bugs, which would have been much more difficult to detect in a more systematic development approach. The operative diagnostic principle or tactic from Linus' viewpoint is expressed in his well-known aphorism that "given enough eyeballs, all bugs are shallow." On the other hand, there have also been critiques of Linux's development. For example, one empirical study of the growth in coupling over successive versions of Linux concluded that "unless Linux is restructured with a bare minimum of common coupling, the dependencies induced by common coupling will, at some future date, make Linux exceedingly hard to maintain without inducing regression faults," though this outcome was thought to be avoidable if care were taken to introduce no additional coupling instances (Schach et al., 2002).

The modular design of Linux's architecture facilitated code development just as the collaborative framework facilitated bug handling. For example, the code for device drivers currently constitutes the preponderance of the Linux source code, in contrast to the code for core operating system tasks like multitasking which is much smaller by comparison. The drivers interface with the operating system kernel through well-defined interfaces (Wirzenius, 2003). Thus, modular device drivers are easy to write without the programmer having a comprehensive grasp of the entire system. This separable kind of structure is extremely important from a distributed development point of view. It facilitates letting different individuals and groups address the development of drivers independently of one another, something which is essential given the minimally synchronized and distributed nature of the open development model. In fact, the overall structure of the kernel that Linus designed was highly modular. This is a highly desirable characteristic of an open source software architecture, because it is essential for decomposing development tasks into independent pieces which can be worked on separately and in parallel, with only relatively limited organizational coordination required. Furthermore, this structure also allows so-called *redundant development* (Moon and Sproul, 2000) where more than one individual or groups of individuals can simultaneously try to solve a problem with the best outcome or the earliest outcome ultimately selected for inclusion in the system.

Linux was portable, functional, and turned out to be surprisingly reliable. As we have noted, over its first several years of development, enough features were added to Linux for it to become competitive as an alternative to Unix. Its portability was directly related to the design decision to base Linux on a monolithic core kernel (with hardware-specific code like device drivers handled by so-called kernel modules). This decision was in turn directly related to enabling the distributed style of Linux development. The structure also allowed Linus Torvalds to focus on managing core kernel development, while others could work independently on kernel modules (Torvalds, 1999b). Several years after the version 1.0 release of the system in 1994, Linux was ported to processors other than the originally targeted 386/486 family, including the Motorola 68000, the Sun SPARC, the VAX, and eventually many others. Its reliability quickly became superior to Unix. Indeed, Microsoft program manager Valloppillil (1998), in the first of the now famous confidential Microsoft "Halloween" memos, reported that the Linux failure rate was two to five times lower than commercially available versions of Unix, according to performance analyses done internally by Microsoft itself.

The scale of the project continued to grow. The size of the distributed team of developers expanded almost exponentially. Despite this, the organizational paradigm remained lean in the extreme. Already by mid-year 1995, over 15,000 people had submitted contributions to the main Linux newsgroups and mailing lists (Moon and Sproul, 2000). A decade later, by the year 2005, there would be almost 700 Linux user groups spread worldwide (http://lugww.counter.li.org/, accessed January 5, 2007). The 1994 version 1.0 release, which had already been comparable in functionality to Unix, encompassed 175,000 lines of source code. By the time version 2.0 was released in 1996, the system had 780,000 lines of source code. The 1998 version 2.1.110 release had a million and a half lines of code (LOC), 30% of which consisted of code for the kernel and file system, about 50% for device drivers, while about 20% was hardware architecture-specific (Moon and Sproul, 2000). The amazing thing was that, to quote Moon and Sproul (2000): "No (software) architecture group developed the design; no management team approved the plan, budget, and schedule; no

HR group hired the programmers; no facilities group assigned the office space. Instead, volunteers from all over the world contributed code, documentation, and technical support over the Internet just because they wanted to." It was an unprecedented tour de force of large-scale distributed development and led to a blockbuster system.

What motivated such an army of dedicated participants? Many of them shared the same kind of motivation as Linus had: they wanted to add features to the system so that it could do something useful that they wanted for their personal benefit. People also wanted to be known for the good code they developed. Initially, Linus provided personal acknowledgements for individuals who made significant contributions. Already by the version 1.0 release in 1994, Linus personally acknowledged the work of over 80 people (Moon and Sproul, 2000). This version also began the practice of including a *credits file* with the source code that identified the major contributors and the roles they had played. It was up to the contributors themselves to ask Linus to be included in the credits file. This kind of reputational reward was another motivation for continued developer participation in a voluntary context like that of Linux.

All participants were by no means equal. Linux kernel developer Andrew Morton, lead maintainer for the Linux production kernel at the time, observed in 2004 (at the Forum on Technology and Innovation) that of the 38,000 most recent patches to the Linux kernel (made by roughly 1,000 developers), 37,000 of these patches – that's about 97% – were made by a subset of 100 developers who were employees paid by their companies to work on Linux! It is worth perusing the Linux credits file. For example, you might try to observe any notable demographic patterns, like country of origin of participants, their industrial or academic affiliations based on their e-mail addresses, the apparent sex of participants, and the like.

Decisions other than technical ones were key to Linux. Managerial innovativeness was central to its successful development. Technical and managerial issues could very well intertwine. For example, after the original system was written for the Intel 386 and then re-ported in 1993 for the Motorola 68000, it became clear to Linus that he had to redesign the kernel architecture so that a greater portion of the kernel could serve different processor architectures. The new architectural design not only made the kernel code far more easily portable but also more modular. Organizationally, this allowed different parts of the kernel to be developed in parallel (Torvalds, 1999a, b) and with less coordination, which was highly advantageous in the distributed development environment. The way in which software releases were handled was also determined by market effects. A simple but important managerial/marketing decision in this connection was the use of a *dual track for release*. The dual track differentiated between *stable releases* that could be used confidently by people who merely wanted to use the operating system as a platform on which to do their applications work – versus *development releases* that were less stable, still under development, and included the newest feature additions. This kept two potentially disparate audiences happy: the developers had flexibility, the end users had certainty. The distinction between developer and stable releases also supported the "release-early, release-often" policy that facilitated rapid development. The *release-numbering system* reflected the categorization and is worth understanding. Odd-numbered release series such as 2.3 (or its sub-tree members like 2.3.1 and 2.3.2) corresponded to developer or experimental releases. Stable releases had an even-numbered second digit, like 2.0, 2.2. Once a stable release was announced, a new developer series would start with the next higher (odd) number (such as 2.3 in the present case). Amazingly, there were almost 600 releases of all kinds between the 0.01 release in 1991 that started it all and the 2.3 release in 1999 (Moon and Sproul, 2000).

Though development was distributed and team-based, the project retained its singular leadership. While Linus displayed a somewhat self-deprecatory and mild-mannered leadership or management style, it was ultimately he who called the shots. He decided on which patches were accepted and which additional features were incorporated, announced all releases, and at least in the beginning of the project reviewed all contributions personally and communicated by e-mail with every contributor (Moon and Sproul, 2000). If it is true that enough eyeballs make all bugs shallow, it also appears to be true that in the Linux world there was a governing single pair of eyes overseeing and ensuring the quality and integral vision of the overall process. So one might ask again: is it a cathedral (a design vision defined by a single mind) or a bazaar?

The choice of the GPL has been decisive to the developmental integrity of Linux because it is instrumental in preventing the divergence of evolving versions of the system. In contrast, we have seen how proprietary pressures in the development of Unix systems encouraged the divergence of Unix mutations, though the POSIX standards also act against this. This centralizing control provided by the GPL for Linux was well-articulated by Roger Young (1999) of Red Hat in a well-known essay where he argued that unlike proprietary development: "In Linux the pressures are the reverse. If one Linux supplier adopts an innovation that becomes popular in the market, the other Linux vendors will immediately adopt that innovation. This is because they have access to the source code of the innovation and it comes under a license that allows them to use it." Thus, open source creates "unifying pressure to conform to a common reference point – in effect an open standard – and it removes the intellectual property barriers that would otherwise inhibit this convergence" (Young, 1999).

This is a compelling argument not only for the stability of Linux but also for the merits of the GPL in rapid, innovative system development.

Writing code may be a relatively solitary endeavor, but the development of Linux was an interactive social act. We have remarked on the organizational structure of Linux development, the motivations of its participants, and the personal characteristics of its unique leader. It is also worthwhile to describe some characteristics of the social matrix in which the project operated. For more detail see the discussion in (Moon and Sproul, 2000). To begin with, Linus' participation in the Usenet newsgroup comp.os.minix preceded his original announcement to the community of his Linux adventure. This was a large online community with about 40,000 members by 1992. The group that would develop Linux was a self-selected subset that sat on top of this basic infrastructure, which in turn sat on top of an e-mail and network structure. Of course, by word of e-mail the Linux group would quickly spread beyond the initial Minix newsgroup.

Communities like those that developed Linux exhibit a sociological infrastructure. This includes their group communication structure and the roles ascribed to the different members. In Linux development, group communication was handled via Usenet groups and various Linux mailing lists. Within months of the initial project announcement, the original single mailing list (designated *Linux-activists*) had 400 members. At the present time there are hundreds of such mailing lists targeted at different Linux distributions and issues. The comp.os.linux newsgroup was formed by mid-1992. Within a few years there were literally hundreds of such Linux-related newsgroups (linuxlinks.com/Links/USENET). The mailing list for Linux-activists was the first list for Linux kernel developers, but others followed. It is worth looking up the basic information concerning the Linux kernel mailing list at www.tux.org. Check some of the entries in the site's hyperlink Index to understand how the process works. If you are considering becoming a participant in one of the lists, beware of which list you subscribe to and consider the advice in the FAQ (frequently answered questions) at the site that warns:

> Think again before you subscribe. Do you really want to get that much traffic in your mailbox? Are you so concerned about Linux kernel development that you will patch your kernel once a week, suffer through the oopses, bugs and the resulting time and energy losses? Are you ready to join the Order of the Great Penguin, and be called a "Linux geek" for the rest of your life? Maybe you're better off reading the weekly "Kernel Traffic" summary at http://www.kerneltraffic.org/.

The *kernel mailing list* is the central organizational tool for coordinating kernel developers. Moon and Sproul (2000) observe that: "Feature freezes, code freezes, and new releases are announced on this list. Bug reports are submitted to this list. Programmers who want their code to be included in the kernel submit it to this list. Other programmers can then download it, test it within their own environment, suggest changes back to the author, or endorse it." Messages sent to the list are automatically resent to everyone on the list. The e-mail traffic is enormous, with thousands of developers posting hundreds of thousands of messages in the course of time. As of 2005, a member of the kernel list could receive almost 10,000 messages per month, so that digest summaries of messages are appropriate to look at, at least initially. The modular architecture of Linux also affects the communications profile of the development since the architecture partitions the developers into smaller groups. This way intensive collaboration is not across a broad population of developers but with smaller sets of developers.

The technical roles of the major participants are divided into so-called credited developers and maintainers. *Credited developers* are those who have made substantial code contributions and are listed in the Linux *credits file* (such as http://www.kernel.org/pub/linux/kernel/CREDITS, accessed January 10, 2007). There are also major contributors who for various personal reasons prefer to keep a low profile and do not appear on the credits list. There were about 400 credited Linux kernel developers by 2000. *Maintainers* are responsible for individual kernel modules. The maintainers "review linux-kernel mailing list submissions (bug reports, bug fixes, new features) relevant to their modules, build them into larger patches, and submit the larger patches back to the list and to Torvalds directly" (Moon and Sproul, 2000). These are people whose judgment and expertise is sufficiently trusted by Linus in areas of the kernel where he himself is not the primary developer that he will give close attention to their recommendations and tend to approve their decisions. The credited developers and maintainers dominate the message traffic on the Linux-kernel mailing list. Typically, 1/50th of the developers generate 50% of the traffic. Of this 50%, perhaps 30% of the traffic is from credited developers while about 20% is from maintainers. The norms for how to behave with respect to the mailing lists are specified in a detailed FAQ document that is maintained by about 20 contributors. For example, refer to the http://www.tux.org/lkml/ document (accessed January 10, 2007) to get a sense of the range of knowledge and behaviors that are part of the defining norms of the developer community. It tells you everything from "What is a feature freeze?" and "How to apply a patch?" to "What kind of question can I ask on the list?" Documents like these are important in a distributed, cross-cultural context because they allow participants to understand what is expected of them and what their responsibilities are. In the absence of face-to-face interactions, the delineation of such explicit norms of conduct is critical to allowing effective, largely text-based, remote communication.

References

Bovet, D.P. and Cesati, M. (2003). Understanding the Linux Kernel, 2nd edition. O'Reilly Media, Sebastopol, CA.

DiBona, C., Ockman, S., and Stone, M. (1999). The Tanenbaum-Torvalds Debate in Appendix A of Open Sources: Voices from the Open Source Revolution. M. Stone, S. Ockman, and C. DiBona (editors). O'Reilly Media, Sebastopol, CA.

Edwards, K. (2003). Technological Innovation in the Software Industry: Open Source Development. Ph.D. Thesis, Technical University of Denmark.

Moon, J.Y. and Sproul, L. (2000). Essence of Distributed Work: The Case of the Linux. http://www.firstmonday.dk/issues/issue5_11/moon/index.html. Accessed December 3, 2006.

Schach, S., Jin, B., Wright, D., Heller, G., and Offutt, A. (2002). Maintainability of the Linux Kernel. IEE Proceedings – Software, 149(1), 18–23.

Torvalds, L (1999a). The Linux edge. Communications of the ACM, 42(4), 38–39.

Torvalds, L. (1999b). The Linux edge. In: Open Sources: Voices from the Open Source Revolution, M. Stone, S. Ockman, and C. DiBona (editors). O'Reilly Media, Sebastopol, CA, 101–111.

Valloppillil, V. (1998). Open source software: A (New?) development methodology, (August 11, 1998). http://www.opensource.org/halloween/. Accessed January 20, 2007.

Wirzenius, L. (2003). Linux: The Big Picture. PC Update Online. http://www.melbpc.org.au/pcupdate/2305/2305article3.htm. Accessed November 29, 2006.

Yamagata, H. (1997). The Pragmatist of Free Software: Linus Torvalds Interview. http://kde.sw.com.sg/food/linus.html. Accessed November 29, 2006.

Young, R. (1999). Giving It Away. In: Open Sources: Voices from the Open Source Revolution, M. Stone, S. Ockman, and C. DiBona (editors). O'Reilly Media, Sebastopol, CA, 113–125.

3.2 Windowing Systems and Desktops

By the early 1970s, computer scientists at the famed Xerox PARC research facility were vigorously pursuing ideas proposed by the legendary Douglas Engelbart, inventor of the mouse and prescient computer engineer whose seminal work had propelled interest in the development of effective bitmapped graphics and graphical user interfaces years ahead of its time (Engelbart, 1962). Engelbart's work eventually led to the development of the Smalltalk graphical environment released on the Xerox Star computer in 1981. Many of the engineers who worked at Xerox later migrated to Apple, which released the relatively low-cost Macintosh graphical computer in 1984. Microsoft released systems like Windows 2.0 with a similar "look and feel" to Apple by 1987, a similarity for which Microsoft would be unsuccessfully sued by Apple (Reimer, 2005), though see the review of the intellectual property issues involved in Myers (1995). The provision of open source windowing and desktop environments for Unix began in the early 1980s with the initiation of the X Window System project. By the mid-1990s the GNOME and KDE projects to create convenient free desktop environments for ordinary users, with GUI interfaces similar to Windows and Mac OS, were begun. This section describes the enormous efforts that have gone into these major open source projects: X, GNOME, and KDE.

3.2.1 The X Window System

The X Window System (also called X or X11 after the version which appeared in 1987) lets programmers develop GUIs for bitmap displays on Unix and other platforms which do not come with windowing capabilities. It was developed for a Unix environment beginning at MIT in 1984 in a joint collaboration between MIT, DEC, and IBM and licensed under the permissive MIT/X open source license by 1985. It is considered to be "one of the first very large-scale free software projects" (X Window System, 2006), done in the context of the budding Internet with extensive use of open mailing lists. The system lets programmers draw windows and interact with the mouse and keyboard. It also provides what is called network transparency, meaning that applications on one machine can remotely display graphics on another machine with a different architecture and operating system. For example, X allows a computationally intensive program executing on a Unix workstation to display graphics on a Windows desktop (X Window System, 2006). X now serves as the basis for both remote and local graphic interfaces on Linux and almost all Unix-like systems, as well as for Mac OS X (which runs on FreeBSD). KDE and GNOME, the most popular free desktops, are higher level layers that run on top of X11. In the case of KDE on Unix, for example, KDE applications sit on top of the KDE libraries and Qt, which in turn run on X11 running on top of Unix (KDE, 2006).

The X Window System is a large application with an impressive code base. For example, X11 had over 2,500 modules by 1994. In an overview of the size of a Linux distribution (Red Hat Linux 6.2), Wheeler (2000) observed that the X Windows Server was the next largest component in the distribution after the Linux kernel (a significant proportion of which was device-dependent). It occupied almost a million-and-a-half SLOC. X was followed in size by the gcc compiler, debugger, and Emacs, each about half the size of X. In comparison, the important Apache project weighs in at under 100,000 SLOC. Despite this, X also works perfectly well on compact digital devices like IBM's Linux watch or PDA's and has a minimal footprint that is "currently just over 1 megabyte of code (uncompressed), excluding toolkits that are typically much larger" (Gettys, 2003).

The system was used on Unix workstations produced by major vendors like AT&T, Sun, HP, and DEC (Reimer, 2005). The X11 version released in 1987 intentionally reflected a more hardware neutral design. To maintain the coherent evolution of the system, a group of vendors established the nonprofit MIT X Consortium in 1987. The project was directed by X cofounder Bob Scheifler. The consortium proposed to develop X "in a neutral atmosphere inclusive of commercial and educational interests" (X Window System, 2006), with the objective of establishing "the X Window System as an industry-wide graphics windowing standard" (Bucken, 1988). IBM joined the consortium in 1988. Over time, commercial influence on the project increased. There were also ongoing philosophical and pragmatic differences between the FSF and the X project. In fact, Stallman (1998) had described the X Consortium (and its successor the Open Group) as "the chief opponent of copyleft" which is one of the defining characteristics of the GPL, even though the X license is GPL-compatible in the usual sense that X can be integrated with software licensed under the GPL. The FSF's concern is the familiar one that commercial vendors can develop extensive proprietary customizations of systems like the X reference implementation which they could then make dominant because of the resources they can plow into proprietary development, relying on the liberal terms of the MIT/X license.

A notable organizational change occurred in 2003–2004. The XFree86 project had started in 1992 as a port of X to IBM PC compatibles. It had over time become the most popular and technically progressive version of X. However, by 2003 there was growing discontent among its developer community, caused partly by the difficulty of obtaining CVS commit access. On top of this, in 2004, the XFree86 project adopted a GPL-*incompatible* license that contained a condition similar to the original BSD advertising clause. The change was supposed to provide more credit for developers, but it had been done in the face of strong community opposition, including from preeminent developers like Jim Gettys, cofounder of the X project. Gettys opposed the change because it made the license GPL-incompatible. Stallman (2004) observed that although the general intention of the new license requirement did "not conflict with the GPL," there were some specific details of the licensing requirement that did. In combination with existing discontent about the difficulty of getting CVS commit access, the new GPL incompatibility had almost immediate disruptive consequences. The project forked, with the formation of the new X.Org foundation in 2004. X.Org rapidly attracted almost all the XFree86 developers to its GPL-compatible fork. The newly formed organization places a much greater emphasis on individual participation. In fact, Gettys (2003) notably observed that "X.org is in the process of reconstituting its governance from an *industry consortium* to an organization in which *individuals*, both at a personal level and as part of work they do for their companies have voice, working as part of the larger freedesktop.org and free standards community" (italics added). X.Org now provides the canonical reference implementation for the system which remains "almost completely compatible with the original 1987 protocol" (X Window System, 2006).

References

Bucken, M. (1988). IBM Backs X Windows. Software Magazine, March 15. http://findarticles.com/p/articles/mi_m0SMG/is_n4_v8/ai_6297250. Accessed December 3, 2006.
Engelbart, D.C. (1962). Augmenting Human Intellect: A Conceptual Framework. Stanford Research Institute, Menlo Park, CA. http://www.invisiblerevolution.net/engelbart/full_62_paper_augm_hum_int.html. Accessed December 3, 2006.
Gettys, J. (2003). Open Source Desktop Technology Road Map. HP Labs, Version 1.14. http://people.freedesktop.org/~jg/roadmap.html. Accessed December 6, 2006.
KDE. (2006). K Desktop Environment: Developer's View. http://www.kde.org/whatiskde/devview.php. Accessed January 10, 2007.
Myers, J. (1995). Casenote, Apple v. Microsoft: Virtual Identity in the GUI Wars. Richmond Journal of Law and Technology, 1(5). http://law.richmond.edu/jolt/pastIssues.asp. Accessed December 6, 2006.
Reimer, J. (2005). A History of the GUI. http://arstechnica.com/articles/paedia/gui.ars. Accessed December 3, 2006.
Stallman, R. (1998). The X-Window Trap. Updated Version. http://www.gnu.org/philosophy/x.html. Accessed December 3, 2006.
Stallman, R. (2004). GPL-Incompatible License. http://www.xfree86.org/pipermail/forum/2004-February/003974.html. Accessed December 3, 2006.
Wheeler, D. (2000). Estimating Linux's Size. Updated 2004. http://www.dwheeler.com/sloc/redhat62-v1/redhat62sloc.html. Accessed December 1, 2006.
X Window System (2006). Top-Rated Wikipedia Article. http://en.wikipedia.org/wiki/X_Window_System. Accessed December 3.

3.2.2 Open Desktop Environments – GNOME

The objective of the GNOME Project is to create a free General Public Licensed desktop environment for Unix-like systems like Linux. This ambition has long been fundamental to the vision of free development for the simple reason that providing an effective, free GUI desktop interface for Linux or other free operating systems is necessary for them to realistically compete in the mass market with Windows and Apple environments. Aside from Linux itself, no other open source project is so complex and massive in scale as GNOME, and so overtly challenges the existing, established, proprietary platforms. The acronym GNOME stands for GNU Network Object Model Environment. It is the official

GNU desktop. In addition to the user desktop, GNOME also encompasses a variety of standard applications and a comprehensive development environment used to develop applications for GNOME or further develop the GNOME platform itself.

The idea for the GNOME project was initiated in 1996 by Miguel de Icaza. Icaza, a recent computer science graduate who was the maintainer for the GIMP project, released (along with Fedrico Mena) a primitive version (0.10) of a GUI infrastructure for Unix in 1997. The development language used was C (de Icaza, 2000). There was a significant free licensing controversy behind the motivation for developing GNOME. There already existed by that time another free desktop project called KDE, but there were licensing controversies associated with KDE. One of its key components, the Qt toolkit library discussed in Chapter 2, did not use an acceptable free software license. To avoid this kind of problem, the GNOME developers selected, instead of Qt, the GIMP open source image processing toolkit GTK+. They believed this software would serve as an acceptable LGPL basis for GNOME. The GNU LGPL permitted any applications written for GNOME to use any kind of software license, free or not, although of course the core GNOME applications themselves were to be licensed under the GPL. The first major release of GNOME was version 1.0 in 1999. It was included as part of the Red Hat Linux distribution. This release turned out to be very buggy but was improved in a later release that year.

There are different models for how founders continue a long-term relationship with an open source project. For example, they may maintain license ownership and start a company that uses a dual open/proprietary track for licenses. In the case of Icaza, after several years of development work on GNOME, he relinquished his role and founded the for-profit Ximian Corporation in 2000 as a provider for GNOME-related services. In order to ensure the continued independence of the GNOME project, the GNOME Foundation was established later that year. Its Board members make decisions on the future of GNOME, using volunteer committees of developers and release teams to schedule planning and future releases. The not-for-profit GNOME Foundation, its industrial partners, and a volunteer base of contributors cooperate to ensure that the project progresses. The GNOME Foundation's mandate has been defined as creating "a computing platform for use by the general public that is completely free software" (GNOME Foundation, 2000; German, 2003).

GNOME is unambiguously *free* in lineage and license – and it's big. Following free software traditions, the development tools that were used to create GNOME are all free software. They include the customary GNU software development tools (gcc compiler, Emacs editor, etc.), the Concurrent Versioning System for project configuration management, and the Bugzilla bug-tracking server software developed by the Mozilla Foundation and available from http://www.bugzilla.org/. These development tools were of course themselves the product of lengthy development during the 1980s–1990s by the GNU project. The project's code base is extensive and increasingly reliable. It is now a very large system with about two million LOC and 500 developers in various categories (German, 2003). As Koch and Schneider (2002) observe, that's actually roughly six million LOC added and four million lines deleted per the project's CVS repository. As already noted, the GNOME desktop has been envisioned as an essential component if the free GNU/Linux environment is to compete in the popular market with Windows and Apple. That vision is emerging as a reality. Thus GNOME represents one of the culminating accomplishments of the free software movement.

GNOME has three major architectural components: the GUI desktop environment, a set of tools and libraries that can interact with the environment, and a collection of office software tools. The scale and organizational structure of the project reflect these components. The GNOME project architecture consists of four main software categories, with roughly 45 major modules and a large number of noncore applications. The categories comprise libraries (GUI, CORBA, XML, etc. – about 20 in total), core applications (about 16: mail clients, word processors, spreadsheets, etc.), application programs, and several dozen noncore applications (German, 2003). The modules, as typical in such a large project, are relatively loosely coupled, so they can be developed mostly independently of one another. When modules become unwieldy in size, they are subdivided as appropriate into independent submodules. The modular organization is key to the success of the project because it keeps the organizational structure manageable. Basically, a relatively small number of developers can work independently on each module.

While most open source projects do not, in fact, have large numbers of developers, GNOME does, with over 500 contributors having write access to the project repository (German, 2003), though as usual a smaller number of activist developers dominate. Koch and Schneider (2002) describe a pattern of participation for GNOME that is somewhat different than that found by Mockus et al. (2002) in their statistical review of the Apache project. Though GNOME's development still emanated from a relatively small number of highly activist developers, the distribution is definitely flatter than Apache's. For example, while for Apache the top 15 developers wrote about 90% of the code, for GNOME the top 15 developers wrote only 50% of the code, and to reach 80% of the GNOME code, the top 50 developers have to be considered. At a more local level, consider the case of the GNOME e-mail client (Evolution). According to its development log statistics, five developers, out of roughly 200 total for the client, were responsible for half the modifications; 20 developers accounted for 80% of the development transactions; while a total of 55 developers of the 200 accounted for 95% of the transactions (German, 2003). This skewed pattern of contribution is not untypical. Refer to the useful libresoft Web site page http://libresoft.urjc.es/Results/index_html for CVS statistics for GNOME, as well as for many other open source projects.

The user environment that had to be created for GNOME was well-defined: it was simply a matter of "chasing tail-lights" to develop it. Requirements engineering for GNOME, like other open source projects, did not follow the conventional proprietary development cycle approach. It used a more generic and implicitly defined approach as described in German (2003). The underlying objective was that GNOME was to be free software, providing a well-designed, stable desktop model, comparable to Windows and Apple's, in order for Linux to be competitive in the mass market PC environment. The nature of the core applications that needed to be developed was already well-defined. Indeed, the most prominent *reference applications* were from the market competition to be challenged. For example, Windows MS Excel was the reference spreadsheet application. It was to be matched by the GNOME gnumeric tool. Similarly, the e-mail client Microsoft Outlook and the multifunction Lotus Notes were to be replaced by the GNOME Evolution tool. An anecdote by Icaza reflects both the informality and effectiveness of this reference model tactic in the design of a simple calendar tool:

> I proposed to Federico to write a calendar application in 10 days (because Federico would never show up on weekends to the ICN at UNAM to work on GNOME ;-). The first day we looked at OpenWindows calendar, that day we read all the relevant standard documents that were required to implement the calendar, and started hacking. Ten days later we did meet our deadline and we had implemented GnomeCal (de Icaza, 2000).

Requirements also emerged from the discussions that occurred in the mailing lists. Prototypes like the initial GNOME version 0.1 developed by Icaza also served to define features. Ultimately, it was the project leader and the maintainers who decided on and prioritized requirements. While fundamental disagreements regarding such requirements could lead to forks, this did not happen in the case of GNOME.

GNOME's collaborative development model relies heavily on private companies. Indeed, much of GNOME's continued development is staffed by employees of for-profit companies. However, the project itself is vendor-neutral. The maintainers of most of GNOME's important modules are actually employees of for-profit corporations like Ximian, Red Hat, and Sun. This arrangement helps guarantee the stable development of the project since essential tasks are less subject to fluctuations at the volunteer level. The paid employee contributors tend to handle design, coordination, testing, documentation, and bug fixing, as opposed to bug identification (German, 2003). Thus, for the Evolution client, about 70% of the CVS commits come from the top 10% of the contributors, *all* of whom are employees of Ximian. Similarly, Sun has extensively supported the so-called GNOME accessibility framework which addresses usability issues including use by disabled individuals. Though paid corporate employees play a major role, the volunteer participants are also pervasive, particularly as beta testers, bug discoverers, and documenters. The volunteers are especially important in the area of *internationalization* – an aspect that requires native language experts and is supported by individuals motivated by a desire to see GNOME supported in their own language. Interestingly, despite the role of voluntarism it also appears to be the case that a career path strategy is often followed or at least attempted by volunteers. Thus, most of the paid workers had started off as project volunteers and later moved from being enthusiastic hobbyists to paid employees of the major corporate sponsors (German, 2003).

Communication among the project participants is kept simple. It is handled in a standard manner, using relatively *lean media* over the Internet communication channel, supplemented by traditional mechanisms like conferences and Web sites. Mailing lists are used extensively for end users as well as for individual development components. Bimonthly summaries are e-mailed on the GNOME mailing list describing major current work, including the most active modules and developers during the report period. These are the forums in which decisions about a module's development are made. Project Web sites contain information categorized according to type of participants, from items for developers and bug reports to volunteer promotional efforts. An annual conference called GUADEC brings developers together and is organized by the GNOME Foundation. IRC or Internet Relay Chat (irc.gnome.org) provides an informal means of instantaneous communication. (Incidentally, the Web site Freenode.net provides IRC network services for many free software projects including GNU.) Of course, the CVS repository for the project effectively coordinates the development of the overall project. A limited number of developers have write access to the repository, having gained the privilege over time by producing patches that maintainers have come to recognize as trustworthy, a tried and true path in open development. Initially, the patches have to be submitted by the developers to the maintainers as diffs or patches, at least until the developer has attained a recognized trustworthy status with the maintainer. Rarely, it may happen that a developer may apply a patch to the repository that is subsequently rejected by the maintainer. Such an outcome can be disputed by appealing to the broader community, but these kinds of events are infrequent (German, 2003).

References

De Icaza, M. (2000). The Story of the GNOME Project. http://primates.ximian.com/ ~miguel/gnome-history.html. Accessed November 29, 2006.

German, D.M. (2003). GNOME, a Case of Open Source Global Software Development. In: International Conference on Software Engineering, Portland, Oregon.

GNOME Foundation. (2000). GNOME Foundation Charter Draft 0.61. http:// foundation.gnome.org/charter.html. Accessed November 29, 2006.

Koch, S. and Schneider, G. (2002). Effort, Co-operation, and Co-ordination in an Open Source Software Project: GNOME. Information Systems Journal, 12(1), 27–42.

Mockus, A., Fielding, R.T., and Herbsleb, J.D. (2002). Two Case Studies of Open Source Development: Apache and Mozilla. ACM Transactions on Software Engineering and Methodology, 11(3), 309–346.

3.2.3 Open Desktop Environments – KDE

The acronym KDE stands for – believe it or not – Kool Desktop Environment. The KDE Web site cogently expresses the vision and motivation for the project: "UNIX did not address the needs of the average computer user. . . . It is our hope that the combination UNIX/KDE will finally bring the same open, reliable, stable and monopoly-free computing to the average computer user that scientist and computing professionals world-wide have enjoyed for years" (www.kde.org). GNOME and KDE to some extent competitively occupy the same niche in the Linux environment. But they are now both recognized for the advances they made in achieving the OSS goal of creating a comprehensive and popularly accessible free source platform. In 2005, USENIX gave the two most prominent developers of GNOME and KDE, de Icaza and Ettrich, its STUG award for their work in developing a friendly GUI interface for open desktops, saying that: "With the development of user friendly GUIs, both de Icaza and Ettrich are credited with overcoming a significant obstacle in the proliferation of open source. . . . Their efforts have significantly contributed to the growing popularity of the open source desktop among the general public" (http://www.usenix.org/about/newsroom/press/archive/stug05.html, accessed January 10, 2007).

The theme of product development by a sole inspired youth repeats itself in KDE. The KDE project was started in 1996 by Matthias Ettrich, a 24-year-old computer science student at the University of Tubingen. Ettrich had been first exposed to free software development via the GNU project and Linux. Actually it was more than mere exposure. Ettrich wrote the first version of the open source product Lyx which uses the open source software system LaTeX, developed for Don Knuth's typesetting system TeX to produce high-quality document output. Ettrich has said that "this positive and successful experience of initiating a little self-sustaining free software community made me brave enough to start the KDE project later" (FOSDEM, 2005).

Ettrich announced his KDE proposal in a now well-known e-mail where he proposed the idea for the project. The objective is reminiscent of the attitude that Firefox's Blake Ross had for Firefox's potential audience. Ettrich wanted to define and implement:

A GUI for end users

> The idea is NOT to create a GUI for the complete UNIX-System or the System-Administrator. For that purpose the UNIX-CLI with thousands of tools and scripting languages is much better. The idea is to create a GUI for an ENDUSER. Somebody who wants to browse the web with Linux, write some letters and play some nice games.

The e-mail was posted at the hacker's favorite mid-morning hour: October 14, 1996, 3:00 A.M., to the Linux newsgroup, de.comp.os.linux.misc. Refer to the KDE organization's http://www.kde.org/documentation/posting.txt for the full text.

In low-key, good-humored style reminiscent of Linus Torvalds, Ettrich continued:

> IMHO a GUI should offer a complete, graphical environment. It should allow a user to do his everyday tasks with it, like starting applications, reading mail, configuring his desktop, editing some files, delete some files, look at some pictures, etc. All parts must fit together and work together.
>
> ... So one of the major goals is to provide a modern and common look & feel for all the applications. And this is exactly the reason, why this project is different from elder attempts.

"IMHO" is the deferential "In My Humble Opinion" acronym derived from Usenet custom.

The inaugural e-mail refers prominently to the author's intention to use the Qt C++ GUI widget library for the planned implementation of the project. Eventually, this use of the Qt toolkit would lead to free licensing concerns regarding KDE. These concerns would be significant in motivating the development of the competing GMOME project. The X referred to in the e-mail later is the X Window System for Unix which provided the basic toolkit for implementing a window, mouse, and keyboard GUI. Motif is the classic open source toolkit from the 1980s for making GUIs on Unix systems. Incidentally, the misspellings are from the original, reflecting the relaxed tone of the e-mail and perhaps the difference in language. The e-mail continues as follows:

> Since a few weeks a really great new widget library is available free in source and price for free software development. Check out http://www.troll.no

The stuff is called "Qt" and is really a revolution in programming X. It's an almost complete, fully C++ Widget-library that implementes a slightly improved Motif look and feel, or, switchable during startup, Window95.

The fact that it is done by a company (Troll Tech) is IMO a great advantage. We have the sources and a superb library, they have beta testers. But they also spend their WHOLE TIME in improving the library. They also give great support. That means, Qt is also interesting for commercial applications. A real alternative to the terrible Motif :) But the greatest pro for Qt is the way how it is programmed. It's really a very easy-to-use powerfull C++-library.

It is clear from the post that Ettrich was unaware that there might be licensing complications with the Qt toolkit. Originally Qt appears to have been proprietary to Trolltech. Actually, there were both free and proprietary licenses available, with the proprietary licenses only required if you were intending to release as closed source a product you developed using Qt. The free license, however, was not quite free. For example, the version described at http://www.kde.org/whatiskde/qt.php (accessed January 10, 2007) requires that "If you want to make improvements to Qt you need to send your improvements to Troll Tech. You can not simply distribute the modified version of Qt yourself," which was contrary to the GPL. There was much legal wrangling on this issue between the KDE developers and the FSF. Finally, in 2000, Trolltech – for which Ettrich then worked – announced that it would license Qt under the GNU GPL. This satisfied reservations among proponents of the Free Software Movement. Per the KDE Web site it is now the case that "Each and every line of KDE code is made available under the LGPL/GPL. This means that everyone is free to modify and distribute KDE source code. This implies in particular that KDE is available free of charge to anyone and will always be free of charge to anyone."

The Qt licensing issue was a political cause célèbre among certain open source advocates, but it does not seem to have been a consideration for users selecting between KDE and GNOME. They were primarily concerned about the functionality of the systems (Compton, 2005). Already by 1998, Red Hat had chosen KDE to be their standard graphical interface for their Linux distributions. Currently, major Linux distributions tend to include both KDE and GNOME in their distributions, with some companies like Sun or Caldera preferring one to the other. A port of KDE to run on a Windows environment is the mission of Cygwin (http://kde-cygwin.sourceforge.net/).

The demographic profile of the KDE participants is fairly standard. KDE has about 1,000 developers worldwide, mainly from Europe, having originated in Germany. It consists mostly of males aged 20–30 years old, many

of whom are students or are employed in IT (Brand, 2004). The KDE
Web site is interesting and quite well-organized. Refer to the organization's
http://www.kde.org/people/gallery.php "Virtual Gallery of Developers" for
biographies of the major developers, with academic, professional, and personal
remarks. About two-thirds of the participants are developers, the remainder
being involved in documentation, translation (about 50 languages are currently
represented), and other activities. According to the survey by Brand (Chance,
2005), the work efforts of individual contributors vary from a quarter-of-an-hour
to half-a-day, per day, with an average of two to three hours per day. In general, as we have noted previously, open development processes are visible and
extensively documented (Nichols and Twidale, 2003) in a way that proprietary,
closed source, corporate developments cannot be, almost in principle. The mailing lists and CVS repository that are the key communications tools establish an
incredibly detailed, time-stamped record of development with readily available
machine-readable statistics. For example, the libresoft Web site mentioned previously, particularly the statistics link http://libresoft.urjc.es/Results/index_html
(accessed January 10, 2007) is an excellent resource for detailed data on many
open source projects including not only KDE but also important other projects
like GNOME, Apache, FreeBSD, OpenBSD, XFree86, Mozilla and so on, with
plentiful data about CVS commits, module activity, and so on. The site also
contains detailed data on committers and their contributions.

KDE started its development at a propitious moment in the evolution of open
software platforms. This first version was both timely and critical because it
helped advertise the product at a time when Linux was rapidly growing. There
was as yet no easy-to-use desktop interface available for Linux, so the product
filled an unoccupied market niche. The initial success of the project was also
bolstered because the project creators were able to recruit developers from
another open source project they had connections with (Chance, 2005). Further
successful development and possibly even the competition with the GNOME
project helped advertise the project even more, leading to additional developer
recruiting. The C++ implementation of KDE (vs. C for GNOME) facilitated
the enhancement of the system's core libraries, again arguably facilitating its
success. Though KDE was initiated in 1996, most developers joined between
1999 and 2002 (Brand, 2004).

Influence inside the KDE project is as usual determined by work-based
reputations. Reputations are based on experience and contributions, but
friendly and cooperative behavior is an asset. Admission to the KDE core team
requires a reputation based on "outstanding contributions over a considerable
period of time" (http://www.kde.org/). The kde-core-devel mailing list is where
decisions are made, but the process is informal and unlike the centralized
"benevolent dictatorship" approach characteristic of Linux development. The

norm tends to be that "whoever does the work has the final decision" (Chance, 2005). Lead architects and maintainers who are authorized to speak for the community are responsible for moving the platform forward. Ettrich has observed that the relatively anarchical structure of the KDE organization makes it hard to do things, commenting that "unless you have a captain," then, even with all the right ideas, "whether we are able to realize them against our own resistance is a different matter" (FOSDEM, 2005). These challenges reflect the classic tension between the Cathedral and the Bazaar: it is hard to do without strong, authoritative leadership in guiding the direction of large projects. The conflicts that have arisen derive mainly from differences concerning the future direction of the project. Secondary sources of conflict include interpersonal reactions to things like refusals to accept patches or ignored contributions. There are also the traditional conflicts between the end users and developers. These typically result from a disjuncture between the technical orientation of the developers versus the preference for stability and ease of use that end users are interested in. A usability group (http://usability.kde.org/) has developed that attempts to mediate the two viewpoints, but its standing is still of limited importance (Chance, 2005). Like GNOME, KDE has placed a strong emphasis on accessibility issues for individuals with disabilities. In terms of future developments, Ettrich himself underscores usability issues as one of his "top 3 favorite focus areas for KDE" (FOSDEM, 2005).

References

Brand, A. (2004). Structure of KDE Project. PELM Project, Goethe University, Frankfurt.

Chance, T. (2005). The Social Structure of Open Source Development. Interview with Andreas Brand in NewsForge. http://programming.newsforge.com/article.pl?sid=05/01/25/1859253. Accessed November 29, 2006.

Compton, J. (2005). GNOME vs. KDE in Open Source Desktops. http://www.developer.com/tech/article.php/629891. Accessed January 20, 2007.

FOSDEM. (2005). Interview with Matthias Ettrich KDE. http://archive.fosdem.org/2005/index/interviews/interviews_ettrich.html. Accessed January 10, 2007.

Nichols, D. and Twidale, M. (2003). The Usability of Open Source. First Monday, 8(1). http://www.firstmonday.dk/issues/issue8_1/nichols/index.html. Accessed December 3, 2006.

3.3 GIMP

GIMP is a free software image manipulation tool intended to compete with Adobe Photoshop. We include it in this chapter on open source platforms because it is an important desktop application (not an Internet-related system like those considered in Chapter 2) and because its toolkit is used in the GNOME desktop. Imaging tools like GIMP are of increasing importance in industrial and medical applications as well as gaming and entertainment technology. The story of GIMP is important for understanding the record of accomplishment of open development for several reasons. Its originators were, prototypically, computer science undergraduates at Berkeley who had themselves been weaned on open source products. Out of personal curiosity they wanted to develop a product that incidentally, but only incidentally, would serve an important need in the open source platform. Their product imitated and challenged a dominant proprietary software tool for an end-user application, unlike most previous free programs. Legal questions about the licensing characteristics for some components of the system created a controversy within the free software movement. The software architecture represented by its plug-in system strongly impacted the success of the project by making it easier for developers to participate. The reaction and involvement of end users of the program was exceptionally important in making GIMP successful because its value and effectiveness could only be demonstrated by its ability to handle sophisticated artistic techniques. Consequently, the tool's development demanded an understanding of how it was to be used that could easily transcend the understanding of most of the actual developers of the system. In other words, the end users represented a parallel but divergent form of sophistication to the program developers. Management challenges arose with the fairly abrupt departure of the originating undergraduates for industrial positions on completion of their undergraduate careers and the replacement of the original leadership with a team of coresponsible developers. Like the other open source products we have examined, the story of GIMP can help us understand how successful open source projects are born and survive.

GIMP, an acronym for the "GNU Image Manipulation Program," is supposed to be a challenge to Adobe Photoshop. It is intended to stand as the free source counterpart to Adobe Photoshop and is an official part of the GNU software development project. Coming out beginning in 1996, GIMP was one of the first major free software products for an end-user applications, as opposed to most of the GNU projects that were oriented toward use by programmers. It provides standard digital graphics functions and can be used, for example, to make graphics or logos, edit and layer images, convert image formats, make animated images, and so on. According to its Freshmeat project description, GIMP is "suitable for such tasks as photo retouching, image composition and image authoring. It can be used as a simple paint program, an expert quality photo retouching program, an online batch processing system, a mass production image renderer, an image format converter, etc." (from "The Gimp – Default Branch"; description on www.freshmeat.net).

Class projects at UC Berkeley have a way of making a big splash. GIMP was developed by Peter Mattis and Spencer Kimball in August 1995, initially for a class project for a computer science course when they were undergraduates. Mattis "wanted to make a webpage" (Hackvän, 1999) so as a result they decided it would be interesting to design a pixel-based imaging program. Following open source development custom, Mattis posted the following question on comp.os.linux.x > Image Manipulation Program Features in July 1995 at the canonical hacker time of 3:00 A.M.:

> Suppose someone decided to write a graphical image manipulation
> program (akin to photoshop). Out of curiousity (and maybe something
> else), I have a few (2) questions:
>> What kind of features should it have? (tools, selections, filters, etc.)
>> What file formats should it support? (jpeg, gif, tiff, etc.)?
> Thanks in advance,
> Peter Mattis

At this point, neither Mattis nor Kimball had anything but a cursory familiarity with image manipulation tools (Hackvän, 1999). However, within six months Mattis and Kimball working alone – not as part of a free-wheeling bazaar format – had released a beta version of GIMP as open source. The announcement was made at 4:00 A.M. on November 21, 1995, on comp.windows.x.apps > ANNOUNCE: The GIMP. The style of the release announcement is worth noting for the specificity and clarity of its statement of the project functionality and requirements. We provide it in some detail as an illustration of how these announcements are heralded:

The GIMP: the General Image Manipulation Program

> The GIMP is designed to provide an intuitive graphical interface to a
> variety of image editing operations. Here is a list of the GIMP's major
> features:

> *Image viewing*
> - Supports 8, 15, 16 and 24 bit color.
> - Ordered and Floyd-Steinberg dithering for 8 bit displays.
> - View images as rgb color, grayscale or indexed color.
> - Simultaneously edit multiple images.
> - Zoom and pan in real-time.
> - GIF, JPEG, PNG, TIFF and XPM support.

> *Image editing*
> - Selection tools including rectangle, ellipse, free, fuzzy, bezier and
>   intelligent.

- Transformation tools including rotate, scale, shear and flip.
- Painting tools including bucket, brush, airbrush, clone, convolve, blend and text.
- Effects filters (such as blur, edge detect).
- Channel & color operations (such as add, composite, decompose).
- Plug-ins which allow for the easy addition of new file formats and new effect filters.
- Multiple undo/redo. . . .

The GIMP has been tested (and developed) on the following operating systems: Linux 1.2.13, Solaris 2.4, HPUX 9.05, SGI IRIX.

Currently, the biggest restriction to running the GIMP is the Motif requirement. We will release a statically linked binary for several systems soon (including Linux).

URLs
http://www.csua.berkeley.edu/~gimp
ftp://ftp.csua.berkeley.edu/pub/gimpmailto:g . . . @soda.csua.berkeley.edu
Brought to you by
Spencer Kimball (spen . . . @soda.csua.berkeley.edu)
Peter Mattis (p . . . @soda.csua.berkeley.edu)

NOTE
This software is currently a beta release. This means that we haven't implemented all of the features we think are required for a full, unqualified release. There are undoubtedly bugs we haven't found yet just waiting to surface given the right conditions. If you run across one of these, please send mail to g . . . @soda.csua. berkeley.edu with precise details on how it can be reliably reproduced.

The first public release (version.54) actually came in January 1996.

Plug-ins played an important role in the expansion of GIMP. The two solo developers had provided a powerful and functional product with important features like a uniform plug-in system, "so developers could make separate programs to add to GIMP without breaking anything in the main distribution" (Burgess, 2003). Spencer noted that "The plug-in architecture of the Gimp had a tremendous impact on its success, especially in the early stages of development (version 0.54). It allowed interested developers to add the functionality they desired without having to dig into the Gimp core" (Hackvän, 1999).

Plug-ins are very important in GIMP also because of its competition with Photoshop. In fact, plug-ins for Adobe Photoshop can also run on GIMP if you use the *pspi* (Photoshop Plug-in Interface) plug-in for GIMP that runs third-party Photoshop plug-ins. Pspi was developed for Windows in 2001 and

for Linux in 2006 (http://www.gimp.org/~tml/gimp/win32/pspi.html). Pspi
acts as an intermediary between GIMP and Photoshop plug-ins, which are
implemented as dlls. According to pspi developer Tor Lillqvist, "The question was 'How would you load and call code in a Windows DLL on Linux'"
(http://www.spinics.net/lists/gimpwin/msg04517.html). As described by Willis
(2006), pspi appears to be a "full, running copy of Photoshop. It provides the
hooks into the menus and functions of Photoshop that the plugin expects to
see, and connects them to the GIMP's extension and menu system." This is
actually extremely significant for the attractiveness of the Linux platform itself.
Professional graphics artists strongly prefer Photoshop under Windows; one
reason being the availability of third-party plug-ins. The availability of pspi for
Linux changes this. There are a few ironies in this story. A software bridge like
pspi is made possible in the first place because of the Adobe policy of encouraging the development of third-party plug-ins through the use of its software
development kit. Thus, Adobe's (natural and logical) plug-in policy, designed to
increase its own marketability, can also by the same token increase its competition's marketability. Furthermore, compiling the pspi source requires the Adobe
development kit, so you need the kit to create the executable for pspi. However,
once this is done, the executable itself is of course freely redistributable, as the
pspi is in the first place. Oddly, up until Photoshop 6 Adobe gave the software
development kit away for free but now requires specific approval. Thus, in a
certain sense an original compilation of pspi for use in GIMP would implicitly
require such an approval by Adobe. In any case, the point is moot because down-
loadable binaries are available for multiple platforms for pspi (Willis, 2006).
The pspi development illustrates the complicated interplay between technical
development issues, software architecture choices, legal issues, high-end graphics user expectations, and the sometimes-unintended consequences of corporate
policies like those that encourage external development.

Perhaps unsurprisingly, licensing issues have also affected GIMP's development. The initial GIMP toolkit for building widgets was based on the proprietary
Motif *widget* library. A *widget* (which is shorthand for "windows gadget") can
be defined as a "standardized on-screen representation of a control that may
be manipulated by the user" (redhat.com glossary), examples being scroll bars,
menus, buttons, sliders, and text boxes. Widgets can be thought of as the basic
building blocks of graphical interfaces and are constructed using *toolkit* programs. Because the Motif widget library was proprietary, an open source widget
library was developed, called GTK+ (standing for GIMP toolkit), in order to
remain fully consistent with the principles of the free software movement. There
was also another more personal professional motivation for replacing the Motif

library. In addition to the developers thinking that Motif toolkit was "bloated and inflexible" (Hackvän, 1999), Mattis personally "was dissatisfied with Motif and wanted to see what it took to write a UI toolkit" for his own edification. The resulting GTK toolkit (eventually enhanced to GTK+) was licensed under the LGPL, so it could be used even by developers of proprietary software (www.gtk.org). GTK was provided with the 1996 release (Bunks, 2000). Subsequent to that release, weaknesses in the beta version of the system, like poor memory management, were resolved. There were also improvements like the use of layer-based images, based on what the developers saw used in Photoshop 3.0. Another beta version was released in early 1997.

By June 1997, Kimball and Mattis had released version 0.99.10 with further improvements, including the updated GTK+ library. That final undergraduate version represented a huge effort. Kimball remarked that he had "spent the better part of two years on Gimp, typically at the expense of other pressing obligations (school, work, life)" and that "probably 95 to 98 percent of the code in 0.99.10 was written by Pete or myself" (Hackvän, 1999). They both share the copyright on the entire project, though in point of fact Kimball concentrated on GIMP and Mattis on the GTK. They never got to release version 1.0 – they graduated from college in June 1997. The authors say that developing GIMP was largely a matter of duty to the cause of free software. For Spencer Kimball, his GIMP development work had been partly his payment on what he felt was a debt of honor, as he said in an interview: "From the first line of source code to the last, GIMP was always my 'dues' paid to the free software movement. After using emacs, gcc, Linux, etc., I really felt that I owed a debt to the community which had, to a large degree, shaped my computing development" (Hackvän, 1999). Similar feelings were expressed by Mattis about having "done his duty" for free software (Hackvän, 1999).

Transitions can be bumpy in open source. Since the model is significantly volunteer-driven, you cannot just go out and hire new talent or leadership (granted, the increasing participation of commercially supported open source developers modifies this). Management problems set in at GIMP upon the graduation of its principals from college because of the vacuum caused by their departure. Spencer and Mattis had moved on. They were holding down real jobs and could no longer put time into the project (Burgess, 2003). Most problematically, "there was no defined successor to S&P, and they neglected to tell anyone they were leaving" according to Burgess (2003). Turnover at even traditional technical companies, where there is an average time between job changes of two years, is a significant negative factor in productivity. This impact is likely exacerbated in the free software community where "the rate of turnover for both volunteer and full-time contributors is probably higher and the resulting losses to productivity and momentum are probably more severe. New developers have the source code, but usually they can't rely upon local experts for assistance with their learning curves" (Hackvän, 1999). Thus, the GIMP project had management hurdles to face that can handicap any project and certainly apply to open source development as well. But a new development model soon emerged – a team of members with designated responsibilities for managing releases, making bug fixes, etc. There was no single team leader, and project decisions were made through the #gimp Internet Relay Channel. The initial effort was "focused almost exclusively on stability" (quote from Spencer in Hackvän (1999)). As far as the viability of the learning curve for the volunteers, even without the guidance of the original pair, Spencer approvingly observed that "I'm not sure how long it took the new maintainers to learn their way around the code, but judging by the stability of the product, they seem to be doing quite well" (Hackvän, 1999). By mid-1998 the first stable version was released. GIMP was ported to Windows by Tor Lillqvist in 1997. A binary installer was developed by Jernej Simoncic that greatly simplified installation on Windows. By 2004, after several years of development, a stable release, supported not only on Unix, but on Mac OS X and Windows was announced. The www.gimp.org Web site now lists almost 200 developers involved in the project beyond the founders Kimball and Mattis.

For products like Adobe Photoshop and GIMP, high-end specialized users set the standards for the product. Indeed, the requirements for an advanced image-processing product are probably more well understood in many respects by its end users than its developers, particularly its professional graphic-artist users. The effective development and application of the product entails the development of sophisticated artistic techniques and demands an understanding of how the tool is to be used that completely surpasses the understanding of most of the actual developers of the system. Thus, as already observed, GIMP's end users represented a parallel but divergent form of sophistication to the program developers. An impassioned base of such users was decisive in establishing the recognition and acceptance of GIMP. Their positive response and word-of-mouth publicity helped spread the word about the product and define its evolution. The Linux Penguin logo was famously made using GIMP. The now-celebrated Penguin was designed by Larry Ewing in 1996, using the early 0.54 beta version of GIMP (Mears, 2003). In what would become common expert user action, Ewing also set up a Web page that briefly described how he used GIMP to make the logo (Ewing, 1996). The whole episode became the first major exposure that GIMP received (Burgess, 2003). The how-to site Ewing setup was the first of many. As Burgess observed regarding GIMP, "what differentiated this program from many others is that a lot of sites sprung up on how to use the program . . . showing off artwork and sharing techniques" (Burgess, 2003).

The bottom line is how do GIMP and Adobe Photoshop compare? It is a confusing issue because there are very different potential user audiences involved, and so the level of functionality needed varies from the mundane to the esoteric. For many applications, GIMP appears to be perfectly suitable. GIMP was initially awkward to install on Windows, but the current download installer is fast and effective. The basic GIMP interface is highly professional. One hears very different comparative evaluations from different sources, and it is not really clear how objective the evaluators are. Overall, GIMP's performance appears to not match that of Photoshop. Photoshop's interface is more intuitive. GIMP is less easy to use, an important distinction for a casual user. The proliferation of separate windows is not always well-received. The quality of the tools in GIMP is arguably uneven. However, GIMP is free of charge and cross-platform. But if you are a professional graphics artist or if the application is a significant one where the graphics output is key to the successful outcome of a costly mission, the charge for the commercial product would likely not be an issue.

References

Bunks, C. (2000). Grokking the GIMP. New Riders Pub. Also: http://gimp-savvy.com/BOOK/index.html?node1.html. Accessed November 29, 2006.

Burgess, S. (2003). A Brief History of GIMP. http://www.gimp.org/about/ancient_history.html. Accessed November 29, 2006.

Ewing, L. (1996). Penguin Tutorial. http://www.isc.tamu.edu/~lewing/linux/notes.html. Accessed January 10, 2007.

Hackvän, S. (1999). Interview with Spencer Kimball and Peter Mattis. Linux World, January 1999. http://www.linuxworld.com/linuxworld/lw-1999-01/lw-01-gimp.html. Accessed January 21, 2004.

Mears, J. (2003). What's the Story with the Linux Penguin? December 26. http://www.pcworld.com/article/id,113881-page,1/article.html. Accessed January 10, 2007.

Willis, N. (2006). Running Photoshop Plugins in the GIMP, Even under Linux. April 10. http://applications.linux.com/article.pl?sid=06/04/05/1828238&tid=39. Accessed November 29, 2006.

4

Technologies Underlying Open Source Development

The free software movement emerged in the early 1980s at a time when the ARPANET network with its several hundred hosts was well-established and moving toward becoming the Internet. The ARPANET already allowed exchanges like e-mail and FTP, technologies that significantly facilitated distributed collaboration, though the Internet was to amplify this ability immensely. The TCP/IP protocols that enabled the Internet became the ARPANET standard on January 1, 1983. As a point of reference, recall that the flagship open source GNU project was announced by Richard Stallman in early 1983. By the late 1980s the NSFNet backbone network merged with the ARPANET to form the emerging worldwide Internet. The exponential spread of the Internet catalyzed further proliferation of open source development. This chapter will describe some of the underlying enabling technologies of the open source paradigm, other than the Internet itself, with an emphasis on the centralized Concurrent Versions System (CVS) versioning system as well as the newer decentralized BitKeeper and Git systems that are used to manage the complexities of distributed open development. We also briefly discuss some of the well-known Web sites used to host and publicize open projects and some of the services they provide.

The specific communications technologies used in open source projects have historically tended to be relatively lean: e-mail, mailing lists, newsgroups, and later on Web sites, Internet Relay Chat, and forums. Most current activity takes place on e-mail mailing lists and Web sites (Feller and Fitzgerald, 2002). The mailing lists allow many-to-many dialogs and can provide searchable Web-based archives just like Usenet. Major open source projects like Linux in the early 1990s still began operation with e-mail, newsgroups, and FTP downloads to communicate. Since the code that had to be exchanged could be voluminous, some means for reducing the amount of information transmitted and for clarifying the nature of suggested changes to the code was required. The *patch* program created by Larry Wall served this purpose. Newsgroups provided a means to broadcast ideas to targeted interest groups whose members might like to participate in a development project. The Usenet categories acted like electronic bulletin boards that allowed newsgroup participants to post e-mail-like messages like the famous comp.os.minix newsgroup on Usenet used by Linus Torvalds to initiate the development of Linux. Another powerful collaborative tool, developed beginning during the late 1980s, that would greatly facilitate managing distributed software development was the versioning or configuration management system. It is this topic that will be the focus of our attention in this chapter.

Versioning systems are software tools that allow multiple developers to work on projects concurrently and keep track of changes made to the code. The first such system was the *Revision Control System* (RCS) written in the early 1980s by Walter Tichy of Purdue. It used diffs to keep track of changes just like later systems, but was limited to single files. The first system that could handle entire projects was written by Dick Grune in 1986 with a modest objective in mind. He simply wanted to be able to work asynchronously with his students on a compiler project. Grune implemented his system using shell scripts that interacted with RCS and eventually it evolved into the most widely used versioning system, the open source *Concurrent Versions System*, commonly known as *CVS*. Brian Berliner initiated the C implementation of CVS in mid-1989 by translating the original shell scripts into C. Later contributors improved the system, noteworthy being Jim Kingdom's remote CVS implementation in 1993 that "enabled real use of CVS by the open source community" (STUG award announcement for 2003, http://www.usenix.org/about/stug.html).

4.1 Overview of CVS

CVS has been crucial to open source development because it lets distributed software developers access a shared repository of the source code for a project and permits concurrent changes to the code base. It also allows merging the changes into an updated version of the project on the repository and monitoring for potential conflicts that may occur because of the concurrent accesses. Remarkably, at any point during a project development, any previous version of the project can be easily accessed, so CVS also serves as a complete record of the history of all earlier versions of the project and that of all the changes to the project's code. It thus acts like what has been metaphorically called a *time machine*. We will overview the concepts and techniques that underlie

CVS (and similar systems) and illustrate its use in some detail, with examples selected from the comprehensive treatment of CVS by Fogel and Bar (2003).

CVS, which is available for download from www.nongnu.org/cvs, is the most widely used version control tool. It is distributed as open source under the General Public License (GPL). It is an award-winning tool; its major developers received the STUG (Software Tools User Group) award in 2003 in which it was identified as "the essential enabling technology of distributed development" (STUG award announcement for 2003; http://www.usenix.org/about/stug.html). As Fogel and Bar (2003, p. 10) observe, "CVS became the free software world's first choice for revision control because there's a close match . . . between the way CVS encourages a project to be run and the way free projects actually do run."

CVS serves two basic functions. On the one hand it keeps a complete historical digest of all actions (patches) against a project and on the other hand it facilitates distributed developer collaboration (Fogel and Bar, 2003). As an example, consider the following scenario. Suppose a user reports a bug in the last public release of a CVS project and a developer wants to locate the bug and fix it. Assuming the project has evolved since the previous release, the developer really needs an earlier version of the project, not its current development state. Recapturing that earlier state is easy with CVS because it automatically retains the entire development tree of the project. Furthermore, CVS also allows the earlier version, once the bug is repaired, to be easily reintegrated with the new current state of the project. Of course, it is worth stating that the kind of development management that CVS does had already been possible before the deployment of CVS. The advantage is that CVS makes it much easier to do, which is a critical factor particularly in a volunteer environment. As Fogel and Bar (2003, p.11) observe: "[I]t reduces the overhead in running a volunteer-friendly project by giving the general public easy access to the sources and by offering features designed specifically to aid the generation of patches to the source."

CVS is a client-server system under which software projects are stored in a so-called *repository* on a central server that serves content to possibly remote clients. Its client-side manifestations let multiple developers remotely and concurrently *check out* the latest version of a project from the repository. They can then modify the source code on the client(s) as they see fit, and thereafter commit any changes they have made to their working copy back to the central repository in a coordinated manner, assuming they have the write privileges to do so. This is called a *copy-modify-merge* development cycle.

Prior to CVS, versioning tools followed a *lock-modify-unlock model* for file changes. Only one developer could have access to a particular file at a time; other developers had to wait until the file being modified was released. This kind of solo, mutually exclusive access requires considerable coordination. If the developers are collocated, or know each other well and can contact each other quickly if a lockout is handicapping their work, or if the group of developers is small so that concurrent accesses are infrequent, then the coordination may be manageable. But in a large, geographically and temporarily distributed group of developers, the overhead of coordinating becomes onerous and annoying – a problematic issue in what may be a preponderantly volunteer community. This concurrent access is one way in which the copy-modify-merge model of CVS smoothes the interactions in a distributed development. The impact of conflicts in CVS also appears to be less than might be expected in any case. Berliner, one of the key creators of CVS, indicated that in his own personal experience actual conflicts are usually not particularly problematic: "conflicts that occur when the same object has been modified by someone else are quite rare" and that if they do occur "the changes made by the other developer are usually easily resolved" (Berliner, 1990).

Diff and Patch

The CVS development tree is not stored explicitly. Under CVS, earlier versions of the project under development are maintained only implicitly with just the *differences* between successive versions kept – a technique that is called *delta compression*. The CVS system lets a developer make changes, track changes made by other developers by viewing a log of changes, access arbitrary earlier versions of the project on the basis, for example, of a date or revision number, and initiate new branches of the project. The system can automatically integrate developer changes into the project master copy on the repository or to any working copies that are currently checked out by any developers using a combination of its update and commit processes. The distributed character of the project's developers, who are working on the project at different times and places, benefits greatly from this kind of concurrent access, with no developer having exclusive access to the repository files; otherwise the project could not be collaborated on as effectively. Changes are generally only committed after testing is complete, so the master copy stays *runnable*. The committed changes are accompanied by developer log messages that explain the change. Conflicts caused by a developer, who is concurrently changing a part of the project that has already been changed by another developer, are detected automatically when the developer attempts to commit the change. These conflicts must then be resolved manually before the changes can be committed to the repository.

Basic programs (commands, utilities, files) required for such versioning system include the following:

1. the diff command,
2. the patch command, and
3. the patch file.

The *diff* command is a Unix command that identifies and outputs the differences between a pair of text files on a line-by-line basis. It indicates (depending on the format selected) whether different lines have been added, deleted, or changed, with unchanged shared lines not output, except as context. Those are the only possible four editorial states.

Conceptually, *diff* takes a pair of files A and B and creates a file C representing their "difference." The output file is usually called a *patch file* because of its use in collaborative development where the difference represents a "software patch" that is scheduled to be made to a current version of a program. Modifications to projects may be submitted as patches to project developers (or maintainers) who can evaluate the submitted code. The core developers can then decide whether a suggested patch should be rejected, or accepted and committed to the source repository, to which only the developers have write access. The so-called *unified difference format* for the diff command is especially useful in open source development because it lets project maintainers more readily recognize and understand the code changes being submitted. For example, the unified format includes surrounding lines that have not been changed as context, making it easier to recognize what contents have been changed and where. Then, a judgment is required before the changes are committed to the project repository.

The *diff* command works in combination with the *patch* command to enact changes (Fountain, 2002). The Unix *patch* command uses the textual differences between an original file A and a revised file B, as summarized in a *diff* file C, to update file A to reflect the changes introduced in B. For example, in a collaborative development context, if B is an updated version of the downloaded source code in A, then:

$$diff\ A\ B\ >\ C$$

creates the *patch file* C as the difference of A and B. Then the command:

$$patch\ A\ <\ C$$

could be used to apply the patch C to update A, so it corresponds to the revision B.

The complementary diff and patch commands are extremely useful because they allow source code changes, in the form of the *relatively small patch file* like C (instead of the entire new version B), to be submitted, for example, by e-mail. After this submission, the small patch changes can be scrutinized by project maintainers before they are integrated into the development repository.

These commands are considered the crucial underlying elements in versioning systems, regardless of whether they are used explicitly or wrapped up in a tool. CVS C-implementer Berliner characterizes the patch program as the "indispensable tool for applying a diff file to an original" (Berliner, 1990). The patch program was invented by Larry Wall (creator of Perl) in 1985.

4.2 CVS Commands

Note: The following discussion is based on the well-known introduction to CVS by Karl Fogel and Moshe Bar (2003), specifically the "Tour of CVS" in their Chapter 2 – though their treatment is far more detailed, overall about 370 pages for the entire text in the current PDF. The present overview gives only a glimpse of CVS and is intended as a bird's-eye-view of how it works. We will use a number of examples from the Fogel and Bar (2003) *tour* which we will reference carefully to facilitate ready access to the original treatise. We also intersperse the examples with contextual comments about the role of CVS. The interested reader should see Fogel and Bar (2003) for a comprehensive, in-depth treatment. We next illustrate some of the key CVS commands.

4.2.1 Platforms and Clients

Naturally, in order to execute the *cvs* program it must have been *installed* on your machine in the first place. CVS comes with most Linux distributions, so in that case you do not have to install it. Otherwise, you can build CVS from the source code provided at sites like the Free Software Foundation (FSF)'s FTP site. The *stable releases* of the software are those with a single decimal point in their release version number. Unix-like platforms are obviously the most widely used for CVS development. The well-known documentation manual for the CVS system is called the *Cederqvist Manual*, named after its original author who wrote the first version in 1992 (Cederqvist et al., 2003). (Incidentally, dates are interesting in these matters because they help correlate noteworthy technological developments related to open source. For example, CVS debuted around 1986, but the key C version by Berliner did not come out until 1989. Linus Torvalds posted his original Linux announcement in August 1991.)

The cvs executable once installed automatically allows you to use it as a *client* to *connect* to remote CVS repositories. If you want to create a repository on your own machine, you use the cvs *newrepos* command and the *init* subcommand to create one. If you then add an appropriate Unix users group, then any of the users can create an independent new project using the cvs *import* command. Refer to Fogel and Bar (2003) for detailed information about where to get source code, compilation, commands, administration, etc.

There are also Windows versions of CVS available. Currently these can only connect as clients to repositories on remote machines *or* serve repositories on their own local machine. They cannot provide repository service to remote machines. The Windows version is typically available as prebuilt binary exe-cutables. A free Windows program called *WinCVS* is distributed under the GPL that provides a CVS client that only lets you connect to a remote CVS repository server. However, it does not let you serve a repository from you own machine, even locally. WinCVS is available as a binary distribution with relatively easy installation and configuration instructions. The WinCVS client lets you make a working project copy from a remote repository to which you can subsequently commit changes, update, or synchronize vis-à-vis the repository, etc.

4.2.2 Command Format

The CVS interface is command-line oriented. Both command options and global options can be specified. Command (or local) options only affect the particular command and are given to the right of the command itself. Global options affect the overall CVS environment independently of the current command and are given to the left of the command. The format to execute a command is

$$cvs \quad -global\text{-}options \quad command \quad -command\text{-}options$$

For example, the statement:

$$cvs \quad -Q \quad update \quad -p$$

runs the *update* command (Fogel and Bar, 2003, p. 27). The token *cvs* is of course the name of the CVS executable. The -Q tells the CVS program to operate in the *quiet* mode, meaning there is no diagnostic output except when the command fails. The -p command option directs the results of the command to standard output. The repository being referenced may be local or remote, but in either case a working copy must have already been checked out. We consider the semantics of the illustrated update command in an upcoming section, but first we address a basic question: how do you get a copy of the project to work on in the first place?

4.2.3 Checking Out a Project From a Repository

The transparency of online open source projects is truly amazing. Using CVS, anyone on the Internet can get a copy of the most current version of a project. While only core developers can make changes to the master copy of a project in the repository, CVS allows anyone to retrieve a copy of the project, as well as to keep any of their own modifications conveniently synchronized vis-à-vis the repository. This is a major paradigm shift. It is the polar opposite to how things are done in a proprietary approach where access to the source is prohibited to anyone outside the project loop. In open source under CVS, everyone connected to the Internet has instantaneous access to the real-time version of the source as well as to its development history: what was done, where it was done, by whom was it done, and when was it done! Of course, the same technology could also be used in a proprietary development model for use by a proprietary development team only, or by individuals or small teams working on a private project.

Remember the nature of the CVS distribution model. There is a single *master copy* of the project that some CVS system maintains centrally in a repository. Anyone who wants to look at the source code for a project in that repository, whether just to read it or to modify it, has to get his or her own separate *working copy* of the project from the repository. Given that a project named *myproject* already exists, a person checks out a working copy of the project with the command (Fogel and Bar, 2003, p. 32):

cvs   checkout myproject

Of course, before you can actually check out a working copy of a project, you first have to tell your CVS system or client where the repository is located that you expect to check out from. If the repository were stored locally on your own machine, you could execute the cvs program with the -d (for directory) option and just give the local path to the repository. A typical Unix example, assuming the repository is located at /usr/local/cvs (Fogel and Bar, 2003, p. 27), would be

cvs   -d/usr/local/cvs   command

To avoid having to type the *-d repository* you can set the environment variable CVSROOT to point to the repository. In the rest of this overview we will *assume* this has already been done (Fogel and Bar, 2003, p. 30). If the repository were located on a remote server reached over the Internet, you would use an access method. The method may allow unauthenticated access to the repository, but it is also possible to have password-authenticated access to the server (via an access method called pserver). Authenticated access requires not only a username, server name, and the path on the server to the CVS repository, but also a login command. The login results in a request by the system for a password. Once this is done, CVS saves the password, sort of like a cookie, so that any subsequent accesses to the server from the same client machine require no login password.

Once the repository is identified, the project can be checked out. When a working copy of a project is checked out, the *latest revisions* of all the project's files are provided in the working copy. In a versioning system like CVS, a revision is a modified version of a project that has been committed to the repository. The smallest unit given a revision number is a file. Individual source code revisions can be accessed by revision number or date. The terms *revision* and *revision number* differ from the *version number* of a project which is an unrelated numbering scheme used for public identification of releases.

4.2.4 Updating a Working Copy

Keep in mind that the following cvs *update* command updates the project working copy, not the official copy of the project in the cvs repository, remote or otherwise. It is the *commit* command that we will examine later that is used to "update" the actual repository copy on the basis of changes made to the working copy.

Consider first how to make a change to the source code in the working copy. Suppose that the project already contains just the following simple C source code file hello.c (Fogel and Bar, 2003, p. 35):

```
#include <stdio.h>
void
main ()
{
    printf ("Hello, world!\n");
}
```

As an example, edit the file so that it includes an additional line with a printf statement as shown later (Fogel and Bar, 2003, p. 35):

```
#include <stdio.h>
void
main ( )
{
    printf ("Hello, world!\n" );
    printf ("Goodbye, world!\n" );
}
```

If we now execute the cvs *update* command, the effect will be to access the repository copy of the project and use it to update the current working copy. Let us reemphasize that these changes are *only to the working copy* and have not yet been committed to the repository. There are several possibilities:

1. If a working copy file is the same as its repository copy, then there is no change to the working file.
2. If some working copy file differs from its repository copy and the differences are all the result of the local changes the user has made to the working file, then again the file is left as the user modified it.
3. If a working and repository file differ, and the changes are all from the repository copy (because it was altered since the user checked it out), then the updated repository copy replaces the local unaltered working copy.
4. If a working and repository file differ, and the changes are partly from the repository copy (because it was altered since the user checked it out) and partly from the user's working copy, then the updated repository copy is merged with the user's current working copy. Of course, the repository copy itself is not changed because this is an update command, not a commit. But the user's copy has been "updated."

The purpose of the update command is to allow the local developer to synchronize his or her own working copy with respect to the current state of the repository. As we shall see shortly, the CVS *commit* command sends changes that have been made to the working copy to the centralized repository and merges them into the repository copy. The *update* command does the reverse. It brings any changes already made by other remote developers to the repository, since the copy was checked out or its last update, back into the local developer's working copy – the developer who executes the update command – *from* the repository. This keeps that developer's local working copy synchronized with the repository whenever the local developer wants the update process done. Remember, it does not keep the repository synchronized with the working copy. It does not even affect the repository. Nor does it affect the working copies of other remote developers. If another developer is working on his or her own working copy concurrently, then an update command will not reflect those changes until that developer commits them to the repository. Practice differs as to when to do updates. One approach is to update against the repository for synchronization before making any significant changes to the working copy. To maintain closer control on the update, you can also name the files that you want to allow to be updated. An example of the update command and its results follow (Fogel and Bar, 2003, p. 36).

cvs update
cvs update: Updating
  M hello.c
  cvs update: Updating a-subdir
  cvs update: Updating a-subdir/subsubdir
  cvs update: Updating b-subdir

The *M* stands for modified. It signals that the file has been modified by this user since the copy was checked out and that those changes have not yet been committed to the repository.

The directories and subdirectories referred to here are assumed to be those for the hypothetical project. These project directories and files are part of our reference example from Fogel and Bar (2003). For simplicity, we assume that they were created separately and then imported into the repository using the *import* command (which we do not address). For later reference we mention that hello.c lies in the directory named *a-subdir*. As it will turn out, there are two other files we have not needed to refer to yet, named fish.c and random.c, that will be assumed to lie in the two project directories a-subdir/subsubdir and b-subdir, respectively (Fogel and Bar, 2003, p. 31).

4.2.5 The Diff Command

The synchronization effect of the *update* command is significant but the output of the update command does not say much except that the file hello.c has been modified (M) but not yet committed to the repository. Thus it reflects that there has been a change to the file, but does not identify the changes. To identify the changes, we need to execute the *diff* command. To compare the current working copy with the repository copy, we execute

$$cvs \quad -Q \quad diff \quad -c$$

The global *Q* (quiet) option makes the command run quietly. The command option *c* (context) makes it provide the surrounding context for any changes. No file has been identified in this command, so any files where there are differences between the working and repository copy will be diagnosed. The command gives the following output (Fogel and Bar, 2003, p. 37):

```
Index: hello.c
===================================
RCS file: /usr/local/cvs/myproj/hello.c,v
retrieving revision 1.1.1.1
diff -c -r1.1.1.1 hello.c
```

```
*** hello.c 2001/04/18 18:18:22 1.1.1.1
- hello.c 2001/04/19 02:17:07
***************
***4,7****
-4,8-
main ()
{
    printf ("Hello, world!\n");
+ printf ("Goodbye, world!\n");
}
```

Since no file argument was given for the command, CVS automatically applied it to any file that could possibly be appropriate. In this case, the working copy of hello.c was compared with the original copy of hello.c in the repository. The repository copy (time-stamped 2001/04/18) is bounded by asterisks (*'s). The working copy (time-stamped 2001/04/19) is bounded by dashes (-'s).

In this example, the *context* and/or changes were in lines 4–7 of the original repository file and in lines 4–8 of the working copy file. The sole difference between the files consists in the newly added printf line which is flagged by the + in the output.

Generally, whenever a pair of files A1 and A2 are diff'ed, the so-called *unified format* patch shows all the contrasting new and old code segments, and the changes they have undergone, as well as their context. The contrasted segments of code are called *hunks*. Corresponding hunks are shown following one another in the diff output. In this case the hunks are delineated by ***4,7 *** and – 4,8 –. Symbols like

+   for a line added in A2 when A1 and A2 are diff'ed,
−   for a line deleted from A1, and
!   for a shared but changed line that appears differently in A1 and A2

make the changes in the paired hunks for A1 and A2 readily recognizable.

The process of using the diff and the associated patch commands, and comparing hunks to see what modifications have been made, is essential in distributed software development. It is basically the information you need in order to see what the other developers are doing and exactly how it differs from what you are planning to do, if it does differ. It does not tell you what the motivations for the changes are or who made them. That is the province of the *log* command. The diff command only provides the overall *What*, the log command provides the *Who* and the *Why* for the ongoing distributed development.

The current example contains only one hunk that requires any notation to indicate that one of its lines was an addition (Fogel and Bar, 2003, p. 37).

```
***4,7****
-4,8-
main ()
{
    printf ("Hello, world!\n");
+ printf ("Goodbye, world!\n");
}
```

The first hunk is empty because there were no repository changes and no lines have been altered (!) or removed (-) in the working copy.

The next example (Fogel and Bar, 2003, pp. 38–39) illustrates the effect of a changed line in a file rather than an added line. The command and its output follow (a few # Perl comment lines have spilled over):

cvs -Q diff -c

```
Index: cvs2cl.pl
==================================
RCS file:
/usr/local/cvs/kfogel/code/cvs2cl/cvs2cl.pl,v
retrieving revision 1.76
diff -c -r1.76 cvs2cl.pl
***cvs2cl.pl 2001/04/13 22:29:44 1.76
- cvs2cl.pl 2001/04/19 05:41:37
***************
***212,218 ****
    # can contain uppercase and lowercase letters,
    digits, `-',
    # and `-'. However, it's not our place to
    enforce that, so
    # we'll allow anything CVS hands us to be a
    tag:
!     /^\s([^:]+): ([0-9.]+)$/;
    push (@{$symbolic_names{$2}}, $1);
    }
  }
- 212,218 -
    # can contain uppercase and lowercase letters,
    digits, `-',
```

```
      # and `-'. However, it's not our place to
      enforce that, so
      # we'll allow anything CVS hands us to be a
      tag:
!        /^\s([^:]+):  ([\d.]+)$/;
      push (@{$symbolic_names{$2}}, $1);
      }
   }
```

The example identifies an assumed Perl script file named *cvs2cl.pl* that has been changed. The corresponding hunks are from lines 212–218 of the repository and working files. Most of the output consists of context lines that are unchanged. The exclamation point notation (!) flags the solitary altered line of the Perl code in line 215: the 0–9 text in the original (where the change is also flagged) has been changed to \ d in the working copy. Had say three of the comment lines been removed in the altered working copy, the line range in the working copy would have been 212,215 and the deleted lines, which would of course still be in the repository copy because the changes have not been committed yet, would be flagged in the repository hunk with – 's to indicate that they were deleted (from the working copy).

We already observed that diff's are important to developers because they allow differences between the current repository copy and proposed changes in the working copy to be clearly identified. However, diff's are also important because they are central in terms of the internal representation of the repository since projects are represented as a sequence of diff's. Indeed, the project, as it was at any past point in time, can be reconstructed by CVS using the diff's. That is, the repository implicitly contains, but only implicitly so, every previous version of the project: the entire *project development tree*. It does not contain these earlier versions explicitly, which would certainly be space-consuming. It only has the current version of the project and the diff's that lead back to the earlier versions, any of which can then be reconstructed on demand by CVS.

The procedure for recreating any previous revision from this implicit development tree is simple and intuitive. Each new revision in the repository copy had in fact been derived by applying a diff to a previous revision. Provided this historical chain of diff's is retained, any earlier copy can be reconstructed, given the most recent revision. For example, consider how to get back to the current repository revision from one's own tentative working revision (without doing another checkout). The diff between the two copies identifies the editorial differences between them, like what lines may have been removed in the original or what lines may have been altered. So we could get back to the original by simply applying these changes to our own uncommitted working copy. That operation would effectively bring us back in time (from the putative next revision represented by the working copy) by applying or following the information in the diff. In a similar manner, one could work back in a step-by-step fashion to any earlier revision of the project tree. This is what has been described as the time-machine-like functionality of the CVS system. Conversely, since the diff supplies symmetric information, then given only the diff between the working and repository copy, and without adverting to the working copy, we could go from the repository copy to the working copy.

Thus, when CVS has to update an out-of-date working copy currently being used by a distributed developer, all CVS has to do is apply the diff command to the working copy's files against the repository copy in order to identify the patch needed to bring the working copy up to date. This is also similar to the way in which a developer/maintainer accepts diff output (which are also called patch files because of how they are used), sent by contributors to a project, and manually applies the diff (or patch) to the repository to enact the change.

4.2.6 The Commit Command

The *update* command updates the local working copy with respect to the current repository copy. This operation requires only *read access* privileges since the repository copy is unchanged, just referenced. On the other hand, the *commit* command stores changes in the repository, so it requires *write access* privileges to the repository. In a major open source project, the write access privileges are reserved to a limited set of core developers or maintainers. Participants who want to submit changes to the repository have to send the changes as patches such as via e-mail. A maintainer/developer can then adjudicate whether the patch is appropriate. If so, it can be committed or written to the repository by the maintainer/developer using the commit command. The typical policy is to try to ensure the master copy of the project in the repository stays in a *runnable* state by only committing changes when they are already both complete and tested (Fogel and Bar, 2003).

The ability to easily recapture any earlier state of a project in CVS makes the commit process less risky in case of an error. If a submitted patch is committed and turns out to have problems, the maintainer can easily recoup the original state of the system, undoing the faulty patch. Of course, as patches build up, this becomes less and less simple since subsequent patches may depend on previous ones.

Here is how the commit command works. If executed by a distributed developer, the command sends the modifications made by the developer to the central project repository. For example, the following example (Fogel and Bar, 2003, p. 43) commits the changes that have been made to the hello.c file but so far only locally, to the repository:

cvs   commit   -m   "print goodbye too"   hello.c

Checking in hello.c;
/usr/local/cvs/myproj/hello.c,v   <– hello.c
new revision: 1.2; previous revision: 1.1
done

The *-m* option tells the system to use the embedded phrase (*"print goodbye too"*) in the log file. This descriptive phrase included by the author on the command line then becomes part of the *log* of messages in the repository. This log can be browsed to see what kind of changes have been made to the repository over time – a capability that is important for keeping developers apprised of what is going on in the development. Notice how the system says that the revised file hello.c has now been *checked in* to the system (repository), complementary to how the project/file had originally been *checked out* via the checkout command. The previous revision number for the file hello.c has also been updated from 1.1 to 1.2. We note that the revision numbers of different files in a project may be very different from one another simply because some of the files may have been updated more frequently than others. Of course, the files that are selected to represent the most current revision of a project are automatically those files with the highest revision numbers.

If the commit command mentions no file, then all the files in the current directory are committed. The following commit command will therefore affect any local files that have been modified, which in this hypothetical example we will assume to be the files named fish.c and random.c, as per the example we are using from (Fogel and Bar, 2003). We mentioned these files previously, at the end of the section on the update command. Once again, let us assume they have been modified in the local copy. The command executed is

cvs   commit   -m   "filled out C code"

The command output is (Fogel and Bar, 2003, pp. 43–44, 52)

```
cvs commit: Examining
cvs commit: Examining a-subdir
cvs commit: Examining a-subdir/subsubdir
cvs commit: Examining b-subdir
Checking in a-subdir/subsubdir/fish.c;
```

```
/usr/local/cvs/myproj/a-subdir/subsubdir/fish.c,v
<- fish.c
new revision: 1.2;        previous revision: 1.1
done
Checking in b-subdir/random.c;
/usr/local/cvs/myproj/b-subdir/random.c,v
<- random.c
new revision: 1.2;        previous revision: 1.1
done
```

Both of the affected files, fish.c and random.c, have had their revision numbers updated which in this case happens to be the identical value 1.2, though that correspondence is purely coincidental. The revision numbers of individual files are of course not generally thus synchronized, but depend on the frequency of modification of the files. Just as when you check out a project from the repository, you get the latest or highest revision numbers for each file in the project, correspondingly when you commit or check in an update, the revision numbers of the checked in files get updated to the next higher revision numbers for those separate files. The user ID, time, and date stamp are also added automatically.

4.2.7 The Log Command

The descriptions given in the developers' comments on changes can be browsed through using the CVS *log* command. The following output is for the hypothetical single file hello.c. It assumes hello.c has gone through a series of revisions that are listed in the output in reverse order (revision 1.4, 1.3, 1.2, 1.1, 1.1.1.1). The revisions are assumed to have been made by two developers who had logged on with names *Bert* and *Harry* (a slight change from the reference example). In this example the last committed change is assumed to have been executed by developer Bert using the commented commit command (Fogel and Bar, 2003, p. 50):

> *cvs   commit   -m   "adjusted middle line"*

The log command that displays these explanatory commented commands and changes is

> *cvs   log   hello.c*

This returns output, with some trivial changes from the original example (Fogel and Bar, 2003, p. 51), that includes

```
RCS file: /usr/local/cvs/myproj/hello.c,v
Working file: hello.c
head: 1.4
branch:
locks: strict
access list:
symbolic names:
      start: 1.1.1.1
      Bert: 1.1.1
keyword substitution: kv
total revisions: 5; selected revisions: 5

description:
------------
revision 1.4
        date: 2001/04/20 04:14:37; author: Bert;
        state: Exp; lines: +1 -1
        adjusted middle line
------------
revision 1.3
        date: 2001/04/20 02:30:05; author: Harry;
        state: Exp; lines: +1 -0
        added new middle line
------------
revision 1.2
        date: 2001/04/19 06:35:15; author: Bert;
        state: Exp; lines: +1 -0
        print goodbye too
------------
revision 1.1
        date: 2001/04/18 18:18:22; author: Bert;
        state: Exp;
        branches: 1.1.1;
        Initial revision
----------------
revision 1.1.1.1
        date: 2001/04/18 18:18:22; author: Bert;
        state: Exp; lines: +0 -0
        initial import into CVS
        =========================
```

A command like the one cvs commit -m "filled out C code" that we used previously, committed two files (fish.c and random.c) to the repository at the same time, so the (same) comment from the command will be logged for both the files. This facilitates recognizing changes that have been committed simultaneously when you browse the log file. You can also get the log entries for explicitly selected files. In fact, because of the difficulty of reading lengthy log information, it may be best to selectively look at the log data for a single file at a time. Log files are useful for developers for getting a quick overview of what has been transpiring in a project. But reading the log command's output is confusing if you want to get an overview of the entire development because the log command gives the log messages for every file. For example, if ten files were submitted at a single commit then their log entries would all appear as separate entries with the same log message. There are tools available that convert the log command's output to a more understandable and concise form. A useful CVS add-on provides so-called GNU style *ChangeLogs* to present the log file data. In the ChangeLog view, all files committed at the same time are shown as a group with the single same shared log message that accompanied the commit.

CVS can also send out so-called *commit e-mails* to notify developers or other interested parties about commits. The e-mails are based on the CVS log file. Commit e-mails are a key opportunity for peer review by project participants (Fogel, 2005). Its public nature reminds people that review is a regular process and gives people the opportunity to participate in the review. The peer review process also makes committers aware of the fact that "what they do is seen and understood" by a panoply of thoughtful observers (Fogel, 2005, p. 33).

4.2.8 Recognizing Conflicts in Modifications

The process of integrating developer changes with the project's master copy or repository is called *merging*. Changes that are disjoint and affect different files can be merged automatically, but overlapping changes cause potential conflicts that have to be resolved *manually*. This approach is automatically entailed if one allows concurrent access to a project without locking out developers.

Thus, suppose two developers are working on the same file hello.c of a project. One developer *Harry* has already added a statement printf ("between hello and goodbye \ n") to the code and has successfully committed this change to the repository. Another developer *Bert* is preparing to work on the same file in his working copy but has *not* made any changes to it as yet. Developer Bert can determine the status of his working copy vis-à-vis the repository by executing the cvs status command:

cvs   status   hello.c

The *status* command does *not* update or synchronize Bert's code with the repository like the update command does. It only reports whether there have been any changes to the repository copy since Bert's current working copy was checked out. In this case, the system warns Bert that his working copy is now out of date and needs a patch to bring it into synchronization (Fogel and Bar, 2003, p. 48):

File: hello.c	Status: *Needs Patch*
Working revision:	1.2 Mon Apr 19 02:17:07 2001
Repository revision:	1.3 /usr/local/cvs/myproj/hello.c, v
Sticky Tag:	(none)
Sticky Date:	(none)
Sticky Options:	(none)

The affected file is hello.c. Its revision number was 1.2. The repository has changed since the file was checked out and now the most recent revision of the file has revision number 1.3. Thus the status of the file is that it needs to be updated (or patched or synchronized) against the repository copy before the developer proceeds to work on the file. Had there been no discrepancies between the repository and working copy, the status command would merely have reported the status as *up-to-date*. Had there been no changes to the repository copy and only local modifications in the working copy, the status would have been reported as *locally modified*.

Suppose developer Bert ignores the warning and makes changes directly to his old revision by adding the statement printf ("this change will conflict \n"), say, at the same place in the code where a change was already committed by the other developer to the repository. If Bert executes the *status* command again, then this time the system warns him (Fogel and Bar, 2003, p. 48) that not only the repository copy of his file has changed, but his copy has also changed and so the situation needs to be resolved by properly *merging* the changes with the new revision:

File: hello.c   Status: *Needs Merge*

Suppose that Bert then updates his working copy; thus

cvs   update   hello.c

CVS once again announces that there is a conflict, but this time it also identifies the potentially inconsistent lines of code. The partial output in the following introduces the situation (Fogel and Bar, 2003, p. 49):

```
RCS file: /usr/local/cvs/myproj/hello.c,v
retrieving revision 1.2
retrieving revision 1.3
```

Merging differences between 1.2 and 1.3 into hello.c

```
rcsmerge:  warning: conflicts during merge
cvs update:  conflicts found in hello.c
C  hello.c
```

The notation *C* next to the file name flags the file involved in the potential conflict. Revision 1.3 is the most recent revision of the file. Revision 1.2 is Bert's older working copy revision of the file. Clear warnings are given that a conflict is present that must be resolved by the receiving developer.

The remainder of the output presents the results of the update command's merge. The merge has only been done in the sense that the two disparate copies were combined in the *developer's copy only*, while of course not affecting the repository. The merged working file hello.c at this point includes the two developers' changes that are appropriately distinguished from one another inside markers (Fogel and Bar, 2003, p. 49):

```
#include <stdio.h>
void
main ()
{
  printf ("Hello, world! \n");
  <<<<<<< hello.c
    printf ("this change will conflict\n" );
    =======
    printf ("between hello and goodbye\n");
  >>>>>>> 1.3
  printf ("Goodbye, world! \n");
}
```

The repeated angular brackets >>> and <<< are called *conflict markers* and follow the format (Fogel and Bar, 2003, p. 49):

```
<<<<<<< (filename)
the uncommitted changes in the working copy
-- change by one of the developers --
=======
the new changes that came from the repository
-- change by the other developer --
>>>>>>> (latest revision number in the
repository)
```

The conflict is only resolved when the developer, possibly working collaboratively with the other developer who made the commits, edits the conflicted file where the conflicts occur and commits the changes. Thus

1. The correct choice of text is decided on.
2. The conflict markers are edited out.
3. The resulting patch can then be committed to the repository with an appropriate log message explaining the change.

This kind of conflict detection is nonetheless fairly limited or myopic in scope. A more nuanced understanding of the nature of potential conflicts has to be kept in mind. Developers still have to be on guard. Source code is replete with numerous interfile dependencies. A classic instance of such dependencies is the effect of changing a header file in a C program. CVS handles these in its usual nonlocking mode. Of course, such a change does not affect just the header file. It impacts every file that uses the header file. In such a case, locking a file, as was done in the conventional lock-modify-unlock model for versioning, would only give a developer a misleading impression that the changes were only local to that file. But as Rooney (2004) warns in his discussion of the similar Subversion versioning system: "Locking gives you the illusion that it's safe to make changes, but in reality you need the same amount of communication among developers that you'd need in the nonlocking mode. Locking just makes it easier to forget that."

4.2.9 Branches in CVS – and Forks

The revisions we have considered so far have evolved from the top of the development tree, that is, from the most recent revision. However, sometimes one may need to develop a new revision by springing off from an earlier revision in the tree. Suppose, for example, that an earlier revision corresponded to a public release of a project. Suppose also that someone has subsequently detected a bug in this earlier release. Obviously, since the bug has been recognized in the context of the previous release, the patch that repairs the bug should be applied against that release rather than more current revisions. This can be easily done with CVS. A new tangential project development like this is called a *branch*.

Branches can be thought of as retrospective, alternate project evolutions that emerge and diverge from earlier versions. A branch of a project is a different line of development that is split off from the main line of development or trunk at an earlier release that has been identified as having a problem only after its distribution. Branching is accomplished by checking out a working copy of that earlier version. The bug is then fixed in that working copy. Then the patch is committed to the branched version. It is not committed, at least at this point, to the current development version which is left unaltered, though of course it may turn out that the current version can be similarly debugged and also patched. If the *same* patch works for both the earlier release that was branched and the current development version, then the branch can be *merged* back to the trunk with the history or record of all these changes still preserved in the repository (Fogel and Bar, 2003).

A branch in a CVS development tree is of course completely different from a fork in an open source project. A branch of the project still belongs to the project. It is merely a technically driven and perhaps temporary split in the project tree. A *fork* of a project, on the other hand, is a political or organizational phenomenon that occurs when some of the developers or participants disagree with the core decision maker(s) about the direction of the project – so much so that they decide to strike off on their own and continue the project in a different direction. They can make a copy of the project (the existing CVS tree), assuming the license allows this, as the GPL would, and start a new project with the current one as the point of departure. Forks are relatively rare in open source development because they upset the whole applecart, breaking up an originally unified project. As an illustration, the Apache Web server project can perhaps be considered as essentially an amicable and successful fork in the NCSA httpd daemon developed by Rob McCool.

4.2.10 Development Practices: Patches and Releases

CVS provides an effective software tool for handling patches in distributed development and ultimately for posting new releases of a project. The question of what practices or policies are used to manage these actions is separate from the technology provided by the tool.

How are patches handled administratively? In any major project, an open source participant does not directly commit a patch to the repository with his or her own commit command because such write privileges to a repository are reserved to a limited group of developers. Participants have *read* access to the repository, so they can checkout copies and modify them. But commits are typically handled indirectly through a developer filter. The normal participant/developer can just submit the patch in an e-mail to a core developer who does have *write* privileges or to a maintainer. The developer/maintainer then commits the patch to the repository, or not, as the case may be. As we have indicated earlier, the time-machine-like functionality of the CVS development tree allows faulty patches to be easily undone, so even these commits are only semidecisive. If it turns out, the patch is ineffective, and it can be undone by backing the development tree up to the previous revision. Of course, the longer it took to recognize an inappropriate patch, the more likely it would be that subsequent patches would be piled on top of the revision, incrementing the difficulty of getting the system integrated back to a satisfactory state. Patches are reviewed and tested carefully and perhaps modified by the maintainer before being accepted. The work is tedious. If the patch is rejected, the maintainer has to explain why and do so in a courteous manner since these are public forums (Fogel and Bar, 2003).

How are releases handled? There are questions as to when to do it, who is in charge of the process, and how it is distributed. Consider first the technical question of distribution of the release. New releases can be distributed in two ways: in toto or as patch increments. Thus they can be provided as a single self-contained *tarball* with all the project files and directories wrapped up into a single archive. This is suitable for users who are just starting off on the project and so have no prior version to build on. For users who already have the previous most recent release of the project, a different approach may be appropriate: they can be provided a patch file that contains all the patches required to bring the earlier version up to date. The user can then download this (much smaller) patch file only and apply it to their previous version, rather than download the complete project as a tarball (Fountain, 2002).

Releases tend to be made when a sufficient number of bugs have been repaired or a sufficient number of new features have been added since the last release, though a new release may sometimes also be done for political reasons because it may serve the purpose of bringing public attention to the product and the project. The actual decision as to when to make the release is made by the core developers who will also typically decide who should be the release manager. It is the responsibility of the release manager to ensure that the new release revision is stable. A common practice is to first initiate a so-called *freeze*. This usually entails a *feature freeze* under which "no significant new functionality is added to the program, but bug fixes are permitted," and perhaps also a *code freeze* wherein "*no* changes are to be made to the code except those absolutely necessary to fix known bugs" (Fogel and Bar, 2003, p. 190). Other relevant terms that reflect the intentions of the release management process include a *soft freeze* where the objective is to avoid destabilizing changes to the project and generally not do "anything big" (Fogel and Bar, 2003, p. 190). In a *hard freeze*, only code changes that repair relatively straightforward known bugs may be allowed.

The restrictions and inconvenience to development imposed by pre-release freezes are mitigated if a project is differentiated into a *development branch* and *stable branches*. The main project trunk can be considered as the development branch. When a decision is made to make a new release, a branch can be made. This release branch can then be evolved until it stabilizes to the release manager's satisfaction. At the same time the main development trunk can continue unaffected. Bugs fixed on the release branch as it is readied for release can of course also be applied to the development branch. As the release approaches stability, a *beta release* may be released which is characterized by being both fairly well-tested and relatively stable. Stability means very few bugs are being reported; thus "once bug reports from the beta have slowed down to a trickle," the release becomes official (Fogel and Bar, 2003, p. 200). Once the release is "released," then development on its offshoot branch can terminate. Future releases can then similarly branch off the continuing main development trunk of the project. In Linux development, both the development and stable versions are always publicly accessible. They cater to different audiences. The stable versions are for people who need reliability. The development versions are for the developers, early adopters, and users who need to use or want to test new features not yet in the stable release. The Linux project introduced a now widely used distinctive numbering scheme to differentiate stable and development versions as we have previously described in our discussion of the Linux platform.

References

Berliner, B. (1990). CVS II: Parallelizing Software development. In: Proceedings of the USENIX Winter 1990 Technical Conference. http://docs.freebsd.org/44doc/psd/28.cvs/paper.pdf. Accessed January 10, 2007.

Cederqvist, Per et al. (1992). Version Management with CVS. Network Theory Limited, Bristol, United Kingdom.

Cederqvist, Per et al. (2003). Version Management with CVS, Network Theory Limited, Bristol, United Kingdom.

Feller, J. and Fitzgerald, B. (2002). Understanding Open Source Software Development. Addison-Wesley, Pearson Education Ltd., London.

Fogel, K. (2005). Producing Open Source Software: How to Run a Successful Free Software Project. O'Reilly Media. Sebastopol, CA.

Fogel, K. and Bar, M. (2003). Open Source Development with CVS, 3rd edition. Paraglyph Press, Scotsdale, AZ. http://cvsbook.red-bean.com/. Accessed August 30, 2007.

Fountain, D. (2002). Creating and Using Patches. http://tools.devchannel.org/devtoolschannel/04/06/02/1521207.shtml?tid=46. Accessed November 29, 2006.

Rooney, G. (2004). Practical Subversion. Apress Publishers, Berkley, CA.

4.3 Other Version Control Systems

CVS still dominates the version control market but there are other important versioning systems available, or Software Configuration Management (SCM) systems as they are also called. These include Subversion, BitKeeper, Git, CodeVille, and Monotone. We will discuss Subversion and BitKeeper in some detail and the others briefly. With the exception of the proprietary BitKeeper, these systems are all open source. A fundamental distinguishing characteristic of a versioning system is whether it is centralized or decentralized; see Wheeler (2004) for a useful overview. CVS and Subversion are both centralized versioning systems, operating according to a client-server model. They maintain a unique centralized repository to which changes are fed from distributed developers. BitKeeper, Monotone, Codeville, and Git are all decentralized systems. They support environments where distributed developers work asynchronously and independently, updating local repositories by pulling in changes from others. The BitKeeper system was used for some time in the Linux kernel development during which it demonstrated the remarkable power of decentralized (distributed) versioning systems to expedite project management. We shall begin with a discussion of Subversion and then turn to the decentralized systems.

4.3.1 Subversion

Subversion is similar to CVS. It uses a distributed nonlocking model for project management and allows both local and remote server-based access to its repository. Subversion was already in development for several years prior to its version 1.0 debut in early 2004. The collaborative software company CollabNet started its development in 2000, intending it as a replacement for CVS, and brought in two major CVS experts Karl Fogel and Jim Blandy for the project. Blandy was a long-time free software advocate and the maintainer for the GNU Emacs project. It was he who came up with the product's transgressive name, and it does have the obvious implication. According to the Subversion Web site its avowed mission is to "Take over the CVS user base." Other developers include Collins-Sussman and a community of open source contributors.

The objective of Subversion was to *not* radically alter the CVS design, but only fix what were believed to be its flaws. In fact, its developers wanted Subversion to look like CVS precisely to minimize the learning curve for new users coming from a CVS environment. Subversion became "self-hosting" in August 2001 (Collins-Sussman et al., 2005). The product is open source, distributed under an Apache-BSD type of license. CollabNet holds the copyright. CollabNet also funds most of the development and some of its employees are full-time developers. Despite the corporate sponsorship and ownership, the project is nonetheless "run like most open-source projects, governed by a loose, transparent set of rules that encourage meritocracy" (Collins-Sussman et al., 2005).

The system is implemented as a collection of C libraries with well-defined APIs and runs on multiple platforms. Windows, Unix, and Mac OS versions are available. The interface is line-oriented like CVS and includes the same basic commands, but the command-line output is *readable* and intentionally *parseable*. Although the system is command-line oriented, a Visual Studio.Net product called AnkhSVN is available for Windows environments that lets you work with most Subversion commands inside the .NET IDE.

Subversion is much less widely used than CVS, though it is probably the second most popular versioning system in use and is increasing in popularity. Its penetration on WebDAV servers increased 25-fold since its release as per the securityspace.com Apache Module Report, though this still represents only a tiny fraction of the overall market. The GNU GCC project now uses Subversion rather than CVS to manage its repository, which is significant, given the prominent status of the GCC project. Significantly, it also serves as the versioning system for Python and the KDE desktop project. On the other hand, Subversion has limitations that make it inappropriate for some projects. For example, Linux development uses distributed repositories. Since Subversion, like CVS, is a centralized source control system, it is not suited to Linux style decentralized development. In fact, Torvalds explicitly disregarded it as a replacement candidate for BitKeeper, which had temporarily been the Linux versioning system.

A major improvement in Subversion over against CVS is that Subversion *versions* directories not just files. According to the Subversion home page, it "versions not only file contents and file existence, but also directories, copies, and renames." All added, copied, or renamed files get a complete new history. Subversion's commits are atomic. It also supports binary files (such as media) and binary diff's. The Subversion home page claims the system is "equally efficient on binary as on text files, because it uses a binary diff'ing algorithm to transmit and store successive revisions." In contrast, CVS is text-oriented because its applications were expected to be about source code development. Versioning systems like CVS have typically handled binary files such as those arising in imaging or multimedia contexts in a clumsy manner if at all, particularly binary diff's. In fact, binary revisions have usually been done by keeping a separate copy of the binary file for each revision. Versioning tools may even corrupt a binary file by adding inappropriate end-of-line conversions that damage the file. Conflicts regarding changes in binary files still have to be handled manually in Subversion, but it facilitates the process. Subversion gives you the copy you checked out, the modified copy, and the current repository copy. You can then use an independent tool to decide how to compare them (Rooney, 2004).

References

Collins-Sussman, B., Fitzpatrick, B., and Pilato, C. (2005). Version Control with Subversion. Red-Bean.com. http://svnbook.red-bean.com/. Accessed January 10, 2007.

Rooney, G. (2004). Practical Subversion. Apress Publishers, Berkley, CA.

Wheeler, D. (2004). Comments on Open Source Software/Free Software (OSS/FS) Software Configuration Management (SCM) Systems. http://www.dwheeler.com/essays/scm.html. Accessed November 29, 2006.

4.3.2 Decentralized Systems: BitKeeper, Git, Monotone, CodeVille

BitKeeper is a commercial, proprietary, decentralized versioning system. It debuted around 1998. Its story is quite well-known in the open source community, partly because it was controversially used for a time in Linux kernel development where it demonstrated the dramatic impact decentralized configuration management could have in expediting project management. BitKeeper's developer Larry McVoy describes it as a "peer to peer system of replicated repositories" (Andrews, 2002). According to its Web site, it provides a system where "every developer gets their own personal repository, complete with revision history, and the tool handles moving changes between repositories" (bitkeeper.com), which is radically different from the centralized CVS model. The BitKeeper license is proprietary. Despite this, its owners had allowed open source developers, of which the Linux kernel project was the most prominent example, to use the software free of charge under certain stipulations. This free-of-charge deployment to the open source community was part of a business strategy by McVoy (a Linux kernel developer himself) for building BitKeeper's market share. In exchange for the free-of-charge use of BitKeeper in a binary-only version, open developers had to agree not to participate in developing competing products like CVS while they were using it, as well as not to try to reverse engineer the product (Corbet, 2005). BitKeeper was, of course, also available under a purely commercial license. The system's biggest platform market is Windows, but it has been ported to many systems including FreeBSD, Solaris, and Mac OS X, though the BitKeeper Web site affirms that "Linux is the platform of choice."

The decentralized character of BitKeeper underlies its tremendous effectiveness in facilitating project management for parallel development. It supports what can be thought of as a layered network structure for the collaboration of developers – a structure that lets a project leader partition and delegate project responsibilities among a number of subsystem managers. This kind of partitioning is possible because under BitKeeper each developer group "can have a shared repository which sits between them and the global repository" (BitKeeper Web Site, 2006). Each developer in a group can then clone this shared repository to establish his or her own work area, and work on his or her own repository independently. This creates a safer and more robust development environment. The staging area that separates each local group from the rest of the project allows "changes to be debugged within a local group, without breaking" the main repository (BitKeeper Web Site, 2006). These features were decisive to Linus' adoption of BitKeeper for kernel development. They made his role as head of the entire project dramatically more manageable by buffering him from software changes, except those that had been vetted through a small number of his trusted lieutenants. As a consequence, he had fewer, less-fragmented changes to review, coming from fewer, more reliable developers, and which had been vetted more carefully prior to being considered for integration into a master repository by Linus. This buffered, partitioned structure makes BitKeeper's project management advantages scalable. Furthermore, it underscores a corresponding vulnerability in the single repository model, where one bad apple can spoil the barrel because systems like CVS lack "staging areas to protect the main tree" from bad check-ins (BitKeeper Web Site, 2006). In CVS, a bad patch, checked into the unique repository tree, impacts everyone as soon as they synchronize with that repository.

The decentralized BitKeeper model works better because it reflects parallel development more faithfully than a single repository system. Critically, a system like CVS will "lose information every time there is parallel development because you are forced to merge before you check in if someone else checked in first. The state of your workspace before the merge is lost forever" (BitKeeper Web Site, 2006). For example, a typical parallel development scenario, which can be handled only clumsily in a centralized system like CVS, occurs when development information is lost in the course of a merge. As an example, consider the following scenario from the product's Web site. Suppose A and B are developers using CVS and that A checks in his work before B does. At that point B has to do a merge before checking in her work. If B later decides that A's work was incorrect and wants to divorce her work from it, then in the CVS environment B will have to manually unmerge the work because the CVS environment doesn't separate B's original premerge work and the results of her merger (BitKeeper Web Site, 2006). In contrast, every one of the distributed repositories in BitKeeper is just like its own all-remembering time machine that can reset to any prior state, even after integrating changes from other developers, because each repository can at any time readily reconstruct its prior development states. BitKeeper keeps track of multifile changes with atomically applied *changesets*. The availability of these changesets in the repository allows the developer/owner of the repository to reconstruct its development tree back to any prior point. Thus the set of distributed repositories lose none of the development states that occur among the distributed developers in a parallel development, unlike in a single repository model. Beyond these important structural features, BitKeeper also provides reasonable GUI facilities for viewing information like differences between files, changesets, and repository history, which are better than those found in a tool like CVS, and it has the ability to propagate file name changes.

The design and capabilities of a tool like BitKeeper are fascinating in themselves, but BitKeeper's story transcends technical issues. Its history not only sheds light on versioning tools and the productivity of project management but is also broadly relevant to open source movement and licensing issues, the relation between commercial products and open communities, and the viability of open business models. In his controversial decision in 2002, Linus Torvalds decided to use BitKeeper for Linux kernel development. He described BitKeeper as unambiguously: "The best tool for the job." Its selection by Linus was at the same time a huge publicity boost for BitKeeper because of the importance of Linux and its centrality in the free software movement. BitKeeper's application to the kernel project dramatically improved productivity during its period of use (Andrews, 2005). Linus himself acknowledged that: "It's made me more than twice as productive, and its fundamentally distributed nature allows me to work the way I prefer to work – with many different groups working independently, yet allowing for easy merging between them" (BitKeeper Press Release, 2004). It also profoundly improved the workflow (Andrews, 2005). But free software advocates such as Richard Stallman strongly objected to using BitKeeper, especially for the signature Linux kernel project, because its license restrictions were a violation of basic free software principles, and it is the tradition in the movement to use only "free" software products for development. The final complication occurred when there was a controversy over the development of a tool called SourcePuller by the OSDL's (the Open Source Development Labs) Samba project leader Andrew Tridgell. McVoy objected that this activity constituted reverse engineering in violation of the BitKeeper free license, though Tridgell vigorously denied this. Linus himself was critical of Tridgell's activity, saying it "only caused problems" and merely "insured its own irrelevance by making BitKeeper no longer available" (McMillan, 2005). The outcome was that McVoy decided in 2005 to stop making the system available for free to open source developers. Interestingly, the Linux kernel tree is still tracked by BitKeeper since many kernel developers commercially license the product, especially "large companies who actively contribute to Linux development such as IBM, Intel, HP, Nokia and Sun" (Andrews, 2005). However, by mid-2005, Linus had started developing an alternative system called Git to do decentralized version control for Linux.

BitKeeper's McVoy contended that disassociating BitKeeper from the Linux kernel development reflected badly on the open source community because third-party applications like BitKeeper were key to the success of any platform. He stated that "no company is going to port their applications to a platform whose stated goal and track record is to reverse engineer everything they find useful. At some point the open source world needs to . . . decide they'll tolerate commercial software" applications without trying to reverse engineer them (Andrews, 2005). Nor was McVoy overtly concerned about competition from new tools developed for Linux kernel work. This was partly because he believed the requirements for commercial versioning tools, which was BitKeeper's real market, differed fundamentally from those for projects like Linux kernel development. For one thing the Linux application is text-oriented and has little need for binary files, while revision management for binary files, which introduce potentially serious storage problems, is critical in commercial applications. McVoy was also generally skeptical of the general ability of free software to support a business model with the exception of some special cases. In particular, he thought a true free license was impossible in principle for a software like BitKeeper, given the relatively small size of its prospective market and because the software costs far more to develop than you can realistically "extract from it in revenue" (Andrews, 2002). McVoy frankly acknowledged that his relationship with Linux had made BitKeeper a "dramatically better product because of the free users." Indeed, the free-of-charge license that the product was supplied under *required* free users to use the *latest* image of the software "because that's where the free users provide value. It doesn't help anyone to get bug reports on problems we've already fixed" (Andrews, 2002). McVoy said BitKeeper relied strongly on its "open source advantage: when we release a new image, it gets tested by a lot of people very quickly. Unless the other SCM people adopt our model, it's tough for them to catch up" (Andrews, 2002). Thus, the open source community connection, even though temporary, was decisive to BitKeeper's competitive advantage versus other SCM systems.

BitKeeper's Replacement: Git

After BitKeeper was dropped from use in Linux kernel development, Linus himself began rapidly developing a General Public Licensed replacement that he modestly called *git*, which is a self-deprecating slang eponym for a "rotten person" (McMillan, 2005). Development began in early April 2005. The prototype was already used for managing kernel release by mid-June, and by the end of July Linus turned the project over to Junio Hamano. His design very intentionally avoided imitating that of BitKeeper with Linus saying: "I respect Larry (McVoy) too much, and I didn't want there to be any question about git being just a clone" (Torvalds, 2006). As it turned out, the choice to do things "radically differently" let git be dramatically effective (Torvalds, 2006). Speed and efficiency were Linus' primary objectives for the system. Speaking in the context of the enormous number of kernel development transactions he was responsible for, Linus commented that git "was designed on the principle that everything you ever do on a daily basis should take less than a second" (McMillan, 2005). As he prototyped the system, he insisted that the main thing when applying patches was to make the process efficient: "If it takes half a minute to apply a patch and remember the changeset boundary etc (and quite frankly, that's _fast_ for most SCM's around for a project the size of Linux), then a series of 250 emails . . . takes two hours. If one of the patches in the middle doesn't apply, things are bad bad bad" (Torvalds, 2005a). Linus proposed as a performance benchmark that "the first 200 patches in the current git kernel archive" be able to be processed at the rate of "three per second" (Torvalds, 2005b). Within days, Linux developer Matt Mackall (2005) had run the benchmark at a little over six patches per second. By 2006, Linus felt confident that git was already better for kernel development than BitKeeper, though this was partly because it had been specifically developed for work on the kernel (Torvalds, 2006). The tool also made development management practices like cherry-picking (merging some but not all of a set of changes) easier and handled branches better. Linus claimed it was "the fastest SCM out there . . . on almost any operation you can name" and had "the smallest disk footprint I've ever heard of" (Torvalds, 2006). Despite this, he graciously acknowledged the brilliance of McVoy's work and that "BK was what taught me what to aim for" (Torvalds, 2006).

Codeville and Monotone

To complete our look at decentralized SCM systems, we briefly mention Codeville and Monotone. CodeVille, developed by Bram Cohen of BitTorrent fame together with his younger brother Ross Cohen, is implemented in Python. It is cross-platform and released under the BSD. At the time of this writing it had not yet reached version 1.0. A distinguishing feature is CodeVille's use of a novel-merging algorithm which helps eliminate possibly unnecessary merge conflicts by using an automatic technique that devolves into a CVS-style manual merge in special cases. The underlying algorithm currently uses a two-way merge between files, and then applies historical information on revisions to "decide which side of each differing section of code wins based on which side's revisions have already been applied" (Cohen, 2005). Monotone is another decentralized SCM system released under the GPL and written in C++. An early release came out in 2003. Monotone runs on Windows, Unix, and Mac OS. It enforces atomic commits like Subversion and unlike CVS.

References

Andrews, J. (2002). Interview: Larry McVoy. http://kerneltrap.org/node/222. Accessed December 6, 2006.

Andrews, J. (2005). No More Free BitKeeper. http://kerneltrap.org/node/4966. Accessed November 30, 2006.

BitKeeper Press Release. (2004). BitKeeper Helps Double Pace of Linux Development. http://www.bitkeeper.com/press/2004-03-17.html. Accessed December 6, 2006.

BitKeeper Web Site. (2006). http://www.bitkeeper.com/. Accessed December 6, 2006.

Cohen, B. (2005). The New Codeville Merge Algorithm. May 5. http://lists.zooko.com/pipermail/revctrl/2005-May/000005.html. Accessed December 6, 2006.

Corbet, J. (2005). The Kernel and BitKeeper Part Ways. April 6. http://lwn.net/Articles/130746/. Accessed January 10, 2007.

Mackall, M. (2005). Mercurial 0.4b vs Git Patchbomb Benchmark. April 29. http://marc.theaimsgroup.com/?l=gitandm=111475459526688. Accessed December 6, 2006.

McMillan, R. (2005). After Controversy, Torvalds Begins Work on Git. Australian PC World, April 20. http://www.pcworld.idg.com.au/index.php/id;1852076002. Accessed December 6, 2006.

Torvalds, L. (2005a). Re: Kernel SCM Saga_. April 7. http://marc.theaimsgroup.com/?l=linux-kernel&m=111288700902396. Accessed December 6, 2006.

Torvalds, L. (2005b). Re: Mercurial 0.3 vs Git Benchmarks. April 26. http://www.gelato.unsw.edu.au/archives/git/0504/2078.html. Accessed December 6, 2006.

Torvalds, L. (2006). Re: VCS Comparison Table. October 20. http://marc.theaimsgroup.com/?l=git&m=116129092117475. Accessed December 6, 2006.

4.4 Open Source Software Development Hosting Facilities and Directories

Software hosting facilities for open source development are Web sites that help distributed software collaborators manage their open source project and also provide source code repositories for development. We describe some of the services typically provided for two of the most prominent Web sites, SourceForge and Freshmeat, as well as the FSF directory. It is also worth noting some of the other prominent Internet sites that are relevant to open source. One particularly well-known site is Slashdot.org (named for the "/." notation in Unix.) Slashdot is a go-to place for current news on open source. O'Reilly.com is another useful site for information and books on open source.

4.4.1 SourceForge

Sourceforge.net is the largest hosting site with over 100,000 software projects listed as of mid-2005. SourceForge is owned by the Open Source Technology Group, which in turn is a wholly owned subsidiary of VA Software which distributes VA Linux. The same group also runs Freshmeat and the DevChannel Web sites. The SourceForge home page lists software project categories ranging from Games, Multimedia, Networking, and Security to Desktop and Financial programs. It provides basic access to its environment free of charge but expanded services are based on an annual subscription fee. As of 2003 over 70% of the SourceForge packages were licensed under the GPL, another 10% under the LGPL, and about 7% under BSD licenses (Wheeler, 2005).

SourceForge provides its own *Collaborative Development System* (CDS). This includes tools like a so-called Compile Farm Service that lets developers use an SSH (Secure Shell) client to access different hosts with different operating systems on which they can compile and test their programs. The supported operating systems currently include POSIX, Unix-like systems, and Mac OS. The site also provides CVS repository services to projects for software storage with standard CVS capabilities, like controlled access to the repository under the project administrator as well as access to a CVS client to use the service. Anonymous CVS access is provided to examine a project repository, but only project developers with access permissions determined by the project administrators can access the CVS tree using an SSH client.

The CDS communication tools provided include mailing lists, forums, and so-called trackers. Both public and project-member-only lists are available. The mailing posts are archived for later Web-based viewing and search. The forums are used for project discussions. Posts to the forums are threaded and searchable. So-called trackers are used to manage user-submitted source code patches, bug reports, requests for support, and feature requests. The bug tracker tabulates reported bugs with links to brief descriptions of the bugs, bug priority, the identity of the submitter, and who if anyone has been assigned to fix the bug. Proposed user patches to problems are identified together with brief descriptions for their rationale. A log or table of user requests for enhanced features describes proposed enhancements, submitters, and possibly assignee. User support requests are handled similarly.

The site enhances project visibility. In addition to the various development and communication services, SourceForge provides increased visibility for projects: firstly, because the site is well-known and also because projects undergoing extensive development or experiencing large numbers of downloads are highlighted on the SourceForge home page. Projects are provided with various Web services, including space for project-related Web content and scripts, secure management of content, and project MySQL databases. Project scripts in Perl, Python, and PHP may be served.

As an illustration of the kind of information provided by SourceForge, we will describe some of the information it provides for one of its currently most popular downloads: *BitTorrent*. The project summary page for BitTorrent describes the purpose of the software: a tool for distributed download. It identifies the project administrators and the list of developers (in this case there were eight). In addition to their e-mail addresses, it provides an option for developers to publicize their skills or expertise. The skill inventory for each developer identifies the developer's language and software development skills, level of accomplishment, and length of experience in the designated skill. A log of skill entries might include

Skill:	Programming
Language:	C
Level:	Wizard
Experience:	> ten years

as well as personal comments by the developer. The development status of the project is also given. BitTorrent is identified as a Stage-5 project that belongs to the SourceForge Production/Stable category. Terms like this are explained by links that also show project statistics. Possible status categories are Planning, Pre-Alpha, Alpha, Beta, Production/Stable, Mature, and Inactive. The intended audience for the software is described. In the case of BitTorrent, the expected product users are end users operating in a desktop environment and system administrators. The licensing characteristics of the software are also indicated. BitTorrent is described as licensed under Other/Proprietary. A reference to the actual BitTorrent Web site at bittorrent.com reveals that the license is actually a modified version of the Jabber Open Source License. The operating system platforms to which the software has been ported are listed. The development languages for the project are given as C and Python. The development activity on a project is one indicator of how healthy an open source project is. The SourceForge Activity Percentile for BitTorrent was over 99% in mid-August 2005. In this case this reflected the popularity of downloads of the program rather than a high development rate during the period. Generally speaking, the *Activity Percentile* is a composite measure that reflects project development actions, page hits, downloads, tracker accesses, and communication metrics like forum posts. Links to the home page of the project are also given. For BitTorrent, the actual home page was not on SourceForge, but at bittorrent.com. The BitTorrent site indicates that it does not use a CVS, BitKeeper, or Subversion repository.

Its code is maintained under the open source version control system Codeville even though the SourceForge site does have a CVS repository for BitTorrent, albeit the latest entries were all at least a year old.

4.4.2 Freshmeat

Freshmeat.net is another major open source development Web site also owned like SourceForge by the Open Source Technology Group under VA Software. Freshmeat is primarily focused on providing information on software releases as well as updates and articles on open source software, though proprietary software is also cataloged. As of 2003, over 70% of the Freshmeat packages were licensed under the GPL or the LGPL and over 5% were under BSD licenses (http://freshmeat.net/stats/, accessed January 8, 2007). Project developers can register their projects on the site and provide ongoing updates. Users can search for software by category such as area of application, licensing requirements, ported platforms, and programming language used. They can download and even rate products. For example, if you search for BitTorrent on the site, an entry appears that describes the product purpose, the nature of its licenses (which in this case were indicated as OSI-approved), intended audience, platforms, the implementation programming languages, etc. This is similar to the basic summary information on SourceForge. Statistics on product popularity and the vitality of the project development are also given. Terms like *popularity* and *vitality* have clear and accessible definitions. For example, vitality is measured by the number of announcements about the project multiplied by its age in days, divided by the number of days since the last announcement. The site does not provide CVS or other software development services.

4.4.3 The FSF Directory

The http://directory.fsf.org/ Web site is another major catalog of "free software that runs under free operating systems." It sponsors many projects including the GNU project. The directory is now also sponsored by UNESCO. Politically this new association is an important international statement about the increasing global recognition of the free software movement.

Products are grouped by category and special attention is given to verifying the license characteristics of the software. For example, in our running illustration, BitTorrent falls under the *Network Applications* category of *Tools* because it facilitates distributed download. The entry links to a page with basic information about BitTorrent. It starts with a useful description of the purpose and rationale for the software. It gives a link to the current home Web site for

BitTorrent. It also links to a compressed tarball copy of the source code for the program as well as to a SourceForge page that provides information and downloads for source and binaries for BitTorrent. Links are also given for the mailing lists for user help, bug reporting, and the developer list. Additional information similar to some of what is available on SourceForge is also provided. The identity and mailing address of the person who verified the type of license for gnu.org are given too. For BitTorrent a link for the license type characterizes it as being under an X11-style, so-called simple, permissive open license. As another comparative illustration, consider looking up the KDE project on the FSF site. One quickly locates the basic information and links for the KDE graphical desktop environment, its license, source code tarball, announcement e-mail list, link to a complete list of credited developers, etc., as well as a link to the KDE home page site.

References

Wheeler, D. (2005). Why Open Source Software/Free Software (OSS/FS, FLOSS, or FOSS)? Look at the Numbers! http://www.dwheeler.com/oss_fs_why.html. Accessed January 8, 2007.

SECTION TWO

Social, Psychological, Legal and Economic Aspects of Open Source

5

Demographics, Sociology, and Psychology of Open Source Development

Open source development is a form of distributed, collaborative, asynchronous, partly volunteer, software development. A new paradigm for cooperation like this invariably introduces new questions about its social characteristics and its affects on human behavior. Matters of interest range from the characteristics of the participants (demographic, motivational, etc.), the social psychology of their interactions, and the effectiveness of their cooperative processes, to the cognitive and problem-solving side effects of this kind of development. The purpose of this chapter is to survey these issues and identify some of the scientific and social concepts that can help in understanding them. We believe these social science perspectives can help provide a conceptual framework for better understanding open development. We will begin by considering the basic demographics of the phenomenon: the characteristics of the developer population, the motivations of developers and community participants, how participants interact, the diversity of projects, and so on. The survey by Kim (2003) is one of a number of useful surveys that have been done on these issues. We also examine relevant concepts from the field of social psychology, including the classic notions of norms and roles, factors that affect group interactions like compliance, internalization, identification and normative influence, the impact of power relationships and group cohesion, and the application of these concepts to open development. There are other useful abstractions available from cognitive science, such as the cognitive biases that affect group interactions and problem solving. Social psychology also provides models for understanding the productivity of collaborating groups in terms of process effectiveness and organizational effects that influence productivity. It has been famously said that "the medium is the message" (McLuhan, 1964). In this spirit we consider the influence of the collaborative medium on these interactions, briefly surveying some of the classic research on the effect of the communications medium on interaction, including the characteristics of the canonical "medium" represented by face-to-face interaction and collocated work. Like social psychology, this research offers a rich array of abstractions and perspectives for interpreting distributed collaboration. Potentially useful concepts range from the impact of so-called common ground, coupling, and incentive structures, to the use of social cues in communication, richness of informational exchanges, and temporal effects in collaboration. We introduce the elements of these ideas and provide simple illustrations of their relevance to open source development.

A methodological caveat is worth mentioning at this point. Much of the data we report on has a fairly straightforward interpretation. Some of it is descriptive, using the terminology and categories of social psychology to describe social phenomena recognized in open source communities. We will illustrate in simple ways how these perspectives might be used to think about open development. Some of the studies we examine reflect more empirical, statistically based research. However, in all cases, it should be kept in mind that the underlying social, psychological, demographic, cognitive, and media phenomena considered and the results reported for them are intrinsically complex, and so they may be subject to multiple interpretations.

5.1 Scale of Open Source Development

A quick way to obtain a general sense of the magnitude of open development is to examine the major open project Web sites, as we have overviewed in the previous chapter and which we briefly recall here. The most important of these sites, which contain directories of open source projects, include the FSF-Free Software Foundation (FSF)'s GNU directory at http://directory.fsf.org/, the SourceForge Web site at www.sourceforge.net, and the Freshmeat Web site at www.freshmeat.net. As of mid-2005, SourceForge, which is the Internet's largest open source repository, had over 100,000 open source projects listed. Freshmeat had almost 40,000 projects and GNU over 4,000 projects. These databases provide descriptions of projects, links to downloads and to home Web pages for projects, licensing information, e-mail lists for project participation, project release histories, and development updates. Sourceforge also provides resources for managing code. Both Sourceforge and Freshmeat are owned by the Open Source Technology Group (OSTG) that is like a networked information utility. Being hosted on a major site like Sourceforge helps increase a project's visibility. According to the site, Sourceforge provides news, articles, downloads, and forums to help IT professionals, developers, and users make informed decisions about information technology products and services (http://www.ostg.com/). It also provides development and project management tools like Concurrent Versioning System (CVS) and Subversion for hosting open source development projects. In terms of corporate relationships, OSTG is a subsidiary of VA Software and also owns Slashdot and other organizations involved with open development. It should not be confused with the OSDL (Open Source Development Labs) that was succeeded by the Linux Foundation in 2007.

As should be expected for a movement that evolved from the Unix community, there is a continuing strong Unix presence on these sites even in the case of end-user programs. For example, consider the 20 most popular projects on Freshmeat, 15 of which were for end users, while the remaining 5 were for developers or system administrators, at the time of Kim's review (2003). Of the 15 most popular end-user applications, all of them – without exception – ran on Unix systems. Just 5 of the 15 could also run on Windows platforms. Interestingly, the top 5 downloads on Sourceforge are all file-sharing programs, like BitTorrent. On the other hand, an examination of the 10 most popular downloads on sourceforge.net in mid-2006 suggests a different picture, with all top 10 downloads being available for Windows with a few also available for Unix-like systems. Of these programs, all were available under the General Public License (GPL).

We are already aware of the many historical reasons for open source being predominantly a Unix phenomenon (though, as our comments on the prominence of Windows platforms for major Sourceforge downloads indicates, this appears to be changing). For example, Kim (2003) recalls that at least part of the reason why source code was provided for Unix systems, while not for Microsoft systems, was the traditional architectural portability of Unix. Since Unix-like systems could be ported to run on many different machine architectures, it was natural for developers to distribute the actual source code for applications rather than merely binaries, so the applications could be compiled to execute on different machines. This objective was in turn facilitated by the fact that Unix systems came with a C compiler, unlike the Microsoft PC systems. The compiled source could be expected to execute, possibly after some modifications. And of course, there had also been the longstanding objective in the free software community of developing a self-contained, nonproprietary environment for computing that would provide programs ranging from software infrastructure tools to end-user applications, specifically for Unix-like systems. In contrast, the Microsoft market was focused on the IBM PC or its commoditized clones, so there traditionally had been less reason to distribute the source code because the binary executables for these essentially equivalent PC's sufficed. It is noteworthy that there are also a significant number of Windows and MS DOS shareware and freeware applications available, such as at www.simtel.net. The shareware programs have traditionally not been open software in the sense of the free/open source movement, though the freeware category does include programs licensed under the GPL.

References

Kim, E. (2003). An Introduction to Open Source Communities. Blue Oxen Associates. http://www.blueoxen.com/research/00007/. Accessed January 10, 2007.
McLuhan, M. (1964). Understanding Media: The Extensions of Man. McGraw-Hill, New York.

5.2 Demographics and Statistical Profile of Participants

This section overviews the basic demographics of the populations involved in free development. Open source participants tend to be young and male, IT professionals or students, with a part-time or volunteer commitment that is limited for most but quite substantial for some. A good overview of their general demographics as well as data on the personal motivations of open developers is available in the surveys by Lakhani et al. (2002), Ghosh et al. (2002), and Robles et al. (2001). The remarkably skewed nature of the gender distribution of OSS participants apparent from these surveys is somewhat astonishing, with all of these major surveys reporting that almost all of their respondents (98%) were male. Age distribution was skewed in a more predictable and less extreme manner, with, perhaps unsurprisingly, about 70% of the respondents being in their 20–30s with an average age in the upper 20s. The preponderance of participants (80%) were from either the United States or Europe. Although about a quarter of the respondents were students, another half of the respondents were employed as full-time professionals in IT. Almost half (about 40%) had completed college degrees, between 10 and 30% had Master's degrees (depending on the survey), while about 20% had completed only high-school degrees. The latter statistic would reflect youth rather than ultimate educational level. For example, recall that Blake Ross of Foxfire was in high school at the time of Firefox's development, but as of this writing is a student at Stanford. Most of the participation was part-time. Up to 50% expend 5 hours or less per week. About 15% or fewer work half-time, expending 20–40 hours per week. Only 5–10% of individuals spent on the order of 40 hours per week on open projects. Similar results were found by the Linux Study and the UNC Open Source Research Team surveys reported on in Feller and Fitzgerald (2002). Those results indicated that the majority of Linux kernel developers (60%) were involved for under a year, with another 20% involved for 1–2 years. The developers were geographically split evenly between the United States and Europe.

The process of entry into open source development groups has both informal and stylized characteristics. Brand (2003) describes the relatively casual process for joining the KDE project. Awareness of the existence of the project by newcomers tended to be by word of mouth or through reading about the project on the Internet, such as through newsgroups. Entry and exit were generally voluntary, with the exception that an individual might be removed from a community for illicitly removing code from the repository. There was a high turnover rate because the organizations include a strong volunteer component; hence, there were always many newcomers or *newbies*. A newcomer could evolve to a developer status by making small contributions to the project code over the course of a half year or so. Progress in the organization was based on the typical reputation-based process. Individuals might lurk for a while on the e-mail list of an open project, eventually making a bid to join by making a small code contribution (Reagle, 2003). The FAQs for the projects are useful sources for their behavioral norms. As Moon and Sproul (2002) observe regarding entry into a group, the Linux kernel mailing list FAQ urges that "a line of code is worth a thousand words," so the best way to advocate a change to the software code is to simply "implement it first, then post to the list for comments." A signature rite of passage for a group member is the ability to *check-in* code or being granted write-access to the CVS repository, a status that allows a contributor to modify the existing source code. In general, check-in code may be one's own code or a patch submitted for approval by a member lacking write-access privileges. Write-access is naturally one of the ultimate symbols of belonging. Persistent denial of write-access to experienced participants may trigger their departure or a fork in the project (Brand, 2003).

References

Brand, A. (2003). The Structure, Entrance, Production, Motivation and Control in an Open Source Project. http://dot.kde.org/1065087742/. Accessed November 29, 2006.

Feller, J. and Fitzgerald, B. (2002). Understanding Open Source Software Development. Addison-Wesley, Pearson Education Ltd., London.

Ghosh, R., Glott, R., Krieger, B., and Robles, G. (2002). Free/Libre and Open Source Software: Survey and Study Final Report. International Institute of Infonomics, University of Maastricht, Netherlands and Berlecon Research GmbH, Berlin. http://www.infonomics.nl/FLOSS/report/. Accessed November 29, 2006.

Lakhani, K., Wolf, R., and Bates, J. (2002). The Boston Consulting Group Hacker Survey. http://www.osdn.com/bcg/BCGHACKERSURVEY-0.73.pdf. Accessed November 29, 2006.

Moon, J. and Sproul, L. (2002). Essence of Distributed Work: The Case of the Linux Kernel. In: Distributed Work, S. K. Pamela Hinds (editor). MIT Press, Cambridge, MA,

Chapter 16. http://www.firstmonday.dk/issues/issue5_11/moon/. Accessed December 3, 2006.

Reagle, J. (2003). Socialization in Open Technical Communities. http://opensource.mit.edu. Accessed November 29, 2006.

Robles, G., Scheider, H., Tretkowski, I., and Weber, N. (2001) WIDI – Who Is Doing It? A Research on Libre Software Developers. Technical University of Berlin. Also at: http://widi.berlios.de/paper/study.html. Accessed November 29, 2006.

5.3 Motivation of Participants

Raymond famously suggested that personal need and curiosity motivate much of the participation in open source development, as reflected in his well-known phrase that "every good work of software starts by scratching a developer's personal itch" (Raymond, 1998). Linus Torvalds, one of the towering figures of free software, says that it is about having fun in doing "something that matters" (Reagle, 2003). Indeed, according to Lakhani and Wolf (2003), the enjoyment of creative work is actually "the strongest and most pervasive driver." This perspective is consistent with classic motivational research that identified the predisposition of engineers for work that is "interesting and challenging" (Reagle, 2003).

Let us consider some of the empirically recognized motivations for open participation, beginning with the simple distinction: which participants work for free and which are paid. According to the Free/Libre survey (Ghosh et al., 2002), there is a fairly even mix of paid and unpaid participants. Half the open source participants who responded to the survey indicated that they received no financial compensation for their efforts. The remaining half were paid to either develop open source software (about 15%), administer it (about 15%), or support it (about 20%). The review and survey by Jørgensen (2001) of the FreeBSD project shows similar results with almost half the participants indicating that their employer paid them to work part- or full time on the project. Thus open development appears equally likely to be development for free, as it is to be development for pay. Kim (2003) provides an obliquely related perspective: one in four persons surveyed received indirect compensation for his work, while one in five persons indicated that his work on open source eventually led to a job. As the FSF's Moglen (1999) observes, the prominence of hybrid corporate strategies that utilize open source means that "an increasing number of people are specifically employed to write free software. But in order to be employable in the field, they must already have established themselves there." Thus prior volunteer participation can be a prerequisite for subsequent compensated participation. Given that corporate employees are so often participants, the next logical, meta-level question of motivation is "why is the corporate sponsor involved?" We address this kind of question in more detail when we look at business models for open source later on. Basically, as Gacek and Arief (2004, p. 36) succinctly observe, corporate actors "usually get involved to gain market share or undermine their competitors, or they simply use open source software so that they won't have to build an equivalent product from scratch." Refer to Hang et al. (2004) for an analysis of motivation according to the roles of the participants, including developers, distributors, and users.

Unsurprisingly, there are differences between the self-reported motivations of volunteers versus paid participants. Almost half the volunteers said that they were interested in the opportunity to improve their skills, versus about 30% of the paid employees (Lakhani et al., 2002). Conversely, the opportunity to do their job more effectively was a motivation for almost two-thirds of the paid participants against only one in five of the volunteers. But regardless of compensation status, knowledge acquisition was key. Both the Free/Libre by Ghosh et al. (2002) and the Boston Hacker survey per Lakhani et al. (2002) indicated that the opportunity to learn and develop new skills was by far the dominant reason to participate. Thus 80% of respondents in the Free/Libre survey indicated this reason and over 90% responded similarly in the Boston Hacker survey (where more than one reason could be checked off). Interestingly, half the Free/Libre respondents indicated that they had a complementary desire to share their knowledge and skills with others as a motivation.

There was a range of other motivations as well, from reputation building and job prospects to philosophical and practical concerns. Frequently reported motivations included participating in the open source scene (30%+), improving open source products (30%+), solving problems that were not able to be handled by proprietary software (30%), a philosophical belief that software should not be proprietary (30%+), and the possibility of improving job opportunities (about 25%). Although a surprisingly slim 5% said the idea was to make money, twice that number wanted to establish a reputation in the open source community and one in four thought that participation would indeed improve their job prospects (Free/Libre, 2002). Obviously, reputation is a two-edged sword: it is about status in a community but it is also fungible with compensation. The survey by Hars and Ou (2002) touches on psychological models of motivation, distinguishing between internal psychological motivations and external motivations from the environment, but yields a similar overall perspective to the other studies.

In summary, self-improvement is a decisive element in the self-reported reasons for participation in open development, while the acquisition of knowledge was also key. Although compensation advantages were not necessarily an immediate objective, a substantial number of participants expected their involvement to enable them to do their full-time job better or to ultimately improve their job prospects.

References

Gacek, C. and Arief, B. (2004). The Many Meanings of Open Source. IEEE Software, 21(1), 34–40.

Ghosh, R., Glott, R., Krieger, B., and Robles, G. (2002). Free/Libre and Open Source Software: Survey and Study Final Report. International Institute of Infonomics, University of Maastricht, Netherlands and Berlecon Research GmbH, Berlin. http://www.infonomics.nl/FLOSS/report/. Accessed November 29, 2006.

Hang, J., Hohensohn, H., Mayr, K., and Wieland, T. (2004). Benefits and Pitfalls of Open Source in Commercial Contexts. In: Free/Open Software Development, S. Koch (editor). Idea Group Publishing, Hershey, PA, 222–241.

Hars, A. and Ou, S. (2002). Working for Free? Motivations for Participating in Open-Source Software Projects. International Journal of Electronic Commerce, 6(3), 25–39.

Jørgensen, N. (2001). Putting It All in the Trunk: Incremental Software Development in the FreeBSD Open Source Project. Information Systems Journal, 11(4), 321–336.

Kim, E. (2003). An Introduction to Open Source Communities. Blue Oxen Associates. http://www.blueoxen.com/research/00007/. Accessed January 10, 2007.

Lakhani, K. and Wolf, R. (2003). Why Hackers Do What They Do: Understanding Motivation Effort in Free/Open Source Software Projects. Sloan Working Paper 4425–03, 1–28.

Lakhani, K., Wolf, R., and Bates, J. (2002). The Boston Consulting Group Hacker Survey. http://www.osdn.com/bcg/BCGHACKERSURVEY-0.73.pdf. Accessed November 29, 2006.

Moglen, E. (1999). Anarchism Triumphant: Free Software and the Death of Copyright. First Monday, 4(8). http://www.firstmonday.org/issues/issue4_8/moglen/index. html. Accessed January 5, 2007.

Raymond, E. S. (1998). The Cathedral and the Bazaar. First Monday, 3(3). http://www. firstmonday.dk/issues/issue3_3/raymond/index.html. Ongoing version: http:// www.catb.org/~esr/writings/cathedral-bazaar/. Accessed December 3, 2006.

Reagle, J. (2003). Socialization in Open Technical Communities. http://opensource.mit. edu. Accessed November 29, 2006.

5.4 Group Size and Communication

In social psychology, group size is considered one of the characteristics most determinative of a group's behavior. Notably, despite the scale of opportunities for group interaction that the Internet provides and the existence of major, very large open source projects, the participant communities involved in the vast number of these projects are generally much smaller than one might expect. In fact, they tend to be tiny.

A useful empirical examination of group size and the communication characteristics of the 100 most active, *mature* open source projects listed on the SourceForge Web site are presented in Krishnamurthy (2002). The projects selected were from a group of about 500 OSS projects that SourceForge categorizes as *mature*, a classification that constitutes a relatively small portion of the Sourceforge repository. The Web site groups projects into six categories: planning, pre-alpha, alpha, beta, production/stable, and mature. When Krishnamurthy's survey was done, there were close to 10,000 SourceForge projects listed as belonging to the planning stage, approximately 10,000 were in the alpha or pre-alpha release stage, and roughly 5,000 were in each of the beta or production/stable stages. Thus of about 30,000 SourceForge projects, the mature category represented only about one in sixty. Of these, only the 100 most active of the mature projects (as determined by their SourceForge activity profile) were considered for the study. This highly selective group was expected to be the most likely to have extensive communities of participants, but to the contrary the data showed that even "the vast majority of mature OSS programs are developed by a small number of individuals" (Krishnamurthy, 2002).

The distribution of the selected SourceForge community sizes was as follows. According to the statistics at SourceForge, the most common number of developers was 1 (!). The median number of developers was 4. The average number was 6 to 7. Even the largest developer group examined, with 42 members, was dramatically smaller than the numbers one usually sees publicized, for example, in the Linux credit lists, which even before the year 2000 had around 350 people. Granted, projects like Linux are successful global projects, so one does not expect them to be typical. About one in five of the surveyed projects had only one developer, another one in five had two or three, 50% had four or less, and only one in five had more than ten developers.

Another metric for project size is the number of administrators. SourceForge uses a designation called *project administrator* and automatically associates to each project it lists at least one project administrator. According to Source-Forge, the administrator is the individual "responsible for the control of that project's presence on SourceForge.net." Project administrators are often the primary authors of the hosted software, though they may also include individuals who "provide support and perform maintenance functions for that project" (http://sourceforge.net). Krishnamurthy presents statistics about the project administrators. Here too, the numbers are smaller than might have been expected. The majority of projects have only one administrator and roughly 70% have at most two. Indeed, the average number of administrators is just over two, with both the median and the mode equal to one.

The scale of communications among participants in the projects considered was also more limited than one might expect. The average project had two forums and two mailing lists. More significantly, the forums tended to have few messages, with one out of three of the projects having no forum messages and the preponderance having few messages over the lifetime of the projects, though some projects had fairly active forums, the highest being a project with 5,000 forum messages over its lifetime. As a statistical pattern, Barabási (2002) proposes a *power-law distribution* for participation in open source groups with the level of participation, as measured by a metric like the number of e-mails sent, being related to status in the group (see also Barabási and Albert (1999)). For example, the kth member might have $1/k$ the metric value associated with the lead member. This is consistent with the case of the development of Linux where it appears that 50% of the correspondence was generated by 1/50th of the contributors (Moon and Sproul, 2002).

References

Barabási, A. (2002). Linked: The New Science of Networks. Perseus Publishing, Cambridge, MA.

Barabási, A. L. and Albert, R. (1999). Emergence of Scaling in Random Networks. Science, 286(5439), 509–512.

Krishnamurthy, S. (2002). Cave or Community: An Empirical Examination of 100 Mature Open Source Projects. First Monday, 7(6). http://www.firstmonday.dk/issues/issue7_6/krishnamurthy/index.html. Accessed December 3, 2006.

Moon, J. and Sproul, L. (2002). Essence of Distributed Work: The Case of the Linux Kernel. In: Distributed Work, S. K. Pamela Hinds (editor). MIT Press, Cambridge, MA, Chapter 16. http://www.firstmonday.dk/issues/issue5_11/moon/. Accessed December 3, 2006.

5.5 Social Psychology and Open Source

Distributed collaborative software development is a relatively new kind of human interaction, regardless of whether it occurs in a voluntary or organizationally based open source mode, or in other kinds of distributed or outsourced development. The traditional social sciences can provide some insight into these enterprises: what drives their growth, what inhibits their development, and how they can be improved. Both sociology and psychology are useful in understanding collaborative development. Although it has been observed that the psychology of groups ultimately reduces to the psychology of individuals (Allport, 1924), there is a useful composite perspective on group interactions called *social psychology*. We will overview some of the basic ideas from this field, including social concepts like norms, roles, normative influence, power relations, and attitudes, and psychological concepts like conflict and distraction, and consider their relevance to open development. A subsequent section on cognitive psychology considers the relevance of cognitive psychology and how cognitive biases affect the behavior of individuals and groups.

5.5.1 Norms and Roles

The norms under which a group operates and the roles of group members are core concepts of social psychology that are useful for understanding how groups behave. Norms and roles help to define member's expectations about what is considered appropriate behavior by the group. For example, we have seen that in open source development there is typically a small group of core developers surrounded by a broader group of contributors or participants. Each of these groups has norms of behavior that govern entry into the groups and how individuals act when in a group. Each group also has roles it plays in the development process. *Group norms* are the agreements, implicit or explicit, reached by members of a group, concerning *what* should or should not be done by its members and *when* it should or should not be done. Norms help minimize potential disorder in group interactions. They are like rules of conduct for the members of a group and represent one basic way in which group interactions are structured. *Roles* on the other hand are implicit or explicit agreements made by members of a group that specify *who* must do something or who must *not* do something. Roles can emerge spontaneously. Zigurs and Kozar (1994) concluded that groups automatically tend to identify two basic types of role specialists: the task-oriented individual who addresses ideas and the likable individual who helps manage socioemotional issues that arise in the group. The satisfaction of group members with group processes and outcomes tends to be correlated with the distribution of roles between the task-oriented and group-building roles. Bormann (1975) classically theorized that there was a natural distribution of role behaviors, with ideally about two-thirds of role behavior being task oriented and one-third oriented to building the group. This is very roughly coherent with open source behavior, where the predominant effort is the technical task itself, but the role of promoting project development and vision is also essential. Our overview of major open source projects shows that such roles have often merged in a single individual who has technological talent as well as highly effective interpersonal abilities. Linus Torvalds is a quintessential example. He guided the design of the Linux system, demonstrating exceptional technical judgment as well as excellent judgment in recognizing the merit of others' contributions, and solicitously nursed the project along by his speedy recognition and adoption of participants' patches. We have seen the same kind of 24×7 nurturing intervention by other successful open developers like Rob McCool for the NCSA httpd daemon and Blake Ross for Firefox.

Norms and roles can be thought of as akin to the protocols that govern the interaction of computer processes in a distributed computing environment. Network communication protocols define standardized expectations for the behavior of the components of a system in response to a range of normal and exceptional processing scenarios. Norms and roles have a similar purpose. Protocols for group interaction that are defined by the members of a group are sometimes called social protocols. They include explicit policies like governance rules for a project and informal patterns of interaction. The often highly elaborate FAQs found on open source Web sites may be thought of as defining their social protocols. Protocols that govern the interactions within a group but which are hardwired into the groupware that supports the interaction are sometimes called technological protocols. Groupware for supporting collaboration necessarily makes many assumptions about the expected behavior of users that are embodied in the technical realization of the system. CVS write privileges are a simple example of an open source technological protocol. Purely social protocols, in contrast, consist of processes that are agreed to by the members of a group, affected by the culture and status of the group participants, and influenced by the organizational structure in which the group is embedded, but which are not enforced by the software environment as is the case for technological protocols (Ellis et al., 1991). For example, Jørgensen (2001) describes an explicit social protocol or norm in the FreeBSD project (Committers' Guide, rule 10) that requires that "a committer shall do pre-commit testing to prevent breaking the build in the development branch." Another broadly recognized open source practice that can be thought of as having the force of a strong social norm is the widespread commitment to the use of free tools for free development. Although this is not universally applied, transgressions of this norm can cause real problems, as happened when the powerful but proprietary BitKeeper tool was temporarily used for Linux kernel management. This provoked considerable controversy in the open community with the result that BitKeeper eventually had to be replaced by the free Git system (see Chapter 4 for further discussion). Another powerful open norm is the avoidance of forks in project development if at all possible. This norm is based on the simple pragmatic rationale that forks wastefully split development resources into noncooperating groups (Feller and Fitzgerald, 2002). Although technologically enforced protocols have convenient characteristics like automatic enforcement, norms or social protocols on the other hand appear to promote collaboration better than technological protocols because the group must collaborate as a team in order to create them. This process also helps create group social identity, which improves the chances of survival and success of the group.

There are of course many other norms in the open development culture. For example, one simple but classic norm is presenting oneself in a humble manner and even engaging in good-humored self-deprecation if appropriate (IMHO, etc.). This demeanor is part of the traditional self-image of the hacker culture, regarding which Weber (2004, p. 140) observes, "Bragging is off limits. The norm is that your work brags for you." However, since contributors are in many respects synonymous with their code contributions, there is an inevitable ego impact, depending on whether one's code is accepted or rejected, so personal competition for status and approval is unavoidable despite the pretense of understatement (Weber, 2004). A variety of norms were tabulated in the treatment of the original MIT hacker culture that appeared in the well-known "Hackers: Heroes of the Computer Revolution" by Levy (1984), which elaborated the idea of a *hacker ethic*. The free software movement drew from the hacker culture and in many ways originated in it. The hacker ethic is a mixture of what might be considered the principles, beliefs, and/or norms of the movement. One of its imperatives was that "access to computers should be unlimited and total," which obviously reflects the prime imperative of the free software movement. Another is that "all information should be free," again a founding norm. There are several other dicta as well, but the idea that "hackers should be judged by their hacking" seems to reflect a quintessential behavioral norm for open interactions. For an analysis that puts this hacker ethos into a broader historical context, relating it to a pre-Protestant work ethic that places a premium on passion for interesting work and freedom from fixed divisions between leisure and labor (see Himanen (2001) and Feller and Fitzgerald (2002)).

Raymond's FAQ style document (Raymond, 2004) describes detailed rules and bluntly stated norms for expected behavior in open source projects in general. As Raymond indicates, it's all part of the process of publicly maintaining and reminding people about the norms for proper questioning. This document is worth reading to get a sense of the social ambience of the environment. One of its features is that there is a decided tendency not to "suffer fools lightly" and one should be prepared for that. The KDE Web site (http://www.kde.org) for the KDE desktop project provides a well-organized introduction to the norms of behavior for its open source project. For example, it carefully describes what the norms are for handling communications with the group. Concerning criticism, Fogel (2005) observes that blunt questions and unvarnished technical criticisms should not be considered as rude. Although this style of interaction may be unfamiliar to newcomers, he argues that it is typical of the hard science disciplines. The blunt technical criticism is even arguably a kind of flattery. Fogel observes that what would actually be rude under these circumstances would be to provide inadequate or superficial criticism, without acknowledging that it is inadequate, perhaps because you lacked the time to be more complete. We have previously mentioned Brand's (2003) overview of entry into the KDE community. Referring to the KDE FAQ links for a discussion of how its various e-mail lists are handled, newcomers will find a discussion that orients them about the kinds of e-mails that are appropriate and how to construct them. Most of these guidelines are addressed to general users of KDE rather than potential or actual developers. A sociological model of initiation rites for project enrollment was suggested by Von Krogh et al. (2003) based on the notion of a so-called *joining script*. Although Stutz (2003) amusingly describes the term as overblown sociological jargon about the "dance that wannabe members of a community must perform in order to become officially sanctioned members," it's actually an interesting term. Jørgensen (2001) describes an initiatory task for the FreeBSD project that requires new committers to add their name to the Developer section of the handbook and remove it from the Additional Contributors section, an accomplishment described as a "good first test of your CVS skills."

5.5.2 Interactions in Groups

This section overviews some general concepts related to the interactions between members of a group, not necessarily an open source group. The primary social factors that affect how members come to agree within groups are called compliance, internalization, and identification (Kelman, 1958). *Compliance* refers to the kind of agreement among members arising from social pressure. *Internalization* refers to agreement that occurs because a proposition or objective corresponds to an individual's own beliefs. *Identification* refers to agreement that occurs when an individual appropriates a group's expectations as his own. For example, the Firefox promotional campaign, which encourages Firefox advocates to "spread the word" about the fox, identify noncompliant Web sites (defendthefox), and generally personally promote the browser, reflects a strategy of persuading Firefox users to self-identify with the product and its mission. Of course, these individuals also presumably agree internally with the mission because they have been satisfied with the performance of the browser and like the idea of free software, though that does not imply they would de facto be interested in proselytizing for the product. Compliance may be mediated by *normative influence*, which refers to the support for an objective or opinion that results from secondary cues like the number of group participants who hold an opinion or the status of those participants. It also refers to the tendency of individuals to defer to what they perceive as the group opinion, without even the need for explicit group pressure, persuasion, or coercion. Web sites that proselytize for a product like Firefox can create a sense of normative influence. Despite its origin in group preferences, normative influence does not necessarily lead to an averaged or bland kind of behavior. In fact, quite to the contrary, groups frequently exhibit a tendency to adopt more extreme positions than individuals under the pressure of normative influence or group polarization. Consider the four familiar characteristics of open communities Reagle (2003) highlights as essential to open source: creation of products that satisfy open source definitional criteria, transparency in their processes, nondiscrimination in product development, distribution, and use, and the right to take off on your own or noninterference. These trivially entail issues of compliance, internalization, and identification. For example, participants comply with the open definitional criteria whose rationale they have also likely internalized and the same holds for development principles like transparency. Especially on the free software side, one expects to find personal identification with the movement's philosophy, and not merely its pragmatic advantages. Striking off on your own or noninterference, on the other hand, would merely reflect a complete breakdown in group identification.

Groups may be subject to socially significant hierarchical factors that affect the relationships among members, especially groups that are embedded in organizations. These factors include the various kinds of *power relationships* that affect group interactions, including expert power (corresponding to domain expertise), charismatic power (corresponding to personal attractiveness), and group leadership. These power characteristics can in turn influence the norms a group operates under. For example, Grudin (1994) observed that groups formed around autocratic individuals may tend toward autocratic norms. Groups whose members are not significantly differentiated by differences in status, power relationships, or task expertise are called *peer groups*. Obviously, most open source projects are decidedly *not* mere peer groups, even though they are egalitarian in their attitude in terms of meritocratic skills, because the core developer group will generally have both the greatest domain expertise and the most intense commitment to the project, so there will be intrinsic asymmetries in a group. In any organizational group, there exist a variety of nonpeer relationships among the members based on hierarchical or power relationships between individuals. In fact, open groups established around a preeminent developer are in many respects fairly authoritarian. Linus Torvalds has a reputation as a nice guy, but it is he who runs the Linux show, together with his approved trusted lieutenants. Python creator Guido van Rossum lightly refers to himself as "Benevolent Dictator for Life" in all things pythonic – just like Linus Torvalds does for Linux. Basically, project management must inevitably be vested in some person or small group (Feller and Fitzgerald, 2002, p. 91). But the root legitimacy of the authority involves leadership abilities and domain expertise rather than mere ego domination. As Linus himself asserted during the Torvalds–Tanenbaum debate (see DiBona et al. (1999) for the e-mail), his own standing in the Linux community was based on the fact that "I know it better than anyone else." However, project authority can also evolve and spread out. For example, in the case of Linux, networking guru Allan Cox became one of Torvalds' "lieu-tenant(s)" (Weber, 2004, p. 105) by virtue of his expert role in implementing Linux's networking capabilities, leading to "the informal, pyramidal hierar-chy that characterizes decision-making for Linux" (p. 105). Weber describes this classic diffusion of power as follows. Initially, power lies wholly in the hands of the originator of the idea for the project who "articulates the core values behind the project" (Weber, 2004, p. 259). But as a community develops around the project, the openness of the environment "moves power away from the leader and toward the followers" (Weber, p. 259). Another dimension of power relationships in open groups involves the role of corporate sponsors. The institutional resources they bring to the table and the nature of their underlying motivations can easily undermine the open process by altering its power rela-tionships. However, as we will emphasize when we consider hybrid horizontal business models in Chapter 7, experienced open source leaders are well aware of the need to prevent such arrangements from distorting open community norms and culture.

An effective group requires a measure of unity. The degree to which exist-ing members are motivated to remain participants in a group is called *group cohesion*. The kind of "stroking" that Raymond (1998) alludes to as necessary to keep a group's interest in a project at a passionate level of commitment requires a leader who is able to communicate not only in a broadcast style to many individuals but also intermittently on a one-on-one basis with individ-ual members. On the other hand, according to so-called social identity theory (Whitworth et al., 2000, 2001), group unity is not primarily driven by inter-personal attraction between group members but rather by identification with the group as a social entity. The evidence for such a social identity factor in group behavior is supported by the observation that groups can be cohesive even when interpersonal relations among the members of the group are poor. The importance of cohesion even when there are various internal tensions act-ing against it is alluded to by Lerdorf (2004) in connection with the transition to a multimember team with Suraski and Gutmans during the development of PHP.

The number of persons with whom an individual is in regular communication is called *social connectivity*. Even before the widespread use of the Internet, it was recognized that computer-supported communication systems increase this connectivity by an order of magnitude (Ellis et al., 1991). It is now obvious that the Internet has dramatically expanded the social connectivity of a substantial segment of the entire human race. Indeed, it was precisely this connectivity that enabled the rapid expansion of collaborative open development. Major open source developers like Linus demonstrate the ability to creatively exploit a surprisingly high level of social connectivity via extensive bilateral technical exchanges with codevelopers. As an illustration, consider that the credits file for version 1.0 of Linux already had 80 individuals and that was only the group of recognized contributors. There are also downsides to this massive connectivity. For example, if you are participating in an open source development, the entire world is your stage: just imagine how many people you may be communicating with. Fogel (2005) makes some amusing remarks about cultivating an awareness of your project social connectivity (though he does not use that term) and its implications for things like whether or not you should really post an e-mail to the group. He humorously suggests that pop-ups should be supplied on such occasions that remind prospective e-mail senders that "your email is about to be sent to several hundred thousand people who will have to spend at least 10 seconds reading it before they can decide if it is interesting. At least two man-weeks will be spent reading your email. Many of the recipients will have to pay to download your email. Are you absolutely sure that your email is of sufficient importance to bother all these people?" (Fogel, 2005, p. 173). Fogel's pragmatic caveat is a bracing reminder about the hidden cost of every message when connectivity is so high.

5.5.3 Human Factors in Groups

Human relationship factors in group interactions must be distinguished from objective performance factors. The significance of this distinction was made prominent by Bales' experimental studies of group interactions (Bales, 1950, 1951, 1955) and has been used by many subsequent researchers like (Franz, 1999). Bales distinguished between task-related interactions, such as those that address solution correctness and quality, in contrast with interpersonal or social interactions, like social influence, group cohesion, and group leadership. This is now called Bales' task versus socioemotional distinction. Bales classified group interactions into 12 categories, depending on whether the interactions exhibited solidarity, tension release, agreement, disagreement, or antagonism, presented a suggestion, gave an opinion, gave information, asked for information, asked for an opinion, or asked for a suggestion (Short et al., 1976, p. 36). The categories fall into two broad classes corresponding to what can be described as the task-related, problem-solving, nonperson-oriented interactions, versus person-oriented interactions that reveal the existence of an attitude between members. Whitworth et al. (2001) introduced an additional group-social component as reflected in expressions of group solidarity or group confidence in a decision, versus an individual-emotional component manifested in expressions of tension or agreement. Group-social effects have practical implications, for example, individuals "who identify with a group tend to accept the group's decisions as their own" (Whitworth et al., 1997, p. 1). Whitworth claimed that such affects do not depend on so-called rich media for their communication, with effective group agreement able to "occur through the exchange of relatively simple position information, or choice valence . . . across distributed lean-text networks" (p. 1). As we have seen, the voting mechanisms used in open source developments like Apache are based on exactly such lean communication mechanisms.

Attitudes can be defined as general, persistent evaluations of a person or issue by another person. They affect how information is processed and have socioemotional as well as objective elements (Fabrigar et al., 1999). In a well-known paper, Festinger (1957) conjectured that the way in which people attend to information is "congruent with their attitudes" and that there is a converse tendency to "avoid information which is incongruent" with their attitudes (Fabrigar et al., 1999, p. 182), so-called *congeniality effects*. He assumed these effects occurred at the "exposure, attention, perception, judgment, and memory stages of information processing" (p. 182). Later empirical studies supported Festinger's thesis, indicating that people tend to negatively evaluate information which is contrary to their preexisting attitudes. The attractiveness of a source of information also has an impact on the credibility of the information. While one rationally expects the credibility of a source to be affected by the source's expertise, the attractiveness of the source also plays an important role. Fabrigar also observed that if there is limited opportunity to scrutinize the contents of a message, then the source's attractiveness affects attitudes even if the attractiveness is irrelevant. In face-to-face exchanges, attractiveness is apparent, but in distributed exchanges it would probably be replaced by generic surrogates for how another individual is perceived, such as their community status in the case of open source.

Groups do not necessarily mitigate behavior. In fact, inflammatory behavior may be more common in group contexts than for individuals. It has long been contended that computer-mediated groups tend to exhibit "more uninhibited behavior – using strong and inflammatory expressions in interpersonal interactions" (Siegel et al., 1986, p. 157). Sproul and Kiesler (1986) attributed the tendency toward "more extreme, more impulsive, and less socially differentiated"

(p. 1496) behavior than in a face-to-face context, as due to the lack of adequate social context cues in information-poor media. The use of uninhibited or angry communications in computer-supported communications is called *flaming*. The pervasive acronym RTFM (Read The F – 'ing Manual) used in computing-related development forums in general, not just for open source, is symptomatic. Normal people would not routinely express themselves this way in face-to-face conversation unless the speaker was arrogant or boorish. Furthermore, interactions in open source groups are also by definition both completely and permanently public, with conflicts exposed not only to the immediate participants, but to anyone who has access to the mailing list, including the media, and to posterity via the archives.

In general, conflict in group interactions may be either detached or emotional, either type requiring negotiation for resolution. Interpersonal conflict between the members of a collaborative group differs from *domain level conflict*, the latter referring to differences regarding technicalities like implementation or design criteria. Conflicts between parties may also be differentiated according to whether they are *conflicts of interest* or *conflicts of viewpoints*. Conflicts of interest lead to so-called hard (win–lose) negotiations, while conflicts of viewpoint lead to soft (win–win) negotiations characteristic of friendly, cooperating parties. Both situations benefit from the use of structured negotiation processes. The argument between Linus Torvalds and Andrew Tanenbaum is a classic example of an important technical design conflict that precipitated interpersonal and domain-level conflict. We previously alluded to this classic incident in our discussion of Linux kernel design. Minix designer Tanenbaum had sarcastically characterized the Linux architecture as obsolete in a famed newsgroup post (see DiBona et al. (1999) for the e-mails). Torvalds responded heatedly within hours with his own e-mail post to the newsgroup. His response included inflammatory remarks like "your job is being a professor and researcher: That's one hell of a good excuse for some of the brain-damages of minix. I can only hope (and assume) that Amoeba doesn't suck like minix does" (response dated: 29 Jan 92 23:14:26 GMT). Amoeba was another operating system project Tanenbaum was working on. The debate lasted quite a while but eventually the tone settled down to a more measured, technological one. The entire exchange was instructive, concerning how open source development works. As Weber (2004, p. 102) observes of the open development process, in general "discussions get down to technical issues, clarifying the trade-offs among design strategies and decisions that matter for the function and performance of software." Tanenbaum's provocation had the positive effect of compelling Torvalds to more explicitly understand and more clearly and effectively articulate his own design rationale than he had done to that point. Ultimately, as Weber (2004, p. 102) observes, the argument had a highly positive outcome because it "pulled people in toward Linux and excited their interest."

Social Proxies

We have already seen that open source development is usually supported by a relatively lean mix of e-mails, CVS, forums, Web sites, and IRC. Simple adjuncts to this environment might prove useful. New mechanisms to support computer-based collaborations are regularly proposed. As an illustration of some additional possibilities, we shall take a brief detour to describe an interesting mechanism called a social proxy. Erickson et al. (1999) describe a simple artifice intended to facilitate social interaction in distributed computer-supported groups by visualizing participation more effectively. It uses a tool for documenting an ongoing conversation, supplemented by a graphical device called a *social proxy* that signals the current state of the interactions. We will describe the proxy and then indicate its relevance to improving distributed interactions. The social proxy Erickson et al. considered was an iconic circle, with colored dots called marbles that corresponded to the participants in the conversation (with different members identified by the color of the marble). Marbles corresponding to individuals participating in the current conversation lay within the circle, near its center. Marbles of individuals who were logged on to the system but not currently involved in the conversation lay outside the circle. The environment the proxy monitored had a list of conversations, only one of which can be active at a given time for a given user. Whenever a conversation was selected, the user's marble moved to within the circle for that conversation, while it moved out when the user deselected the conversation. A user's marble moved nearer to the center the more frequently the user contributed to the conversation, while it moved gradually out toward the perimeter as the user participated less, eventually moving outside the circle if the member remained logged on to the system but ceased to participate in the conversation. Marbles of listeners not currently actively participating would lie toward the perimeter of the circle. This simple artifice "gives a sense of the size of the audience, the amount of conversational activity, as well as indicating whether people are gathering or dispersing, and who it is that is coming and going . . . (and) it focuses attention on the group as a whole" (Erickson et al., 1999, p. 75). The "conversations" were shared sequential documents, one per conversation, which persisted over time. New entries were added with time stamps, with user names at the head of the document similar to some bulletin boards. The combination of the conversational documents plus the social proxy icon provided both content and social cues as to what was going on. Thus, a number of characteristics could be readily recognized: the formality or informality of the conversation could be recognized from the text; the tempo of the exchanges could be identified from the time stamps; the number and frequency of participants from the proxy; norms for the conversational style were signaled by the length of the exchanges, and so on. The sequential, scrolling layout of the conversational document provided a "low overhead way for participants to signal agreement, encouragement, and empathy" (p. 74), key mechanisms for fostering group identity.

Social proxies create a sense of social translucence in computer-supported conversation. *Socially translucent* systems "provide *perceptually* based social cues which afford awareness and accountability" (Erickson et al., 1999, p. 72). To illustrate this concept, consider two ways one can make a swinging door safe. In one case, a door can have a sign posted on it that says "open slowly" lest anyone on the other side of the opening door get hit by the door as it swings open. The textual sign is understandable but this kind of sign will gradually cease to be noticed especially by those who use the door regularly. Contrast the result of placing a see-through window in the door, so people using the door can see someone on the other side. The window provides a perceptually based social cue. It allows us to readily detect movement and faces on the other side and instinctively reacts to them more effectively than to a printed sign. The window mechanism is also immediate, while the sign is only a warning. With the window, a person sees someone on the other side: they do not just get warned about a general possibility. This direct awareness also brings social norms into play since under such norms we are expected to not push a door into someone. Furthermore, the effect is bilateral: we not only know someone is on the other side, but the other person knows we know they are there, further reinforcing the sanctions provided by the social norms. Thus the mechanism provides both social awareness and accountability. Erickson et al. suggest such socially translucent mechanisms, of which the software social proxy they designed was an instance, make it "easier for users to carry on coherent discussions; to observe and imitate others' actions; to engage in peer pressure; to create, notice, and conform to social conventions" (p. 72). These beneficial group-building effects are achieved by a lean tool: a scrolled conversation supplemented by a perceptual social proxy. A collaborative tool like CVS arguably provides a limited measure of social translucence since the related activity of other users can be discerned with commands like update, but the mutual awareness is intermittent and requires an explicit action like a commit or update to achieve awareness. The CVS *watches* option provides a slightly greater degree of translucence by enabling contributors to be automatically notified regarding who is working on files that they may be interested in.

References

Allport, F. H. (1924). Social Psychology, Houghton-Mifflin, Boston, MA.

Bales, R. (1950). A Set of Categories for the Analysis of Small Group Interaction. American Sociological Review, 15, 257–263.

Bales, R. (1951). Interaction Process Analysis. Addison-Wesley, Reading, MA.

Bales, R. (1955). How People Interact in Conferences. Scientific American, 212, 3–7.

Bormann, E. G. (1975). Discussion and Group Methods: Theory and Practice, 2nd edition. Harper and Row, New York.

Brand, A. (2003). The Structure, Entrance, Production, Motivation and Control in an Open Source Project. http://dot.kde.org/1065087742/. Accessed November 30, 2006.

DiBona, C., Ockman, S., and Stone, M. (1999). The Tanenbaum-Torvalds Debate in Appendix A of Open Sources: Voices from the Open Source Revolution, M. Stone, S. Ockman, and C. DiBona (editors). O'Reilly Media, Sebastopol, CA.

Ellis, C., Gibbs, S., and Rein, G. (1991). Groupware Some Issues and Experiences. Communications of the ACM, 34(3), 39–58.

Erickson, E., Smith, D. N., Kellogg, W. A., Laff, M., Richards, J. T., and Bradner, E. (1999). Socially Translucent Systems: Social Proxies, Persistent Conversation, and the Design of Babble. In: Proceedings of the CHI'99 Conference on Human Factors in Computing Systems. ACM, New York, 72–79.

Fabrigar, L. R., Smith, S. M., and Brannon, L. A. (1999). Application of Social Cognition: Attitudes as Cognitive Structures. In: Handbook of Applied Cognition, F. T. Durso (editor). John Wiley & Sons, New York, Chapter 7, 173–206.

Feller, J. and Fitzgerald, B. (2002). Understanding Open Source Software Development. Addison-Wesley, Pearson Education Ltd., London.

Festinger, L. (1957). A Theory of Cognitive Dissonance. Stanford University Press, Stanford, CA.

Fogel, K. (2005). Producing Open Source Software: How to Run a Successful Free Software Project, O'Reilly Media, Sebastopol, CA.

Franz, H. (1999). The Impact of Computer-Mediated Communication on Information Overload in Distributed Teams. In: Proceedings of 32nd Hawaii International Conference on System Sciences, Maui, Hawaii.

Grudin, J. (1994). Groupware and Social Dynamics: Eight Challenges for Developers. Communications of the ACM, 37(1), 93–105.

Himanen, P. (2001). The Hacker Ethic. Random House, New York.

Jørgensen, N. (2001). Putting It All in the Trunk: Incremental Software Development in the FreeBSD Open Source Project. Information Systems Journal, 11(4), 321–336.

Kelman, H. C. (1958). Compliance, Identification, and Internalization: Three Processes of Attitude Change. Journal of Conflict Resolution, 2(1), 51–60.

Lerdorf, R. (2004). Do You PHP? http://www.oracle.com/technology/pub/articles/php_experts/rasmus_php.html. Accessed November 29, 2006.

Levy, S. (1984). Hackers: Heroes of the Computer Revolution. Penguin Books, New York, NY.

Raymond, E. (2004). How to Ask Questions the Smart Way. http://www.catb.org/~esr/faqs/smart-questions.html. Accessed November 29, 2006.

Raymond, E. S. (1998). The Cathedral and the Bazaar. First Monday, 3(3). http://www.firstmonday.dk/issues/issue3_3/raymond/index.html. Accessed December 3, 2006.

Reagle, J. (2003). Socialization in Open Technical Communities. http://opensource. mit.edu. http://opensource.mit.edu. Accessed November 29, 2006.

Short, J., Williams, E., and Christie, B. (1976). The Social Psychology of Telecommunications. Wiley, London.

Siegel, J., Dubrovski, V., Kiesler, S., and McGuire, T. W. (1986). Group Processes in Computer Mediated Communication. Organizational Behavior and Human Decision Processes, 37, 157–187.

Sproul, L. and Kiesler, S. (1986). Reducing Social Context Cues: Electronic Mail in Organizational Communication. Management Science, 32, 1492–1512.

Stutz, D. (2003). The Business Schools of Harvard and MIT Consider Free/Open Source. http://www.synthesist.net/writing/osspatents.html. Accessed November 30, 2006.

Von Krogh, G., Spaeth, S., and Lakhani, K. (2003). Community, Joining, and Specialization in Open Source Software Innovation: A Case Study. Research Policy, 32, 1217–1241.

Weber, S. (2004). The Success of Open Source. Harvard University Press, Cambridge, MA.

Whitworth, B., Gallupe, B., and McQueen, R. (1997). Generating Agreement in Dispersed, Computer-Mediated Groups: An Integrative Theoretical Framework. Department of Management Research Report, University of Waikato, 1–42.

Whitworth, B., Gallupe, B., and McQueen, R. (2000). A Cognitive Three-Process Model of Computer-Mediated Group Interaction. Group Decision and Negotiation, 9, 431–456.

Whitworth, B., Gallupe, B., and McQueen, R. (2001). Generating Agreement in Computer-Mediated Groups. Small Group Research, 32(5), 625–665.

Zigurs, I. and Kozar, A. (1994). An Exploratory Study of Roles in Computer-Supported Groups. MIS Quarterly, 18, 277–314.

5.6 Cognitive Psychology and Open Source

Computer-supported collaborative work is a relatively new phenomenon, and open source development is a unique type of distributed collaboration. It is natural to inquire as to whether research in cognitive psychology on group cognition sheds any light on how to think about this phenomenon? We believe it is beneficial to understand the perspective of such research because at a minimum it can provide reference points or templates for how to think about some aspects of these projects and it may provide a matrix for interpreting them. We present a few elementary cognitive models, contrasting them with software methodologies, and then we examine some of the interesting cognitive biases that can hamper problem solving by individuals and groups.

5.6.1 Cognitive Models

Cognitive psychology *describes* how people think. This is different from software methodologies that *prescribe* how people should develop software. Open source development usually takes a fairly lean approach to software methodology, but the role of cognitive psychology in the process is more of an unavoidable given because it represents how the human mind addresses problem solving by individuals or groups. We briefly consider some models for cognitive process and how cognitive factors affect problem solving in software engineering particularly for groups.

A software method prescribes a systematic process for doing software development. The process consists of a set of recommended rules and procedures to use during development. By structuring development, software methods facilitate not only the identification and sequencing of tasks, but also the distribution of tasks to members of the development group. Software methods also facilitate coordinating the activities of a group by explicitly specifying the processes the development group should engage in and the outcomes of those processes, simplifying and improving group coordination. Finally, by defining expected outcomes and landmarks, software methods also provide consistent frameworks for the social processes that accompany software development, including the norms and roles involved in group interactions (Hohmann, 1997).

In contrast to software methods, cognitive models describe the mental processes that are used by software developers at both an individual and a group level. Generally speaking, a *cognitive model* may be defined as a model of how people think or a description of how they solve problems (Hohmann, 1997). A cognitive model may explicitly describe how people think naturally and spontaneously when problem solving *or* it may propose or prescribe ways to think effectively about problems based on empirical studies of successful problem solving, a kind of cognitive engineering. As an illustration of the descriptive mode, consider that according to one cognitive model of software development, developers solve the key parts of a problem by preliminarily mentally scanning their own personal, preexisting cognitive library of solution plans until they identify a plan that suits the problem at hand which they then apply or adapt. This kind of cognitive strategy underlies what is called *opportunistic design* (Hohmann, 1997). This is obviously prominent in open source development. For example, Raymond's remarks (Raymond, 1998) about the decisive importance of reusing or rewriting previously existing code in open source underscores the strong opportunistic design characteristics of open source development. In fact, one of the underlying purposes of the open source movement is to increasingly expand the universally available library of software solutions that people have to work with, creating a software commons for reuse by all.

An instructive descriptive model of group cognition which views groups as *information processors* that behave in ways that are in many respects analogous to how individuals think is presented in (Hinsz et al., 1997). Before describing this model, let us first consider some of the salient features of individual cognition. Individual cognition requires establishing *objectives*, paying *attention* to the information needed for a task, *encoding* information in some manner, *remembering* and *retrieving* it, *processing* information, using *feedback* to adapt one's processing, and producing *responses*. Individuals acquire information, by attention, in a *context* that also defines the "processing objective for the information" (Hinsz et al., 1997, p. 44). This information is then encoded by a process that involves structuring, evaluating, and interpreting the information into an *internal representation* stored in the individual's memory for subsequent access. These processes of attention and retrieval "enable information to enter awareness (in order to be) . . . processed on the basis of an objective" (Hinsz et al., 1997, p. 44). Subsequent to processing, an individual makes a response that can be an *alternative, conclusion, judgment,* or *solution*, depending on the type of task.

Group cognition parallels the elements of individual cognition described earlier. In the case of groups, processing objectives arise from several possible sources: an organizational context, the nature of the task, the roles of the members, procedures, and so on. Formal procedures like using *agendas* can help set "processing objectives and control the way groups process information" (Hinsz et al., 1997, p. 51). Newsgroup announcements of new open source projects, like Linus' famous initiating e-mail for Linux, have often historically set the preliminary agenda for open projects. To-do lists are another simple example. Unlike the case for individuals, where the issue does not arise, congruence among the objectives of group members is critical. The worst-case scenario from an open project's point of view is a failure in congruence that leads to a fork in the project. Just like in individual cognition, groups must "attend to information to process it" (p. 46). Factors related to group attention include how the attention of the group is brought to bear on available material or issues, how groups affect the focus of attention of their members, and how information is distributed in a group. For example, it is known that groups, merely in and of themselves, can distract the attention of members because the presence of others may cause individuals to become self-conscious and focus attention on themselves or how others perceive them rather than on the task. Fogel's (2005) observation about the unnerving exposure of their work that novice open source developers may experience when their repository commits are e-mail notified to a huge audience of anonymous project observers for critique is one occasion of such self-consciousness. In general terms, the distribution of available information also affects what becomes the focus of attention and is subject to notable social effects. For example, Olson and Olson (1999) observe that "it appears that information must be held by at least two people in the group before it will be brought to the attention of the group as a whole" (p. 419). A possible reason for this is that information held by a single individual may lack adequate "social validation (for) the value or accuracy of the information" (Hinsz et al., 1997, p. 47). On the other hand, in open source the process is intentionally kept public and transparent. The norms are against private discussions. As Fogel (2005) observes, "As slow and cumbersome as public discussions can be, they're almost always preferable in the long run. Making important decisions in private is like spraying contributor repellant on your project." In terms of their general propensities, collaborating groups will tend to share information better if the group perceives that there is a single correct solution to a task. Research differs as to whether the encoded representations of information by groups are more or less complex than those of individuals. Differences in such mental representations among members can lead to conflicts whose causes may not even be evident until after group discussion. Groups tend to be superior to individuals in terms of their ability to store and retrieve information, the greater reliability of retrieval being due to the group's ability to correct faulty individual memories. Obviously in computer-supported groups and open source projects there are extensive mechanisms for institutional memory ranging from e-mail archives to CVS repositories that can readily reproduce any previous state of a project and the logged rationales for modifications. The response of groups is also affected by consensus rules. For example, if a majority vote rather than merely a unanimous one decides an issue, then groups show greater flexibility in moving away from an alternative they had previously accepted. We have previously observed how the IETF (Internet Engineering Task Force) development structure, based on the motto of "rough consensus and working code," informed the process and voting model for key open projects like Apache (Moody, 2001). For certain kinds of open development issues, like whether a given interface seems appropriate, nonbinding polls of broader populations of user-participants can be used to guide consensus. Groups generally appear to use "information-processing rules or strategies more reliably and consistently" (p. 50) than individuals, though this does not necessarily correlate with correctness, just with consistency. A consistently recognizable pattern in group processing is that "groups generally decrease variability in the way information is processed, compared with individuals" (p. 53), including "narrowed focus of attention, redundant memories, accentuation of processing strategies, and shared distribution of information" (p. 53). Hinsz et al. (1997) also consider the so-called "combination of contributions" model for small-group collaboration, a model which supplements their own view of groups as information processors. Some of the issues that arise from the viewpoint of the latter combinations model are how to identify the resources, skills, and knowledge that members bring to an interaction and what processes are involved in combining or transforming those individual contributions to produce the group outcome. In the case of open projects, the core developer group tends to be relatively small and so the individual strengths of their members are well known to one another, which is in fact one reason for the low bureaucratic overhead of these groups.

The application of cognitive psychology to the analysis of group collaboration has sometimes been criticized for paying inadequate attention to both the social and the physical context of collaboration (Olson and Olson, 1999). The emerging field of distributed cognition represents an attempt to remedy this by characterizing cognitive processes "not only in terms of activity inside the heads of individuals but in the patterns of activity across individuals and in the material artifacts that mediate this activity" (p. 418). In distributed cognition, the "social setting and the artifacts" (p. 418) include processes like those that support short-term memory, such as having someone remind us what we were talking about prior to an interruption occurring, or that support long-term memory, like remembering who else knows something so that we do not have to commit it to memory or artifacts like paper-and-pencil calculation to facilitate processing. The Olson's claim that the "most important implication of the theory of distributed cognition is that we can *design* the artifacts and the social processes to embody cognition . . . design new technology-based artifacts or . . . design the processes that help distributed cognition thrive in new way" (p. 419). Obviously in open software development the ultimate artifact is the code, as well as the descriptions of the problems to address and the rationales for solutions. The simple exchange of program source code during development via the FTP network protocol was one of the earliest advances in exchanging design artifacts. The introduction of CVS during the late 1980s and early 1990s together with the Internet accessibility of the CVS repositories represents the embodiment of the distributed cognition underlying open source development.

5.6.2 Cognitive Biases

Like any other process, cognition is subject to biases that undermine its effectiveness. The field of cognitive psychology has identified a number of these biases. They are worth being aware of because they represent typical errors that individuals (or groups) are predisposed to. A *cognitive bias* refers to the propensity of individuals to be consistent or predictable in their cognitive behavior, especially with respect to the kind of errors they make. These biases can operate at the individual and group level. Biases by groups can be more potent than those of individuals. According to a well-known thesis in cognitive psychology, groups tend to "display more homogeneous cognitive processes than their members" (Hinsz, 1997, p. 54). This homogenization can lead to either accentuation or attenuation of those processes or biases, that is, either "exaggeration or diminution of an information processing tendency" (p. 54). In terms of cognitive biases, accentuation means that if a tendency toward the bias is present in the members of a group, then the group bias will tend to be more extreme, while if a bias tends to be uncommon among the members, then it will tend to be even further attenuated or diminished in the group. The phenomenon of *group polarization* according to which groups shift toward an extreme of an already preferred tendency is one example of this pattern.

A practical method for improving one's critical thinking is to familiarize oneself with the kind of errors we tend to make. Toward this end, it is instructive to be aware of the kinds of cognitive errors researchers have identified. They represent a kind of syllabus of errors to be on guard against when thinking. Awareness of these errors can help sharpen one's thinking skills by alerting one to common errors in problem solving and helping one recognize the errors more rapidly when they do arise. Biases that both individuals and groups are subject to include cognitive inertia, cognitive stability, availability bias, cognitive simplification, representativeness bias, input and outcome bias, confirmatory bias, and process bias. So-called cognitive effects include cognitive dissonance and cognitive synchronization. We briefly comment on each and examine several in the context of software development.

Consider first tunnel vision in thinking. In cognitive psychology this tendency of an individual or group to narrowly focus on a single or a few thematic lines of thought is called *cognitive inertia*. It is related to other cognitive behaviors like cognitive dissonance. While awareness of this tendency can help reduce its occurrence, it can also be decreased by explicit process structures or countermeasures. For example, it is recognized that during an idea-generation task, cognitive inertia can be reduced by randomly exchanging sets of ideas among group members (Dennis et al., 1990), thereby expanding the range of discussion rather than contracting it. This research also supports the observation that the simultaneous multiple conversational exchanges that occur in electronic meeting systems are often relatively independent of one another, thereby helping to reduce cognitive inertia. *Groupthink* is a related phenomenon, which is defined by Janis (1982) as an extreme form of group polarization. One of the causes of cognitive inertia is *cognitive dissonance*, a widely studied effect defined as the tendency to resist viewpoints whose adoption would require a global rethinking of one's current solution to a problem. Cognitive dissonance occurs if an individual must choose between two equally appealing, but incompatible, alternatives, as Festinger (1957) observed in his classic study of dissonance. A group bias related to cognitive inertia is *cognitive stability* defined as the tendency of a group to resist a change in the subject of discussion because of social inhibitions against repeatedly changing the focus of a discussion. Cognitive stability may often serve a logical purpose. For example, if you post a question to an open source technical forum where it's considered off-topic, then you'll be either ignored or dismissed as a "loser" (in hacker jargon). The rationale for this is "to try to protect their communications channels from being drowned in irrelevance" (Raymond, 2004). A related but slightly different cognitive effect is *cognitive synchronization*, which is the nonbias, group cognitive process that occurs when members synchronize to make sure they have a common, shared representation of a problem or ensure all the members of the group are "on the same page" (Robillard and Robillard, 2000). Stabilization of the source code prior to a project release is a kind of product synchronization that requires cognitive synchronization by the project members.

The information you decide to attend to tends to drive how you think. For example, there are biases related to how easily information is remembered or recalled. A tendency to estimate the frequency of occurrence of a case or situation as greater than it actually is, because the case is more readily thought of, more interesting, or more vivid, is called *availability bias* (Stacy and Macmillan, 1995). It occurs when the likelihood of an event is overestimated because of the ease with which instances of the event can be recalled. Of course, ease of recollection may have nothing to do with frequency of occurrence, because it puts a premium on striking events that are more easily remembered and recalled. As an example, availability bias may lead a developer to assume that the particular code features that a developer has worked on are characteristic of an entire program's code and that conversely unfamiliar code features are infrequent. Another example is related to mental representations. In software development, developers retain mental representations, which reflect their view of an application but which may be very different from how end users view the same application. A developer's representation may be strongly influenced by those components of a system that were difficult to implement or debug, even though this may reflect a skewed view of the system from the viewpoint of its actual use. Availability bias will incline a developer to understand the system in terms of such a biased mental representation. Availability bias can be explained in terms of models like ACT, an activation-based model of cognition developed by Anderson (1976) that originally focused on higher cognition (Pirolli, 1999). The ACT explanation for availability bias is that remarkable information may become encoded in cognitive *chunks* that have high activation values, making them more readily brought into working memory when an individual is cognitively stimulated by appropriate triggering patterns, even when the details of the triggering patterns are not relevant to the chunk retrieved.

As availability bias reminds us, the readily recollected is not always the most frequent. The next bias we consider illustrates that what is familiar is not necessarily universal. The tendency to expect the local characteristics of a limited data sample to be characteristic of the data in general is called *representativeness bias* (Stacy and Macmillan, 1995). From a software development point of view, representativeness and availability biases can result in misallocating testing resources to unrepresentative cases by affecting the selection of test cases when verifying program correctness. One way to limit the impact of these biases is to use an empirical approach. For example, if the issue is how often certain code constructs occur, automated tools should be used to find out what actually occurs, or if the objective is to optimize code, one should first identify where the code spends most of its execution time by empirically profiling the code's execution-time behavior.

There are a number of other biases that reflect data, outcome, and process predispositions. Thus *cognitive simplification* is related to availability bias and is defined as the preference for easily available as opposed to actually significant data – or the tendency to base conclusions on small samples of data (Nosek, 1998). *Input bias* is a cognitive bias that predisposes one to favor certain kinds of data and includes a reluctance to use qualitative data, oversimplification of complex data, a priori dismissal of disconfirmatory evidence, overemphasis on outlying data, or a preference for people-oriented versus problem-oriented data (Hohmann, 1997). For example, one of the difficulties in obtaining objective comparative data on the relative merits of specific open source versus proprietary applications is that studies and individuals often have a stake in one category or the other and may ignore disconfirmatory evidence (an input bias). *Outcome bias* is a predisposition to favor certain kinds of outcomes for decision making. This includes aversion to outcomes that can handle complex cases, a tendency to reject novel solutions, or aversion to thoroughly testing solutions (Hohmann, 1997). A cognitive bias in favor of specific kinds of processes in decision making is called a *process bias* and includes an excessive dependence on Standard Operating Procedures (SOPs), a preference for overly lengthy processes, excessive preference for group processes, excessive analogizing, aversion to detailed examination of assumptions, and oversimplification (Hohmann, 1997).

Especially when testing software, it's important to be willing to be proved wrong. *Confirmatory bias* refers to the tendency to seek or attend to evidence that confirms our current viewpoint and is related to *cognitive dissonance*. Confirmatory bias looks for evidence that verifies expected results rather than for evidence that refutes expectations. This bias plays a role in the failure to detect code errors during inspection because of a priori expectations about behavior. The broad volunteer tester pool of users for open source products, a group that is disjoint from and even anonymous to the core developer pool, makes representative testing far more likely, decreasing this type of bias, at least for projects with a large user community. Hutchins (1991) provides a mathematical model for how confirmatory bias arises in groups. A counterintuitive result of his model is that "increasing the richness of communication may result in undesirable properties at the group level" (p. 297), such as incoherent shared interpretations that arise when "the importance of sharing an interpretation with others outweighs the importance of reaching a coherent interpretation" (p. 299). Confirmatory bias is related to *positive-test bias*, which may be reduced by explicitly searching for errors rather than attempting to verify or confirm one's viewpoint (Stacy and Macmillan, 1995). As an illustration of this bias, it appears to be the case that programmers are much more likely to propose test cases that demonstrate that a program works correctly than they are to propose cases that demonstrate that a program fails (Teaseley et al., 1993).

The problem solving and cognitive styles of individuals vary widely because the cognitive activities engaged in by individuals and groups do not follow lines laid out by prescribed methods. This is to be expected since no one knows how we think or how to systematically make us think better, though the objective of software and problem solving methods is to chip away at the ad hoc character of problem solving and, in specific problem domains, to identify and establish standardized techniques to improve the efficiency of problem solving and make it more systematic. The term *cognitive style* is commonly used to refer to the kind of cognitive processes an individual may be predisposed to use to solve problems, the extremes of which are adaptation and innovation. In adaptation, problems are solved within existing frameworks by adjusting existing solutions. In innovation, newly invented structures are preferred (Hohmann, 1997). As we have seen, a recurrent pattern in open source development is the premium placed on recycling existing solutions, Raymond's Fetchmail program being a well-documented example. This reflects an adaptive approach, at least as the preliminary default choice. On the other hand, the effective open project leader must be alert to innovative designs suggested by others, another classic observation about how successful effective open projects work.

References

Anderson, J. R. (1976). Language, Memory, and Thought. Lawrence Erlbaum, Hillsdale, NJ.

Dennis, A. R., Easton, A. C., Easton, G. K., George, J. F., and Nunamaker, J. F. (1990). Ad hoc versus Established Groups in an Electronic Meeting System Environment.

In: Proceedings of the 23rd Hawaii International Conference on System Sciences, III, 23–29.

Festinger, L. (1957). A Theory of Cognitive Dissonance. Stanford University Press, Stanford, CA.

Fogel, K. (2005). Producing Open Source Software: How to Run a Successful Free Software Project, O'Reilly Media, Sebastopol, CA.

Hinsz, V. B., Tindale, R. S., and Vollrath, D. A. (1997). The Emerging Conceptualization of Groups as Information Processors. Psychological Bulletin, 121(1), 43–64.

Hohmann, L. (1997). Journey of the Software Professional. Prentice Hall, Upper Saddle River, NJ.

Hutchins, E. (1991). The Social Organization of Distributed Cognition. In: Perspectives on Socially Shared Cognition, L. B. Resnick, J. M. Levine, and D. Teasley (editors). American Psychological Association, Washington, DC, 283–307.

Janis, I. (1982). Groupthink: Psychological Studies of Policy Decisions and Fiascoes. Houghton Mifflin, Boston, MA.

Moody, G. (2001). Rebel Code. Penguin Press, New York.

Nosek, J. (1998). The Case for Collaborative Programming. Communications of the ACM, 41(3), 105–108.

Olson, G. and Olson, J. (1999). Computer Supported Cooperative Work. In: Handbook of Applied Cognition, F. T. Durso (editor). John Wiley & Sons, New York, Chapter 14, 409–442.

Pirolli, P. (1999). Cognitive Engineering Models and Cognitive Architectures in Human-Computer Interaction. In: Handbook of Applied Cognition, F. T. Durso (editor). John Wiley & Sons, New York, Chapter 15, 443–477.

Raymond, E. (2004). How to Ask Questions the Smart Way. http://catb.org/~esr/faqs/smart-questions.html. Accessed November 30, 2006.

Raymond, E. S. (1998). The Cathedral and the Bazaar. First Monday, 3(3). http://www.firstmonday.dk/issues/issue3_3/raymond/index.html. Ongoing version: http://www.catb.org/~esr/writings/cathedral-bazaar/. Accessed December 3, 2006.

Robillard, P. N. and Robillard, M. P. (2000). Types of Collaborative Work in Software Engineering. Journal of Systems and Software, 53, 219–224.

Stacy, W. and Macmillan, J. (1995). Cognitive Bias in Software Engineering. Communications of the ACM, 39(6), 57–63.

Teaseley, B., Leventhal, L. M., and Rohlman, S. (1993). Positive Test Bias in Software Testing by Professionals: What's Right and What's Wrong. In: Empirical Studies of Programmers: Fifth Workshop, C. R. Cook, J. C. Scholtz, and J. C. Spohrer (editors). Ablex, Norwood, NJ.

5.7 Group Problem Solving and Productivity

The kind of problem a group is trying to solve through collaboration strongly affects its productivity. This section considers some generic types of problems and the impact of the problem type on the problem solving effectiveness or productivity of a group. The discussion follows the approach laid out in Steiner's (1972) widely referenced analysis of group problem solving work, which remains a classic in the field of social and cognitive psychology. Steiner analyzed many of the fundamental issues of problem solving in groups. Unlike the distributed collaborative group work done over the Internet, Steiner mainly addressed groups working in a face-to-face context, but many of his concepts are applicable to the distributed collaboration that occurs in open source development. We will briefly describe Steiner's conception of the relationship between group productivity and what he calls process losses and process gains, as well as the impact of the type of task on the problem solving and communication processes of the group. This process gain/process loss model is widely used in contemporary analyses of computer-supported group interactions. We also elaborate on Steiner's classification of tasks as divisible, unitary, disjunctive, or conjunctive and consider its relevance to open source development.

5.7.1 Task Type and Group Productivity

The performance of a group on a task depends on three factors:

1. the resources the group has available to perform the task,
2. the requirements of the task itself, and
3. the processes which the group uses to solve the task.

Development resources can be human, tangible, or fiscal. In open source, the human resources are voluntary participants or corporate employees. The tangible resources include the underlying Internet collaborative medium, itself largely created through open development, and software tools like CVS, which are largely free software. Fiscal resources include governmental support, corporate sponsorships, donations by individuals, or support (like in the case of GNU) from foundations like the FSF. The task is the software system or application to be developed, with subtasks for particular aspects of the development like programming, bug reporting, and documentation. The processes are like those we have described for projects such as Apache and Linux, built around the relatively lean framework of e-mail lists + CVS + Web sites + forums + IRC. Steiner defined the potential productivity of a group as the productivity of the group if it arranges its processes to optimally utilize its available resources to solve the requirements of the task. Invariably, there will be some factors beyond the control of the group like the resources available to perform the task or the requirements of the task, but a group may have considerable control over the processes it uses to solve the task. To the extent that the processes the group applies are faulty, the resulting actual productivity of the group will be less than its potential (ideal or optimal) productivity. Steiner expressed this relationship as follows:

Actual productivity = Potential productivity – Losses due to faulty processes.

The actual productivity depends strongly on the type of task since the processes a group can apply are affected by the kind of task the group faces. Indeed, task type may account for half the variation in group productivity (Poole et al., 1985). A commonly used classification of tasks in social psychology was defined by McGrath (1984) and partitions tasks along two axes: a cognitive – behavioral axis and a cooperative – conflicting axis, with the attributes affecting the relative importance to the group of information versus values (McGrath and Hollingshead, 1994, p. 67). The classification identified four general kinds of task: generating ideas or plans, choosing solutions, negotiating conflicts with respect to ideas or interests, and executing tasks (cooperatively or competitively). Steiner's classification of tasks, which we focus on, is based on their structure. It distinguishes between divisible and unitary tasks, disjunctive and conjunctive tasks, as well as a few other categories. We describe these in the following.

Divisible Tasks

Divisible tasks are those that lend themselves to partitioning into subtasks. The subtasks can be worked on independently by individuals or subgroups. This kind of divisibility has obvious implications for group effort and is essential to the feasibility of open development. In software development, in general, tasks tend to be partitioned into a well-defined hierarchy of subtasks. Of course, the most successful open projects like Linux and Apache have intentionally designed their software architectures in a modular fashion to support partitioned distributed development. A logically large group, which is by definition combined of members who represent a significantly broader range of knowledge and skills than any individual member, can successfully solve a divisible task even if none of its members working independently has either the skill or the capacity to solve the task. Logically large or broad domain expertise by the set of participants is a well-known characteristic of open groups, complemented by domain specialization at the individual level. The division of labor that a divisible task permits can also increase the reliability with which the task can be accomplished. Thus while the disjoint skills of the individuals in a group may make a task feasible, the redundant skills and mutual oversight provided by the group may increase the reliability of the solution.

Partitioning divisible tasks into subtasks may be more art than science. There may be innumerable ways to subdivide a task, but a successful decomposition defines a set of subtasks that can be solved relatively independently and allo-cated or assigned to individuals in the group who are most capable of performing the subtasks. Task partitioning (divide and conquer) is an established technique in software and algorithm development. This problem solving tactic reflects how people naturally partition tasks in ordinary activities. It raises the obvious kinds of questions: in what ways or in how many different ways can a task be divided? How should individuals be assigned to the divided subtasks? How can individuals or the group combine, integrate, or synthesize their activities or outcomes on the subtasks to solve the original or root task? Is there a required or optimal sequence in which the subtasks should be done since the initiation of some tasks may depend upon the completion of other tasks? In software development, a standard technique for task partitioning is based on designing a system such that it can be implemented in a modular fashion, so its modules can then be independently worked on by subgroups. Linux is an example where the solution design was strongly motivated not only by the requirements of the underlying operating system problem, but also by the ability of the design to support independent distributed work. The kernel modules in Linux can be worked on separately and independently. Without this framework, the Linux project could not have developed at the rate it has. Naturally, the decentralized repository model of project management used in Linux fits in with this parti-tioned problem and domain expertise structure, with configuration management systems like Git and BitKeeper designed to faithfully reflect this structure.

Unitary Tasks

Unitary tasks are problems that do not benefit from partitioning, because they cannot be practically divided into subtasks each of which can be performed independently and the results of which can be conveniently combined. Despite the "bazaar" aspects of open source development, the originating design of a project is usually unitary or at least the result of a cohesive partnership. It is easy to think of examples of unitary tasks from everyday life. For exam-ple, can you partition tying your shoelaces into subtasks which could then be combined? It seems puzzling to recognize how two people could share the task of tying the shoelaces into a bow at the end? This action does not seem easily partitioned into separate tasks. It is even hard to articulate how the task is done in the first place because the act itself has been transformed by habit into an almost autonomous action. The lack of such a recognizable specifi-cation for the final task is one barrier to its decomposition or partitioning. Another obstacle is the coordination that decomposition would entail because the elements of the task seem so tightly coupled. The required coordination seems best centralized through a single individual's mind because of the subtle timing and sensory feedback it requires. In what respects is the initial design of a software system like this and is that why design tends to be considered as inseparable? Another thought experiment for understanding task divisibility is driving a car. Suppose one person handles the steering wheel, while another works the brakes, while both parties look out the front window to direct the car! Unlike tying shoelaces, in this case the separate responsibilities are at least more readily identified or specified in terms of what has to be done and by whom: one person steers, the other person brakes or accelerates, both direct or guide based on visual feedback. However, once again complications arise because of the difficulty of coordinating the separated tasks that are still tightly coupled in a feedback loop that affects the overall process. Ordinarily, this coupling is transparent, involving the real-time eyes–hands–feet coordination of a single individual. But when tasks are split between two separate persons, the feedback loop that works conveniently for a single person becomes clumsy at best for a pair of cooperating individuals. Thus a task may turn out to be unitary because of the difficulty of specifying a partition for the task or because of the difficulty of separating the task into subtasks that are not tightly coupled.

Although a unitary task is indivisible by definition, it could be collaborated on by a group by selecting or combining individually generated solutions to obtain a group response. The specific selection or combination method depends on the task. For example, reasoning problems done under time constraints are typically considered as unitary because they do not lend themselves to subtasking to separate individuals (Steiner, 1972). This is perhaps one reason why individual programmers check out code from a CVS repository and work on it in temporary isolation. If a group works on a unitary problem, it acts as a group of individuals working independently on the same problem. How a group response would be produced depends on how the individual efforts feed into the group product. For example, it may be that exactly one of the proposed individual answers can be correct. This kind of unitary task is said to be disjunctive because a group decision or response is like an exclusive-or of the separate responses generated by the members. One solution is selected as the correct response using some form of group judgment, like voting, and the rest are rejected. For example, we have previously described how in the case of the Apache project the protocol was for a developer (self-charged to solve a certain problem) to collect alternative solutions from contributors, forward them to the developer mailing list for feedback and evaluation, and then subsequently develop the actual solution himself based on what was gathered from the proposed solutions. This seems like a disjunctive approach, though it may have some elements of the conjunctive category we describe next.

Other Categories of Tasks

A task is said to be conjunctive if the group outcome depends on the outcomes of every individual of the group. In a conjunctive task each individual must produce a satisfactory result on his assigned subtask or else the group cannot correctly complete the overall task. The word conjunctive derives from the use of the term in logic where the conjunction of two propositions is true if and only if both propositions are true. For conjunctive tasks the information separately available to each member of the group or the subtask solved by each member is needed to correctly solve the overall problem. The performance of the group is limited by the performance of the poorest performing member. If a member fails to understand the rules, the productivity of the entire group suffers. Thus the problem is said to be conjunctive. As a trivial example, successfully finding a searched-for element of an array that has been partitioned among individuals requires only a single individual to correctly locate the element but if that member errs then the entire outcome may be wrong. Furthermore, a negative outcome where the searched element is not in the array requires a correct negative response from every member and so a failure by any member to correctly solve his subtask invalidates the entire group outcome. Conjunctive tasks also occur in a pipelined decomposition of a nonunitary task where all the pipelined tasks are necessary and indeed each of the pipelined tasks may depend on the successful prior completion of precedent tasks. Other tasks Steiner defines are additive and discretionary tasks. In additive tasks the group result is the sum of the individual results and so every member's contribution has an impact. In discretionary tasks the group can use any mechanism it decides on to combine the individual results, such as simple averaging.

The performance of a group may be measured in a variety of ways such as by the number of tasks the group performs correctly. Unless there exists a single member of a group who is the most competent on every subtask, the potential performance of a group exceeds that of any of its individual members. A classic instance of a problem where groups perform better is traversing a maze where groups can learn faster by combining the learning experiences of individual members. The potential productivity of a group working on a disjunctive task depends on the capability of its most capable member, as well as on the group process for accepting solutions. Conjunctive tasks affect group productivity in the opposite way because the performance of the group depends upon its least capable member. For divisible tasks, the productivity of the group also depends on the resources allocated to the individuals performing the subtasks. While group heterogeneity may increase the potential productivity of a group because of the broader skill set of its members, partitioning the work efforts entails matching members to subtasks since the outcome of a subtask depends on the competency of a member to perform that subtask. This may increase process losses for reasons ranging from the need for the most competent individual to dominate group decision making in disjunctive tasks to the impact of having greater differences in social status than in homogenous groups.

5.7.2 Effects of Group Characteristics

Group composition refers to the membership characteristics or subject demographics of a group. Members may be differentiated by status characteristics: they may be peers or there may be a hierarchical order. Group composition may be homogeneous or heterogeneous with respect to a particular attribute. The logical size of a group is a related notion. A group has a small logical size if the domain knowledge of the group is comparable to that of an individual member as a result of redundancy in member expertise. As mentioned previously, logically large groups in contrast have a greater range of knowledge than any individual member and are obviously what is needed for any substantial open source project. Homogeneity of the dispositions of the group members appears to promote collegiality, but it may also adversely affect motivation. Homogenous dispositions tend to enhance member satisfaction with the group, but this increased satisfaction does not necessarily manifest itself in increased task productivity. The dispositional characteristics of the members decline in importance if appropriate roles are prescribed that can guide behavior. Heterogeneity should in principle tend to produce an initial diversity of views in a group discussion, thereby possibly enhancing the quality of decisions, but the relation between initial group diversity and heterogeneity is unclear. However, psychological studies do indicate that heterogeneity on the dominance characteristics of individuals can significantly affect group performance (Steiner, 1972). For open source communities, there are some notable attributes that characterize group composition. The most obvious is the gender uniformity that surveys invariably indicate, with almost all participants being male, as well as the relatively youthful age distribution. Open development projects obviously have a preponderantly technical membership, including their administration, but noncore, nontechnical users also participate in the roles of bug reporters and testers, especially for mass-market tools like browsers and desktop application.

Assembly effects are differences in performance due to group composition. They have been examined in the context of so-called ad hoc groups, which are groups without prior histories of working together. Ad hoc groups are intentionally constructed, for purposes of experiment design, to be homogeneous or heterogeneous on some attribute. The objective is to configure the group and so one can analyze how its behavior depends on the homogeneity/heterogeneity of the attribute used in the construction of the group. Despite the intent of such an experimental design, it is difficult to interpret the experimental results of such configurations because there may be significant correlations between the characteristics that have been used to construct the designed group and other unrecognized characteristics that influence the group behavior. This complicates any subsequent statistical analysis since the factors that actually cause experimentally observed effects may not in fact be the explicitly constructed characteristics but only unrecognized correlated characteristics. For example, Olson and Olson (1997) observe that changes in the physical size of a group tend to simultaneously affect other variables. Thus larger groups tend to be less homogeneous, status effects become more of a factor, and structural effects like the emergence of a leader tend to appear. To circumvent this, they recommend that instead of examining the effects of group size, one should directly examine variables based on the characteristics of group members, organizational context or type of task. Refer also to the research by McGrath (1984) and Morgan and Lassiter (1992).

The process gain versus process loss model of group productivity analyzed by Steiner for face-to-face groups serves equally well to analyze interactions in computer-supported collaborations. The next few sections will look at various process gains and losses that arise in computer-supported environments and their apparent impact on productivity and problem solving.

References

McGrath, J. E. (1984). Groups: Interaction and Performance. Prentice Hall, Englewood Cliffs, NJ.

McGrath, J. E. and Hollingshead, A. B. (1994). Groups Interacting with Technology. Sage Pub, Thousand Oaks, CA.

Morgan, B. B. and Lassiter, D. L. (1992). Team Composition and Staffing. In: Teams: Their Training and Performance, R. W. Swezey and E. Salas (editors). Ablex, Norwood, NJ.

Olson, G. and Olson, J. (1997). Making Sense of the Findings: Common Vocabulary Leads to the Synthesis Necessary for Theory Building. In: Video-Mediated Communication, K. Finn, A. Sellen, and S. Wilbur (editors). Lawrence Erlbaum Associates, Mahwah, NJ, Chapter 4.

Poole, M. S., Siebold, D. R., and McPhee, R. D. (1985). Group Decision-Making as a Structuration Process. Quarterly Journal of Speech, 71, 74–102.

Steiner, I. D. (1972). Group Process and Productivity. Academic Press, New York.

5.8 Process Gains and Losses in Groups

What is the impact of computer-supported communication on group productivity and how can productivity be enhanced by such processes? This section discusses these issues in terms of Steiner's model for group productivity as determined by the task to be solved, the resources available to the group, and the processes used to solve the task. The characteristics its processes can affect a group's productivity. We will examine several phenomena that affect productivity and how they can be influenced by computer support.

Before considering specific process gains and losses related to software development, it is worth remembering the global picture of how software development itself progressed with the advance of the technology created by open development. For example, in the case of Unix, original development was slower and far less distributed because the tools for distributed development remained inchoate. Networking capabilities like those provided by BSD 4 had a meta-effect on software development. Version 4, for example, didn't merely improve the capabilities of an operating system. It fundamentally altered the very way in which software development collaboration could be done because it provided an infrastructure for digitally transmitting not only communication messages but also large amounts of source code between remotely located developers. This created a shared workspace where the actual production artifacts could be worked on in common. The Internet then precipitated even more dramatic increases in the scale and rate of development. The organization of collaborative processes also had a dramatic impact on software development. One need only contrast the rate of development of the GNU GCC Compiler project, after it was managed in bazaar mode, versus its prior traditional development. The bazaar mode of development for EGCS (the Experimental GNU Compiler System) followed the Linux development model and was initiated in 1997, while the very same project continued ongoing development according to the conventional nonbazaar mode. The two projects progressed at strikingly different rates, with the bazaar mode so dramatically outpacing the conventional one that by 1999 the original GCC project was sunset and development was placed entirely under the EGCS project. Thus, it is obviously a given that computer-supported mechanisms have led to revolutionary process gains in development. The following discussion addresses some aspects of the impact of computer support. This and subsequent sections provide additional perspectives through which to view open development.

5.8.1 Process Gains and Losses

Computer-supported collaboration enables processes that improve group productivity in a variety of ways. For example, it allows remote, parallel, relatively instantaneous communication and supports a digitized group memory, all of which facilitate problem solving. Steiner (1972) viewed group productivity as a resultant of process losses that subtract from a potential or ideal productivity to yield actual productivity. The ideal productivity of a group was defined by Steiner as its productivity if a group arranges its processes to optimally utilize its available resources to solve the requirements of a task. The actual productivity of a group will be less than its ideal productivity to the extent to which the processes the group applies cause inefficiencies. Organizing group processes optimally is more easily said than done. Even in an elementary model like that of Hohmann (1997), the basic operations of group problem solving are potentially complex tasks: identify the subtasks required to solve a problem, distribute these subtasks among the group members to work on, coordinate these distributed activities, and integrate the distributed results to complete the original task. The performance of the group depends on all these complex factors. Some factors, like the resources available to perform a task or the nature of the task itself, may be outside the control of the group; however, groups may exercise considerable control over other aspects of their processes. For example, it is often the case that the nature of the "work task" in open development is already unlike that in the typical "work" model. The task itself is far more likely to be under the control of the "workers" because it has been chosen for reasons of personal interest or passion, rather than assigned by an external agent. Of course, this is obviously less true in a corporate-sponsored environment that assigns its own workers to the project.

Computer-supported collaboration may lead to process gains as well as process losses for a group. Process gains are factors that increase performance in a collaborative environment or are efficiencies associated with the intrinsic characteristics of a process. They include, for example, the synergies and learning that can occur in a group environment (Nunamaker et al., 1991b) or the advantages associated with parallelism in a computer-supported environment. As we have previously observed, the process gain of "learning" is in fact recognized as one of the most prominent self-identified motivators for open source participants. The process gain represented by parallelism is the root of the famed open source "given enough eyeballs, all bugs are shallow" principle. Process losses are factors that decrease performance or are inefficiencies associated with the intrinsic characteristics of a process (Dennis, 1996). Dennis and Valacich (1993) examine the process gains and losses associated with computer communication. Together with Nunamaker et al. (1991a, b), they identify literally dozens of potential losses. The most prominent of these include production blocking and evaluation apprehension, which we examine in the following. Although their work was done in the context of a specific and now somewhat dated type of interaction environment, many of the concepts and problems they addressed are still pertinent.

5.8.2 Production Blocking

Production blocking is the kind of process loss that occurs in a face-to-face environment when more than one participant wants to speak concurrently. This loss is mitigated in computer-supported collaborations, resulting in the elimination of a process loss. Since speaking requires mutually exclusive access to the floor, only one person can speak at a time. Access to this nonshareable resource ("the floor") is sometimes called airtime, and various social protocols can be used to manage its allocation. The delay caused by this access contention and its cognitive side effects is a key source of productivity loss in face-to-face group problem solving. Detailed implicit turn-taking protocols and cues are used in face-to-face and synchronous auditory or visual environments to manage this access. Computer-supported communications ameliorate production blocking by allowing simultaneous or parallel communication, thus diminishing blocking. The blocking is actually reduced by the combination of two capabilities of computer-supported environments. Firstly, parallel communications enable more than one participant to communicate at a time. Secondly, extensive logging of communications enables later access to these communications. Together these abilities reduce the blocking that occurs in physical meetings.

There are also secondary process gains that arise from these capabilities. The logged communications in computer-supported environments provide a group memory by recording communications for later use. This reduces the need for members to continually keep abreast of and remember exchanges, reduces the cognitive effort required by listening, and facilitates reflecting on what has been said. In any event, synchronous exchanges are already a problem for geographically dispersed developers working under different schedules in different time zones (McCool et al., 1999), so asynchronous and logged communications are a precondition of any distributed collaboration. Since group support systems capture significant amounts of information in the form of meeting logs, these logs can, in principle, also serve as knowledge repositories that preserve a group's collective memory. For open source groups, the logged information is contained in public e-mail and forum archives, as well as in CVS log statements. As group membership changes, new members can access the experience of their predecessors. These repositories may provide simple search functions, but they also represent opportunities to develop intelligent search tools to help access the information they contain. One would like participants to be able to "drill down" through the information in a log to help understand a current situation. It would be useful to develop intelligent agents that can more effectively mine repository data (Nunamaker, 1999). In the case of open source projects, archives provide both institutional memory and direct, online transparency about the operation of the project, which is one of the key characteristics of open development.

Production blocking can lead to a range of process losses. For example, participants who are not allowed to speak at a given point may subsequently forget what they were going to say when they are finally able to speak. Alternatively, after listening to subsequent discussion, participants may conclude that what they had intended to say is now less relevant, less original, or less compelling, once again suppressing their remarks. The participant may or may not be accurate in this assessment of their intended remarks, but in any case the group does not know what they were thinking, which could in turn affect how the overall group discussion proceeds. Another effect of blocking is that individuals who are waiting to express an idea have to concentrate on what they are about to say instead of listening to what others are saying or thinking productively about the problem, thus distracting themselves by trying to remember an idea rather than moving on and generating new ideas. All of these process losses are mitigated in a computer-supported environment.

As we have seen in Chapter 4, software versioning systems are used by developers to keep track of changes to a project as it evolves. Early software versioning systems exhibited a type of production blocking or access contention. Modern systems allow simultaneous access to the files of a project. This is useful even for a local development group but essential for the productivity of distributed development and now a fundamental feature of open development. The most widely used versioning tool is the CVS described in detail in Chapter 4. Before the development of CVS, versioning tools used a lock-modify-unlock protocol for file handling that permitted a certain level of concurrency. However, under that model only one developer at a time was allowed to have access to a given file. Other developers had to wait until the file being modified was released. Such mutually exclusive access could require significant coordination and obviously constituted production blocking. Collocated developers might be able to contact one other quickly if such a lockout was blocking their development work. Similarly, if a development group was small enough so that access collisions were infrequent, the blocking might be acceptable or the coordination might be manageable. However, in large distributed groups such collisions and their coordination are troublesome, especially in a significantly volunteer community. An especially irksome and common coordination problem was the phenomenon of so-called stale locks (Rooney, 2004). This occurred when a person checked out a file and took out a lock on the file so that it could be modified. The developer might work on the file for a while, perhaps eventually even returning it to its original state after some failed efforts at modification, and then "temporarily" turn his attention to some other files with the intention of returning to the original file later, but then forget to return the lock. In the meantime, another developer attempting to work on the locked file would be pointlessly blocked out.

In contrast to this older, blocking versioning system, consider CVS. Once again the software projects are stored in a repository on a central server. More than one distributed developer can concurrently check out the latest version of a project from the repository. They can then modify the source code on the client concurrently even when they are working on the same file. When the changes are eventually committed back to the server, the CVS detects if there are any conflicts in the changes made by one developer with concurrent changes to the same information made by another developer. If a conflict arises, the developer making the most recent change is automatically notified of this situation by the CVS and told in a very readable notation exactly what the conflicting elements appear to be. The developer can then adjust his modification as appropriate, without having been blocked from working on the files in the first place. This copy-modify-merge capability dramatically reduces the chance of such production blocking.

Unsurprisingly, the computer-supported mechanisms that reduce effects like production blocking can themselves cause process losses. Despite its benefits, there are possible complications and costs associated with these parallel, synchronous or asynchronous communications. For example, McGrath and Hollingshead (1994) observe that there is a potentially high cognitive load, and there are possible sequencing complications to interaction discourse caused by these communications:

If (message) composition takes different amounts of time for different members, and transmission takes some finite additional time, then not only is receipt of a message separated in time from composition, but messages may also be received and sent in different sequences by different members. Furthermore, because multiple sources can transmit at the same time, the reading load is likely to increase rapidly with small increases in group size (McGrath and Hollingshead, 1994, p. 20).

The time-honored e-mail mailing lists used in open source are certainly subject to these effects. Real-time mechanisms like IRC can both alleviate and exacerbate these effects. The kind of sequencing anomalies that may occur can disrupt the semantic flow of exchanges that would occur naturally in face-to-face conversation. This holds even more so for asynchronous communications where the pattern of responses of users to messages may be unknown, possibly leading to significant confusion. For example, in a synchronous system if a user does not reply within a reasonable time frame, one may conclude the choice is deliberate. But in an asynchronous system, "the assumption that all potential receivers have in fact read and understood a message within a short span of time is not likely to be warranted. Hence ambiguity is increased in an asynchronous computer system because the sender cannot be confident that the failure of any given member to reply to a given message in a timely fashion reflects that member's deliberate choice" (McGrath and Hollingshead, 1994, p. 21).

5.8.3 Evaluation Apprehension and Anonymity

Evaluation apprehension is another process loss, most prominent in a face-to-face environment, which is triggered by fear of being criticized for an opinion one expresses. Like other process losses we have considered, it too can be mitigated by computer-supported collaboration. Evaluation apprehension prevents individuals, especially timid or low-status individuals, from expressing their ideas. It causes that type of process loss where members of a group do not express their ideas because they fear negative evaluation by others in the group (Dennis and Valacich, 1993). One rudimentary process structure proposed to decrease evaluation apprehension is enforcing a moratorium on criticism at those points in a discussion where individuals propose their opinions, a kind of temporary self-censorship that can be implemented in either a face-to-face or computer-supported environment. However, such a policy may be more easily enforced in a face-to-face context because once a critical comment is posted in a computer-supported environment, it cannot be easily retracted.

Anonymity is a standard technique for reducing evaluation apprehension. In a computer-supported environment it can be achieved by anonymous communication. Sometimes anonymity is just a side effect of keeping barriers to participation low, like allowing people to access project information or provide bug reports without going through a full-scale registration process (Fogel, 2005). More fundamentally, anonymity allows individuals to present their ideas without fear of being openly embarrassed by critical comments and without having to openly challenge the opinions of others. The risk of embarrassment or even retaliation in an organizational environment is substantially decreased if no one can be sure who made a comment. Anonymity is relatively straightforward to implement in a computer-supported environment, though there may be technical issues related to system security and the trustworthiness of the software in guaranteeing anonymity. Furthermore, if group members know each other well, they may be able to guess the author of an anonymous exchange, though this is more likely in a small group than in a large group (Nunamaker et al., 1991a).

Anonymity leads to a number of process gains. It reduces an individual's public association with the ideas they generate, with a corresponding decrease in the kind of personal, premature commitment to one's opinions that can lead to cognitive inertia as well as hostility to adverse ideas. Anonymity makes it easier to present new or challenging ideas because it separates out personalities from the ideas being proposed and lets participants change their previous opinions without having to admit that they have done so. It facilitates devil's advocacy and reduces the likelihood of a few individuals dominating a process (Gallupe et al., 1992). The most significant benefits of anonymity arise in situations where there are power and status differences with fewer benefits accruing in peer groups (Nunamaker et al., 1991b). Anonymity empowers group members with lower social or organizational status who will be less likely to hold back on presenting their ideas because of evaluation apprehension. In addition to reducing apprehension, anonymity also tends to reduce conformity, especially if a discussion is heated and critical, or there are status differences among the members. In fact, anonymity tends to have little benefit if the issues considered are not perceived as risky, while its benefits increase when the perceived risks are substantial, such as may occur in an organizational context where there are significant differences among individuals and potentially significant costs for nonconformist opinions or for errors in proposed judgments or recommendations. In the case of open source development, many of the potential risks of anonymity or the lack thereof are related to reputation gains and losses. Given the increased participation of corporations as sponsors of the work efforts of open developers, impacts on the organizational status of individuals become more of an issue than it had been when these were predominantly volunteer efforts. Furthermore, individuals also now represent their organizations and so their skills reflect not only on themselves but also on their companies.

When a known participant makes a contribution to an open project, it is available for scrutiny and critique by any observer. These observers can perfectly well be anonymous. The anonymity of these potentially critical voices operating in such a public arena may well unnerve even members of the core development team whose work is subject to such scrutiny. While the anonymity may decrease the apprehension of the critics, it may increase the evaluation apprehension of the individuals whose work is a target of the criticism. As Fogel (2005) observes in the context of the common e-mail commit notices that are triggered automatically when commits are made to a CVS repository, the developers may feel that "now you're asking them to expose their code to the scrutiny of random strangers, who will form judgments based only on the code. . . . These strangers will ask lots of questions, questions that jolt the existing developers . . . To top it all off, the newcomers are unknown, faceless entities. If one of your developers already feels insecure about his skills, imagine how that will be exacerbated when newcomers point out flaws in code he wrote, and worse, do so in front of his colleagues" (Fogel, 2005). Nonetheless, it is precisely the awareness of and feedback from such scrutiny that brings the best work out of the developers.

Anonymity tends to be most useful at the start of collaboration "when you're exploring ideas and eliciting options" because it promotes candor (Nunamaker, 1999, p. 70). While it might seem that anonymity could destabilize group behavior and social norms, possibly leading to increased flaming in response to anonymous critical comments, Nunamaker et al. (1996) observe that in their experience this does not happen. Indeed, anonymity is useful for team building because it allows candid exchanges in a safe environment. However, there is a trade-off between anonymous, free expression of ideas, which are consequently not owned or sponsored by anyone, versus public expression of ideas for which an individual may gain merit for a contribution (or possibly demerit and humiliation for a perceived error). Because of this trade-off, anonymity is less useful in groups where individuals are awarded on the basis of individual effort.

Can computer-supported anonymity increase the creativity of problem solving? The effects of anonymity have been extensively studied for the special case of idea generation or brainstorming tasks in a series of papers by Nunamaker, Dennis, Valacich, and Vogel (such as Nunamaker et al., 1991a). Previous research found that anonymous groups apparently generated more ideas during brainstorming than nonanonymous groups when using computer-supported communication, at least for tasks with low levels of conflict and under certain circumstances. The groups involved also perceived the interaction process as more effective and satisfying. Similar results were obtained in a variety of different experimental settings, occurring, for example, for both groups that had preexisting group histories and groups that did not, for groups of varying sizes, and for groups from public and private organizations (Nunamaker et al., 1991a). Jones (1988) observed that while so-called Negotiation Support Systems increased idea productivity or generation of alternative solutions in low-conflict situations, these systems did not appear to have a significant impact on idea generation in high-conflict situations. While some have proposed using interaction processes that require a noncritical tone for group interactions to enhance idea generation, in fact conflict and criticality of tone seem intrinsic to such processes. See such as Connolly et al. (1993), which evaluated the effect of anonymity versus evaluative tone. The impact of anonymity on idea productivity is most pronounced in groups with high-status differentials, with behavior changing as one migrates from a peer group to a charged status group where some participants may not want to express themselves at all. There is little impact from anonymity in groups where there are no preexisting power structures, no preexisting vested interests in outcomes, and no fear of negative consequences for nonconformity, but there are significant impacts from anonymity for individuals in groups with existing organizational contexts (such as Nunamaker et al., 1991a).

References

Connolly, T., Routhieaux, R. L., and Schneider, S. K. (1993). On the Effectiveness of Group Brainstorming: Test of One Underlying Cognitive Mechanism. Small Group Research, 24, 490–503.

Dennis, A. R. (1996). Information Exchange and Use in Group Decision Making: You Can Lead a Group to Information, but You Can't Make It Think. Management Information Systems Quarterly, 20(4), 433–457.

Dennis, A. R. and Valacich, J. S. (1993). Computer Brainstorms: More Heads Are Better Than One. Journal of Applied Psychology, 78(4), 531–537.

Fogel, K. (2005). Producing Open Source Software: How to Run a Successful Free Software Project. O'Reilly Media, Sebastopol, CA.

Gallupe, R. B., Dennis, A. R., Cooper, W. H., Valacich, J. S., Nunamaker J., and Bastianutti, L. (1992). Electronic Brainstorming and Group Size. Academy of Management Journal, 35(2), 350–369.

Hohmann, L. (1997). Journey of the Software Professional. Prentice Hall, New Jersey.

Jones, K. (1988). Interactive Learning Events: A guide for Facilitators. Kogan Page, London.

McCool, R., Fielding, R., and Behlendorf, B. (1999). How the Web Was Won. http://www.linux-mag.com/1999-06/apache_01.html. Accessed November 30, 2006.

McGrath, J. E. and Hollingshead, A. B. (1994). Groups Interacting with Technology. Sage Pub, Thousand Oaks, CA.

Nunamaker, J. F. (1999). Collaborative Computing: The Next Millennium. Computer, 32(9), 66–71.

Nunamaker, J. F., Briggs, R. O., Romano, N. C., and Mittleman, D. (1996). The Virtual Office Workspace: Group Systems Web and Case Studies. In: Groupware: Collaborative Strategies for Corporate LANs and Intranets, D. Coleman (editor). Prentice Hall, Upper Saddle River, NJ.

Nunamaker, J. F., Dennis, A. R., Valacich, J. S., and Vogel, D. R. (1991a). Information Technology for Negotiating Groups. Management Science, 37(10), 1325–1346.

Nunamaker, J. F., Dennis, A. R., Valacich, J. S., Vogel, D. R., and George, J. F. (1991b). Electronic Meeting Systems to Support Group Work. Communications of the ACM, 34(7), 40–61.

Rooney, G. (2004). Practical Subversion. Apress Publishers, Berkley, CA.

Steiner, I. D. (1972). Group Process and Productivity. Academic Press, New York.

5.9 The Collaborative Medium

There are a wide range of environmental and media characteristics that affect collaboration. This section considers some of them. We briefly discuss the concepts of interaction environments, collocated work, common ground, coupling, incentive structures, and technological readiness. We consider the role of cues in communication, how to establish shared understanding, the structure of conversations, the effect of environment on social cues, the consequences of what is called information richness, and the impact of time-related effects on interaction.

5.9.1 Collaborative Infrastructure

The interaction environment of a collaboration is the modality through which the group interaction occurs. Face-to-face interactions are the prototypical human interaction environment and are fundamentally different from computer-supported ones. For example, the latter provide fewer of the cueing factors that facilitate shared cognitive attention, factors like gesturing, deictic reference, and nonverbal expression. A rich cueing environment makes it easier for a group to attain a common understanding or shared context for its discussions, effectively letting everyone in a group be on "the same page." The scarcity of such cues in computer-supported interactions reflects a process loss. Of course, computer-supported interactions also have media-related process gains. For example, these interactions are more documentable, reviewable, and may be more precise than their face-to-face counterparts (Nunamaker, 1999). Current technological limitations on what cueing characteristics are available in computer-supported environments may be mitigated with advances in technology, but other limitations are intrinsic to remote communication.

To understand the nature of the physical and media factors that affect distributed collaboration, consider the simplest collaborative environment: collocated work (Olson and Olson, 2000). Collocated work, or proximal interaction, refers to collaboration where participants are located at a common site, with workspaces separated by at most a short walk, and where the work is done synchronously. There is a shared space where members of the group can meet and all group members have convenient access to shared static media like blackboards, bulletin boards, and so on. Collocation and physical proximity are known to have a strong positive effect on the initiation of collaboration. For example, it is known that academic researchers on the same floor of a building are far more likely to collaborate than researchers on different floors, even after organizational factors like collocating individuals with similar roles or interests near each other are taken into account (Kraut et al., 1990). The explanation for this effect is understood to be the far greater frequency of communication, especially informal communications, between nearby individuals, a phenomenon especially important during the initiation and planning of collaboration.

Many of the characteristics of a collocated environment are based on the "spatiality of human interaction" (Olson and Olson, 2000). Interactions in such an environment are characterized by rapid feedback (allowing for quick correction), multiple information channels (vocal, facial, postural, and gestural), coreference (such as deictic reference by gaze), spatiality of reference (participants are in the same physical space), opportunistic information exchange, shared local context, implicit cues, and easily nuanced information exchange. Each of these forms of expression can convey subtleties transcending textual communications. Except for the communication blocking that occurs in a physical interaction, the interactions are real time. The discrete communication represented by text cannot match the easy continuum of nuances that occur in a proximal context. For example, the elementary issue of identification of participants is trivial and immediate since the source of a communication is obvious. All the participants share the same local context, including the same time of day and circadian state. Having the same spatial frame of reference, so-called coreference, simplifies deictic reference, the ability to point to objects by gesturing and the use of the words *this* or *that* as references. There is also substantial individual control, with participants able to readily focus discussions. Most of these characteristics derive from the shared spatiality that embeds both the individuals, work products, and artifacts in a single space. Each of these features of a collocated workspace has certain positive implications for collaboration. For example, the rapid real-time feedback makes it easy to nip misunderstandings and errors in the bud. The instant personal identification of sources makes it easier to evaluate information in the context of its source. The availability of spontaneous, unplanned interactions that are less likely to occur in a computer-supported context permits opportunistic exchange of information, as well as facilitates individual and group cohesion (Olson and Olson, 2000). This is not to imply that face-to-face interactions always represent a "gold standard" for interactions (Olson and Olson, 2000), since remote collaborations may sometimes be more suitable. For example, a variety of factors from safety to cost may require a remote approach, and distance from the immediate work environment may lend a perspective that cannot be achieved locally. Obviously in the case of open source development, remote access greatly expands the pool of potential participants. In fact, this is exactly why open collaboration increased so dramatically subsequent to the expansion of access to the Internet. It also opens new opportunities for collaboration since it makes it easier to find out what other developers in other parts of the world are working on, communicate with them, and gain access to their work artifacts. Collocated work is certainly not excluded for open development. In fact, companies like IBM and Red Hat have made increasing use of collocated open source development (Feller and Fitzgerald, 2002). Such an approach combines the advantages of distributed collaboration with the many fundamental advantages we have described for face-to-face interaction.

Many factors are involved in facilitating collaboration. The most fundamental factor, called common ground, refers to the primitive environmental factors that make it possible to establish a shared collaborative experience (Olson and Olson, 2000). Common ground characteristics include factors that enhance cueing, such as the copresence of participants, the visibility of participants to each other, audibility, cotemporality (which allows immediate reception of communications or messages), simultaneity (which allows all participants to send and/or receive messages simultaneously), and sequentiality (which ensures that speaker and communicator items cannot get out of order). The richer the interaction environment or medium, the more cues it supports for establishing a commonly recognized, shared understanding. Copresence, for example, entails all the advantages that come with convenient deictic reference. If we take an extended notion of what constitutes common ground, then the Internet can be considered as creating a virtual, albeit partial, facsimile of actual spatial common ground, supported by mechanisms like CVS that emulate some of the attributes of common ground (generalized copresence, generalized visibility, generalized audibility, cotemporality, and simultaneity). Of course, it is not an ideal common ground, but then again it creates a whole universe of community that did not even exist before.

Characteristics that enhance the quality of communications are also relevant to common ground and they can be strongly affected by temporal factors. These include revisability of messages (which means messages can be revised by the sender before their final transmission) and reviewability of messages (which means messages from others can be reviewed after receipt) (Olson and Olson, 2000). The temporal differences between face-to-face and distributed interactions affect both these characteristics. Indeed, one striking difference between copresent and computer-supported interactions is the acceptability of a delay in response (Adrianson and Hjelmquist, 1991). In fact, one reason why reviewability and revisability are limited in a face-to-face environment is that it is awkward or unacceptable to have significant delays between the turns of face-to-face speakers. In contrast, computerized interactions rely primarily on the production and perception of textual messages. These can be composed without the need for the relatively instantaneous generation of verbal content required in a face-to-face environment. Furthermore, these messages can be planned, rewritten, and edited by the sender, and read, reread, and thought about by the receiver after reception. Given that we are considering computer-supported versus face-to-face interactions, we might note that there are relative differences between the speeds of entering keyboard data and reading text versus speaking and listening, though these are not likely to be significant for our present purposes. As McGrath and Hollingshead (1994) observe, "Most people can talk much faster than even very skilled typists can type," but "most people can read faster than they can listen" (p. 19). In other words, spoken output in face-to-face communication is faster than keyboard output in computer-supported environments, but computer-supported input via reading is faster than face-to-face input by listening.

A fundamental temporal characteristic that differentiates between interaction environments is whether they are synchronous or asynchronous. Face-to-face communications are synchronous by nature, while computer communications can be synchronous or asynchronous. These different modes lead to different patterns of communication. Synchronous communications are strongly constrained by temporal constraints that tend to limit the length of communications, while asynchronous communication tends to encourage lengthier messages and possibly more simultaneous discussion topics (McGrath and Hollingshead, 1994). Collaboration in open source is mainly asynchronous, with an emphasis on media like e-mail, mailing lists, Web sites, and forums as opposed to synchronous mechanisms, though tools like IRC have also played a role. Feller and Fitzgerald (2002) remark on the important self-documenting advantage of asynchronous tools, as well as their compatibility with a globally distributed environment that is spread across multiple time zones.

The significant role played by visual factors in face-to-face group exchanges is underscored by Olson and Olson (2000). These cues may eventually become more widely available when video support in computer communications becomes more prevalent. However, current environments are limited in these respects and so are extraordinarily sparse from the viewpoint of typical human exchanges. This sparseness can be a breeding ground for all sorts of misunderstandings and ambiguities. Although it is possible to create substitutes for some of these factors in a computer-supported environment, it is worthwhile to be aware of the deeply textured, instinctive, and transparent support for visual factors that are automatically provided in face-to-face communication.

The absence of some of these common ground characteristics in computer-supported environments is the basis of some amusing stories about Internet anonymity and identity that CVS/Subversion guru Karl Fogel tells. One telling tale is told by free software developer Jim Blandy about a bug reporter who regularly submitted exceptionally clear bug reports to the project when Blandy was working on GNU Emacs. At a certain point some required copyright paperwork had to be sent to the individual by the FSF for legal purposes. As it happened, the paperwork was sent back incomplete, without an indication of the person's employer. After a few further interactions, it turned out that the conspicuously capable participant was a 13-year old living at home with his parents (Fogel, 2005). But that identity was not evident on the Internet where it was the person's work and writing that spoke for him. In a similar anonymous vein, Fogel alludes to a New Yorker cartoon by Paul Steiner that depicts a dog at a computer terminal slyly confiding to another dog: "On the Internet no one knows you're a dog." Perhaps videoconferencing would have betrayed the canine! On a more serious note, Fogel (2005) observes that open source Internet-based collaboration is "psychologically odd because it involves tight cooperation between human beings who almost never get to identify each other by the most natural, intuitive methods: facial recognition first of all, but also sound of voice, posture, etc." (Fogel, 2005, p. 89). As an admittedly limited surrogate for an "online face," he recommends using a "consistent screen name." The appellation should be used for everything from e-mail to your repository committer name. It should be intuitively related to your real name rather than a make-believe moniker. Even if you use a pseudonym for purposes of anonymity, it too should have the same kind of realistic characteristics.

Coupling, Incentives, and Technological Readiness
There are other decisive conditions that affect the ability to collaborate. These include the degree to which work is tightly coupled, the desire of the participants to collaborate, and the technological preparedness of a group to work in a distributed environment. We briefly discuss each of these factors.

The concept of coupling is widely used in software engineering to refer to the extent to which separate software modules are interlinked. In cooperative work, coupling is determined by both the characteristics of the task and the abilities needed for the individuals to implement the task. If a task requires close, timely interactions between diverse group members who work on the task, then the task is said to be tightly coupled. Tight coupling requires rapid, frequent communications, particularly for ambiguity resolution or repair. A tasklike design is typically tightly coupled, while a tasklike coauthoring is only moderately coupled (Galegher and Kraut, 1992). Tightly coupled tasks are hard to implement using computer-supported distributed collaboration (Olson and Olson, 2000). On the other hand, remote implementation may be feasible if the component tasks of a project are packaged appropriately. The design of the Linux kernel is a textbook example of designing an operating system so that it can be developed in a distributed manner by many participants working parallelly and independently (Torvalds, 1999). Design can also be simplified, as it is often in open source, if there is a well-known shared application being imitated in taillight fashion and whose availability therefore moots much of the design issue in the first place.

The willingness of participants to collaborate in the first place is tied to the incentive structure of the work defined as the system of rewards that encourage performance of an activity. Collaboratively sharing and seeking information from or with others requires an appropriate organizational incentive structure. As an example of an incentive structure hostile to collaboration (remotely or locally) consider one that awards participants based on individual claims to ownership of ideas. In such a context, a collaborative environment that clouds ownership may be perceived as contrary to an individual's benefit (Olson and Olson, 2000). Thus, for successful collaboration to occur, the organizational culture must value and promote sharing. Existing patterns of interaction in an organization should also reflect a collaborative attitude, like being aware of other's information requirements and making one's own information available if it is thought to be relevant to others. The open source movement certainly promotes sharing so that incentive is present. It also allows reputation building, which as we have seen may be a surrogate for career mobility, another incentive. While GPL'd content is copyrighted in the name of its owner/originator, the license allows modifications to be copyrighted by the contributor of the modification, which is certainly an incentive. On the other hand, open GPL'd projects like MySQL that are dual licensed may have a policy of meticulously reimplementing code contributions from volunteers, precisely so that the ownership of the original and now extended copyrighted product is not clouded or diluted.

In addition to an organization having the appropriate collaborative culture, it also needs to be at the correct stage of technological readiness to be a good candidate for successful distance collaboration (Olson and Olson, 2000). Historically, the technologies underpinning collaboration were adopted by organizations in the following order: telephone, fax, e-mail, telephone audioconferencing, voice mail, e-mail with attachments, videoconferencing, Web sites of static information, shared calendars, and so on. We have mentioned elsewhere the enabling developments in technology, from FTP to the widespread dispersion of the Internet, to the creation of versioning systems like CVS, which were preconditions for the kind of open source environment we see today. These represented the technological readiness conditions for the entire paradigm. The impact of technological characteristics on distributed open collaboration, as opposed to traditional face-to-face collaboration, is examined in empirical studies of the open source FreeBSD and GNU GCC projects by Yutaka Yamauchi et al. (2000). One of the conclusions of the study is that the conventional model of precoordinated work is inapplicable in these projects. The project work tends to be coordinated after the fact, using mechanisms like e-mail, CVS, and to-do lists to provide an appropriate balance between the spontaneous, independent work contributions of individuals and the centralized control.

5.9.2 Conversational Interactions

Any kind of communication, whether computer supported or proximate, requires extensive coordination between speakers (senders) and listeners (receivers) (Whittaker and O'Conaill, 1997). In the first place, there must be coordinating processes for initiating and terminating entire conversations (called availability), as well as processes for coordinating how speakers and listeners alternate turns during an initiated conversation (turn taking). In addition to process coordination, conversations also require content coordination, which refers to the way in which the participants in the conversation establish a shared understanding. Even something as apparently simple as turn taking in proximate spoken communication is remarkably subtle. For example, collisions, which occur when speakers overlap, happen only 5% of the time, so for 95% of the time only a single person is speaking. Despite this extensive mutual exclusion, the delays between turns in spoken communications often occur at the millisecond level! The turn-taking process determines how these transitions are negotiated. Availability refers to the initiation of entire conversations. Potential participants must identify when partners are available to converse and also recognize whether the moment is opportune to initiate a conversation. These processes require awareness and alertness on the part of participants to cues that signal turn taking and availability, including understanding the social protocols that reflect readiness to begin a conversational process or to switch turns between speaker and listener. A simple relationship here is to the CVS update command or the repository conflicts identified after commits. These are different from one another but both are related to potential collisions in changes made on a particular file. The CVS system does not preclude these collisions but does at least notify the developer affected that a collision has occurred and exactly what the nature of the resulting potential confusions is. The developers involved are not really having an explicit conversation, but it is nonetheless like a dialog mediated through the repository.

The role of nonverbal cues in face-to-face conversational exchanges is well known. Argyle (1969) classified nonverbal cues into mutual attention (evidence of attention by the other), channel control (nods and looks that negotiate turn taking), feedback (to track agreement), illustrations (gestures for deixis or emphasis), emblems (like a head shake to indicate "no"), and cues that reflect interpersonal attitude (like facial expression, proximity, gaze, etc.). Such nonverbal cues "are always combined with other cues and usually with a verbal message" (p. 63), and in their absence, the participants will modify or adapt their actions to attempt to accommodate the deficit. For example, a click on a downloaded copy of a program's license agreement may be the gesture that confirms or assents to the contractual text of a license. The click that down-loaded the product in the first place is a conceptually separate artifact and has no licensing implications. In a sense this is a primitive conversational exchange with verbal and nonverbal elements, though in this case it is the underlying legal content that represents the substance of the interaction. On the other hand, for the GPL it is the very act of modifying or distributing the software that connotes assent to the license agreement rather than explicit acts of agreement like clicks (Fitzgerald and Bassett, 2003).

Establishing a shared understanding is far more complex than simply navi-gating a conversation. For one thing the literally expressed meaning of a com-munication underspecifies what the speaker fully intends. What is unspoken has to be inferred by the listener from the discussion context, prior understandings, and contextual environmental cues in the physical environment. Some of this inferred understanding can be gathered from the preposited shared source rep-resented by common ground. For example, common ground facilitates deictic reference, which lets participants easily identify artifacts in the environment. As part of establishing shared understanding, conversations require a feedback loop so that speakers can confirm that listeners have correctly understood the intent of their communications.

Human conversation, face-to-face or computer-supported, can be viewed as a series of interlocked communication cycles, each cycle involving a "series of operations on a given message: composition, editing, transmission, recep-tion, feedback (acknowledgment of receipt), and reply," the time to complete the cycle depending on the communication media (McGrath and Hollingshead, 1994, p. 8). Much of the information used to support conversations is based on visual cues automatically available in face-to-face environments, includ-ing communicative cues about other participants in the interaction and cues about the shared environment itself. Communicative cues include gaze, facial expression, gestures, and posture. Communicative processes like turn taking may depend on information from multiple channels, such as gaze, gesture, and posture. Each of these cues in turn is complex. For example, gaze information depends on where a person looks, how long he looks, and the manner in which he looks. When a listener gazes at a speaker, the listener picks up important visual cues that clarify the content of the speaker's words. When a speaker gazes at a listener(s), this supplies critical feedback as to whether the speaker is being understood and, if not, the speaker can adjust or clarify the message accordingly until cues indicating understanding manifest.

Significantly, nonverbal signaling can proceed concurrently with verbal com-munication without interrupting the verbal communication (Short et al., 1976). The effects are subtle in terms of their impact on the conversational process.

For example, a "negotiated mutual gaze" (Whittaker and O'Conaill, 1997, p. 29) between speaker and listener signals that the speaker is yielding the turn to the listener. Or, the speaker can gaze at the listener to prompt attention on the listener's part. A gaze can be modulated to indicate the speaker's affective attitude to the listeners or the affective content of what the speaker is saying: trustworthy, sincere, skeptical, amicable, and so on. The characteristics of a person's gaze behavior are also revealing. For example, an individual who looks at his conversational partner only a small part of the time will tend to be evaluated as evasive, while a person with the opposite behavior may be interpreted as friendly or sincere. Facial expressions are an even richer source of communicative information and feedback than gaze. They range from head-nod frequency to cross-cultural expressions of affect. A glance is another useful visual behavior that can allow a participant to determine whether another person is available for conversation, or not present, or engaged in another activity or conversation. Glances also serve as useful "prompts to the identity of a potential participant" (Daly-Jones et al., 1998, p. 34).

Conversational dialog is a prototypical interaction and so it is useful to understand the structure of such dialogs. Models of discourse like the conversation analysis of Sacks et al. (1974) and the interactionist model of Clark and Schaeffer (1989) have been used to analyze the structure of conversations. The Sacks model takes a regulatory view of dialog, emphasizing the role of turn taking in discussions and factors like how often the speakers in a conversation overlap, the length of gaps between speakers, the lengths of individual turns, interruptions, and breakdowns in the dialog. It tends to interpret breakdowns in conversational flow as failures of communication and a smooth flow of turn taking as indicating conversational success. The alternative interactionist model interprets the underlying issue in a dialog as attaining a shared understanding, not about regulating turn taking. This approach interprets interruptions and overlaps in speech not as disruptions of a normative smooth sequence of turns, but as necessary to produce a common ground of shared understanding, which is the real objective of the dialog.

Human interactions have multiple components, including making contact in the first place, turn-taking disciplines, attention monitoring, comprehension feedback, and various kinds of deixis to objects or persons (Whittaker and O'Conaill, 1997). Each of these components can be supported by auditory or visual cues. Both parties can use auditory or visual signals. Visual signals appear to be more important when larger the number of participants. Turn taking can use either visual or auditory cues, the latter including affects like vocal changes in pitch, which serve as turn regulators. Beyond the issue of attention, there is also the question of agreement. Visual cues like "postural congruence or mirror imaging of body orientation may signal similarity of views" (Whittaker and O'Conaill, 1997, p. 25) but explicit auditory verifications of interpretations may be required in addition to the visual cues. So-called back-channel cues are also used to implement reciprocity. These include auditory references like "OK" and visual back-channel cues like nods. Both auditory and visual deixis provide important support for collaboration because they facilitate reference to "the artifacts used in cooperative tasks (which) support distributed cognition in that they allow people to externalize their thought processes so that they can be shared by others" (p. 26). Shared artifacts can play an important role in mediating and coordinating negotiations. Increased conversational interaction aids understanding more than mere listening. The putative explanation for this effect is that "conversation involves participants trying to establish the mutual belief that the listener has understood what the speaker meant . . . a collaborative process called grounding" (Grayson and Conventry, 1998, p. 37). This mutual view of conversational understanding contrasts with the autonomous view of understanding according to which "merely hearing and seeing all that happens and having the same background knowledge is sufficient to understanding fully" (Grayson and Conventry, 1998, p. 37).

5.9.3 Social Cues

Social context cues are generally attenuated in computer-supported systems. For example, the detailed real-time feedback that face-to-face interactions provide allows remarks that are recognized as offensive, on the basis of social cues after being spoken, to be quickly retracted on the grounds they were actually misinterpreted or unintended. This is less feasible in a computer-supported environment because the subtle cues signaling offense are less available. Sproul and Kiesler (1986) claimed that the diminution of such cues tends to result in behavior that is "more extreme, more impulsive, and less socially differentiated" (p. 1496) than in a face-to-face context, with negative behaviors exhibited ranging from flaming to decreased inhibition about delivering negative information. They explain this behavior as resulting from reduced static and dynamic social cues. Static social cues refer to artifacts symbolizing status, like an overwhelming entrance lobby to a corporate building that is intended to connote the status and power of the enterprise. Dynamic social cues refer to body expressions like nods of approval or frowns. Adrianson and Hjelmquist (1991) note there are some benefits to nonrich computer-supported environments. The absence in computer-supported systems of nonverbal signals, like the signals available in face-to-face communications for conveying attitudes and feelings and "regulating interaction" (p. 282), helps explain the more egalitarian communication that appears to occur in such systems. This is partly because the attitudes whose signals are absent include those used to convey status or dominance. The communication of these attitudes depends significantly on face-to-face effects like "gaze, posture, position, gestures," and so on (p. 282).

Fewer social cues may also lead "to psychological distance, psychological distance leads to task-oriented and depersonalized content, and task-oriented depersonalized content leads in turn to a deliberate, un-spontaneous style," according to Spears and Lea (1992, p. 34), while conversely a richer, face-to-face environment makes interpersonal factors more salient. The limited range of social cues in computer-supported groups is often used to explain antisocial behaviors like decreased inhibition and the benchmark behavior of group polarization. Group polarization refers to the "tendency for the (average) attitudes or decisions of individuals to become more extreme, in the direction of the already preferred pole of a given scale, as a result of discussion within a group" (p. 37). This disturbing phenomenon is one of the most well-established characteristics of group behavior. There are different explanations for why it happens. Spears and Lea claim that computer-supported communications exacerbate group polarization because they "undermine the social and normative influences on individuals or groups, leading to a more deregulated and extreme (anti-normative) behavior" (p. 37). The usual explanation for group polarization had been different. It claimed that the egalitarian, uninhibited behavior of computer-supported groups increases the number of so-called "persuasive arguments," reenforcing the general direction of group opinion. The fact that there are a reduced number of social cues in the environment then leads to more extensive exchanges of arguments and progressively more extreme arguments. Factors like deindividuation and depersonalization come into play. In social psychology, deindividuation refers to "the loss of identity and weakening of social norms and constraints associated with submergence in a group or crowd" (p. 38). It is encouraged by the anonymity and reduced feedback typical of computer-supported environments which in turn provoke more asocial behavior. Depersonalization also occurs in these groups because the decreased number of social cues redirects the attention of participants to the objective task and away from the social context. These two psychological effects combine to allegedly make the group less interpersonally oriented and more information-oriented. The group is then more affected by the impact of "persuasive arguments," with the resulting tendency toward group polarization. In contrast to this conventional social–psychological explanation for group polarization, Spears and Lea explain polarization as a consequence of the fact that people are more likely to be affected by group influence "under de-individuating conditions because the visual anonymity (provided by computer-supported environments) will further reduce perceived intra-group differences, thereby *increasing the salience of the group*" (p. 47, italics added). According to this explanation, group polarization is not a manifestation of the socially barren computer-supported environments but merely reflects the convergence of the group on an extreme group norm. These are interesting but complicated analyses for why behavior like group polarization occurs, but the basic point is that group polarization is an empirically recognized phenomenon.

5.9.4 Information Richness

Information richness refers to the information-carrying capacity of a medium. In an analysis written before the widespread use of e-mail and the Web, Daft and Lengel (1984) rated face-to-face contact at the high end of information richness, followed by telephone communication (rated high), personal memos and letters (rated moderate), and formal written documents (rated low). Since the exchange of information represents the most basic level of functionality in a group collaboration, it is worth understanding what kinds of information tend to be used by whom and how. For example, managers differed from nonmanagerial workers in the kinds of information they use. They rated face-to-face communication highest because of its immediate feedback capabilities, multiple cues, natural language use, auditory, and visual character. In contrast, traditional textual communications suffered from slow feedback and no audiovisual cues, though e-mail would of course be radically different in respect to the potential rate of feedback, which could be both almost instantaneous and pervasively available. Managers reacted to media characteristics based on their need to "make sense of ill-defined, complex problems about which they may have little or unclear information." Consequently, they tended to use rich media when addressing the "unpredictable human dimensions of organizations." Because of their more rapid feedback characteristics and multiplicity of cues, information-rich media, such as face-to-face contact, let managers "communicate about and make sense of these processes" more effectively.

The preference of managers for face-to-face interactions is informed by the importance of intangible social and emotional factors in these communications and the managerial significance of the "poorly understood aspects of the organization" (Daft and Lengel, 1984, p. 201). For a manager, "rich media" is a broad category, including everything from site visits, breakfast meetings, and special tours for personal contact, to phone calls for informal, personal communications. According to Mintzberg (1973), managers (at that time) spent over 80% of their day on communicating but made only modest use of formal communications, extensively relying instead on internal and external contacts, gossip, rumor, and so on. Although that study is a dated one, it seems plausible that the technologies available have not radically altered the types of information sought. Leaner media in contrast may "oversimplify complex topics and may not enable the exchange of sufficient information to alter a manager's understanding," though they provide sufficient information for more routine problems (Daft and Lengel, 1984, p. 192). Although this analysis was done before e-mail became commonplace (e-mail is not one of the written forms considered), it still resonates.

A preference for rich information sources increases with the uncertainty and complexity of a problem, while less rich sources of information are perceived as suitable for more routine matters. A medium is considered more information rich, the more rapidly it allows users to disambiguate lack of clarity (Lee, 1994). Information richness reflects how effective a medium is for producing timely shared understanding and for its capacity to support learning. This is relevant to managerial concerns like equivocality, defined as uncertainty about the meaning of information because the information can be viewed from more than one perspective. Face-to-face communication provides many cues to reduce equivocality. Uncertainty or lack of information about a situation can be reduced by obtaining additional information, but equivocality is unaffected by further information and only resolved or clarified through a negotiating discussion that is used to converge on a consensus interpretation that minimizes equivocality (Hohmann, 1997). Such a process of negotiation is highly social and interpersonal. According to Kraut et al. (1990), high equivocality leads decision makers into a fundamentally social interaction because they are essentially involved in a process of "generating shared interpretations of the problem, and enacting solutions based on those interpretations" (p. 7). This research even claims that "organizations reduce equivocality through the use of sequentially less rich media down through the hierarchy" (p. 212). Such a conclusion would be consistent with the notion that nonrich, computer-supported communications are better suited for reducing uncertainty or lack of information, as opposed to reducing equivocality or the existence of multiple interpretations of information. The reliance of open source development on lean as opposed to rich information sources in the sense just described may be related to the commonly expressed concerns about the limited ability of open development to thoroughly understand user needs (Messerschmitt, 2004).

References

Adrianson, D. and Hjelmquist, E. (1991). Group Process in Face-to-Face Computer Mediated Communication. *Behavior and Information Technology*, 10, 281–296.
Argyle, M. (1969). *Social Interaction*. Methuen, London.

Clark, H. H. and Schaeffer, E. (1989). Contributing to Discourse. Cognitive Science, 13, 259–294.

Daft, R. and Lengel, R. (1984). Information Richness: A New Approach to Managerial Behavior and Organizational Design. In: Research on Organizational Behavior, vol. 6, L. Cummings and B. Staw (editors). JAI Press, Homewood, IL.

Daly-Jones, O., Monk, A., and Watts, L. (1998). Some Advantages of Video Conferencing over High-Quality Audio Conferencing: Fluency and Awareness of Attentional Focus. International Journal of Human–Computer Studies, 49, 21–58.

Feller, J. and Fitzgerald, B. (2002). Understanding Open Source Software Development. Addison-Wesley, Pearson Education Ltd., London.

Fitzgerald, B. and Bassett, G. (2003). Legal Issues Relating to Free and Open Software. In: Essays in Technology Policy and Law, vol. 1, B. Fitzgerald and G. Bassett (editors). Queensland University of Technology, School of Law, Brisbane, Australia., Chapter 2.

Fogel, K. (2005). Producing Open Source Software: How to Run a Successful Free Software Project. O'Reilly Media, Sebastopol, CA.

Galegher, J. and Kraut, R. E. (1992). Computer-Mediated Communication and Collaborative Writing: Media Influence and Adaptation to Communication Constraints. CSCW, New York, 155–162.

Grayson, D. and Coventry, L. (1998). The Effects of Visual Proxemic Information in Video Mediated Communication. SIGCHI Bulletin, 30(3), 30–39.

Hohmann, L. (1997). Journey of the Software Professional. Prentice Hall, New Jersey.

Kraut, R. E., Egido, C., and Galegher, J. (1990). Patterns of Contact and Communication in Scientific Research Collaborations. In: Intellectual Teamwork: Social and Technological Foundations of Cooperative Work. Lawrence Erlbaum, Hillsdale, NJ, 149–171.

Lee, A. S. (1994). Electronic Mail as a Medium for Rich Communication: An Empirical Investigation Using Hermeneutic Interpretation. MIS Quarterly, 18, 143–174.

McGrath, J. E. and Hollingshead, A. B. (1994). Groups Interacting with Technology. Sage Pub, Newbury Park, CA.

Messerschmitt, D. (2004). Back to the User. IEEE Software, 21(1), 89–91.

Mintzberg, H. (1973). The Nature of Managerial Work. Harper and Row, New York.

Nunamaker, J. F. (1999). Collaborative Computing: The Next Millennium. Computer, 32(9), 66–71.

Olson, G. and Olson, J. (2000). Distance Matters. Human–Computer Interactions, 15, 139–178.

Sacks, H., Schegloff, E. A., and Jefferson, G. A. (1974). A Simplest Systematics for the Organization of Turn-Taking in Conversation. Language, 50, 696–735.

Short, J., Williams, E., and Christie, B. (1976). The Social Psychology of Telecommunications. Wiley, London.

Spears, R. and Lea, M. (1992). Social Influences and Influence of the "Social" in Computer-Mediated Communication. In: Contexts of Computer Mediated Communication, M. Lea (editor). Harvester Wheatsheaf, London, Chapter 2, 30–65.

Sproul, L. and Kiesler, S. (1986). Reducing Social Context Cues: Electronic Mail in Organizational Communication. Management Science, 32, 1492–1512.

Torvalds, L. (1999). The Linux edge. Communications of the ACM, 42(4), 38–39.

Yamauchi, Y., Yokozawa, M., Shinohara, T., and Ishida, T. (2000). Collaboration with Lean Media: How Open-Source Software Succeeds. In: Proceedings of Computer Supported Cooperative Work Conference (CSCW '00). ACM, New York, 329–338.

Whittaker, S. and O'Conaill, B. (1997). The Role of Vision in Face-to-Face and Mediated Communication. In: Video-Mediated Communication, K. Finn, A. Sellen, and S. Wilbur (editors). Lawrence Erlbaum Associates, Mahwah, NJ, Chapter 2, 23–49.

6

Legal Issues in Open Source

Much of the impetus for the free and open software movement arose as a reaction to legal issues related to software licensing. Consequently, questions concerning what is commonly called intellectual property have been a habitual feature of the open source landscape. Intellectual property includes creations like copyrighted works, patented inventions, and proprietary software. The purpose of this chapter is to survey some of the relevant legal issues in this domain in an accessible manner informative for understanding their relevance to free and open development. The legal and business mechanisms that have been developed to protect intellectual property are intended to address the core objective of protecting creations in order to provide appropriate incentives for innovators. Traditionally, such protection has been accomplished through exclusion. For example, under copyright law, one is not allowed to distribute a copyrighted work without the authorization of the owner of the copyright. The General Public License (GPL) that lies at the heart of the free software movement takes an unconventional perspective on the use of copyright. It focuses not on how to exclude others from using your work, but on how to preserve the free and open distribution of your work when you do allow others to modify and redistribute it (Weber, 2004). We will consider the basic legal concepts associated with intellectual property and how they have been brought to bear in the open source movement. We describe the characteristics of the flagship free software license (the GPL) and various other open and proprietary licenses, particularly the so-called OSI-certified licenses sanctioned by the Open Source Initiative (OSI). We address the basic concepts of copyright, derivative works, public domain, patents, software patents, contracts, and licenses. We also touch on related matters like trade secrets, nondisclosure agreements, trademarks, reverse engineering, the novel concept of copyleft, enforcement issues, the next version of the GPL (GPLv3), and the nature of derivative works of software. Our primary frame of reference is the U.S. legal system, so caution must be exercised when interpreting the concepts examined here in a global context. There are important international differences especially in the area of software patents, as well as in copyright enforcement, contract, and the acceptability of techniques like reverse engineering, which we address only briefly.

Disclaimer: The discussion in this chapter should not be considered legal advice. It is an overview by nonlawyers of legal and licensing issues pervasive in the free software movement and a discussion of relevant historical context. It is not intended to replace competent legal counsel for which you must consult a lawyer.

6.1 Copyrights

A *copyright* gives the creator of a work the *exclusive* right to

1. make a copy of the work,
2. distribute copies of the work for sale or for free,
3. disclose or display the work publicly, and
4. create so-called derivative works that are derived from the original product.

The protection of such intellectual property was considered so fundamental in U.S. history that it was included under the powers granted to Congress as the so-called "Patent and Copyright Clause" in the U.S. Constitution; namely, that the Congress had the power and obligation "To promote the Progress of Science and useful Arts, by securing for limited Times to Authors and Inventors the exclusive Right to their respective Writings and Discoveries" (Article 1: The Legislative Branch, Section 8: Powers of Congress, of the U.S. Constitution). Over time, progress in technology led Congress to update the laws on intellectual protection on multiple occasions. Software was explicitly defined and added to this protection in 1980. The Digital Millennium Act in 1998 made some further refinements and extended copyright protection to 70 years after the death of the author. Copyrights can be applied to software products, including both programs and data files like images.

The protection provided by copyright starts automatically as soon as a work is fixed in *tangible* form. The notion of tangibility is treated in a broad and forward-looking way in the law. Thus the Copyright Act of 1976 defined it as referring to works "fixed in any tangible medium of expression, now known or later developed, from which they can be perceived, reproduced, or otherwise communicated, either directly or with the aid of a machine or device," making the meaning of "tangible" technologically invariant! You can establish proof of the starting date of the copyright by dating the product in a manner that guarantees the authenticity of the date. According to the Berne Convention for the Protection of Literary and Artistic Works (which is followed by most nations), a copyright generally lasts for a minimum of 95 years after the death of the author, rather than from the date of the original copyright. Under U.S. law copyrights for new works last for the author's life plus 70 years, or, for works made for hire, 95 years from publication or 120 years from creation, whichever is shorter, after which the work passes into the public domain. The fact that copyrights have been largely internationally harmonized under the Berne Convention is important because it makes their application more uniform than contract law, which is more subject to local or national vagaries (Fitzgerald and Bassett, 2003).

A notice of copyright on a product has the form Copyright @ 2006 Don Knuth, indicating the beginning date (year) of the copyright and the copyright *owner* (or owners). Although the notice of copyright is not required, it is very important in infringement suits because it eliminates the defense of unintentional infringement. In the United States a copyright may be registered with the Library of Congress (refer to www.copyright.gov for the process). Although under international law, registration is not a condition of copyright protection, registration does serve as a substantial proof of authorship in the event of an infringement suit. Furthermore, "registration *is* required to initiate litigation to enforce the copyright" and "early registration provides added protection in the form of statutory damages and attorney's fees if litigation becomes necessary" (Rosen, 2005, p. 18). There is a requirement for what is called *mandatory deposit* under which "copies of all works under copyright protection that have been published or distributed in the United States must be deposited with the Copyright office within 3 months of the date of first publication" (www.copyright.gov), though failure to do so does not result in a loss of copyright protection. The copyright owner has the right to sell his copyright or transfer it to another. A distinction, especially noteworthy in the case of software production, is that the author of the work is not necessarily synonymous with the owner of the copyright. If the work is done as part of the author's employment, the owner of the default copyright is the author's employer, not the author. This is also the case for works that are done "for hire" for another party. Interestingly, copyrights in works not done for hire that have been transferred appear to revert to the original owner after a 35-year period, under certain conditions.

Copyright protects only the tangible implementation or expression of an idea, *not* the idea itself. Thus it is not a violation of copyright to produce a similar product that is inspired by the overall look and contents of an original copyrighted product, subject to the criterion of *substantial similarity*, as discussed later. This aspect of copyright is particularly relevant to open source development, a fair amount of which has been based on implementing open source systems that mimic the appearance and functionality of proprietary systems. A work formed by collecting together previously or separately copyrighted works whose copyrights are still preserved in the collection is called a *compilation*. For example, in the case of a software system consisting of copyrighted components, the system would include permissions from the copyright owners of its components. The need for an appropriate paper trail to substantiate the legal pedigree of open source code is increasingly recognized as essential. The Free Software Foundation (FSF) has actually long required that "each author of code incorporated in FSF projects provide a copyright assignment," which is the only way the FSF believes it can ensure the code is and remains free (http://www.gnu.org/licenses/why-assign.html). On the other hand, the Linux project until 2004 did not require contributors to assign their copyrights over to Linus Torvalds or even to confirm that they were the copyright owner of their contributions. Each individual contributor maintained his copyright, like in a compilation. Post-2004, Linux contributors had to state that they owned the contributions they were making, though they do not have to assign their copyright. In a related vein, Brian Behlendorf of Apache observes that while the Apache project did not require contributors to sign a copyright assignment, they had always used a contributor license agreement that gives Apache the right to distribute the code under any license it desired (Andersen, 2004).

Infringement and Derivative Works

The violation of a copyright condition is called a copyright *infringement*. A form of copyright infringement, in the case of software, is redistributing multiple copies of a copyrighted software product, whether for free or for sale, a practice called *software piracy*. Even making additional copies for personal use, unless as authorized by a software license agreement, is an infringement since the copyright owner is the only one who has the right to make copies. Whether the owner sells or gives away the software for free, he still retains the original "copyrights," except insofar as they are transferred to the user via a licensing agreement or assignment. In the case of derivative works (to be defined shortly), a key legal test for the existence of a copyright infringement is based on *substantial similarity* between an allegedly infringing work and the copyrighted work. Two works are said to be substantially similar if a lay observer would recognize the infringing work as at least partly copied from the original copyrighted work (Jassin and Schecter, 1997). Copyright infringement whether intentional or not is subject to civil and criminal liability. The copyright owner can sue in the case of infringement for actual financial losses. Alternatively, the law also allows a plaintiff to sue for so-called *statutory damages*, which are damages specified under law or statute, to a maximum of $150,000 per infringement, even in the absence of demonstration of actual loss for so-called willful infringements. A striking example of the financial implications of copyright infringement is demonstrated by the MP3.com case, where plaintiffs were awarded $25,000 per uploaded CD for a total of over $100 million dollars (Landau, 2000). Such damages can even apply for what might appear to be minor copyright infringements. A court can also issue an injunction against continued infringement.

The U.S. Copyright Act defines a *derivative work* as a work that is based on a previously copyrighted work, but this law does not address the case of derivatives of software works (Webbink, 2003). An ordinary copyright *preserves* to its owner the copyright for any derivative works based on the copyrighted work, but for software the definition of what constitutes a derivative work is sometimes tendentious. For example, simple translation of a copyrighted work into another language, such as another programming language, is prohibited by the Berne Convention without the permission of the original copyright owner. Generally, a software product is considered as derivative if it contains original, modified, or translated source code from an original program. But it is not considered as derivative if it merely links to a preexisting copyrighted program library or plugs into a copyrighted program designed to accept plugins, absent indications of intent, such as "whether the resulting program is being sold as an enhanced version of the original" (Rosen, 2003), though the legal issues do not appear to be settled. A key legal test is whether the work is *substantially similar* to the original in its "total concept and feel" (see Fitzgerald and Bassett, 2003; Fishman, 2004a). Refer to the work by Fishman (2004b) for a treatment of copyright in open source. To get a sense of what might or might not constitute substantial similarity, consider a case referred to by Fitzgerald and Bassett (2003). They describe a challenge to the legal status of an improved computer game where the difference was that the game characters could move faster and could float. The court decided that the modification did not constitute an infringement of the original game's copyright.

Fair Use

Copyrighted materials are generally subject to what is called a fair use provision. *Fair use* refers to the copying and use of limited parts of a copyrighted work for a limited period of time, under the assumption of proper attribution of the owner of the copyright, for such purposes as education and research, but without requiring the explicit permission of the copyright holder. Such use does not constitute copyright infringement and is explicitly allowed by the U.S. Copyright Act. However, there are strict guidelines on how much of a work may be copied.

A key consideration in the application of fair use is the question of damage to any commercial value of the product. However, in the case of software, fair use in the traditional sense becomes immediately problematic since the program's useful functionality requires copying the entire code, which is contrary to fair use restrictions even in the case of educational use.

Public Domain

Software or other creative works that are not under copyright protection are said to be in the *public domain*. Anyone can copy, modify, redistribute, or sell such a work as if it were his own. Previously copyrighted works become public domain when their copyright expires. Works created by government employees are automatically in the public domain. The original owner of a copyrighted work can allow his work to enter the public domain by relinquishing the copyright, though this appears to be rarely done and the mechanisms for doing it also appear unclear. The Judicial Improvement Act of 1990 provides some mechanism related to the Library of Congress that allows the owner of software copyrights to donate his software to the public domain (Samuels, 1993). Once a work enters the public domain, it remains public. However, derivative works based on a public domain work are automatically the property of their author. This also applies to modified versions of public domain software. An interesting case is Don Knuth's TeX system, which he has repeatedly indicated should be considered as public domain, though the TeX name is registered as a trademark, so versions that others produce cannot be called TeX. Knuth has also stated that the version of TeX extant at his death will be "forever left unchanged" for the reason that he believes an unchanging permanent system "has great value" (Knuth, 1990, p. 145). In contrast, the LaTeX language for TeX is free software (though its license is not GPL-compatible). Curiously, even though no one owns a public domain work, a collection of such works based on some distinctive selection criteria can nonetheless be copyrighted as a whole. Finally, we note an application of the concept of public domain that is somewhat pertinent to free software issues, the so-called abstraction–filtration–comparison test used by courts to decide whether or not a program is a derivative work. One of the steps in the test involves filtering out the public domain elements from the software (Webbink, 2003).

Clearly, open source and free software are obviously not in the public domain, since their licenses rely on preexisting copyright ownership of the software, while public domain software has by definition no copyright protection. In fact, the FSF Web site recommends using the term "public domain" only in its strict meaning of "not copyrighted," though if the source code for a program is in the public domain, the site (gnu.org/philosophy/categories.html, accessed

December 19, 2006) does characterize it as "noncopylefted free software." A cautionary perspective about trying to just give software away is provided in Rosen (2002), who observes that, in addition to the fact that such software can subsequently be enclosed in proprietary products (which may or may not be your intention), providing it as a "gift" exposes the giver to potential warranty and liability claims. Disclaiming warranties and liabilities and distributing software "as is" requires a license in the first place. Rosen suggests that if you want to give software away, an appropriate solution is to "use a simple license such as the MIT license" (Rosen, 2002).

6.2 Patents

The legal notion of a patent is a longstanding one, but software patents have become available only much more recently. Their use is still evolving and controversial, and there are significant differences between nations. The FSF strongly opposes the application of patents to software, believing that this will severely undermine the free software movement. We shall discuss some of the objections, but we will first elaborate on the basic principles and practice of patenting. In contrast to copyright, where there has been considerable international harmonization, the law on patents varies considerably across countries, and especially so in the case of software patents.

In the United States, it is the United States Patent and Trademark Office (USPTO) (http://www.uspto.gov) that administers the approval of patents. The USPTO defines a *patent* as "the grant of a property right to the inventor" by the government, for a *novel*, *useful*, and *nonobvious invention*. The patent gives the owner the "right to exclude others from making, using, offering for sale, or selling" the patented invention. This does not give the patent owner the right to exploit the patent, because the patented invention may itself be an improvement over a previously patented invention whose patent is still in effect. However, in that case the owner of the original underlying patent could license his own invention to the new patent owner for a royalty fee. A patent covers the idea underlying an invention and not just a specific expression or implementation of the concept. A patent can also cover the ideas embedded in software. A patent application should be applied for *before* any public demonstration of the invention, else patent rights can be lost (such as 12 months after publication in the United States). The patenting process itself is not cheap. The Patent Office indicates that it costs "a minimum of about $4,000 over the life of the patent" in patent office fees, but additional attorney's fees add up quickly, so the total costs are likely to be significantly more, and the stronger the patent claim, the more expensive the legal process will be. A patent applies for 20 years "from the date on which the application for the patent" is filed. This is a significantly shorter period of time than the duration of a copyright. A patent from the U.S. Patent Office will apply only in the United States. The United States is one of the few nations that bases patents on a first-to-invent as opposed to first-to-file principle, though the first person to file obviously has a default presumption in his favor.

A patent requires disclosure of the idea underlying the invention in an application to the Patent Office. This disclosure is part of the quid pro quo between the government and the inventor. The inventor discloses – which promotes progress because other inventors can build on his invention. The government protects the inventor's intellectual property – so that he can at least potentially benefit commercially from the invention. The disclosure is basically a written description of "how to make and use" the proposed invention. An accelerated process for review of a patent proposal provides a decision about patentability within one year, while the normal process takes an average of almost two years. Naturally, the rationale for an expedited process follows from the very purpose for intellectual protection given in the U.S. Constitution. The Patent Office Web site describes this as an "accelerated examination (that) can provide innovators with the early certainty they may need to attract investors or protect their inventions against infringers," which immediately connects the patent to commercial prospects and legal protection. Under the accelerated process, the inventor must search for the relevant *prior art* that lies close to the invention, identify what that prior work teaches, and distinguish the proposed invention from the art.

Patents differ from copyrights in that patents protect the idea of an invention, while copyrights protect the expression of a creation. For example, in the case of software, while a copyright may be circumvented without infringement by implementing a program differently from a copyrighted program, this would not avoid software patent infringement and the possibility of significant damages. A software patent has a very different impact than a software copyright. Since a copyright protects only the expression of an idea, it does not prevent developers from creating an alternative implementation with very similar functionality. A patent on the other hand protects the idea behind a piece of software and not merely its implementation. Thus while just rewriting some code could circumvent a copyright, this would but not necessarily avoid a patent on the software.

Software Patents

Until recently the U.S. Patent Office had allowed patents only for "processes, machines, articles of manufacture, and compositions of matter." Patents had traditionally not been allowed for "scientific truths" or "mathematical expressions," the latter of which software and computer algorithms were deemed to be. The first landmark decision leading to the recognition of software patents came in the case of Diamond v. Diehr in 1981 when the U.S. Supreme Court first allowed a patent to be sustained for an application that involved software control of a manufacturing process. The next decisive case was that of In v. Iwahashi decided by the U.S. Supreme Court in 1989 when a patent for a voice recognition algorithm was approved that did not involve an associated device. The U.S. Patent Office issued detailed guidelines for software patent handling in 1996. Significantly, U.S. courts supported a presumption of patent validity, making it even easier to obtain patents.

Well-known software patents include those on the LZW compression algorithm, which is used in the algorithm for creating GIF files, Karmarkar's renowned algorithm for linear programming for which AT&T Bell Labs was the patent assignee (patent filed 1986, granted 1990), and the MP3 music format. A famous legal case involving software patents is that of the U.S. corporation Eolas, which obtained a patent for browser plug-ins. The patent was initially rejected by the U.S. Patent Office and widely disputed by both open source advocates Microsoft and even World Wide Web inventor Tim Berners-Lee. Despite this, the company sued Microsoft in 1999 for patent infringement and eventually won a half-billion-dollar settlement against Microsoft, which was let stand by the U.S. Supreme Court in 2005. Interestingly, Eolas indicated it would license the patented method free of charge to not-for-profit companies.

The basic objection of the FSF to software patents is that they make software development a veritable minefield of intellectual property entanglements. Stallman's article on software patents and GIFs (gnu.org/philosophy/gif.html) is instructive on these issues. The following observation by Stallman (2005) crystallizes some of the concerns:

> Developing a large and complex program means combining many ideas, often hundreds or thousands of them. In a country that allows software patents, chances are that some substantial fraction of the ideas in your program will be patented already by various companies. Perhaps hundreds of patents will cover parts of your program.

As an illustration of the magnitude of the problem, a study by Open Source Risk Management (2004) identified almost 300 patent exposures in Linux. Although a third of the patents were owned by Linux-friendly companies like IBM and Red Hat, almost 30 were owned by Microsoft. Notably, both IBM and Red Hat have promised not to assert their patents against the Linux kernel (Carver, 2005). In fact, IBM has pledged access to 500 key patents to "individuals and groups working on open source software" (IBM Press Release, 2005). In another interesting development related to free software patent protection,

Microsoft and Novell entered a mutual agreement to deploy and increase the interoperability of Linux (specifically SUSE Linux Enterprise) and Windows and to "provide each other's customers with patent coverage for their respective products" (Microsoft, 2006), though it will take time to understand what the implications of this kind of agreement truly are. Another line of defense against the threat posed by software patents may lie in the very code being developed by the open source community. Patentable inventions must by law be novel and nonobvious in terms of prior art. Since the free software community is in the process of "building the largest repository of software prior art in existence," it may be increasingly difficult to establish a claim that a patented software process is an advance over previous art (Carver, 2005, p. 464).

Despite the relatively recent emergence of software patents as a legal device, there are an extraordinary number of such patents being granted. According to Evans (2002) the number of software patents granted yearly has dramatically increased from about 800 in 1986 to over 7,000 in the year 2000. The presentation by Stallman referred to earlier observes that there are currently "a hundred thousand software patents each year," a figure which if accurate can only be described as astonishing. It has been argued that software patents tilt the market in favor of proprietary developers (Bessen, 2002). Commercial companies are more likely to have the financial and legal resources to even file a patent. They can also acquire pools of patents, which they can use to negotiate royalty-free use of another company's patents (Shapiro, 2001). Despite the high profile of the free software movement in opposing the use of software patents, the open community's objections are applicable to both open and closed source software, though since open source is disclosed by definition, it is obviously a more evident target for charges of infringement. Advocacy organizations like the Public Patent Foundation can assist developers against individual charges of infringement, but this is arguably only a temporizing measure.

The magnitude of the threat to free software from patents is cogently and ominously described in a discussion by open source legal advocate Bruce Perens (2004 and 2006), who underscores the potentially damaging cost of protection against patent suits for free software developers and any but very large corporations including those with proprietary software models. Remarkably, even invalid patents can lead to huge awards. Perens describes, for example, the case of Blackberry v. NTP. Based on a patent, the NTP company sued Blackberry for patent infringement and subsequently received a half-billion-dollar settlement, which was not reversed by the adjudicating court even after the U.S. Patent Office had ruled the patent itself invalid! Furthermore, even the mere threat of litigation can be incapacitating since, as Perens observes, "the cost of a patent defense is many times the net worth of the typical Open Source developer." Indeed, accusation of infringement can even become a predatory business model with individuals and smaller enterprises willing to pay license fees to settle an allegation rather than embark on expensive litigation. Given that the entire intent of the Patent and Copyright Clause of the U.S. Constitution was to promote the advancement of commerce, science, and the arts and to encourage inventors to make their inventions public, so other inventors could build on earlier work, it is strange that patent law itself now seems to threaten software invention. Ironically, the mere act of making oneself aware of existing patents, and thus exposing oneself to the accusation of being aware of a preexisting patent that one is accused of violating, can expose an individual to what are called *treble* damages in law.

The corporate and international landscape with regard to software patents is confusing. For example, despite being itself a target of major patent infringement claims, proprietary giant Microsoft has played a not inconsiderable role in advocacy for the promotion of software patents. Although Microsoft had initially relied solely on copyrights and a closed source software model for protection, in 1994 it advocated software patents at a U.S. Patent Office hearing. Internationally speaking, software patents are treated quite differently in different countries. India rejected software patents in 2005, but software patents have been widely issued in Europe. In mid-2006 the European Patent Commission announced a surprising decision to exclude software from patentability, an action that on the surface represented a significant change in its anticipated direction. However, the commission allows patents on software ideas. The FSF strongly opposes this practice partly because such patents can be used to instill fear by the threat of litigation. A successful litigation by a patent holder can lead to significant fines, seizure of assets, and even imprisonment for the alleged infringer. Even if most suits eventually fail, the mere threat of such litigation can have a chilling effect on both software users and developers.

6.3 Contracts and Licenses

A *contract* is a legal agreement between two parties that identifies what each party promises to do as part of an exchange. For example, the agreement may be that party A will pay for goods or services provided by party B. A *license* is a contract between the owner of a product and a prospective user that grants the user certain rights regarding the use of the product that would otherwise be illegal. For example, a landowner could grant a person license to walk on his property but subject to some time of day restrictions and perhaps keeping quiet. It's a two-way agreement between the parties. As a more pertinent example, suppose a person owns a copyright on a work. As the copyright owner, the person can grant or transfer to a prospective user of the work some of the privileges that come with copyright protection under U.S. law, under conditions stated in a license agreement. For example, the license could say that the licensee can run the software (an act that represents a copyright privilege) but is allowed to do so only for personal and not commercial applications (which would represent a restriction imposed by the copyright owner in the terms of the license). If the licensee violates any of the conditions of the license, the licensor can consider the license terminated at that point and sue the licensee for copyright violation since the licensor only conditionally transferred some of the copyright privileges and at this point that agreement would be voided. Thus, while a contract is enforced under the provisions of contract law, a software license that transfers copyright under restrictions can be effectively enforceable under the provisions of copyright law. Generally speaking, in the context of copyrights or patents for intellectual property such as software, a license is an agreement by the owner or licensor of the software property or invention to allow the licensee or license holder to use the software, but only under certain conditions. The most common kinds of software licenses are proprietary licenses for commercial applications and the various open software licenses like the FSF GPL and the OSI-certified licenses like the BSD, MIT, and Mozilla Public License (MPL). In subsequent sections, we shall look at the kinds of conditions such licenses impose.

The following discussion very briefly examines some relations between copyrights, licenses, and contracts (refer to the Rosen (2005) for a more complete treatment). A key principle to remember is that under copyright law, one cannot exercise the "exclusive rights of a copyright owner or patent owner without a license" (Rosen, 2005, p. 54). Therefore, open software requires a license for its distribution. The GPL licenses its copyrights (but not copyright ownership) through what is called a *bare license*. A bare license is not considered a contract, because among other reasons it does not require an explicit manifestation of assent, which is one of the requirements for a valid contract. The GPL is unusual in that it relies solely on copyright law rather than also on contract law (Rosen, 2005). Its license states that "you are not required to accept this License, since you have not signed it. However, nothing else grants you permission to modify or distribute the Program or its derivative works." Thus there is no manifestation of assent required as needed for a contract. There are significant legal differences between bare licenses and contracts. Since bare licenses are not contracts, they cannot be enforced under contract law, so a violation of the GPL can be enforced only under copyright law. Furthermore, only a copyright owner has the legal standing to sue for infringement to enforce a bare license like the GPL, while "a contract can be enforced by a licensor even if he doesn't own the underlying copyrights" (p. 58). In principle, a bare license "can be revoked by the licensor . . . while a contract . . . can be enforced under contract law and so that it cannot be revoked" (Rosen, 2005, p. 62). Indeed, a licensed distributor can "enforce a license even if he or she doesn't own the copyrights in the underlying works" (p. 139). Although both copyright and contract law vary worldwide, Rosen observes that the "global requirement for consistency of commercial transactions . . . helps ensure that contracts are interpreted in much the same way around the world" (Rosen, 2005, p. 58). It is not hard for a license to be handled as a contract. In fact it does not even require a change to its text, only that it be "offered and accepted as a contract" (for some "consideration" – another requirement of a valid contract) (Rosen, 2005, p. 56). The required assent can be indicated when you click to agree to a license that is presented to you before accessing software. We note that Eben Moglen (2001) of the FSF has a very different perspective on the significance of these issues, as we describe in the subsection on enforcement of the GPL later in this chapter (also refer to Jones (2003)).

It is elementary but noteworthy to observe that the terms of a software license generally impose no constraints on the owner of the software, only on the person to whom the software license is granted; for example, restrictions in a license on how the licensee is allowed to use the software apply to the licensee, not the licensor. Of course, in the case of software the situation may be dynamic. Thus, suppose the licensed software is part of an open source development project and a contributor submits a patch he authored for which he owns the copyright. The patch is designed to improve the original software, and its incorporation would then constitute a derivative work of the original. However, for the original licensor to create the derivative work, the licensor must now obtain the contributor's permission to incorporate the copyrighted contribution into the improved derived work. The derivative work in a sense is a type of compilation, since it now consists of a number of separately copyrighted elements, albeit they may have been modified and integrated or merged in some fashion. Alternatively, the author of the patch can transfer copyright ownership to the project.

The right to *sublicense* is particularly relevant in open source development because open projects develop recursively, with one developer building on the work of another. Rosen (2005) discusses sublicensing in some detail. Since open software is built up as a sequence of contributions to an original work, the question that arises is "from whom does the person at the end of the chain of title get a license to use, copy, etc" (Rosen, 2005, p. 87). The answer depends on whether the license is sublicensable. Nonsublicensable projects just refer to the copyright and other notices for any component in the source files. On the other hand, if a license is sublicensable, "then any distributor has the right to grant a license to the software, including its components, directly to third parties" (p. 88). The open source MIT license (though not the BSD) is an example of a license that is sublicensable, thus providing the advantage that "a distributor can provide to his customers all the rights needed to the entire work without expecting (them) to follow the chain of title to its beginning" (Rosen, 2005, p. 90).

Other relevant license issues include patent rights, liabilities, and warranties. For example, licenses like the IBM-originated, OSI-certified, corporate *Common Public License* include an explicit "grant of license to any patents concerning the software that the author holds" (Capek et al., 2005), lest users of the software inadvertently infringe such patents. As Rosen (2005, p. 167) observes, the patent grant is not absolute but only for "those specific uses and combinations . . . contemplated at the time of (the) initial Contributions." This condition affects the creation of derivative works that notably "may not exceed the scope of the initial patent license" (Rosen, 2005, p. 167). The MIT open source license illustrates the question of license warranties for noninfringement. Its "as is" condition, in addition to the standard indication that there are no warranties "for fitness for a particular purpose," also explicitly states that it provides no warranty protecting you against claims of infringement if one of the licensed components turns out to have a copyright or patent problem, a responsibility which in any case "would be an impossible burden to impose upon an open source licensor" (Rosen, 2005, p. 90). Ironically, Zittrain (2004) observes, in contrast, how "a proprietary firm can stand behind the pedigree of its code, both because the code presumably originated in controlled and known circumstances and because the absence of accompanying source code makes the firm's offerings difficult to examine for evidence of theft." Software licenses commonly contain a provision renouncing or seriously limiting the licensor's liability for the licensee's use of the software. *Liability* refers to a condition where the use of a defective product causes harm. In general, the developer or seller of a product may be legally liable for financial damages in such cases. Licenses for software products typically require the user to agree to limit liability for damages to the purchase price as a condition of use. For example, if you read the Microsoft EULA (End-User License Agreement), you will see that the warranty is limited to 90 days and your exclusive remedy is basically a refund of the cost of the product if it proves defective within that period.

6.4 Proprietary Licenses and Trade Secrets

Software licenses fall into a variety of types: proprietary licenses that typically do not disclose source code and have various restrictions, reciprocal licenses like the GPL that require derivative works to follow the same license, and intermediate licenses including academic licenses like the BSD that provide source code but do not preclude derivative works from being closed source (Rosen, 2005), effectively letting the user do anything. We begin our discussion of the different kinds of software licenses with proprietary licenses. We shall also discuss a number of related topics, including trade secrets, reverse engineering software obfuscation, and nondisclosure agreements.

6.4.1 Basics of Proprietary Licenses

Proprietary software (assuming it is distributed for use by others) is the software that is usually licensed by the owner under terms that restrict its use and redistribution. Zittrain (2004) observes that "proprietary software in mass distribution almost uniformly reserves all rights to the author except a license to 'run' the software on the purchaser's computer." It is generally distributed as closed source in the form of a binary executable. Zittrain characterizes this practice as a "hallmark of proprietary software, complementing the creator's exercise of a legal right to prevent the use of source code in new works, with a technical barrier to unauthorized use." This type of distribution is done both in order to protect the secrecy of the source code and because for most users the executable is the most usable format for the product because it does not require a separate compilation operation, which would be problematic for most users. Closed source software is generally taken as synonymous with proprietary, but the point is sometimes made that closed and open are opposites, while the opposite of proprietary is public domain.

An *End-User License Agreement* or *EULA* is the most common kind of software license. It is typically proposed to a user for acceptance during software installation as a precondition for use of the software. A EULA is usually agreed to by checking a box on a form to indicate you have read the license and agree to its terms, which seems to be the digital equivalent of signing a contract. These licenses generally have extensive disclaimers about liability for the use of the software, as well as restrictions on the use and sharing of the software. Proprietary licenses typically indicate that fair use "does not include decompiling, reverse engineering, or other such uses," or copying, except for purposes of backup (Webbink, 2003). Despite their prevalence, these licenses appear to be very infrequently read, at least by average users (refer to Magid (2005) for an amusing experiment that the security Web site PC PitStop devised to illustrate this). The Web site included a clause in one of its own EULAs that promised the reader consideration and possibly money if they e-mailed an address that was listed in the license. Four months and 3,000 downloads later, only one person had responded – and was rewarded $1,000 for his effort! The fact that few people read the license was the likely explanation for the lack of follow-up on the tempting offer, rather than prudence on the part of a legion of meticulous license readers. In any case, it is unsurprising that these licenses go unread by most users. People generally don't read the fine print. However, licenses may be very important *to developers* since they affect the extent to which the developer can adapt the software and under what restrictions, as well as to corporate users with deep pockets who could be seriously legally exposed for violations of the license requirements.

Trademarks

Trademarks can be incredibly relevant to both proprietary and open source products. In fact as Rosen (2005, p. 37) observes, "Often the key to marketing success for open source projects are their product or brand names, or trademarks." *Trademarks* are names or symbols that are used to brand the name of a product for such purposes as protecting the reputation of the product or differentiating the product from competitors. They identify the product as that of a particular source or party. They are especially useful in environments like open source where it is easy to enter derivative products into the market; in such a case, established names can command customer loyalty as well as attention. The existence of a trademark for an open project also tends to limit forking in the project because only the main trunk of development has access to the trademark recognition. This is important for the stability of development in the open source movement. Trademarks can be registered with the USPTO, but only marketing for public awareness and use of the trademark on products can make a trademark valuable. For example, Red Hat^{TM} is a valuable trademark that indicates that a premium organization is behind the software and so connotes a superior product, and similarly for products like Apache^{TM} and MySQL^{TM} (Rosen, 2001a). To understand the impact of a trademark, consider a product like Coca-Cola^{TM}, which is based on a secret formula or trade secret. As a matter of fact it appears not to be too expensive to reverse engineer this formula chemically. But the value of the product is really in the trademark that is internationally recognized, distinguishes the product in the marketplace, and is accepted as a symbol of quality. Thus even in the case of a physical product like Coca-Cola^{TM} the market value of the product is inextricably linked to a rather abstract intellectual property, not the intellectual property represented by the trade secret, but the registered symbol represented by the trademark.

6.4.2 Trade Secrets, Nondisclosure Agreements, Reverse Engineering, and Obfuscation

Software can be kept secret in a variety of ways, such as making it available only in binary executables or only allowing access to its functionality over a network without availability of the executables at all. Distributed software can also be protected in other ways. Legal mechanisms like nondisclosure or confidentiality agreements protect software by the threat of penalties for its disclosure. Agreements like these for the Unix system were at the root of the grievances that led to the free software movement. Although code can be hidden in various ways, it can also be revealed by techniques like reverse engineering. On the other hand, reverse engineering can be thwarted or at least complicated by technical countermeasures like obfuscation. We briefly consider these issues because they are intimately related to the very possibility of proprietary code.

Trade Secrets and Nondisclosure Agreements

Trade secrets are a way of keeping product information hidden. A *trade secret* refers to undisclosed information about a product that provides a commercial advantage to its owner. The secret can be enforced by using mechanisms like confidentiality or nondisclosure agreements, which employees of the company owning the product are required to sign in order to be able to work for the company. A *nondisclosure agreement* means that party A acknowledges receiving information from party B and is bound to protect its confidentiality. This is an extremely important commitment on the part of A. Thus if A subsequently develops a related product even after leaving this employer, then it is up to A, if challenged by litigation by B, to prove he did not use information obtained under the *confidentiality* or nondisclosure agreement to develop the new product. For example, the original AT&T Unix license required nondisclosure agreements by individuals receiving the software. Violation of such agreements can entail significant monetary damages. Naturally, the owner of the protected property also has a responsibility and is expected to exert considerable caution in protecting the secret. Given that such precautions are in place, illegal means to obtain the secret constitute industrial or *economic espionage*. This crime is severely prosecutable under the federal Economic Espionage Act of 1996. Violators, including both the perpetrators and the receivers of the protected information, can be imprisoned for 10 years, as well as fined for up to half a million dollars

($5 million for a corporation). The penalties are even more severe if foreign entities are involved.

The concern with trade secrecy is not always merely a matter of their remaining permanently secret. For example, in a case in 2006 an employee of Coca-Cola™ obtained a sample of a new drink under development by the company that was not yet on the market. The employee made the sample available to industrial spies. The business risk or loss to Coca-Cola™ was not so much the disclosure of the product per se so that it could be reverse engineered by a competitor, as the disclosure of a sample of the product before it came to market, thereby undermining the company's strategic advantage in being the first to market this type of product. Rapid successful entry of such products to market can affect not just a company's immediate market share but also the longer term share. The same holds for software products.

Unlike patents, trade secrets have the advantage of not requiring public disclosure of the hidden information, but conversely they are also not legally protected by reverse engineering, though this may possibly be prohibited by a software license (though see Samuelson, 2002). It is worth recalling that Richard Stallman's own first personal experience with nondisclosure agreements had a memorable impact on him. It happened during the 1970s. He had been trying to modify the printer driver for a Xerox printer but could not obtain the source code from his university or colleagues because of their nondisclosure agreements. As Stallman observes, "This was my first encounter with a nondisclosure agreement, and I was the victim. . . . nondisclosure agreements have victims" (Stallman, 2001).

Reverse Engineering and Obfuscation

Reverse engineering is basically about "trying to figure out how something works" (Jones, 2005). It refers to the analysis of a system for the purpose of identifying its internal components and their interrelationships. This may be done to create a representation of the system in an alternative form or a representation at a higher level of abstraction. Alternatively, it can refer to the extraction of design information from a system's behavior, yielding an inventory analysis of a system's scope and functionality. Reverse engineering may be motivated by competitive reasons or benignly, to design a product that can interoperate with a proprietary product. Generally, black-box reverse engineering refers to reverse engineering a software product on the basis of an inventory analysis of a system's scope and functionality. White-box reverse engineering, on the other hand, refers to reverse engineering a software product by a process like decompiling that exposes the implementation of its object code. Either may be legal if done for purposes of interoperability. But it may not be done to avoid or circumvent a protection mechanism. The review article by Jones (2005) is quite instructive on these issues, as is the work by Payne (2002), which considers how disassembling and comprehending code compiled by an optimizing compiler can be a formidable task.

Reverse engineering of manufactured products has often been viewed as a competitive counterbalance to trade secrets. However, the legal issues entailed by reverse engineering for software products can be complex and vary significantly among countries. Reverse engineering may also be encumbered by the presence of copyrights or patents, as well as restrictive software licenses that forbid reverse engineering, such as the license for Microsoft Windows (Jones, 2005). If copyrighted software is reverse engineered in order to develop a competitive product then in order to avoid charges of copyright infringement, it is customary to split the development process between two separate groups. One group does the reverse engineering and produces an abstract specification of the desired product. A completely separate group then uses this specification to implement the new product. This approach is not applicable if the product is protected by patents, since patents would protect the idea not merely its implementation.

The cloning of the original IBM PC is a classic example of a highly significant case of reverse engineering. The reversal was done not for the device hardware but for the BIOS firmware code that underlay its functionality. The IBM PC was a very successful machine and so was a natural target for reverse engineering. Companies like Phoenix Technologies Ltd. and Compaq wanted to create a cloned machine that would be "IBM compatible." The BIOS for the IBM PC, which was available in an IBM technical manual, was copyrighted, so its code could not be just duplicated (Hollaar, 2002). Phoenix legally circumvented the copyright protection by organizing its development team into two separate noncommunicating groups, the so-called *clean-room* or Chinese wall approach (Schwartz, 2001). The first Phoenix group studied the original BIOS code to determine exactly what it did and created a complete functional specification of the system. The second group then took these functional specifications and wrote its own new code to implement the specifications. This did not constitute a copyright infringement, since copyright protects only the expression of code, not its actual behavior or function. In fact, portions of such code could even be substantially similar as long as this was "dictated by function" (Hollaar, 2002). On the other hand, had the code, for example, just been rewritten in piecemeal segments based on the original code, this would have constituted serial infringements or a sequence of derivative works. The clean-room approach constituted legally viable reverse engineering of the BIOS without copyright infringement. The rest of this story is history since the IBM

PC thereafter became commoditized, eliminating IBM's monopoly in the market.

Decompiling is a specific type of reverse engineering based on attempting to reverse the effects of compiling source code into object code by converting object code back to some high-level language that can be more readily understood. Decompilers, such as the Reflector tool for.NET, are generalizations of disassemblers that convert machine code back into assembly language. It is not always possible to decompile object code or create a humanly meaningful high-level version of the code because of the intermixture of code and data in a program and the loss of symbol tables (containing the originally meaningful names) that are typically no longer available in the executable code. See such as Tonella et al. (2000) for an application example and further references. There are also active countermeasures available to inhibit techniques like decompiling. One of these methods used to make such white-box reverse engineering of software more difficult is obfuscation. *Obfuscation* refers to scrambling code and changing symbolic names so that the altered code's behavior remains equivalent to the original but the code is confusing for human readers and much harder to reverse engineer. Tools like *Dotfuscator* are called obfuscators, and these automate the process. Obfuscation may also be combined with encryption. Software obfuscators make it harder to decompile object code and so are obviously technically useful in protecting intellectual property. The type of code that managed code compilers like Microsoft's.NET compilers for C# and VB.NET translate source code into is called *Intermediate Language* (IL), as opposed to native assembly language code. IL code is intended to be cross-platform and cross-language, but it lends itself to reverse engineering because of its consistent structure. As a consequence, Microsoft includes obfuscation tools to make the IL code harder to decompile. The .NET framework code itself however is not obfuscated (Downen, 2005). It is worth noting in this connection that the OSI criteria for open source software explicitly requires that the source code itself cannot be obfuscated.

6.4.3 Miscellaneous Types of Proprietary Software

Before addressing the fundamental issue of the types of open licenses available, we shall briefly digress to remark on some other kinds of software distributions, such as freeware, shareware, and liteware.

Freeware is software provided *free of charge* by its developer or author, but its distribution or redistribution remains under the control of the developer. The software license may permit limited copying and redistribution, but these copies cannot typically be sold by the user and commercial use may also be restricted. The developer retains the right to modify the software in the future or decide at some point to charge for future copies. The software is usually provided without source code, which prevents, or at least makes it problematic, to modify. There are some very important examples of freeware. Both *Adobe Acrobat Reader* and *Internet Explorer* are freeware. The free Adobe Reader represented a business strategy for popularizing the PDF format and the for-sale Adobe Professional. The free Internet Explorer essentially destroyed the market share of the Netscape browser. Freeware is decidedly different from *free* software in the sense of the free software movement where the term *free* refers to freedom of use rather than absence of a fee for use.

Shareware is also called try-before-you-buy software or *trialware*. It is usually delivered digitally free of charge to the user, but the user is expected on the basis of an honor system to pay some small amount for the product after a trial usage period if the user retains the product. *Liteware* is a specific kind of shareware that omits some of the functionality of the complete version. Upon purchase, the user's copy is typically registered with the shareware's distributor and a more complete version of the product may be supplied, as well as access to future product updates and possibly some level of technical assistance or support. The shareware product is copyrighted, so users cannot redistribute it as their own. An important aspect of the underlying business model is the direct one-to-one relationship between the user of the product and the shareware product developer, rather than through an intermediary in a retail outlet. However, shareware vendors with extensive catalogs of shareware products may also distribute products for a fee. This business or marketing model was developed in the early 1980s and successfully used to market some basic PC utilities. *Nagware* is shareware that regularly reminds the user that the program is not free of charge and should be paid for. The reminders typically occur as pop-up messages during the execution of the program. One of the most widely used examples of nagware is the WinZip utility for file compression in Microsoft Windows. Despite the reminders in WinZip, this utility still remains fully functional even after the initial trial period. Free-of-charge software that displays advertisements is called *adware*. The Opera browser is adware that lets the user eliminate the ads for a fee. Stallman (1996/2001) discusses the various terms used to describe software, particular from the viewpoint of their relation to free software.

The *Microsoft Shared Source Initiative* refers to software distributed under a Microsoft initiative that uses a range of software licenses for different products that gives selected customers and developers access to some of Microsoft's source code for their own use, such as the Windows template library. Possible restrictions include nondisclosure agreements or prohibitions against modifying code. The initiative is quite broad with almost 700,000 developers currently reported to be using shared source (Zittrain, 2004). Rosen warns that for software developers planning "to write software that might potentially compete with Microsoft's copyrights or patents, there is great risk in looking at Microsoft's source code" since you may become an infringer if there is "substantial similarity between your commercial software and theirs" (Rosen, 2005, p. 258). Some Microsoft products like WiX (a batch-oriented build tool suitable for Microsoft developers) have been released under open source licenses, like the Common Public License (Walli, 2005). Researchers can modify the source, though not for redistribution without appropriate Microsoft approval or licensing and the same holds for allowed modifications that are distributed for commercial purposes.

An emerging and controversial type of licensing arrangement is represented by so-called *Trusted Computing*. In this model of software licensing, a user can run software but is otherwise not able to "tamper" with it. The systems communicate with the software owners (not the licensee) to ensure registration and protect against software piracy and other activities considered to be license violations. This approach derives from the Digital Rights Management Model used by the Disney Corporation to prevent purchasers of CDs from copying them. Major chip manufacturers such as Intel are expected to incorporate hardware to support this approach. Some of the proposed objectives of trusted computing are to increase the security of systems to the benefit of end users and protect against identity theft. However, this approach is strongly opposed by the FSF, which calls it 'treacherous computing' for reasons ranging from the loss of Internet anonymity to the argument that it is likely to increase vendor lock-in and enable "remote censorship." The topic is discussed extensively in (Anderson, 2003a, b).

6.5 OSI – The Open Source Initiative

The previous sections have introduced some basic concepts of intellectual property: copyright, derivative works, patents, software patents, contracts, licenses, and so on, as well as more narrowly focused but relevant issues like reverse engineering, obfuscation, trademark, and nondisclosure agreements. These ideas provide basic conceptual tools for understanding the purpose and features of the various free and open software licenses we consider next. The OSI is an organization established to foster a better relationship between the free software movement and business. The OSI is a counterpoint to the FSF. It has defined explicit standards for what it calls OSI-certified open source licenses and has a process for approving them. This section reviews the OSI and considers illustrative OSI-certified licenses. We address the definitions and legal characteristics of these licenses, their historical context, implications of the license requirements, different reciprocity characteristics, GPL compatibility, and the important MPL license in particular.

6.5.1   Open Source Initiative and OSI-Certified Licenses

The OSI (www.opensource.org), established by Eric Raymond and Bruce Perens in 1998, is a nonprofit foundation, whose mission is to promote the use of open source software, particularly in commercial applications. The creation of the organization was triggered by the perceived opportunity represented by Netscape's opening of its browser code. The FSF, founded in 1985 before the Internet revolution had represented a more activist or ideological position that advocated the eventual complete disappearance of proprietary software, an attitude that arguably fostered suspicion in the business community (see Rosen (2005) and the useful book review by Rosenberg (2005)). The OSI was founded to counter these commercial concerns about what free and open source software mean. The pragmatic, nonideological approach of the OSI is reflected in the following sound bite from its Web site that describes in a nutshell what open source is all about:

> Open source promotes software reliability and quality by supporting independent peer review and rapid evolution of source code. To be OSI-certified, the software must be distributed under a license that guarantees the right to read, redistribute, modify, and use the software freely (http://www.opensource.org/advocacy/faq.php).

Even more strongly, the history document at the OSI site characterizes the motivation for the new organization and thus

> We realized it was time to dump the confrontational attitude that has been associated with "free software" in the past and sell the idea strictly on the same pragmatic, business-case grounds that motivated Netscape (http://www.opensource.org/docs/history.php).

The very term "open source" that is now so universally recognized originated at this time, much later than the phrase "free software" promoted by the FSF. The term came about as a result of a meeting occasioned by the Netscape's opening of its Navigator code in 1998. It was coined by Chris Peterson and was motivated by both the ambiguity of the word "free," which at least sounded like it meant "free of charge," and the impression that the free software movement could be perceived as being anticommercial, even though this was not the intent of the FSF. But the new description was also a "proxy" for a wider spectrum of issues in the open source community about the community's relation to the business world (see the opensource.org site for a history of the organization and timelines).

The establishment of the OSI formalized the other major branch of the free software movement, the one that had built its projects under the legal matrix provided by licenses like the BSD and MIT, which appeared more attractive for commercial applications. The organization reflected the beliefs of prominent open source developers like Marshall McKusick of the BSD project, Jim Gettys of the X Window System, and Michael Tiemann, author of the GNU C++ compiler, later CTO of Red Hat and current OSI President. It is noteworthy that OSI cofounder Bruce Perens left the organization only a year after its founding, stating in a well-known e-mail (Perens, 1999a) that "Open Source has de-emphasized the importance of the freedoms involved in Free Software. It's time for us to fix that. We must make it clear to the world that those freedoms are still important, and that software such as Linux would not be around without them."

The OSI Foundation maintains a list of approved software licenses which it recognizes as consistent with the basic principles of open source development. Software distributed under any of these licenses can be labeled as *OSI Certified Open Source Software*. All of the FSF's licenses satisfy these criteria a *fortiori*, but some of the OSI licenses do not satisfy the FSF requirements. In an analysis of open source license types, Ueda et al. (2004) found that about 30% of the OSI-certified licenses listed on the OSI site were not free per the FSF list, while conversely about 30% of the FSF licenses were not OSI certified, though in the latter case they could be OSI certified since the FSF conditions are tighter than the OSI criteria. Licenses like the BSD are provided as templates in the sense that you only have to enter the appropriate owner, organization, and year to adapt the license to your own software. Typically to apply a license to your own software, you include the license in a separate file and then reference the file from *each* of your source files, as well as provide the identity of the copyright holder, the license name, and the copyright date.

The OSI Web site lists the criteria or standards that determine whether a new license will be eligible to be described as OSI certified. These criteria were derived from the so-called Debian Free Software Guidelines (see debian.org). The reader may also refer to Perens (1999b) for a useful history by a leader of the Debian project who was also a founder of the OSI and the author/editor of the licensing criteria. The process for having a new license OSI certified requires one to submit an explanatory document, created with the aid of a lawyer, explaining how your proposed license satisfies the OSI criteria. This document must be e-mailed to the OSI via license-approval@opensource. org.

OSI License Certification Criteria

There are ten *certification criteria* that *OSI-certified* licenses must satisfy. They are presented here. These descriptions are paraphrased from the official statement on the OSI Web site for brevity. We have also italicized the qualifiers: *cannot restrict*, *must be*, *must allow*, and so on to underscore the force of the different criteria. The reader should refer to the opensource.org Web site for complete statements and more detailed explicit rationales for each condition.

1. Free redistribution: The license *cannot restrict* the licensee from either selling the software or giving it away for free.
2. Open source: The source code of the program *must be* readily available, such as through free Internet download. The code *must not* impede subsequent development by being intentionally obfuscated.
3. Derivatives: The license *must allow* derivative works. It *must allow* these to be redistributed under the same license.
4. Code integrity: The license *may require* derivative works to be distributed as the original base source code plus separate patches in order to ensure that modifications are readily distinguishable from the original.
5. Nondiscrimination: The license *cannot discriminate* against any group or individual, since this would impede open development.
6. Commercialization: Fields of application, like commercial use, *cannot be restricted* and indeed are encouraged.
7. License distribution: The license rights *automatically apply* to anyone to whom the software is redistributed without requiring another license.
8. No product restrictions: The license *cannot make* the rights depend on the software remaining a "part of a particular software distribution."
9. No codistribution restrictions: The license *cannot restrict* what software it is allowed to be distributed with. For example, open source can be distributed with closed source.
10. Technology: The license *cannot require* "gestures" like click-wrap to "establish a contract between the licensor and the licensee," since these may not be available in some technologies.

Open source licenses as defined under the OSI do not necessarily apply restrictions on how derivative works are themselves licensed. The types of licenses that satisfy these criteria are often broken into subcategories like academic or reciprocal, permissive or nonpermissive, protective or nonprotective, copyleft or not copyleft, and GPL compatible or not. There are other categories as well, but these are the common ones. For example, Webbink (2003) distinguishes between two broad categories of what he calls non protective versus protective open source licenses. *Nonprotective* open source licenses refer to open source licenses like the BSD and Apache licenses that impose no restrictions on the distribution of derivative works, including the inclusion of such redistributions in proprietary code (Webbink, 2003); that is, for such licenses while the open code itself is disclosed, derivative code based on it need not be disclosed. On the other hand, the term *protective* open source license refers to open source licenses, such as the GPL and the Lesser GPL (LGPL), which impose restrictions on the distribution of derivative works to ensure that the original code and derivative works will remain open. The less restrictive, non-protective licenses reflect a dynamic that is as yet unresolved in the computing industry. In economic terms, the issue is the trade-off to be made between the irrevocable "decision to disclose technology" and the "ability to appropriate the returns from that technology" (West, 2003). The article by Warrene (2005) is also a useful primer on the different kinds of licenses. Rosen's book (2005) is a canonical resource for license explications that are both nuanced and lucid. Rosen uses the academic versus reciprocal license terminology.

6.5.2 Illustrative Academic OSI-Certified Licenses

We will now briefly describe the BSD, Apache, and MPL. These are all examples of the so-called academic or permissive licenses that either relax or do not include some restrictions/conditions in the GPL.

BSD-type licenses are the most popular alternative to the GPL. The *BSD (Berkeley Software Distribution) license* was first used for BSD UNIX in 1980. It is widely used such as in major free operating systems like FreeBSD. See www.opensource.org for a copy of the license. The so-called *modified BSD* license (or *new BSD*) is generally considered preferable to the original BSD. (The old BSD had a so-called advertising clause that made it incompatible with the GPL; it was removed in later new, revised or "3-clause" versions of the BSD.) The key characteristic of the BSD is that it allows BSD-licensed code or modifications to be incorporated into closed, proprietary software whose source code can be subsequently kept secret, unlike so-called reciprocal or copyleft licenses like the GNU GPL. On the other hand, BSD-licensed code can also be released under the GPL license as well because of the complete flexibility of the BSD. As a consequence of these licensing characteristics "chunks of BSD code" can be found not only in the Linux kernel and Mac OS X, but also in Solaris and Windows NT (Feller and Fitzgerald, 2002, p. 20).

The BSD license contains the usual "as is" warrantee disclaimers, permits redistribution in either source code or binary form, requires that the original copyright notice be included to allow proper attribution of modified works, and forbids using the names of the open source contributors for endorsement without their approval. One of the objectives of the University of California in defining the BSD license was "to avoid having to pay damages if a user was injured in any way by the software." It accomplished this by including the express warranty and liability disclaimers in the license (Rosen, 2005, p. 76). An even simpler but related license is the MIT X Window license. The BSD-style license seems to offer more obvious guarantees to prospective corporate sponsors of development than the more restrictive GPL. For an example of how commercial circumstances and license conditions can combine to influence the attitudes of even committed GPL-oriented developers, consider the case of the.NET-type framework *Mono*. Mono was initially under development by the open source company Ximian. It is licensed at least partially under an X11 (BSD-type) license. Ximian cofounder Miguel de Icaza of free GNOME fame has explained the pragmatic reasons for the choice. He believes this type of license helps ensure "that the Mono project will attract a growing pool of talented developers, while enabling their companies to control and protect their Mono-based products and services" (Evans, 2002).

The modified BSD license is said to be "compatible with the GPL" according to the FSF Web site, but the relationship between the BSD and the GPL is asymmetric (Lerner and Tirole, 2005). It is compatible in the sense that a GPL project could incorporate open software licensed under the BSD, but this is only because the BSD license itself does not care about license restrictions added by the more restrictive GPL. The BSD pretty much lets you do anything you want to do. While one usually thinks of compatibility as a two-way street, the compatibility referred to by the FSF in this instance is not symmetric. A BSD project could not incorporate software licensed under the GPL into a project that was to be BSD licensed and, say, went proprietary, because while that closed distribution would be compatible with the BSD, it would not be compatible with the GPL and so would violate the GPL license's requirements. In other words the BSD project could use the GPL only by becoming GPL itself and eliminating options available in the BSD. Thus the compatibility works only in one direction.

The *Apache license* (version 2.0) for the Apache Web server is of the BSD type, though the version 2.0 statement of the license from 2004 is much more detailed than the BSD license. For example, it is fairly explicit about derivative works and excludes from them works that "remain separable from or merely link (or bind by name) to the interfaces of the work." The license protects the Apache™ trademark name from being applied to derivative works. It allows modified versions of the source code to be redistributed in closed products, so Apache-style licenses are compatible with proprietary licenses (McMillan, 2002) just as the BSD. However, the FSF does not consider the Apache license as compatible with the GPL, because the license includes "certain patent termination cases that the GPL does not require" (gnu.org). See www.apache.com or www.opensource.org for a copy of this OSI-certified license.

The *MPL* is an increasingly popular license, though not nearly as widely used as the BSD or GPL (Wilson, 2005). It is the license, for example, that the Firefox browser is released under and one of the two licenses Netscape introduced at the release of its source code for the Mozilla Web browser (the open source version of Netscape). The other less well received license was the Netscape Public License (NPL). Recall that this Netscape initiative was part of the climax of the so-called browser wars. Netscape could not have distributed the browser under the GPL for various reasons, even if had so wished. The reasons included the browser's use of cryptographic codes, which at that time could not be exported due to U.S. security regulations, as well as its incorporation of third-party components the company was not privileged to disclose. Consequently, the company introduced the twofold MPL and NPL combination. The NPL was unsuccessful and is in any case not OSI certified. However, the MPL has become well accepted.

Rosen (2005) provides an extremely detailed and informative discussion of the MPL and its rationale; Wilson (2005) is also useful. As is the case for the GPL, publicly distributed derived works that modify *existing* MPL-licensed files were required to remain under the conditions of the license. However, the license also allowed completely proprietary files, provided they contain no original code or modifications of the original code, to be combined with the open source code, while remaining outside the terms of the MPL license. Per Wilson's (2005) discussion, "Put simply, someone can take an MPL-licensed work and build upon it with new components. The resulting work can be distributed, with the MPL covering the use of the original work, and *any* license covering the rest." Rosen (2005) praises the MPL definition for being "a high-quality, professional legal accomplishment in a commercial setting" (p. 142), "the first of the industrial strength open source licenses" (p. 156), and the "model for most of the important commercial open source licenses that followed" (p. 142), representing a carefully defined compromise between academic licenses, like the BSD, and reciprocal licenses, like the GPL. We will elaborate on the license's so-called reciprocity characteristics in more detail when we discuss the GPL. The MPL is OSI-certified license but is incompatible with the GPL. It also has notable patent-related conditions (Engelfriet, 2005). It requires contributors to a Mozilla-licensed project to grant royalty-free patent license on their contributions to everyone, while, conversely, users of the licensed software can assert their own patents only if they pay royalties for any past use of the MPL'd product.

6.6 The GPL and Related Issues

The GPL is the flagship license of the free software movement. Its simple purpose is to keep software licensed under it permanently open. The FSF also defines the LGPL for use with software libraries and regards this license as suitable under special circumstances. There are subtleties in how the implications of these licenses are interpreted, such as those revolving around the issue of what constitutes a derivative work of software. We also briefly consider international and enforcement issues for the GPL and discuss the GPL version 3.

6.6.1 General Public License

The GPL license grew out of the GNU project begun in 1983 by Richard Stallman. The purpose of the GNU project (an acronym for "GNU is not UNIX") had been to provide a nonproprietary, UNIX-compatible operating system built on openly available source code that could be copied, modified, and redistributed under terms compatible with the free software movement and none of which was subject to the original AT&T proprietary software licenses for UNIX. The project was intended to comprise a collection of system programs and software development tools, including text editors and compilers, like the now widely used GNU GCC compiler for C. Eventually, the Linux kernel, initiated later on by Linus Torvalds, was integrated with the GNU system to form the GNU/Linux system. The initial GNU software was distributed under a variety of ad hoc licenses until 1989 when the more convenient and generally applicable GPL was defined.

Shortly after the GNU project was started, Stallman founded the FSF in 1985 to financially support the GNU project and advocate the principles of free software. The FSF defined the GNU *GPL* which would become the most widely used license of the free and open source movement. It was authored by Richard Stallman. The current version 2 (GPLv2) was introduced in 1991 (version 1 came out in 1989). It was created with the vision of allowing downstream developers or users of programs distributed under the license to *preserve* most of the freedoms and privileges of the original copyright holder. These privileges included the *freedom* to

1. run the programs without restriction on use (including commercial and military uses),
2. view the source code of the program and be able to study it,
3. modify the source code to improve it if desired,
4. redistribute the program or modifications of the program, but

5. redistribution must provide any modifications under the same conditions as the original GPL.

The last item in this list is obviously a license restriction, but it is precisely the condition that ensures that the other rights granted in the license are indeed propagated to subsequent, downstream receivers of the program and its modifications. Thus, though sounding like a restriction (which it is), it is intended to be a freedom-enabling condition, passing the freedoms of the original license onto software posterity. This unique "self-perpetuating feature" is arguably the primary factor in the widespread use of the GPL (Carver, 2005, p. 448). The GPL is intended to establish a permanently free commons of software, available to all, and where distributed improvements must be made public. Although framed in idealistic language, it has some extremely important practical side effects. One key benefit is that by keeping product evolution public, it helps prevent the kind of proprietary divergence that occurred with Unix that tends to lead to both software incompatibility and vendor lock-in (Rosen, 2005).

The preamble to the GPL states that users of software licensed under the GPL must be made aware of their rights to copy, modify, redistribute, and so on. In order to distribute software under the GPL, you place a copyright notice in your own name, such as at the top of each source file, and a notice stating that the program is being distributed under the terms of the GPL. You must *also* include a copy of the GPL somewhere in your distribution, such as in a separate file. The license FAQ explains that "including a copy of the license with the work is vital so that everyone who gets a copy of the program can know what his rights are" (http://www.gnu.org/licenses/gpl-faq.html#WhyMustIInclude, accessed December 20, 2006). Thus this is a requirement that serves to propagate awareness of the GPL. If you want to distribute changes you have made to the software you received under a GPL license, then you must ensure that any modified files "carry prominent notices stating that you changed the file and the date of the change" (http://www.gnu.org/licenses/gpl.html). This continues the chain of title for modifications and preserves the integrity of the original authors' source code, similar to OSI requirements and motivations. The developer of the original program retains his copyright ownership of the program. The copyright for the text of the GPL license itself belongs to the FSF, but the copyright for the work protected by the license belongs to the author of the work and only the author has the right to sue in the case of copyright infringement.

With respect to the issue of free as in free of charge, the GPL explicitly allows charging a distribution fee, but explicitly prohibits imposing a license fee for distributed GPL'd software, though it makes no objections to fees for services, warranty protection, or indemnification (insurance against monetary loss). Thus the software does not have to be offered for free, though if an individual receives a copy for a charge, he can nonetheless redistribute that copy free of charge, and if the software is downloaded, a binary copy cannot be cheaper than a source copy.

Modifications of GPL'd software can remain private and do not have to be distributed, but if they are distributed then this must of course be done under the GPL. While the license explicitly precludes the inclusion of GPL-licensed software in *publicly* distributed proprietary programs, this does not affect programs used only internally in an organization. This also applies to using the program or a modification on a public Web site to operate the site (Fishman, 2004a). Thus the requirement for GPL licensing of modifications does *not* mean you have to distribute modifications, only that if you do so, they must be under the GPL (OSS Watch, 2006). You are perfectly free to use the modifications in any way you want if the software is not distributed. Distributed copies must include the original copyright notice and the exclusion of warranty. The exclusion of warranty condition as usual protects the owner of the code from liability in the case of failure of the code to carry out its expected purpose.

Patents are addressed in the Preamble and Section 7 of the GPL. These indicate that patents that apply to any of the GPL'd code "must be licensed for everyone's free use or not licensed at all"; that is, if the code cannot be distributed royalty free then it cannot be distributed at all for which reason this condition is called the "Liberty or Death" clause. Thus distribution of the software is tantamount to an implicit grant of patent license. However, with the proliferation of software patents this matter is increasingly significant, and so for a number of reasons an *express* grant of patent rights from the copyright owner to the user is included in the proposed (draft version of) version 3 of the GPL, in addition to other new, patent-related conditions.

The GPL is the most popular form of license used for open source software, representing the license for almost 70% of open source projects (Rosen, 2005), with the Linux kernel being perhaps the most prominent example. See www.gnu.org for the complete text of the license, as well as www.fsf.org for a discussion of common issues. Although the definition of the GPL was strongly motivated by ideological or philosophical concerns, there is also a strong case to be made that it is a pragmatic choice for a software license. For example, not having a truly GPL-compatible license may in fact be a practical disadvantage for successful project development on the grounds that otherwise "there's a significant risk that you'll fail to receive enough support from other developers to sustain your project" (Wheeler, 2003). Dual licensing is another option for free software distribution. In this connection, it is worth remembering what should be obvious: the copyright owner of a project that distributes its product under a GPL license is *not* restricted by the terms of that license; that is, the copyright owners can license the product any way they want. In particular, as in the case of the company that distributes MySQL, the owner can *dual license* the product as GPL for some users or versions, but as proprietary for others such as commercial users.

Reciprocity and Copyleft

The GPL incorporates a novel licensing concept introduced by the free software movement called *copyleft*. Copyleft is intended to avoid some of the downside associated with putting a product in the public domain, particularly the consequence that public domain software can be embedded in proprietary products. While under the law copyright limits the right of others to copy and redistribute a work, copyleft has a complementary intent, whence its oddly reversed name. Copyleft requires that anyone who receives a copy of a work, such as the source code for a program, receives the right to copy, modify, and redistribute the original work and derived modifications of the work, but only as long as they agree to the obligation that if they distribute such modifications, they do so under the same liberal conditions under which they received the work. As described by gnu.org, "Copyleft says that anyone who redistributes the software, with or without changes, *must pass along the freedom to further copy and change it*." This copyleft intent is asserted in the license that accompanies the original work that requires that all redistributed copies of the work and its derivatives must be distributed under this same license, which is tantamount to a recursive propagation of the original copyleft-restricted license. The owner of the original work still preserves his own copyright ownership. OSI general counsel and prominent open source advocate Lawrence Rosen recommends using the term *reciprocity* instead of copyleft because it is "less alarming and more descriptive than the word copyleft" (Rosen, 2005, p. 106), though he acknowledges that copyleft still has "rhetorical value" (p. 106). Another appealing way of describing copyleft is to say that it merely reflects a "share and share alike" principle. If you want someone to share his code with you, then you must share alike any improvements you make to that code, at least if you distribute them (Carver, 2005). The underlying purpose of such reciprocity arrangements is to create free software in a sense similar to and in the spirit of scientific freedom. As Rosen (2005) describes it, reciprocal licenses "contribute software into a *public commons* (italics added) of free software, but they mandate that derivative works also be placed in that same commons" (p. 70). This is in contrast with software distributed under so-called academic licenses like the BSD that "create a public commons of free software, and anyone can take such software for any purpose – including for creating proprietary collective and derivative works – without having to add anything back to that commons" (p. 70).

The more permissive open source licenses exhibit so-called *weak copyleft*. If software is licensed under the GPL, that license is by definition inherited by the software's descendants (derived works) under the copyleft proviso. In contrast, an open source license that does not require all derivative works to follow the original license exhibits weak copyleft. The MPL is a prominent example. It requires original and modified files licensed under the MPL to remain under that license. As described by Fishman (2004b), "The MPL's copyleft provision entails only changes to files subject to the MPL or new files that contain MPL-licensed code. New files that don't contain MPL-licensed code do not fall under the MPL." OSI-certified licenses like the Apache and BSD licenses that do not require copyleft are sometimes called no-copyleft licenses. Rosen (2005) lucidly explains the reciprocity characteristics of the MPL: "If you create and distribute a Modification to one of the files containing Original Code or previous Modifications, or create and distribute a new file containing Original Code or previous Modifications, those files must be released under the same MPL license" (Rosen, 2005, p. 143). MPL reciprocity is thus more narrowly applied than in the GPL and has the objective of encouraging "the use of open software as building blocks to create Larger Works," which may even be derivative works (Rosen, 2005, p. 147). However, "those Larger Works may be open or proprietary; with respect to them, the MPL acts like an academic license. But the individual building blocks are licensed with reciprocity obligations. If you distribute improvements to those building blocks, you must license those improvements under the MPL as open source software" (Rosen, 2005, p. 147).

Enforcement of the GPL

The enforcement of GPL license requirements has traditionally been handled privately through "negotiation and settlement agreements" (Carver, 2005, p. 464). In fact, there has not been even a U.S. court ruling on the enforceability of the GPL since the release of GPLv2 in 1991, though the case of SCO versus IBM may change that, as described in Carver (2005). Since it is the copyright holder who licenses the software, it is only the copyright holder who can make a claim if there is a violation of the license terms. The FSF is the copyright holder for some free software products and is the author of the GPL, but it is not the enforcer for the GPL, except for the products it owns. However, the FSF investigates reports it receives about GPL violations as part of its role in the free software movement. When appraised of a violation, it negotiates with the violator directly not for the purpose of seeking monetary damages but just to obtain compliance. Refer to the FSF compliance site for its policy (http://www.fsf.org/licensing/compliance, accessed December 20, 2006). As an example, an intervention by the FSF in the case of a popular Linksys wireless router that was distributed without the source code for its GPL'd software is described in Carver (2005). After the FSF negotiated with corporate owner Cisco, the company complied, providing the GPL software for dozens of its devices. This response had the beneficial side effect that the router became popular with hackers who developed projects to install more GPL'd applications on it.

Eben Moglen of the FSF puts the very absence of court cases on the validity of the GPL in a decidedly positive light (Moglen, 2001). He says that it follows from the simple, but effective and low-key, way that the FSF handles compliance, which they do frequently and successfully every year. They have never won – or lost – a case in court, simply because no one ever wants to go to court after the FSF talks to him. The discussion in Moglen (2001) conveys the unorthodox spirit of the General Counsel of the FSF, which is simultaneously legally savvy, witty, and street-smart. Moglen observes that the GPL has to be accepted only when copies are redistributed and since "no one can ever redistribute without a license, we can safely presume that anyone redistributing GPL'd software intended to accept the GPL" (Moglen, 2001). If there is a compliance problem, the FSF quietly contacts the violator, rarely publicizing the case or insisting on damages. However, it does make sure that the perpetrator understands the many consequences of noncompliance, including enormous bad publicity for violating cherished free software principles, widespread loss of goodwill, a level of ignominy such that no accomplished programmer would ever want to work for them again, all followed if they persist by a certain loss in court because of the clear violation of copyright law involved. With deadpan good humor Moglen says, "Look at how many people all over the world are pressuring me to enforce the GPL in court, just to prove I can. I really need to make an example of someone. Would you like to volunteer?" (Moglen, 2001). It is difficult to argue with his record of success. In fact it is arguably the strongest empirical argument for the solidity of the GPL and seems even more convincing than legal arguments about its validity.

Private individuals can directly try to enforce the GPL on their own copyrights. A notable case was that of Harold Welte, head developer for Netfilter (a firewall for GNU/Linux widely used in hardware routers) who pursued a number of GPL violations of Netfilter (Carver, 2005). In one case, Welte made an out-of-court settlement with the violator who subsequently made a substantial donation to FSF, Europe. A later case, with Sitecom Germany GmbH, again involving a violation where a router vendor was not providing the source for the GPL'd Netfilter firewall program used in the router went to a German District court. The court quickly issued an injunction against the violator and quickly decided for Netfilter. The decision was based on the simple termination clause in the GPL that says, "You may not copy, modify, sublicense, or distribute the Program *except as expressly provided under this license*" (Carver, 2005, p. 469, italics added). Significantly for the GPL's enforceability, the termination clause was held to be valid under German law.

As previously noted, no U.S. court has at this point ruled on the GPL. However an important case was brought in 2003 when the SCO Group sued IBM, alleging it had illegally contributed SCO UNIX code to Linux in the course of IBM's sponsorship of Linux development. IBM made a counterclaim that SCO had violated GPL'd IBM code in the Linux kernel (on which IBM holds copyrights to almost 800,000 lines of GPL'd code) in various ways, including "that SCO was distributing sixteen of IBM's own contributions to the Linux kernel while rejecting the GPL license that covered them" (Carver, 2005, p. 476; see also Stone 2004). According to analyst Carver, the most likely outcome of the case is a victory for IBM and the GPL analogous to the Welte case in Germany. However, the case is still not settled as of this writing, though the discovery judge dismissed most of SCO's claims in mid-2006.

International Enforcement

The recognition of intellectual property rights varies greatly across different nations. As a social construct, it is "deeply embedded in the ethos of some nations (like the U.S.) and not in others" (Meeker, 2006, p. 1). Copyrights are strongly enforced in the United States and the European Union (EU). Treaties like the Berne Convention and the Patent Cooperation Treaty aim to establish a degree of worldwide uniformity in copyright and patents, but realistically that does not mean there is anything even approximating global uniformity in their enforcement. Patents vary even more widely than copyrights, especially the relatively new software patents. As we observed previously, tens of thousands of software patents have been at least granted in the United States, though their validity can of course be challenged, but their status is not settled in the EU and India rejects them. There are also differences between the enforcement of legal mechanisms like contract and copyright, Meeker critically observing that "while most countries have some tradition of enforcing contracts, in many countries . . . copyright law is a joke" (p. 2). Major nations like China, India, and Russia provide minimal copyright enforcement, a circumstance especially relevant to the free/open source movement, since these countries are also increasingly major software developers. This combination of their weak copyright enforcement and their robust software development seems to undermine the enforceability of the GPL that relies on license termination in the case of violation, followed by legal action against copyright infringers to enforce compliance. Indeed, one might speculate that under such circumstances, "international outsourcing companies may become the software equivalent of money launderers" (Meeker, 2006, p. 4).

Meeker ironically characterizes open source software as "free software without enforcement" (Meeker, 2006, p. 4), where *free* as used here refers to reciprocal licenses like the GPL, while open source refers to nonreciprocal licenses like the BSD. Despite the cogency of this analysis, one could argue that most software development currently occurs in countries with strong copyright traditions. This provides a broad, geographically rooted enforcement matrix that protects GPL-based development. Global corporations then become implicated in GPL compliance because their operations encompass the copyright-stable regions. Furthermore, outside this legal matrix, the intrinsic practical benefits of the GPL still keep it attractive. Its public disclosure requirements ensure the rapid evolution of software because "each favorable acquired characteristic of others' work can be directly inherited" by other versions of the software (Moglen, 1999). It also has the critically important practical advantage that it protects a project from proliferating into multiple disjoint proprietary forks. The fact that the software is mandated to be published as it develops creates a centripetal force on the development process since different development versions can converge on the evolving visible changes which would otherwise tend to diverge. Major practical factors like these help to maintain robust GPL-based projects that can attract collaborators worldwide, including even those regions beyond where copyright is currently reliably enforced.

The Next Version of the GPL: GPLv3

The current version of the GPL, GPLv2, debuted in 1991. An updated GPLv3 currently under development will address issues like internationalization and software patents. A key objective of GPLv3 will be to ensure that it is "understood and enforceable" in an international context (Peters, 2006, p. 4). For example, as a trivial illustration, since the GPL license is based on copyright, the term for the license should be for the period recognized by applicable copyright law. In addition to internationalization, GPLv3 is intended to address software patents more explicitly and strongly. The draft version includes an explicit patent license grant, which is intended to improve internationalization and respond to some of the dangers software patents pose to free software. For example, currently GPLv2 relies on an *implied grant* of patent license, which is unacceptable in some countries. This is replaced in the GPLv3 draft by an "express patent license grant" (Peters, 2006, p. 4). The draft language is not simple to understand, so we will quote a paraphrase "the distributor is granting a royalty-free, worldwide patent license covering all patent claims the distributor controls or has the right to sublicense, at the time of distribution or in the future, that '*would be* infringed or violated by the covered work or any reasonably contemplated use of the covered work'" (Peters, 2006, p. 4, italics added). The GPLv3 response to problems posed by the proliferation of software patents is also reflected in a new patent-related restriction that applies even to the private use of GPLv3'ed software! Recall that GPLv2 asserts limitations and conditions only when the software is actually distributed. In contrast, the most recent GPLv3 draft states that you lose the right to "make and run privately modified versions of the Program . . . if you bring suit against anyone for patent infringement of any of your essential patent claims in any such version" (http://gplv3.fsf.org/gpl-draft-2006-07-27.html). Distributors also incur an obligation to protect downstream users. A distributor of GPLv3-licensed code "who knowingly relies on a patent license to protect itself from liability in connection with the distribution" must also "shield downstream users from that same liability . . . through the grant of a sublicense . . . indemnification, or similar mechanism" (Peters, 2006, p. 7). As another modification, users will apparently also be able to combine code under licenses previously deemed incompatible," like the Eclipse and Mozilla Public License (Peters, 2006, pp. 6–7). The eventual impact and form of the GPLv3 license is not yet clear. For example, in early 2007, Linus Torvalds and a group of Linux kernel developers expressed reservations such as about the treatment of Digital Rights Management and patent provisions in the GPLv3.

6.6.2 The Lesser GPL and Derivative Works

The GNU *Lesser General Public License* or LGPL, previously called the Library GPL, uses weak copyleft. The LGPL is an open source license that is intended to be useful for open source software libraries because it allows such libraries to be used or called (linked to) by closed source, proprietary programs, without the proprietary programs being affected or "contaminated" by any GPL requirements.

   Most GNU libraries are licensed under the LGPL, but the FSF has tactical motivations for when this license should or should not be used. In contrast to the LGPL, were an open source library licensed under the ordinary GPL, then any program that used the library would itself have to be licensed as GPL and hence could not be proprietary. This is what Stallman says in his gnu.org essay on "Why you *shouldn't* use the Library GPL for your next library" (italics added). Actually a key point in this essay is other than a legal one. It is tactical; namely, that it is better for the ultimate success of the free software movement if free developers chose to release libraries they develop under the GPL (rather than the LGPL) because this gives the free software movement a competitive advantage vis-à-vis proprietary developers who already have the considerable advantage of immense private funding. This development/licensing tactic provides the community of free developers with a software library advantage that proprietary developers cannot avail themselves of. That is why the FSF might recommend the GPL for such situations, even though the FSF also has the library-related LGPL license available. On the other hand, if there are already other equivalent libraries that a proprietary developer could use, then in that case Stallman recommends that the new free library under consideration be released under LGPL so that it can better compete with the existing proprietary libraries. In either case, from the FSF's point of view, it is less a matter of principle than of competitive advantage as to which licensing choice is made.

Derivative Works – Static and Dynamic Linking – APIs

The relationship between the GPL, derivative works of software, and how a new program interacts with existing GPL'd code presents licensing issues that may be subtle or potentially confusing. The following discussion attempts to address some of these issues, but the final interpretations do not all seem conclusive. There appear to be conflicting points of view on some of these issues that do not appear to have been settled yet by judicial decisions.

One consideration is whether there is a difference between the impact of static linking as opposed to dynamic linking in the context of GPL, or depending on the nature of the APIs that a program interfaces with. Consider first the case of static linking. In software development, *static linking* refers to the resolution by a linker of all the unresolved references that an application program's compiled (object) code makes to external library modules, until the separate modules have all been knitted together into a single executable file. From a copyright point of view, it seems that the resulting unified object code *seems likely* to thereby constitute a derivative work of a GPL'd open source library, and hence be subject to the GPL because the application code and library parts are now inseparable (Asay, 2003). On the other hand, consider the implications of *dynamic linking*, which refers to the resolution by a linker of the unresolved references that an application's compiled (object) code makes to external modules – but absent combining the application and external module objects into a single executable file. Thus the executables remain separate. From a copyright point of view, the resulting interacting programs *do not appear* to constitute a derived work of the original external modules. The article by Rosen (2001b) addresses these issues and, in this context, also challenges the notion of the GPL as a viral or contagious type of licensing arrangement. In particular, concerning dynamic links, Rosen indicates that they *do not* create a derivative work, because they are transitory relations that do not modify the code of the original program that is linked to.

The relationship between software interfaces and the GPL can be viewed from other viewpoints as well. For example, well-known Linux commentator Jonathan Corbet (2003) asserted, "It is reasonably widely accepted that a program which simply uses a *well-documented* API does not become a derived work of the code implementing that API" (italics added). The same should apply to an ABI, an Application Binary Interface, which is defined in terms of the object code rather than the source code interface. The Linux kernel system call interface is an example of such a well-known and well-documented, stable interface. Indeed in the case of Linux, "the COPYING file supplied with the kernel explicitly states that programs using the system call interface are not considered to be derived works" (Corbet, 2003). Furthermore, the Linux kernel license even includes the following clarification: "This copyright does *not* cover user programs that use kernel services by normal system calls – this is merely considered normal use of the kernel, and does *not* fall under the heading of 'derived work'" (Epplin, 2001; Raymond, 2001; and the Linux kernel COPYING file referred to there). It seems to be general practice/belief that such an interaction allows a GPL'd library, accessed as in Linux system calls, to act as "as an acceptable platform to build" on, letting proprietary application programs "leverage (the platform's) functionality without stealing" it, in a manner consistent with the open source requirements of licenses like the GPL (Asay, 2003). But while the stable and well-known external Linux interface based on Unix system calls is one thing, internal Linux modules that are not part of this stable interface are another matter according to Torvalds (Corbet, 2003). A pertinent distinction is that the stable interface represents a recognized "boundary for derived works" (Corbet, 2003), while that was not the intent for low-level kernel modules. Another consideration would be whether the external module was "implemented independently of Linux," like in the case of new device drivers.

The FSF's Eben Moglen (2003), on the other hand, appears to offer a different interpretation. In response to a question as to whether a newly composed Java application that uses a JAR (a zipped Java class library) that is licensed under the GPL must itself also necessarily be licensed under the GPL, Moglen said, "The situation is no different than the one where your code depends on static or dynamic linking of a GPL'd library, say GNU readline. Your code, in order to operate, must be combined with the GPL'd code, forming a new combined work, which under GPL Section 2(b) must be distributed under the terms of the GPL and only the GPL. If the author of the other code had chosen to release his JAR under the Lesser GPL, your contribution to the combined work could be released under any license of your choosing, but by releasing under GPL he or she chose to invoke the principle of share and share alike." A noteworthy difference between this and the Linux system-call case may be that the JAR is not an operating system built on an existing stable API like the Linux platform.

References

Andersen, T. (2004). Behlendorf on Open Source. http://www.itwriting.com/ behlendorf1.php. Accessed December 1, 2006.

Anderson, R. (2003a). 'Trusted Computing' Frequently Asked Questions, Version 1.1. http://www.cl.cam.ac.uk/~rja14/tcpa-faq.html. Accessed December 1, 2006.

Anderson, R. (2003b). 'Trusted Computing' and Competition Policy – Issues for Computing Professionals. Upgrade. The European Journal for the Informatics Professional, 4(3), 35–41.

Asay, M. (2003). Open Source's General Public License: Why Microsoft Is So Scared. Wasatch Digital IQ, 3(1). http://www.wasatchdigitaliq.com/parser.php?nav= article&article_id=49. Accessed December 1, 2006.

Bessen, J. (2002). What Good is Free Software? In: Government Policy toward Open Source Software, R. W. Hahn (editor). Brookings Institution Press, Washington, DC.

Capek, C., Frank, S., Gerdt, S., and Shields, D. (2005). A History of IBM's Open-Source Involvement and Strategy. IBM Systems Journal, 44(2), 249–257.

Carver, B. (2005). Share and Share Alike: Understanding and Enforcing Open Source and Free Software Licenses. Berkeley Technology Law Journal, 20, 443–481.

Corbet, J. (2003). Binary Modules and Derived Works. http://lwn.net/Articles/61490/. Accessed December 1, 2006.

Downen, M. (2005). Obfuscation. Posted May 26. http://blogs.msdn.com/CLRSecurity/. Accessed December 1, 2006.

Epplin, J. (2001). Using GPL Software in Embedded Applications: Wind River's Worries. http://www.linuxdevices.com/articles/AT9161119242.html. Accessed December 1, 2006.

Engelfriet, A. (2005). Patent Risks of Open Source Software. http://www.iusmentis.com/ computerprograms/opensourcesoftware/patentrisks/. Accessed December 1, 2006.

Evans, D. (2002). Politics and Programming: Government Preferences for Promoting Open Source Software. In: Government Policy toward Open Source Software, R. W. Hahn (editor). Brookings Institution Press, Washington, DC.

Feller, J. and Fitzgerald, B. (2002). Understanding Open Source Software Development. Addison-Wesley, Pearson Education Ltd., London.

Fishman, S. (2004a). Open Source Licenses Are Not All the Same. 11/18/2004. http:// www.onlamp.com/pub/a/onlamp/2004/11/18/licenses.html. Accessed December 1, 2006.

Fishman, S. (2004b). Web and Software Development: A Legal Guide. Nolo Pub., Berkeley, CA.

Fitzgerald, B. and Bassett, G. (2003). Legal Issues Relating to Free and Open Software. In: Essays in Technology Policy and Law, vol. 1. B. Fitzgerald and G. Bassett (editors). Queensland University of Technology, School of Law, Brisbane, Australia,, Chapter 2.

Hollaar, L. (2002). Legal Protection of Digital Information. BNA Books. http://digital-law-online.info/. Accessed January 20, 2007.

IBM Press Release. (2005). IBM Pledges 500 U.S. Patents to Open Source in Support of Innovation and Open Standards. January 11. Armonk, New York.

Jassin, L. and Schecter, S. (1997). Copyright Permission and Libel Handbook: A Step-by-Step Guide for Writers, Editors and Publishers. John Wiley & Sons, New York.

Jones, P. (2003). The GPL Is a License, Not a Contract, Which Is Why the Sky Isn't Falling. December 14. http://www.groklaw.net/article.php?story= 20031214210634851. Accessed December 20, 2006.

Jones, P. (2005). Software, Reverse Engineering, and the Law. http://lwn.net/Articles/ 134642/. Accessed December 1, 2006.

Knuth, D. (1990). The Future of TEX and METFONT., Nederlandstalige TeX Gebruik-ersgroep, *MAPS* 5, 145–146. www.ntg.nl/maps/maps5.html. Accessed January 5, 2007.

Landau, M. (2000) "Statutory Damages" in Copyright Law and the MP3.com Case. http://chnm.gmu.edu/digitalhistory/links/pdf/chapter7/7.24b.pdf. Accessed December 1, 2006.

Lerner, J. and Tirole, J. (2005). The Scope of Open Source Licensing. Journal of Law, Economics, and Organization, 21(1), 21–56.

Magid, L. (2005). It Pays to Read License Agreements. http://www.pcpitstop.com/ spycheck/eula.asp. Accessed December 1, 2006.

McMillan, R. (2002). Patent War Pending? Lawrence Rosen on How Open Source Can Protect Itself from Software Patents. http://linuxplanet.com/linuxplanet/ interviews/4575/1/. Accessed December 1, 2006.

Meeker, H. (2006). Only in America? Copyright Law Key to Global Free Software Model. LinuxInsider. May 16.

Microsoft. (2006). Microsoft and Novell Announce Broad Collaboration on Windows and Linux Interoperability and Support. Microsoft Press Release. November 2. http://www.microsoft.com/presspass/press/2006/nov06/11–02MSNovellPR. mspx. Accessed January 20, 2007.

Moglen, E. (1999). Anarchism Triumphant: Free Software and the Death of Copyright. First Monday, 4(8). http://www.firstmonday.org/issues/issue4_8/moglen/ index.html. Accessed January 5, 2007.

Moglen, E. (2001). Enforcing the GNU GPL. http://www.gnu.org/philosophy/enforcing-gpl.html. Accessed December 20, 2006.

Moglen, E. (2003). Professor Eben Moglen Replies. February 20. http://interviews. slashdot.org/interviews/03/02/20/1544245.shtml. Accessed February 18, 2007.

Open Source Risk Management. (2004). Results of First-Ever Linux Patent Review Announced, Patent Insurance Offered by Open Source Risk Management. August 2. http://www.osriskmanagement.com/press_releases/press_release_080204.pdf. Accessed December 20, 2006.

OSS Watch (2006). The GNU General Public License – An Overview. Open Source Advisory Service. http://www.oss-watch.ac.uk/resources/gpl.xml. Accessed December 1, 2006.

Payne, C. (2002). On the Security of Open Source Software. Information Systems Journal, 12(1), 61–78.

Perens, B. (1999a). It's Time to Talk about Free Software Again. http://lists.debian.org/debian-devel/1999/02/msg01641.html. Accessed January 5, 2007.

Perens, B. (1999b). The Open Source Definition. In: Open Sources: Voices from the Open Source Revolution, M. Stone, S. Ockman, and C. DiBona (editors). O'Reilly Media, Sebastopol, CA, 171–188.

Perens, B. (2004). The Problem of Software Patents in Standards. http://perens.com/Articles/PatentFarming.html. Accessed December 1, 2006.

Perens, B. (2006). The Monster Arrives: Software Patent Lawsuits against Open Source Developers. June 30. http://technocrat.net/d/2006/6/30/5032. Accessed January 5, 2007.

Peters, D. (2006). Software Patents and Open Source Software: An Overview of Patent Provisions in the First Draft of GPLv3. American Intellectual Property Law Association 2006 Spring Meeting, May 3–5, Chicago.

Raymond, E. (2001). Email from Raymond to Torvalds. Subject: Controversy over Dynamic Linking – How to End the Panic. June 21, 2001, 14:14:42. Linux Kernel Mailing List Archive. http://lwn.net/2001/0628/a/esr-modules.php3. Accessed February 18, 2007.

Rosen, L. (2001a). Naming Your Open Source Software. http://www.rosenlaw.com/lj6.htm. Accessed December 1, 2006.

Rosen, L. (2001b). The Unreasonable Fear of Infection. RosenLaw.com, 32. September 23, 2001. http://www.rosenlaw.com/html/GPL.PDF. Accessed December 1, 2006.

Rosen, L. (2002). Why the Public Domain Isn't a License. Tuesday, 2002–10–01, 01:00. Linux Journal. http://www.linuxjournal.com/article/6225. Accessed December 19, 2006.

Rosen, L. (2003). Derivative Works. http://www.linuxjournal.com/article/6366. Accessed December 1, 2006.

Rosen, L. (2005). Open Source Licensing: Software Freedom and Intellectual Property Law. Prentice Hall, Upper Saddle River, NJ.

Rosenberg, D. K. (2005). Open Source Licensing: Software Freedom and Intellectual Property Law: Book Review. Open Source Licensing Page, Stromian Technologies.

Samuels, E. (1993). The Public Domain in Copyright Law. Communications Media Center at New York Law School. Journal of the Copyright Society of the USA, 41, 137–182. http://www.edwardsamuels.com/copyright/beyond/articles/public.html. Accessed December 6, 2006.

Samuelson, P. (2002). Reverse Engineering under Siege. Communications of the ACM, 45(10), 15–20.

Schwartz, M. (2001). Reverse-Engineering. http://www.computerworld.com/softwaretopics/software/appdev/story/0,10801,65532,00.html. Accessed December 1, 2006.

Shapiro, C. (2001). Navigating the Patent Thicket: Cross Licenses, Patent Pools and Standard Setting. In: Innovation Policy and the Economy, A. Jaffe, J. Lerner, and S. Stern (editors). National Bureau of Economics. http://faculty.haas.vberkeley.edu/shapiro/thicket.pdf. Accessed December 1, 2006.

Stallman, R. (1996/2001). Categories of Free and Non-Free Software. http://www.gnu.org/philosophy/categories.html. Accessed January 20, 2007.

Stallman, R. (2001). Free Software: Freedom and Cooperation. www.gnu.org/events/rms-nyu-2001-transcript.txt. Accessed December 1, 2006.

Stallman, R. (2005). Fighting Software Patents – Singly and Together. http://www.gnu.org/philosophy/fighting-software-patents. Accessed December 1, 2006.

Stone, L. (2004). The Linux Killer. Issue 12.07. http://www.wired.com/wired/archive/12.07/linux.html. Accessed December 1, 2006.

Tonella, P. Antoniol, G., Fiutem, R., and Calzolari, F. (2000). Reverse Engineering 4.7 Million Lines of Code. Software Practice and Experience, 30, 129–150.

Ueda, M., Uzuki, T., and Suematsu, C. (2004). A Cluster Analysis of Open Source Licenses. In: Proceedings of 1st International Conference on Open Source Systems, Genova.

Walli, S. (2005). Perspectives on the Shared Initiative. http://www.onlamp.com/pub/a/onlamp/2005/03/24/shared_source.html. Accessed December 1, 2006.

Warrene, B. (2005). Navigating Open Source Licensing. http://www.sitepoint.com/article/open-source-licensing. Accessed December 1, 2006.

Webbink, M. (2003). Understanding Open Source Software. New South Wales Society for Computers and Law Journal, 51. http://www.groklaw.net/article.php?story=20031231092027900. Accessed December 1, 2006.

Weber, S. (2004). The Success of Open Source. Harvard University Press, Cambridge, MA.

West, J. (2003). How Open Is Open Enough? Melding Proprietary and Open Source Platform Strategies. Research Policy, 32(7), 1259–1285.

Wheeler, D. (2003). Make Your Open Source GPL-Compatible. Or Else. Revised November 2006. http://www.dwheeler.com/essays/gpl-compatible.html. Accessed December 1, 2006.

Wilson, R. (2005). The Mozilla Public License – An Overview. Open Source Advisory Service. http://www.oss-watch.ac.uk/resources/mpl.xml. Accessed December 1, 2006.

Zittrain, J. (2004). Normative Principles for Evaluating Free and Proprietary Software. University of Chicago Law Review, 71(1), 265.

7

The Economics of Open Source

This chapter looks at open source development from an economic and business point of view. We have two objectives. One is to understand the economic matrix in which open source development operates, what characteristic economic factors affect its viability, and what proven business models have been established. The other objective is to consider some of the classic motivational questions about why people do open development from an economic perspective. Some standard economic factors we consider are the influence of vendor lock-in, network effects (or network externalities), the total cost of use of software, the impact of licensing on business models, the potential for customizability for open source versus proprietary products, implications of complementary products, and the effect of commoditization. We also examine some of the successful open source business models that have evolved over time. The longstanding question about open business models is basically how can people make money off a product that is given away for free? Who pays for the cost of developing this software? We consider various approaches that have proved successful, including dual licensing, consultation on open source products, provision of open source software (OSS) distributions and related services, and hybrid business models like the use of open source for in-house development or horizontally in a strategic synergistic combination with proprietary products such as in the case of IBM's involvement with the Apache Foundation and Linux. With respect to the competitive prospects of a product, a key economic characteristic is the extent to which the product's function has become standard, routine, or commoditized (in economic terminology). Commoditization deeply affects the competitive landscape for proprietary products. It also appears to be a fundamental force or driving factor in open source applications development. We will present some explanations that have been set forth to understand the role of this factor in open source success and its implications for the future. Speculation about whether individuals participate in open development for psychological, social, or other reasons has also long intrigued observers of the open source scene. We consider some economic interpretations of motivations for participation. One of these models, which derives its data from an empirical study of the Apache Project, uses a so-called signaling interpretation to explain why individuals find it economically useful to volunteer for open source projects. Another model argues that international differences in economic conditions alter the opportunity cost of developer participation and that this is the decisive factor in variations between participation rates for different geographic regions.

7.1 Standard Economic Effects

The success of an open source product in the marketplace is influenced by a range of factors. What does the product do? Is it easy to use and reliable? Is it secure, or fast, or portable? The answers to these questions vary greatly with the application involved and who the expected users are. The considerations for a Web server, or an Internet utility, or a systems administration tool are vastly different from those involved for mass market tools like Web browsers or special-purpose tools like graphics or accounting utilities. One common element is the impact of basic economic effects like vendor lock-in, network effects, and total cost of use. We consider how each of these affects the marketplace for software products in general and for open versus proprietary products in particular. Vendor lock-in, for example, has been argued to provide an advantage to proprietary giants like Microsoft with respect to its Windows platform. Network effects are feedback effects that make the level of market share increase as a function of market penetration. Such a pattern can influence the selection of marketing strategies for software products. Total Cost of Ownership (TCO) is a standard composite business metric. It is often used to evaluate products and to compare proprietary to open source products, often in the context of a claim by proprietary providers that whereas open products may be initially cheaper because they are (relatively) free of charge, their long-term costs are actually less attractive.

7.1.1 Vendor Lock-in

A user of a product is said to be locked-in to a particular brand if the direct and indirect costs of switching to another brand are prohibitive. This is also called *vendor lock-in*. The switching costs may be due to the cost of training workers to use another system, contrasted with the fact that they are already familiar with the tools they need in the current system. Or there may be switching costs due to program or file incompatibilities that would result if the user migrates to another system. Vendor lock-in is not just a technical effect: it can also be based on perceptual effects like market recognition. For example, Microsoft is a well-recognized and widely accepted operating system, whatever its faults and limitations are. In the absence of strong countervailing reasons, the decision to use Microsoft Windows or products is thus often likely to be perceived as a "safe" decision when it is purchased for corporate or organizational use. If for some reason it turns out that there are problems with this choice because the system does not perform satisfactorily, then the decision maker is at least less likely to face repercussions for having made an idiosyncratic choice; after all, it's a standard solution and there's safety in numbers.

The effects of vendor lock-in can arise with either proprietary or open systems, but are more likely to occur with proprietary systems. Thus proprietary Unix vendors produced different versions of the openly defined Unix system during the late 1980s–1990s that, while "Unix-like," were sufficiently incompatible that users of one Unix environment could not readily use components from another. So lock-in can occur even in relatively similar environments. The use of OSS in general and the GPL in particular tends to protect against lock-in for the obvious reason that any distributed code and functionality must be public, and so users are much less likely to become married to a particular vendor. The users, or at least sophisticated users, in principle have control over the open code, which gives them at least a measure of control over the underlying technology, making them more independent of the vendor. The rationale for why open source promotes vendor-independence over vendor lock-in is succinctly expressed by Bob Young of Red Hat regarding open source (Broersma, 2002):

> It's like buying a car with a hood that you can open, as opposed to the traditional model in the software industry where the hood is locked shut. If you can open the hood it means you can fix your car, but it also means you have access to 10,000 car repair shops . . . Whereas if the hood's locked shut, and if your vendor . . .

In other words, open source provides users freedom and control and relative independence of vendors; however, keep in mind that this is only for sophisticated users with the resources to exploit the control that is theoretically available.

The Windows operating system is usually considered the most prominent example of vendor lock-in. Windows and its accompanying applications represent a highly attractive, unified, packaged environment where the parts are designed to interoperate within that environment. Furthermore, the availability of the Microsoft Windows Application Programming Interface (API) allows many third-party programs to be written for the Windows platform, which also contributes to helping lock users into the environment. This lock-in effect even applies to the developers of independent software for Windows environments because their applications tend to be heavily dependent on the Windows API and so not readily ported to other operating systems. However, the level of user lock-in to Windows because of third-party applications should be decreasing with the availability of Wine for running Windows apps on non-Windows platforms. Vendor lock-in can also arise in cases where proprietary hardware must be used to access a service – a current example being the interaction between the Apple's iPod device and the Apple iTunes Music Store.

7.1.2 Network Effects

Network effects, which are also called network externalities, refer to an increase in the value of a product or service the greater the number of people who use the product or service. For example, the more people use services like e-mail or Web services like eBay, the more valuable the services become because the potential social connectivity of any given user becomes greater. Similarly, the more Web sites or resources on the Internet, the more benefit others gain from the Internet – a classic feedback factor in the original exponential development of the Internet. Likewise, the more people use a software product like Microsoft Word, the more useful it becomes for a given user to use the same package. This is because anyone else using the same software can have complete access to the documents made by the original user. For example, one benefit is that it is easier for collaborators to share a document if they all have access to the same word processing program.

The network effect is obviously not limited to software products and in fact it was first examined in other contexts. For example, the English language has become increasingly important because so many people speak it, making the value of learning it greater, thereby extending the number of speakers in a positive feedback cycle. Of course, not everything behaves in this way. Obvious examples are resources like highways that are constrained by their limited carrying capacities. In this case, the more people who use a highway, the less valuable it becomes to other users, at least at a certain point, because traffic speed and throughput decreases as the road gets more crowded. This corresponds to a negative network effect (or negative externality). It obviously applies to communication networks in general, where increased demand inversely affects access to a network. Social examples where network effects are inverted include products where uniqueness is prized, like a stylish dress valued because it's the only one of its kind. Or a valued rare metal like gold whose value would plummet if it became commonplace and hence commoditized. The work by Liebowitz and Margolis (1998) extensively and critically analyzes the application of this and related concepts (see also Liebowitz (2002) as well as the seminal work by Leibenstein (1950)).

Certain software products such as operating systems have positive network effects because the larger the market for the system, the more likely it is that products will be developed for the system, thereby increasing its value to users. Of course, this phenomenon is not always relevant to the success of a popular software product. For example, the dominant provider of financial and tax software is Intuit which markets Turbo-Tax and Quicken, both of which are widely used. However, unlike, say, the documents generated by word processors which are often exchanged with other users, the type of information these products deal in is not widely exchanged among users, so there are limited network effects. These products are dominant and successful because they are the best products in the field in terms of their functionality (Liebowitz and Margolis, 1998), albeit word of mouth regarding the quality of the product spreads in a network-like fashion.

The attempt to exploit network effects explains certain market strategies like Netscape's original free-of-charge browser strategy that was expected to have the side effect of enhancing the market for other Netscape products. The strategy initially worked, leading to a dominant market share for the Netscape browser partly through network effects. Of course, as we have noted previously, the effect was not permanent. Mismanagement by Netscape and slow-and-steady technical progress by Microsoft's Internet Explorer, combined with the arguably predatory Microsoft practice of bundling its browser and shipping it for free, eroded Netscape's short-lived victory. Freeware products like the Adobe Reader are also motivated by the strategy of exploiting network effects. In the case of Adobe, the Reader is essential for the utility of the product. Without it, most of the public that receives such documents would be unable to read them, which would greatly undermine the utility of the full Adobe software package for the full-function users who create and disseminate these documents. Of course, Netscape was released as open source, while Adobe Reader is proprietary freeware, so the network effect impacts both categories of software similarly. However, a symbiotic combination of network effects for both users and developers does have a relationship to open source development. For example, Firefox's rapid spread created a word-of-mouth network effect among its users. As its market share expanded, the scale of distribution of the project, at that point, helped make it a more attractive target of interest for open developer contributions, who were able to participate in development precisely because of the open nature of the product. Their contributions were then able to further expedite the appeal and spread of the product.

Network effects also manifest themselves significantly in the case of certain Web services where user *contributions* to a site are decisive to the success and even the functionality of the site in the marketplace (O'Reilly, 2005). Important examples of this phenomenon include the services provided by the online encyclopedia Wikipedia, all of the contributions to which are completely user provided and edited. The value of an auction site like eBay also derives from the number of participants it attracts to its auctions.

7.1.3 Total Cost of Ownership

The *total cost of ownership* for software consists of all the direct and indirect costs involved in purchasing (licensing), deploying, using, training and supporting, administering, and maintaining the software. It includes any costs triggered by the purchase of the product, from migration and integration costs to the cost of lost business or even damage to one's business reputation if the product is unsatisfactory. Understanding the TCO of a product is obviously a prerequisite to correctly estimating the return on investment of the decision to purchase the software. Obviously free software is free of charge and so its purchase price is nominally a major advantage. However, the TCO is frequently used by proprietary software providers as a metric to discourage the use of open source. The free-of-charge initial license is said to save up-front costs but to mask hidden, downstream costs. Certainly, up-front purchase costs should be and are recognized as only one element of a quantitative decision process. For example, a report by the Gartner Group estimated original purchase costs of software as less than 10% of total cost, with 90% of total costs being for various indirect costs (Gonzalez, 2002).

TCO is a complex, composite metric. A report by the Computer Sciences Corporation (Hohn and Herr, 2004) breaks down TCO into four major categories: planning and deployment, support and learning, human resources or people, and ongoing costs. Planning and deployment include acquisition, installation, and data migration, as well as the cost of researching the decision, experimenting, and meetings. Support and learning include disruption during migration and incompatible tools, skills, and experience. Human resources include costs for hiring and training new staff and for consultants. Ongoing costs include those for administration and technical support, including administration of licenses, professional development, and opportunity costs. This elaborate model surfaces many cost drivers. Clearly an implication is that understanding these costs is a nontrivial matter and that acquisition costs are only a single, and possibly small, part of the overall cost picture.

Concerning the comparison of costs for open and proprietary platforms, there are detailed, objective analyses that have examined the conditions under which a Linux platform may be less expensive than a Microsoft platform in the TCO sense. Thus the Gartner Report by Smith et al. (2003) considered how TCO can be applied in decision making for office software. They compare the use of Microsoft Office, Linux, and StarOffice. The analysis identifies a preliminary savings of $150 in hardware and software costs for the initial *acquisition* costs for a Linux environment with StarOffice, versus about half that if StarOffice is installed on a Windows platform. However, to even have a chance of savings in TCO, the Linux environment had to be "locked down." The system was largely sealed, with the user having little control over anything but the interface, and was not even able to reinstall the operating system.

An increasingly important case is represented by situations where so-called large multipliers occur that amplify acquisition and deployment costs. For example, the impact of the initial purchase cost is magnified in the case of digital appliances that have embedded software. This occurs, for example, when a manufacturer embeds software in a device like a PDA or cell phone. Since millions of these devices may be distributed, the availability of free-of-charge OSS components immediately provides a huge savings in costs because of the multiplier involved. The same multiplier effects can also benefit organizations with large numbers of desktop PCs. Hohn and Herr (2004) observe that in the case of the Computer Sciences Corporation, the company had 40,000 desktops, which establishes a huge immediate cost savings multiplier when open source decisions are made.

The detailed and well-respected Web site by Dave Wheeler (Wheeler, 2005) contains extensive links to articles comparing the TCO for open source versus proprietary products. The theoretical and empirically supported arguments he advances for often cheaper TCO for open products include lower maintenance and upgrade costs, lower licensing administration costs, and lower costs for hardware including the reuse of low-end and obsolete machines. Wheeler references and overviews a lengthy list of empirical studies. The examples are too extensive to conveniently summarize, but a few stand out. For example, one study indicated that Intel saved $200 million by switching from Unix to GNU/Linux servers. Another study showed Windows versus Linux TCO savings in the range of 20–40% for Linux. The results depend strongly on the application areas, and there are many factors that can affect the relative advantages of the products, but overall there is a great deal of evidence supporting claims of lower total cost of use for open solutions in many venues.

7.2 Open Source Business Models

The longstanding paradoxical quandary about open source business models is basically how can people make money off a product that is sold for free? Who pays for the cost of developing this software? There are a number of approaches that have been successful. The following are some of the basic possibilities:

1. dual licensing,
2. consulting on OSS,
3. providing open software distributions and services,
4. hybrid proprietary/open model – vertical development with OSS, and
5. hybrid proprietary/open model – horizontal arrangements.

For example, the owners of the copyright for an open product can use dual licensing models that differentiate customers based on individual versus commercial use. The myriad of cost factors that we have seen lie behind a TCO analysis serve to reveal many other opportunities for a viable business model as well. Most of these factors come into play after the acquisition of an open source product, but even during the systems analysis and selection phase there are business opportunities. A complex and variegated business can be built on providing expertise in consulting for a repertoire of open source products, with consultation running the gamut from choice of products and system configuration to service support and local adaptation of the software. Open software can be provided with provisions for training and support on a for-charge basis. A business that is primarily running on proprietary software can complement its software operation with open source components adapted for internal use only and not for distribution. There are other possibilities as well for commercial venues for open development. Thus commercial companies can provide products or services that are complementary to open products – an approach that has been called "living symbiotically" with the open source community, a prime example being the strategy adopted by the IBM corporation which invested over $1 billion in 2001 alone in this type of relationship (Lerner and Tirole, 2004). A related approach, which represents the most profitable area for open source to date, is vertical use of open source combined with in-house proprietary software. An underlying trend that also arises, especially in both the dual-licensed and software distributions models, is an emphasis on branding the open product, so it becomes synonymous in the customer's mind with qualities like reliability, thus making it the default trusted product of choice (Moczar, 2005).

7.2.1 Dual Licensing

Dual licensing lets the owner of a copyrighted licensed product provide free and open distribution for nonprofit users but requires a separate paid approach for commercial users. We introduced our discussion of this model in Chapter 2. The MySQL database system is offered under a dual license by the company MySQL AB that owns the software. The noncommercial license is free of charge and pure GPL. The GPL version helps keep the product connected to the creativity of the open source community. The commercial license provides an enhanced version of the software, called MySQL Pro that, according to the Web site, is more secure and reliable, as well as provides service support for a fee. The company has a variety of other products as well and will also develop custom enhancements to the product, which their expertise in the product's implementation puts them in an ideal position to do. Naturally, if any licensed user embeds MySQL in an existing General Public Licensed application, thereby modifying that product, then the resulting application has to be distributed as GPL, if it is redistributed at all, because it comes under the force of that other product's GPL. However, the proprietary MySQL license presents quite different terms and opportunities. It allows commercial developers or companies to not only modify the MySQL source code but also integrate it with their own proprietary products, and redistribute and sell the resulting system as a proprietary closed source system! MySQL can do this, even though such conditions are contrary to the requirements of the GPL, precisely because the MySQL AB company *owns* the copyright to the software and so, as owner, is not restricted by the provisions of one of its licenses, including the fact that it obviously preserves its right to release its product under different licenses! The commercial license requires a fee currently ranging up to $5,000 per year for their high-end server (as of 2005). Thus, if you purchase MySQL under its commercial license, then you do *not* have to comply with the terms of the GPL. Naturally, you cannot infringe on the trademarked MySQL™ name in any derivative product – an issue that arose particularly in the dispute between MySQL and NuSphere (MySQL News Announcement, 2001). The commercial license provides product support from MySQL AB as well as product warranties and responsibilities that are not in the free General Public Licensed copy of the product that is offered only on an as-is basis. This proprietary form of the license is required even if you only sell a commercial product that merely requires the user to download a copy of MySQL, or if you include a copy of MySQL, or include MySQL drivers in a proprietary application. Most of MySQL AB's income derives from the fees for the proprietary license, with additional revenues from training and consultancy services. According to Valimaki (2005), most of the fee income comes from embedded commercial applications. The income from these services and fees adds up to a viable composite open source/proprietary business model.

7.2.2 Consulting on OSS

The broad array of existing open source products also constitutes a fertile and natural opportunity for consulting. These products comprise a large inventory of important, viable, and possibly even best-of-breed open products, with regard to which any business can establish expertise because the internals of the products are public. The range of products is clearly complex and widely enough used such that expertise would present a considerable level of business value. The British OSS consulting firm *GBdirect* is an excellent example of a business model that is based on a company's expertise across a broad spectrum of open source products. The corporate Web site (http://software-support.gbdirect.co.uk/, accessed January 20, 2007) gives a very instructive overview of the market needs that such a company serves. It describes their services as having traditionally involved the design, implementation, installation, integration, and handcrafting of open source solutions. More recently the company offers a wide collection of open source packaged solutions. Its effectiveness depends on having a highly experienced staff of open source experts. The site describes how many of the standard, mature open source packages are "written for experts" so that even technically very capable systems people without the proper experience may have difficulty maintaining them, or modifying and adapting them if needed. It also describes how the company can expedite the conventional proprietary "escalation" of technical assistance by providing software fixes directly from the software author (!) or by designing it themselves, all without any legal impediments, due to the open nature of the licenses. The company's embedding in and familiarity with the open source developer community lets it tap into the expertise of multiple individuals as well as that of other open source companies. The latter opportunity is much less usual in a proprietary framework but is common among open source providers who have a longstanding community tradition of sharing skills since they all work on the same kind of software. The public, open nature of the code also allows the firm to invoke the help of other companies when their own workload is strained, so it can respond more effectively to its clients. The open solutions of other companies can also facilitate innovation because the solutions are available without having to be reverse-engineered.

Expertise like this is increasingly relevant to in-house software developers. Over the past decade, in-house software development has increasingly relied on integrating off-the-shelf components to implement software systems.

Previously this process had emphasized the selection and integration of COTS (Commercial-Off-The-Shelf) products, but there are increasing opportunities for mature, OSS components with the appropriate characteristics, including commercial levels of support, reliability, licensing, etc. (Wang and Wang, 2001). For example, Serrano et al. (2004) briefly overview a project where open source components were determined to be the better selection than traditional COTS components. This change in methodology also increases the general market-place need for companies with expertise in consulting on a range of open systems.

7.2.3 Providing Open Software Distributions and Services

A company like Red Hat^{TM} represents a different business model than either MySQL AB or GBdirect. It constructs and sells software distributions rather than software products. For example, Red Hat is unlike MySQL AB which owns the MySQL copyright so that it maintains the right to dual license its own product. It is also unlike a company such as GBdirect that primarily capitalizes on its expertise and experience in working with a broad array of open products on the basis of which it can then provide consulting services, software mod-ification, system integration, etc. Instead, Red Hat specializes in creating and providing its own *distributions* of Linux, as well as providing extensive train-ing, documentation, and support for its distributions. Red Hat does not own the Linux copyright, nor does it only consult on products. Of course, there are many possible different components in such a system, with multiple options for con-figuration and installation. Red Hat assembles updated, tested combinations, or prepackaged suites of the newest stable Linux versions, combined with the requisite open system components such as GNU compilers, Apache servers, IO drivers, and windowing infrastructure like X11. Companies like the German Linux distributor SUSE follow a similar model. The Debian GNU/Linux distri-bution is an example of a noncommercial distribution. It tends to be about twice the size of the Red Hat distributions but has less frequent releases (Gonzalez-Barahona et al., 2005). The extremely widely used Ubuntu Linux distribution for personal computers is based on the Debian distribution. A fundamental advantage of such distributions is that the user does not have to be a Unix or Linux expert in order to install and configure the system. The user does not have to know what software libraries or programs to use or where to put files. Distributions intentionally handle such details for nonexperts, including the management of ongoing software releases for the components (so-called release engineering). In fact, distributions are now a matter of choice even for Linux experts. The Red Hat installation program is called *Anaconda* and is also General Public Licensed. Separate applications and services are segregated into so-called *packages* which can be selectively installed using a package management system. Red Hat provides multiyear commercial "subscriptions" for distributions like its Red Hat Enterprise Linux system that it guarantees (as per its product descriptions) to have the "latest, extensively tested security patches" with "quality-controlled features, updates, and upgrades" that are regularly and automatically revised, and Web-based administration tools for "updating and managing your system." These are equivalent to full-fledged off-the-shelf proprietary environments, like Microsoft Windows XP with its repertoire of user tools.

Thus, in some respects Red Hat acts like a proprietary software provider except that the systems it sells and its services are based on open source components. Though it offers what may be a commodity product, its mission is to have the preeminent trusted brand name in the Linux distribution market. The branded distribution of trusted commodities is a classic way to run a successful business. As Red Hat cofounder Bob Young described it, commodity industries "base their marketing strategies on building strong brands. These brands must stand for quality, consistency, and reliability" (Young, 1999). Furthermore, perception and product control are key. As Young (1999) observes: "Heinz owns 80% of the ketchup market because they have been able to define the taste of ketchup in the mind of ketchup consumers."

7.2.4　Hybrid Proprietary/open Model: Vertical Development with OSS

According to PHP creator Rasmus Lerdorf (as of this writing a prominent software engineer at Yahoo), the most promising business model for open source is neither distribution nor even dual licensing models, but in-house, proprietary, vertical development utilizing open source platforms and components. He observes that: "the real money . . . in open source is in the verticals. It's about taking open source software, applying it to a problem and selling the resulting solution. That's where you will find the billion-dollar companies" (Schneider, 2003). The extensive use of open source infrastructure to implement the Yahoo environment is one example. Google is another instance of proprietary services that have been developed on top of open source platforms. The Google development model is extensively committed to using open source in general, though of course its search engine is proprietary. Internally, Google uses the Linux core as posted on the Linux kernel Web site to support its proprietary search services, rather than Linux distributions like Red Hat. It also extensively utilizes other open products like Python, MySQL, Apache Tomcat, the GCC compiler, and Java (albeit the Java virtual machine is not open), according to Google open source programming manager Chris DiBona (Shankland, 2005). In fact, Google now provides a Subversion-based open development hosting service. Neither Yahoo nor Google distributes its software; instead each keeps the software internal and private and distributes the services provided by their software solution to solve valuable consumer problems. As we have noted elsewhere, most software, in general, is developed for in-house use in any case. From a labor economics point of view, the marriage of open source and proprietary code for successful in-house development, whether it is done for purely in-house use or to distribute services based on the software, is a significant positive development for programmers.

7.2.5 Hybrid Proprietary/open Model: Horizontal Arrangements

Though there has long been major industrial support and participation for open source development, its importance is increasingly widely recognized and the involvement of corporate sponsors more direct. These arrangements represent a business strategy for the sponsors where open source serves as an adjunct, rather than as a full-fledged driver, for their businesses. Fogel (2005, p. 72) lucidly analyzes some of the reasons for industrial involvement, ranging from helping companies spread the burden, cost, and risk of software development across multiple enterprises to allowing companies to support open source projects that play a supportive or complementary role to their own commercial products. Project participation can also benefit a company by associating it with a prominent open source brand. For hardware vendors, open source can provide low-cost added value for their hardware products. Participation may also be used as part of a corporate strategy to indirectly challenge a dominant competitor on market share and vendor lock-in. IBM's involvement with Linux serves this purpose with respect to Microsoft Windows. On the open community side, a lessened risk of project failure is a major psychological benefit of corporate participation. As Fogel observes, if "IBM backs an open source project, people pretty much assume the project won't be allowed to fail," a perception which can become a "self-fulfilling prophecy" (Fogel, 2005, p. 71).

However, these corporate sponsorships have to be handled adroitly to be successful, otherwise the arrangements can kill the goose that lays the golden egg of passionate volunteer participation and enthusiasm. In effect, while a company may financially support a project and pay employees to participate, the participation must remain *meritocratic* as exemplified by the collaborative participation between Apache and IBM. There will also be a built-in cultural tension between the hierarchical structure of a commercial organization versus the "semi-decentralized volunteer communities of free software projects" (Fogel, 2005, p. 71). A successful relationship requires that the norms for open source participation not change merely because a company becomes involved. The corporate sponsor needs to appreciate that its contributions must fit into "the community's vision for the software. You may have some say in that vision, but you won't be the only voice" (Fogel, 2005, p. 71). The sponsor must establish a relationship of trust with the open source community, not just through support, but by, for example, releasing new code back to the community's software commons. Establishing an effective participatory environment is not simple. Jim Gettys of the X Window System project observes, in a cautionary manner, that X.org had to restructure itself from "from an industry consortium (X Consortium) to an organization in which individuals, both at a personal level and as part of work they do for their companies have voice, working as part of the larger freedesktop.org and free standards community" (Gettys, 2003).

IBM is an example of a company that has established a symbiotic relationship with open source. On the one hand, IBM uses open source products, but it also supports open communities that are involved in developing products that can benefit IBM's own proprietary software. IBM's portfolio of proprietary products tends to focus on middleware and enterprise level applications. IBM's WebSphere is an example and is used for a variety of applications like load-balancing across servers. But WebSphere is built using the Apache server as a key component (Capek et al., 2005), so IBM receives a corporate gain from supporting and participating in the Apache project. IBM ports its proprietary products like Lotus, WebSphere, and DB2 to Linux, thereby "Linux-enabling" them as part of its strategy of integrating its software with free and open platforms. Such porting of proprietary software to open platforms is one of the most prominent commercial strategies for using open source. IBM's corporate expectation is that "Linux will do for applications what the Internet did to networks" (http://www-03.ibm.com/servers/eserver/linux/passport.swf, accessed January 5, 2007). Another major way the company benefits from open source is by supporting open source development tools like Eclipse. While such development tools are not in themselves profitable for IBM, it needs to invest in them because of their side-benefits for its profitable proprietary products. Software tools like Eclipse positively affect IBM products like WebSphere, increasing their value to its customers. The Eclipse Web site defines the product as an open, extensible integrated development platform that provides a "plug-in based framework that makes it easier to create, integrate and utilize software tools" (eclipse.org). By supporting the Eclipse project, IBM can not only help the tool evolve but to some extent influence its evolution, not only for the benefit of the open source community but also for its own corporate benefit. IBM is also heavily involved in Linux development, helping to bolster its role in mission-critical, enterprise level applications. The major areas of the company's open source involvement are the Linux, Apache, Eclipse, and Globus projects, with more than 700 of its employees contributing to the projects (Capek et al., 2005). IBM's open source strategy is to "contribute to key OSS projects that are functionally connected with some of our key products. The joint participation of commercial developers and independent OSS developers creates a synergy that enhances the open-computing *ecosystem*" (Capek et al., 2005, p. 254).

From the viewpoint of economic theory, IBM can be considered as supporting commoditized open products that are *complementary* (in the economic sense) to its core proprietary products. This has the effect of making its core products more attractive since the complementary products they work with are free or inexpensive (Spolsky, 2002). At the same time, IBM is also conducting a platform war against its most prominent competitor Microsoft, with Linux as the commoditized proxy. To the extent that Linux erodes Windows market share, IBM is strengthened because its products run on Linux, while Microsoft is simultaneously weakened, reducing the financial resources it can bring to bear in its competitive battles. The involvement also helps IBM promote open standards with open source implementations – a strategic objective that strengthens IBM against the exploitation of proprietary standards by competitors like Microsoft. The company additionally benefits from the expertise it gains in open source products and development techniques that it can apply internally to its own products as well as in connection with its consulting services. On the legal infrastructure side, IBM has also promoted the use of more rigorous processes for ensuring the copyright integrity of code contributions in open source projects – an area in which many open projects had been somewhat lax and which could in principle affect their commercial viability. It also introduced the Common Public License, an OSI-certified license that it believes serves as a model for commercial use. Eclipse uses the Eclipse License, a modified version of the CPL, with rights owned by the independent Eclipse Foundation.

References

Broersma, M. (2002). Q&A: Red Hat: Linux Can't Compete with Windows. Interview with Bob Young, February. http://news.zdnet.com/2100–3513_22–828802.html. Accessed December 1, 2006.

Capek, C., Frank, S., Gerdt, S., and Shields, D. (2005). A History of IBM's Open-Source Involvement and Strategy. IBM Systems Journal, 44(2), 249–257.

Fogel, K. (2005). Producing Open Source Software: How to Run a Successful Free Software Project. O'Reilly Media, Sebastopol, CA.

Gettys, J. (2003). Open Source Desktop Technology Road Map. HP Labs, Version 1.14. http://people.freedesktop.org/~jg/roadmap.html. Accessed December 6, 2006.

Gonzalez, J. A. (2002). Letter to General Manager of Microsoft, Peru. April 8th. Letter copied in: MS in Peruvian Open Source Nightmare by T. Greene. http://www.theregister.co.uk/2002/05/19/ms_in_peruvian_opensource_nightmare/. Accessed December 1, 2006.

Gonzalez-Barahona, J., Robles, G., Ortuno-Perez, M., Centeno-Gonzalez, J., Matellan-Olivera, V., Barbero, E., and Quiros, P. (2005). Analyzing the Anatomy of GNU/Linux Distributions: Methodology and Case Studies (Red Hat and Debian). In: Free/Open Software Development, S. Koch (editor). Idea Group Publishing, Hershey, PA, 27–58.

Hohn, S. and Herr, G. (2004). Open Source: Open for Business. A Report from Computer Science Corporation: Leading Edge Forum, September.

Leibenstein, H. (1950). Bandwagon, Snob, and Veblen Effects in the Theory of Consumer's Demand. Quarterly Journal of Economics, 64, 183–207.

Lerner, J. and Tirole, J. (2004). The Economics of Technology Sharing: Open Source and Beyond. National Bureau of Economic Research, Cambridge, MA.

Liebowitz, S. J. (2002). Rethinking the Networked Economy: The True Forces Driving the Digital Marketplace. AMACOM, New York, NY.

Liebowitz, S. J. and Margolis, E. (1998). Network Externalities (Effects). In: The New Palgrave Dictionary of Economics and the Law. MacMillan. http://www.utdallas.edu/~liebowit/palgrave/network.html. Accessed December 1, 2006.

Moczar, L. (2005). The Open Source Monopoly. IT Manager's Journal, February 02. http://www.itmanagersjournal.com/feature/3146. Accessed December 1, 2006.

MySQL News Announcement. (2001). FAQ on MySQL vs. NuSphere Dispute. http://www.mysql.com/news-and-events/news/article_75.html. Accessed November, 29 2006.

O'Reilly, T. (2005). What Is Web 2.0. Design Patterns and Business Models for the Next Generation of Software. http://www.oreillynet.com/pub/a/oreilly/tim/news/2005/09/30/what-is-web-20.html. Accessed December 1, 2006.

Schneider, J. (2003). Interview: PHP Founder Rasmus Lerdorf on Relinquishing Control. http://www.midwestbusiness.com/printer/article.asp?newsletterID=4577. Accessed December 1, 2006.

Serrano, N., Calzada, S., Sarriegui, J., and Ciordia, I. (2004). From Proprietary to Open Source Tools in Information Systems Development. IEEE Software, 21(1), 56–58.

Shankland, S. (2005). Google Throws Bodies at OpenOffice. http://news.com.com/Google+throws+bodies+at+OpenOffice/2100–7344_3–5920762.html. Accessed December 1, 2006.

Smith, D., Simpson, R., Silver, M., and Fiering, L. (2003). Linux on the Desktop: The Whole Story. Technical Report AV-20–6574, Gartner. http://www.gartner.com/DisplayDocument?id=406459. Accessed December 1, 2006.

Spolsky, J. (2002). Strategy Letter V. June 12. http://www.joelonsoftware.com/articles/StrategyLetterV.html. Accessed December 20, 2006.

Valimaki, M. (2005). The Rise of Open Source Licensing: A Challenge to the Use of Intellectual Property in the Software Industry. Turre Publishing, Helsinki, Finland.

Wang, H. and Wang, C. (2001). Open Source Software Adoption: A Status Report. IEEE Software, 18(2), 90–95.

Wheeler, D. (2005). Why Open Source Software/Free Software (OSS/FS, FLOSS, or FOSS)? Look at the Numbers! http://www.dwheeler.com/oss_fs_why.html. Accessed December 1, 2006.

Young, R. (1999). Giving It Away. In: Open Sources: Voices from the Open Source Revolution, M. Stone, S. Ockman, and C. DiBona (editors). O'Reilly Media, Sebastopol, CA, 113–125.

7.3 Open Source and Commoditization

The process of the commoditization of software, under which successful proprietary software products tend to become commodified over time, is a fundamental economic phenomenon which has been proposed as a major factor in open source development. First, let us recall that a *commodity* traditionally refers to a widely demanded generic product like timber, crude oil, and iron. Some characteristics of traditional commodities are that they are produced and consumed in mass quantities. They serve as the building blocks of industrial and commercial processes and products. Because of their fundamental and pervasive character, commodities are produced not only in large quantities but also by many different producers. In the world of computer hardware, the commoditization of the standardized IBM PC is considered a paradigmatic example of the potentially disruptive power of this kind of phenomenon (Christensen, 1997). A commodity made by one producer can be used interchangeably with that of another producer. Because they are multisourced, such products are expected to adhere to uniform and open standards of performance (Stutz, 2004b). Commodities are generally not brand-driven products, though they can certainly be branded. The implications of the commoditization of software have been the subject of considerable discussion by analysts in the software industry. For example, commentators like Martin Fink (2003) compare the effect of OSS to that of commoditized, generic drugs in the pharmaceutical industry, producing lower prices and greater vendor competition, albeit in the case of pharmaceuticals only after the original grace period afforded by the patent for the drug.

There is an intimate relation between the forces that drive commoditization and the principles of open source development. The well-known Microsoft software engineer David Stutz, for example, contends that it is the commoditization of software that represents "the critical force behind the rise of open source software" (Stutz, 2004b). Software companies can only optimize their products' potential market by maximizing "their product's potential for useful combination with other software, while at the same time minimizing any restrictions upon its further re-combination," according to Stutz (2004b). However, it is precisely this kind of open-ended flexibility that is intrinsic to the principles underlying the open source movement. Stutz also contends that data is more influential than software in these developments and that the software industry is in the process of "reorganizing itself around the network exchange of commodity data." For example, the MP3 (Mpeg Audio Layer 3) process for audio compression became recognized, and thereafter commoditized, after it became widely used as a standard for exchanging digital music. From this point of view, it is the *data* that is exchanged and stored (XML files, HTML files, MP3 files, etc.), that is, the commodity-like invariant, *not* the constantly evolving *software* that processes the data.

Proprietary software producers like Microsoft are under pressure, not merely from competitive open source operating systems like Linux, but from open source applications across the board. Open applications that run in Windows environments threaten to undermine Microsoft's closed, packaged software, business model, gradually causing an "erosion of the economic value of software" (Stutz, 2003). Granted, the open software approach can be temporarily circumvented when dominant companies bypass it by introducing proprietary extensions of standards, as for example, in Microsoft's implementation of Kerberos. However, though such tactics may have temporary success, the trend toward commoditization seems inevitable because open source excels at creating innovative, individual applications that do not require buying into extensive software suites like MS Office or platforms like Windows. Indeed, over time, open source is app-by-app "*accreting* (italics added) into a legitimate alternative to Windows" (Stutz, 2003).

Another principle Stutz proposes is that resources that lend themselves to many uses are likely to "penetrate society more fully than resources that are special-purpose" (Stutz, 2004b). This has implications for the relative attractiveness of open source versus proprietary products in terms of what are called *economies of scope* where the idea is to leverage consumer demand for a commodity by "reusing the underlying commodity in many different ways." For example, the Unix API is more interoperable; it is more familiar because it is open; and much of it has even been formally and openly standardized, so it represents a standard item that is "good enough" for other software to be built on top of it. This simpler Unix API is therefore more likely "to emerge as the successful cross-platform standard for non-graphical software construction than the complex and monolithic Windows API" (Stutz, 2004b). Or, consider the conventional Microsoft Word document format, which is "complex and encumbered by proprietary behaviors that make it hard for software producers to conform to its detailed, and undocumented, layout" (Stutz, 2004b), so that it appears destined to eventually lose ground as a document standard (granted, there is movement toward a more open standard for the document format).

A further factor related to open development is the impact of open standards. Software agents like servers and browsers are interchangeable because they are all constrained to implement the underlying HTTP and HTML standards or formats (O'Reilly, 2004). In a network-driven environment governed by open standard protocols, not only open source but also proprietary software become effectively commoditized. There are commoditized Web servers like Apache on the one hand and commoditized Web browsers like Internet Explorer on the other hand. O'Reilly (2004) contends that had Microsoft controlled both ends of the HTTP protocol pipeline between server and browser with proprietary Microsoft products, then the continued open nature of the product evolution could have been undermined. Thus it is essential for the standards themselves to be kept honest and open. One way to maintain this is for organizations like the W3C consortium to reject standards that are realized only by proprietary or patent-encumbered implementations.

Some level of commoditization of software products appears inevitable. In the long term even highly successful proprietary platforms become commodified (Stutz, 2004a). The reason is that if a proprietary product becomes dominant in the market or even highly successful, then its functions, interface, etc., tend to become static over time. Once this happens the product becomes a natural reference target for development by cloners who eventually commodify the product, as has happened in the open source efforts to clone Windows and MS Office with competing reference products like GNOME that are similar to the Windows interface. Generally, well-defined systems make easy targets for cloning: one just follows their taillights. Stutz (2004a) describes the phenomenon, in the context of software, as follows: "because mature and successful platform ecosystems are so well-defined and so difficult to change, the vendors who build them invariably place themselves at risk of commoditization through cloning." In other words, the potential for commoditization inexorably "occurs through a hardening of the external shell presented by the platform over time. As a platform succeeds in the marketplace, its APIs, UI, feature-set, file formats, and customization interfaces ossify and become more and more difficult to change"; that is, a phenomenon of "ossification followed by cloning" occurs, with an initially "value-laden proprietary platform" becoming over time a "replaceable component" (Stutz, 2004a).

Since stable products become commodified, products are actually at their most profitable when they are *not* so transparently good enough as to satisfy customers. At that point, producers try to make proprietary configurations of the products that make them competitive or superior in performance with the best performing products dominating the market. Thus, the fulcrum of product evolution depends on when a product is "good enough" for the needs of consumers

(Christensen, 2004; O'Reilly, 2004; Stutz, 2004a). Eventually, production of a version of the product with good enough performance becomes sufficiently routine that manufacturers or producers can no longer differentiate themselves. Profit margins on these commoditized products then decline. The key factors in consumer product preference then become "speed to market and the ability to responsively and conveniently give customers exactly what they want" (Christensen, 1997, 2004). At this point, producers are led to use modular approaches for software product architecture. The opportunities for "attractive profits" tend to move elsewhere in the value chain, for example, to "subsystems from which the modular product is assembled" (Christensen, 2004). In other words, as the product becomes commoditized, the subsystems of which the product is composed become decommoditized (Christensen and Raynor, 2003). Stutz believes that the value opportunities at this point are not primarily in the infrastructure software components that arise, but in the opportunities represented by the ability to distribute "platform-standardized information" such as digital media and Web content (Stutz, 2004a).

Commoditization may seem to be a destroyer of value, but new value opportunities simply emerge elsewhere. The business implications of software commoditization appear to be negative: it removes monetary value from the market. In place of the tens of billions of dollars in revenue generated by the not-yet-commodified Microsoft products, the outcome would appear to be a vast decline in business value as the result of replacement of the proprietary products by the essentially discount distributors of commodity packages like Red Hat Linux. Are companies like Microsoft, which themselves benefited from the commoditization of the PC, destined to suffer a similar decline when their products are commoditized (Stutz, 2004b)? On the one hand, the answer is *yes* because the commoditization outcome appears historically inevitable. On the other hand, the answer is *no* because there are always emerging alternative value opportunities. The economic value that disappears at one point in the value chain may in fact merely end up reappearing as new opportunities at other points in the value chain (Christensen, 2004). Of course, in order to be realized, these opportunities must first of all be recognized and then seized, the way IBM seized the idea of becoming a major software services provider after the commoditization of the PC, rather than trying to hold on to its old role of being a proprietary hardware provider. Similarly, the commoditized OSS that underlies the Internet has opened up enormous opportunities for proprietary software services that rely on this commoditized infrastructure, including as a compelling example the kind of proprietary extensions of Linux that inhabit google.com's tens of thousands of Web servers (Christensen, 2004). There is an ongoing dynamic between large established firms and start-ups. Established firms have structural characteristics that can make them less effective at recognizing opportunities for exploiting new technologies, while small firms may have a disruptively successful ability to recognize opportunities for adopting emerging technologies. However, the advantages of small firms in these situations may be temporary, possibly lasting only until large firms decide to enter the market (Park, 2005); see also Christensen (1997), Schumpeter (1934), and Schumpeter (1942).

References

Christensen, C. (2004). Law of Conservation of Attractive Profits. In: Breakthrough Ideas for 2004: The HBR List. Harvard Business Review, February, 17–18.

Christensen, C. and Raynor, M. (2003). The Innovator's Solution: Creating and Sustaining Successful Growth. Harvard Business School Press, Boston, MA.

Christensen, C. (1997). The Innovator's Dilemma: When New Technologies Cause Great Firms to Fail. Harvard Business School Press, Boston, MA.

Fink, M. (2003). The Business and Economics of Linux and Open Source. Prentice Hall, Upper Saddle River, NJ.

O'Reilly, T. (2004). Open Source Paradigm Shift. http://www.oreillynet.com/pub/a/oreilly/tim/articles/paradigmshift_0504.html. Accessed December 1, 2006.

Park, J. (2005). Opportunity Recognition and Product Innovation in Entrepreneurial Hi-tech Start-ups: A New Perspective and Supporting Case Study. Technovation, 25, 739–752.

Schumpeter, J. A. (1934). Theory of Economic Development. Harvard University Press, Cambridge, MA.

Schumpeter, J. A. (1942). Capitalism, Socialism and Democracy. Harper, New York.

Stutz, D. (2003). Advice to Microsoft Regarding Commodity Software. http://www.synthesist.net/writing/onleavingms.html. Accessed December 1, 2006.

Stutz, D. (2004a). The Natural History of Software Platforms. http://www.synthesist.net/writing/software_platforms.html. Accessed December 1, 2006.

Stutz, D. (2004b). Some Implications of Software Commodification. http://www.synthesist.net/writing/commodity_software.html. Accessed December 1, 2006.

7.4 Economic Motivations for Participation

This section considers two economic explanations for why developers get involved in open source. One uses a labor economics model based on so-called signaling theory; the other uses a cost–benefit model that analyzes geographically dependent wage differences to understand differences in participation. The models are not merely theoretical. They are based on statistical analysis of extensive empirical project data.

7.4.1 A Signaling Model for Motivation

Participation in open source development does not per se lead to higher wages. But it appears to have an indirect effect in that "higher status in a merit-based ranking" does have a significant impact on wages. This was one conclusion of the empirical investigation of the Apache project by Hann et al. (2002). Their study considers a range of possible explanations for what motivates participation, from the cultural and social-psychological to the economic. They conclude that the benefits of purely social or cultural recognition for a developer are not credible as determinative motivations, since similar benefits could be expected to largely accrue in a commercial environment (Lerner and Tirole, 2000) and would not in any case be limited to the field of software. (An argument against this is that open source participation, to a significant extent, disintermediates the presumptive employer, who would gain much of the recognition for the product the programmer works on.) A traditional economic analysis of the motivation would view the decision about participation as driven by a cost–benefit analysis by the programmer, whether or not done consciously. The major cost factor would be the opportunity cost of the decision to participate and would be represented by what other projects the programmer could have spent time on. The benefits balanced against this cost include delayed effects like peer recognition or higher evaluation by prospective employers, as well as immediate benefits like craftsman-like satisfaction in creating something interesting or solving a personally useful technical problem. A labor economics perspective, on the other hand, suggests models of motivation based on enhancement of human capital or so-called signaling theory interpretations. The human capital model is a familiar one. Participation in open source simply provides training in marketable skills. This motivation is clearly applicable and is consistent with the results of statistical surveys of motivation for open source participation, such as Kim (2003). From this viewpoint, the involvement is tantamount to traditional technical and professional training which is expected to enhance one's wage prospects like any other type of training. However, the signaling model of motivation appears to be even more effective in explaining the data.

How do you *signal* how good you really are, if you're a software developer? That's where the signaling theory of labor markets comes in (Hann et al., 2002). Official status or crediting in open source projects signals that you're really good – and that's very attractive to prospective employers. As Moglen (1999) observes, free software participants receive "reputational compensation for their activity" with "Famous Linux hackers ... known all over the planet as programming deities" with obvious implications for economic betterment. From the viewpoint of signaling theory, open source development provides an even sharper interpretive indicator than mere participation because an individual's level of accomplishment can be used to calibrate his or her productive ability. This is a decisively important attribute for programmers who are known as a group to vary greatly in terms of their productivity. Furthermore, their open source work products are accessible, as is their level of recognition by the project group. Open source by definition allows access to the code created by a developer in a way that is not possible with closed source. There are no nondisclosure agreements to worry about, and publicly verifiable sources like the Concurrent Versions System (CVS) log permanently document contributions. Furthermore, the productivity represented by code contributions is a surrogate for a variety of other critical, though more amorphous and less easily measured attributes like "the depth of their understanding, the efficient design of the solution, and their ability to persuade, to get people 'on board' with their ideas and strategies, that represent the true quality of their contribution" (Hann et al., 2002). Recognized effective participation in open source development can serve as a "proxy" reflecting the presence of such key desirable characteristics. In other words, "If potential employers can use open source participation as a signaling mechanism, then the existence of a 'credential' or observable measure of successful participation would allow firms to make inferences about a developer's productive capacity" (Hann et al., 2002).

Apache Software Foundation (ASF) projects provided the experimental data for the signaling interpretation of motivation in Hann et al. Their study investigated the rank of participants within several ASF projects as the putative signaling mechanism because "Membership in the ASF is by invitation only and is based on a strict meritocracy." The study focused on the outcomes for participants in three major Apache projects: the well-known Apache HTTP Web server project, the Jakarta project, which encompasses all the Apache server-side Java projects, and the Mod_Perl project, which is intended to integrate Perl as an Apache HTTP module. These are the largest Apache projects with respect to numbers of developers, numbers of contributions, and the amount of archival data readily available (e-mail archives, forum data, CVS records, etc). The project archival data was supplemented by the results of a survey of Apache participants in these projects.

The key reference variable interpreted as a *signal* was the *ASF project status attained* by the participants. These were the observable ranks in the ASF organization, which from the lowest to highest rank are as follows:

1. developer,
2. committer,
3. project manager,

4. committee member,
5. ASF member, and
6. ASF Board member.

Progression through this meritocratic gauntlet works as follows. Developers who make consistent significant contributions over time can be nominated to become committers (who can commit code changes to the CVS repository without prior approval by an intermediary). Members of the Project Management Committee must be nominated by the committers and approved by the ASF Board and have responsibility for managing all the aspects of a subproject. ASF members are nominated by other ASF members on the basis of their contributions as well as their collaborative skills and must be approved by the ASF Board. The ASF Board members are in turn elected by ASF members and are responsible for the overall governance of the entire Apache organization.

The study showed a strong correlation between status and subsequent employment salary. The preliminary conclusion was that "contributions, as measured by number of patches submitted, per se do not increase wages. On the other hand, the wage of contributors with rank committer or above is on average about 29% higher than that of developers after controlling for education, programming experience, work experience, job switch, and firm characteristics" (Hann et al., 2002).

7.4.2 An Opportunity-cost Model Based on Geographic Differences

Are the actors in open source driven by an opportunity-cost calculus? The thesis seems to be supported by a geographical analysis of wages versus participation rates. The study by Lancashire (2001) attempts to understand the driving factors of open participation using a model that combines economic theory with empirical data analysis. It proposes that a careful review of the differential economic trends (wages and job opportunities) across countries, versus the international geographic distribution of open developers (nationality), suggests that the attraction of programmers to open development is a reflection of the opportunity costs of the involvement as perceived by local developers. Though Lancashire's analysis acknowledges that cultural arguments do provide a degree of explanation for the "dynamic of involvement" of participants once they are engaged in the process (Lancashire, 2001), he counters that such sociological/cultural explanations fail to explain why open source development occurs in the first place. According to this investigation, data analysis shows that "differentials in international market conditions appear to play a decisive role in determining the relative vibrancy of open source communities worldwide" (Lancashire, 2001).

Constructing a utilitarian, economic model for participation requires deconstructing some of the noneconomic models. Recall Raymond's influential essay which proposed an essentially noneconomic understanding of the motivations of open source participants, namely, that the utility function such participants were in fact optimizing "is not classically economic, but is the intangible (product) of their own ego satisfaction and reputation among hackers" (Raymond, 1998a). Lancashire (2001) rejects this by arguing that purely cultural and sociological explanations of open involvement are romanticized. They reflect an underlying group myth that accepted, uncritically and from a variety of sources both intellectual and literary, notions that romanticized hackers "as unique for their cultural proclivity to reject the materialist trappings of modern life" (Lancashire, 2001). The influences that encouraged this myth range from a post-materialistic, political thesis about behavior in industrially advanced cultures elaborated in Inglehart (1990) to fictionally expressed attitudes in works of science fiction and cyberpunk by authors like Heinlein (1966) and Gibson (1984). These stories romanticized engineers as "elite actors in a society where social boundaries are drawn primarily in terms of technical expertise" (Lancashire, 2001). The idea that the intellectual background of Raymond's seminal discussion reflects these influences is consistent with Raymond's tone in his "A Brief History of Hackerdom" (Raymond, 1998b). Ghosh's (1998) effort at formalizing Raymond's ideas in terms of rational economic decisions arguably fails to adequately explain why people initiate open source projects in the first place. He falls back on Raymond's memorable explanation that it's about scratching an itch (Raymond, 1998a), that is, solving some personally useful software problem or creating some needed software functionality. Though Ghosh's theory may help explain "why existing projects gain snowballing support," it does not, according to Lancashire (2001), explain where, when, or why new projects emerge, succeed, or fail – a paradoxical issue in theories of collective action, first observed by Olson (1971). The reputation game explanation for participation can also be critiqued on the grounds that such games are never ends-in-themselves but only means-to-ends or intermediate variables, with a victory in the game merely acting like a signal of capability as in a signaling model (Lerner and Tirole, 2000). The latter also suggests that, in fact, open source developers tend to be attracted to projects that have the greatest likelihood of exhibiting strong signaling effects. This is the case, for example, with software where performance is a key metric of success, because competing products can be easily compared in terms of their level of performance (Edwards, 2003).

How can one disentangle the causes of open source participation from the hodgepodge of causal factors that potentially affect open involvement, especially given the enormous variety of kinds of open projects? A so-called *crucial case analysis* may be the most promising method for dissecting the real motivating factors (Lancashire, 2001). The idea in this approach is to identify cases of project development which appear to be the most challenging for an economic analysis to explain, while most suitable to explain by a cultural analysis. What are the possibilities? Noncomplex software applications can be disregarded because the barriers to entry into such markets are low and hence so are the profits, so that economic interests would not be compelling in any case. Additionally, an application that attracted for-profit companies because the application currently had little market competition should be disregarded since it is tinged with economic appeal, so the cultural and economic factors in participation could not be sorted out. What's left would seem to be open source projects which are highly complex, requiring significant effort for their creation, but that are also antiproprietary in the sense that there already exist effective, low-cost, commercial alternatives when the project is initiated. These types of projects would appear to intuitively offer the strongest proof that the motivation for participation was basically cultural or ideological because the projects are anticommercial. If one could demonstrate that the motivation for participation in such apparently economically unattractive projects was still classically economic, then one would have refuted the cultural hypothesis, precisely in those cases where it should have been strongest.

There are relatively few open source projects that fall into the complex/ antiproprietary category. Two prominent examples are Linux and GNOME. They seem like the best litmus tests for this culture-versus-economics contest. The Linux system began as a free alternative for proprietary Unix systems. The GNOME environment began partly as an alternative for the proprietary Microsoft Windows desktop. Both projects are highly complex. There are also reasonable commercial alternatives for each. Lancashire's (2001) argument is that "if strong arguments supporting economic causation can be made for these two projects ... we should treat theories about cultural causation with much greater skepticism."

It appears that geographic data about wages versus participation rates for GNOME and Linux do not support the cultural, sociological explanation for participation. Lancashire used project data about national origin of participants (garnered from e-mail addresses as per first appearance on Credits lists in the case of Linux) to geographically locate developers for Linux and GNOME. When this data is normalized to reflect population sizes as well as national levels of Internet access, it turns out, contrary to first impression, that Northern

European countries are "disproportionately represented among the top-tier of developers in both projects." Indeed, it appears that after this normalization, the United States remarkably falls to a "position of relatively inactive development," ranking slightly behind countries in Southern Europe. Countries in Northern Europe stay in the forefront and indeed "appear to be undertaking a completely disproportionate amount" of the actual development work. Mexico, Canada, and England exhibit an average level of participation. The discrepancy with respect to U.S. participation is so pronounced that, in economic terms, the United States is arguably "free riding on a collective good provided predominantly by non-Americans." This is completely contrary to what one would expect from "Raymond-style arguments about post-scarcity gift cultures" (Lancashire, 2001). The most prosperous nation on the field is thus, relatively speaking, among the lowest of the "contributors to open source development." There are also historical anomalies because this underparticipation occurs in the context of a free software movement that "originated in the U.S. and was strongly associated with the U.S. through the 1980s." Furthermore, this "decline in commitment goes contrary to the snowballing 'network externality effects' expected in countries with an initially well-established open source community." One wonders how there could be such a decline in support by the country that originally started and led the entire movement?

Economic analysis suggests a very plausible explanation for the migration of interest in open development from the United States to Europe over time; namely, the opportunity cost of involvement in open development for U.S. programmers has changed over the years. During the period of Lancashire's (2001) study, the demand for and wage rate of U.S. programmers had become considerably higher than that for their European counterparts. This increased the "opportunity cost of coding free software over commercial applications, and thereby decrease(d) the amount of free software production" in the United States (Lancashire, 2001). This increase in demand and compensation for IT workers in the United States was a consequence of the very high level of U.S. investment in IT during the 1990s, which, for example, greatly exceeded that in Europe during this period, and which in turn increased the demand for IT professionals in the U.S. market. Furthermore, it is also clear that:

> if the opportunity cost of working on open source projects is lower for European developers than for their American counterparts, the potential benefits Europeans gain from working on them are much greater as well. In a global economy lacking perfect labor mobility and characterized by wage-inequality across countries, we expect individuals to produce free software *if* doing so can help them shift to a higher wage-level. This implies . . . that developers may embrace open source work as a way to tap into lucrative corporate networks abroad (Lancashire, 2001).

The same reasoning also explains the relative youth of open source participants because older participants would have less time to "establish a monetizable reputation than their younger, more mobile counterparts, given less time in which to amortize its immediate costs" (Lancashire, 2001).

Even the initial history of open source in the United States supports arguments for an economic interpretation. The opportunity-cost explanation for the significant change in the distribution of open development is bolstered by the underlying economic, industrial, and governmental matrix in which this development first emerged in the United States. Much of the early open development in the United States was in environments where there was substantial corporate or public support or subsidization for long-term development. Free software may be free for the user and free of restrictions, but its development was not for free. In particular, Lancashire contends that:

> early open source work thrived because its development took place in an immature and publicly-subsidized market. While academics and researchers were no doubt driven by a desire to "scratch an itch" and perform work they found stimulating, it is significant that they performed labor for which there was essentially very little immediate private-market demand. Is free software truly free? It may be something for which developed countries have already paid: through early funding for academic research and development and support for public research *at times when the market for certain types of software was immature*. It is hardly accidental that early "hacker" communities emerged at organizations with the resources and will to subsidize long-term development.

Thus, once again one comes to the conclusion that cultural motivations appear less fundamental than economic ones in fostering open source development and less probative for explaining why developers tend to get involved with open development in the first place, even in the litmus case of projects that are complex and antiproprietary.

These utilitarian/economic critiques of cultural explanations aside, one must keep in mind the "nonmaterialistic" motivation represented by the aesthetic joy and pleasure taken in participating in the creative act of programming – first well described by Brooks (1995). It is an activity where systems that are useful to others, dynamic and unpredictable in their effects, or beautiful in their operation are created as products of the pure thought of the developer. This is a creative act akin to creating art, or mathematics, or music, and this process of creation is simultaneously an exercise in learning. As with any artist, it is not always the case that man lives by bread alone. This applies not only to works that are the product of a solitary artist or craftsman, but also to the act of collaborating in the creation of a collectively designed work of art – like a cathedral.

References

Brooks, F. P. (1995). The Mythical Man-Month – Essays on Software Engineering, 20th Anniversary Edition. Addison-Wesley Longman, Boston, MA.

Edwards, K. (2003). Technological Innovation in the Software Industry. Ph.D. Thesis, Technical University of Denmark.

Ghosh, R. (1998). Cooking-Pot Markets: An Economic Model for the Trade in Free Goods and Services over the Internet. First Monday, 3(3). http://firstmonday.dk/issues/issue3_3/ghosh/index.html. Accessed December 1, 2006.

Gibson, W. (1984). Neuromancer. Penguin Putnam, New York.

Hann, I., Roberts, J., Slaughter, S., and Fielding, R. (2002). Why Do Developers Contribute to Open Source Projects? First Evidence of Economic Incentives. 2nd Workshop on Open Source Software Engineering. In: 24th International Conference on Software Engineering. Orlando, FL.

Heinlein, R. (1966). The Moon Is a Harsh Mistress. Tom Doherty Associates, Inc., New York.

Inglehart, R. (1990). Cultural Shift in Advanced Industrial Society. Princeton University Press, New Jersey.

Kim, E. (2003). An Introduction to Open Source Communities. Blue Oxen Associates. http://www.blueoxen.com/research/00007/. Accessed January 10, 2007.

Lancashire, D. (2001). Code, Culture, and Cash: The Fading Altruism of Open Source, Development. First Monday, 6(12). http://www.firstmonday.dk/issues/issue6_12/lancashire/index.html. Accessed December 3, 2006.

Lerner, J. and Tirole, J. (2000). The Simple Economics of Open Source. National Bureau of Economic Research. http://papers.nber.org/papers/W7600. Accessed December 1, 2006.

Moglen, E. (1999). Anarchism Triumphant: Free Software and the Death of Copyright. First Monday, 4(8). http://www.firstmonday.org/issues/issue4_8/moglen/index.html. Accessed January 5, 2007.

Olson, M. (1971). The Logic of Collective Action. Harvard University Press, Cambridge, MA.

Raymond, E. S. (1998a). The Cathedral and the Bazaar. First Monday, 3(3). http://www.firstmonday.dk/issues/issue3_3/raymond/index.html. Ongoing version: http://www.catb.org/~esr/writings/cathedral-bazaar/. Accessed December 3, 2006.

Raymond, E. S. (1998b). A Brief History of Hackerdom. In: Open Sources: Voices from the Open Source Revolution, M. Stone, S. Ockman, and C. DiBona (editors). O'Reilly Media, Sebastopol, CA, 19–30. Online version: http://www.catb.org/~esr/writings/cathedral-bazaar/hacker-history/. Accessed December 1, 2006.

SECTION THREE

Free Software: The Movement, the Public Sector, and the Future

8

The GNU Project

The Open Source Initiative represents the formalization of one stream of the free and open software movement. We have described its establishment in 1998 by Raymond and Perens, and Peterson's coinage of the term *open source* as an alternative to what was thought to be the more ideologically laden phrase *free software*. Of course, ever since the mid-1980s, the other distinct stream of the movement represented by the Free Software Foundation (FSF) and the GNU project had already been active. The FSF and Richard Stallman initiated the free software concept, defined its terms, vigorously and boldly publicized its motivations and objectives, established and implemented the core GNU project, and led advocacy and compliance for the free software movement. They have been instrumental in its burgeoning success. We have already discussed the FSF's General Public License (GPL) in Chapter 6. This chapter describes the origin and technical objectives of the GNU project that represents one of the major technical triumphs of the free software movement. We also elaborate on some of the responsibilities, activities, and philosophical principles of the FSF, particularly as expressed by FSF General Counsel Eben Moglen.

8.1 The GNU Project

The GNU project was founded to create a self-contained free software platform. The project was begun in 1983 by Stallman. It had an ambitious and arguably almost utopian vision. The acronym GNU stands for "GNU's Not Unix," a kind of recursive acronym that was popular at MIT where Stallman worked. Stallman's objective was to create a complete, open source version of Unix, together with a comprehensive environment of software development tools. All of these were to be not merely "not closed source," but were to be licensed in such a way that neither the software nor any derivative software based on it

297

could *ever* be distributed as closed source. As Stallman described it, his software would be *free* software, as in the sense of a *free* person who can never have his or her *freedom* or *free* expression taken away. The *free* character of the software would be inalienable. And the domain of free software would be broad enough that a programmer could live there without ever again having to depend on using proprietary code. It was like building a "Brave New World" and the GPL was its Declaration of Independence and its Constitution.

Stallman's vision was based on regaining what he regarded as a "Paradise Lost." During his experience as an operating systems' programmer at the MIT AI Lab, it had been traditional for programmers to freely share their code with programmers at other universities as well as at companies – and in turn other people would freely let them see their code, change it, or use it to make new programs (Stallman, 2002a). But by 1982, when the AI Lab purchased a new PDP, the culture had changed. The operating system was no longer "free" in the sense of the programmer community that Stallman had matured in. He thought it was absurd that this community now faced a situation where "you had to sign a nondisclosure agreement even to get an executable copy" of an operating system – never mind not having open access to its source code (Stallman, 2002a). He believed this was a morally reprehensible situation, and one that he could not in good conscience participate in. Stallman in fact quit MIT in early 1984, precisely, so MIT itself could have no proprietary claim on any software he developed. He intended his software, along with its progeny and descendants to continue to be freely available – permanently.

It was a point in time when two paths diverged in the computing world. Stallman thought he knew the road to take. With the open and sharing programming community he so admired in the process of dissolving, Stallman asked himself if there was anything he personally could do to change what was happening. Since he was a programmer, he posed the question: "Was there a program or programs that I could write, so as to make a community possible once again?" (Stallman, 2002a). To Stallman the answer became crystal clear: "What was needed first was an operating system. That is the crucial software for starting to use a computer" (Stallman, 2002a). Unix was the obvious reference system, and so that was the system for which he set out to create a free version, including all the miscellaneous and sundry tools that have to be included in every development environment. As he observed: "In the 1970s, every operating system worthy of the name included command processors, assemblers, compilers, interpreters, debuggers, text editors, mailers, and much more. ITS had them, Multics had them, VMS had them, and Unix had them. The GNU operating system would include them too" (Stallman, 2002a). Every new movement deserves a proclamation. Within a year, Stallman had articulated his ideas in his famous *GNU Manifesto* (Stallman, 1985/2005). The Manifesto expressed the objectives and philosophy of the GNU project. Stallman and other volunteers would create a body of software that they would freely share with others and that was broad enough that its users would never need any software that was not free. He described the essence of its *free* characteristics as being that, in addition to being open source, "Everyone will be permitted to modify and redistribute GNU, but no distributor will be allowed to restrict its further redistribution. That is to say, proprietary modifications will not be allowed. I want to make sure that all versions of GNU remain free" (Stallman, 1985/2005). This emphatically also meant that GNU would not be in the public domain – because if it were, modifications to it or to the original code itself could be subsequently concealed in distributed proprietary products.

The first tool Stallman developed for the GNU project was *Emacs*. Emacs is well-known to aficionados as the "King of all Editors." In fact, Stallman won the 1990 Grace Hopper award from the ACM for his work on developing Emacs. He also won the distinguished MacArthur Foundation award the same year. Emacs is a very powerful programmable text editor. It was implemented by Stallman at the MIT AI Lab in late 1984. He had written an earlier version at MIT in 1975. Although he had officially quit MIT by that point, the director of the lab had allowed him to continue to use the facilities. Emacs has since continued to be developed by the FSF through multiple releases and is supported on many platforms (gnu.org/software/emacs/emacs.html). One of the interesting features of Emacs is that it has modes that let it adapt itself to handle not just text files but also specialized texts, like the source code for programming languages, LaTeX, or HTML documents. It includes features like syntax highlighting and specialized editing commands. Stallman initially distributed Emacs via an anonymous FTP server at MIT. Later he made it available for distribution by magnetic tape to customers who could not access the FTP site. He charged $150 for this service. The current Emacs distribution is available from http://ftp.gnu.org/pub/gnu/emacs/ and its project development tree is available under the CVS system at http://savannah.gnu.org/cgi-bin/viewcvs/emacs/. The fact that Stallman's organization sold copies reflects a few things. First of all, as we must underscore, the term *free* did not necessarily mean *free of charge*. As Stallman said: "I had no job, and I was looking for ways to make money from free software" (Stallman, 2002b, p. 20). The free software movement was about freely accessible software. Secondly, despite the fact that the title of the movement's Manifesto might remind one of another very famous historical manifesto – the Communist Manifesto of Karl Marx and Frederick Engels proclaimed in 1848 – the GNU Manifesto is not at all anticommercial in tone.

The GNU project developed many important and very highly recognized free programs. Perhaps the most prominent of these is the GNU compiler collection or GCC released in mid-1987. The collection originally contained only an optimizing C compiler but was extended to C++, Fortran, Java, and other languages and their libraries (http://gcc.gnu.org). The compilers were written mainly in C and have been ported to many architectures including the x86 series, Motorola 68000, Alpha, VAX, etc. The collection includes a debugger named GDB that works for many programming languages. The quality and impact of the GCC compiler has been dramatic. Michael Tiemann, an early GNU developer and advocate who made major contributions to the first versions of GCC, won the 1996 STUG award which described the GNU C compiler as having "unparalleled influence upon the availability of efficient and standard code on a vast number of hardware platforms" (STUG announcement for 1996, usenix.org). Tiemann himself also recognized early on the commercial potential of free software, which he believed was "a business plan in disguise," even though he thought the GNU Manifesto on the surface appeared to read like "a socialist polemic" (Tiemann, 1999, p. 139). Tiemann helped found Cygnus Solutions in 1989 (later merged with Red Hat Linux) to market and support free software.

Software may be free of charge, but developers aren't. So as interest in the GNU project grew, Stallman decided in 1985 to establish what he called the *Free Software Foundation* to seek funding to support the work that needed to be done. The foundation was established as a tax-exempt charity (http://www.gnu.org). Its purpose was to support the development of free software, in particular to pay developers to create software for the GNU project. The organization was also generally intended to promote the development of freely redistributable software. The FSF ran the initial Emacs tape distribution as a business. Most of its business still comes from selling copies of free software, free manuals, and custom-built free software collections for specific hardware platforms.

Stallman realized that free software needed a corresponding license. So in 1985, he introduced a software license based on a variation of the notion of copyright, called *copyleft*, a term coined by software developer Don Hopkins. Copyleft gave the user the right to copy, change, and redistribute modified programs which were based on the licensed software, but prohibited anyone from adding restrictions on the use of that redistribution (http://www.gnu.org/gnu/thegnuproject.html). Developers could redistribute their own variations but they could do so only under the same terms as they had received the free software in the first place. Later these concepts would be formally embodied in the GNU GPL.

Developers for Stallman's FSF created additional critical packages. Roland McGrath developed the C library, though many others contributed to it (see the GNU Web site). Other FSF developers produced a free version of the Bourne shell (*bash*) and a GNU *tar* command (which combines a set of files into one file while still preserving file system information). All of these packages were sine qua nons for a full Unix-like system. Significantly, the C library would be licensed under a different license than the GNU GPL, called the GNU library license (later called the *Lesser GPL*) and which, unlike the ordinary GPL, allows proprietary software to link to the library code. The strategy behind this choice of license for the free C library was a matter of tactics rather than principle as we discussed in Chapter 6. The idea was that this kind of licensing would encourage the use of the library software. Every proprietary C compiler or Unix-like system needs a C library, so why not encourage that to be the free C library?

Ultimately, the FSF created many of the software accoutrements surrounding an operating system kernel, but the kernel itself never quite came together. Instead, Linux with its kernel burst onto the scene and thereafter a complete free system quickly became available as the free GNU/Linux combination. As a side-comment, the designation for GNU + Linux distributions has been the subject of some controversy. The combination of the GNU utilities with the Linux kernel is commonly called Linux though the FSF strongly prefers the term GNU/Linux. The FSF believes the longer designation more properly reflects the broad scope of the GNU project and its planned objective of building a complete operating system and implicitly acknowledges the key role of the FSF in the success of this project. However, there are others who claim that such distributions also include large amounts of software such as from the X Window System and other non-GNU components like KDE and Apache. It is worth noting that embedded systems like mobile devices primarily use the Linux kernel and so have few if any GNU components, so for such systems there is no ambiguity in the Linux designation.

References

Stallman, R. (1985/2005). The GNU Manifesto. Dr. Dobb's Journal of Software Tools, 10(3). Also: http://www.gnu.org/gnu/manifesto.html. Accessed January 5, 2007.

Stallman, R. (2002a). The GNU Project. http://www.gnu.org/gnu/thegnuproject.html. Accessed December 1, 2006.

Stallman, R. (2002b). Free Software Free Society: Selected Essays of Richard M. Stall-
    man. Edited by J. Gay, The GNU Press, http://www.gnu.org, Free Software Foun-
    dation, Boston, Massachusetts. Accessed June 21, 2007.
Tiemann, M. (1999). Future of Cygnus Solutions: An Entrepreneur's Account. In: Open
    Sources: Voices from the Open Source Revolution, M. Stone, S. Ockman, and C.
    DiBona (editors). O'Reilly Media, Sebastopol, CA, 71–90. .

8.2 The Free Software Foundation

We have described how the FSF (http://www.fsf.org/) was founded by Richard
Stallman in the mid-1980s (1985) after he had initiated the GNU project. It
was, as we suggested, an effort by Stallman to regain the Eden of his early MIT
career when the relatively free distribution of source code was a given. The
objective of his foundation was to promote the free software movement of which
Stallman was now a leader. As described in the previous section, it was also
intended to obtain sponsorship and support for the GNU software project with
its fundamental mission of creating a fully free, Unix-like, comprehensive, self-
contained development environment, permanently unconstrained by proprietary
restrictions. Stallman defined the *General Public License* intending it to serve
as the uniformly used license for distributing free software. The license, first
released in 1989, was a generic version of licenses that had been used for
individual previously released GNU products. It is now far and away the most
widely used free or open software license. The related Lesser GPL for software
libraries was introduced two years later in 1991. As Moglen (1999) observes,
the success of the free software movement in general and the GNU/Linux
project in particular has been and remains critically dependent on the legal
matrix provided by the GPL because it provides "the legal context in which the
labor is mobilized" that creates these projects. The FSF owns the copyrights
to most GNU software and is responsible for legally enforcing the GPL on the
software it owns, but it also assists owners of other GPL copyrights in seeking
compliance from license violators. It has so far been highly effective in the area
of compliance, with no successful court challenge to the license to date and
most disputes resolved outside the judicial forum.

The Web sites at www.gnu.org and www.fsf.org are interesting, informative, and complementary sources of information about the movement. The
FSF site links to numerous documents, interviews, and speeches by Stallman
on www.gnu.org where the philosophy of the movement is set forth (such as
www.gnu.org/philosophy/philosophy.html). The GNU site focuses on the GNU
project, its history, philosophy, and programs. It also includes many interesting
essays by Stallman. These cover a broad range of topics: what free software

is, the famed GNU Manifesto (http://www.gnu.org/gnu/manifesto.html) on the necessity of a comprehensive free software environment, why only free software should be used in schools, its reliability, licensing issues, the harmful nature of software patents, and so on. It characterizes the difference between the free versus the open software movement as a matter of values. While the open source movement views the issue as a *practical* matter, a better way of developing better software, the free software movement views it as a question of ethical responsibility and social *values*. Indeed, for the FSF, the entire movement to create free software is only "part of the long struggle in the history of human beings for the creation of freedom" (Moglen, 2003b, p. 15). The FSF site focuses on the foundation's mission of protecting and promoting free software and provides many useful services, including a directory of free packages.

The analyses of free software issues on the GNU site are a treasure trove. For example, there is a detailed essay on why the GNU Web site does not use GIF files (Stallman, 1997/2006). Although the point is now moot, the discussion is fascinating because it involves an eclectic mix of algorithmic issues, like the Unisys and IBM patents on the LZW compression algorithm used in the GIF representation, the legal statements of those companies regarding their patents, the charitable status of the FSF, the legal implications of making GIFs for companies that redistribute free software, the difference if GIFs are only decoded rather than generated, the general attitude of the FSF toward software patents, alternative patent-free compression formats, references to activist sites like http://www.burnallgifs.org/archives/ (accessed January 5, 2007) dedicated to discouraging the use of GIFs, software patents on the compaction algorithms present in the widely used MP3 format. The organization's position is precisely and meticulously articulated in a discussion that is simultaneously technical, legal, and nuanced. The updated 2006 version of the essay notes that "after 1 October 2006, there will be no significant patent claims interfering with employment of the GIF format" (Stallman, 1997/2006). Software patents are a major strategic concern of the FSF because even though such patents may be transparent to the users of such files, they can have a significant impact on software developers who must pay license fees if they develop software to make these files – a circumstance that can inhibit open source development. Refer also to the informative essays at fsf.org/licensing/essays.

The FSF today focuses on legal and sociopolitical issues related to free software. Consistent with this, there are both lawyers and computer scientists on its current Board of Directors. Stallman is President. Eben Moglen, a member of the Board and Professor at Columbia University Law School, serves as its General Counsel. Moglen, who worked as a professional programmer in his teens, has a diverse background in literature, philosophy, history (in which he has a doctorate), and also law.

The ideological or political character of the FSF's mission remains a sharply distinctive feature of the organization. Its idealistic, humanitarian, and intellectual perspective is attractively expressed in a discussion of the process for defining the GPLv3 where Stallman and Moglen write that the FSF's "goals are primarily social and political, not technical or economic" and, moreover, that the FSF regards "free software as an essential step in a social movement for freer access to knowledge, freer access to facilities of communication, and a more deeply participatory culture, open to human beings with less regard to existing distributions of wealth and social power" (Stallman and Moglen, 2005). From the viewpoint of the history of culture and science, they propose that free software "is the only ethically satisfactory form of software development, as free and open scientific research is the only ethically satisfactory context for the conduct of mathematics, physics, or biology" (Stallman and Moglen, 2005).

However, the FSF's advocacy is not always so mild. For example, the tone of Moglen's *dotCommunist Manifesto* (Moglen, 2003a) is evocatively and provocatively revolutionary. The title and rhetoric are redolent of Marx and Engels' *Communist Manifesto* with the Internet *dot* thrown in for context. Consider the following rhetorical appeal against what are called the dominant owners of culture (Moglen, 2003a, p. 6):

> To the owners of culture, we say: You are horrified at our intending to do away with private property in ideas. But in your existing society, private property is already done away with for nine-tenths of the population. What they create is immediately appropriated by their employers, who claim the fruit of their intellect through the law of patent, copyright, trade secret and other forms of "intellectual property." Their birthright in the electromagnetic spectrum, which can allow all people to communicate with and learn from one another, freely, at almost inexhaustible capacity for nominal cost, has been taken from them by the bourgeoisie, and is returned to them as articles of consumption – broadcast culture, and telecommunications services – for which they pay dearly. Their creativity finds no outlet: their music, their art, their storytelling is drowned out by the commodities of capitalist culture, amplified by all the power of the oligopoly of "broadcasting," before which they are supposed to remain passive, consuming rather than creating. In short, the property you lament is the proceeds of theft: its existence for the few is solely due to its non-existence in the hands of everyone else.

Or Moglen (2003a, p. 7):

> We, the creators of the free information society, mean to wrest from the bourgeoisie, by degrees, the shared patrimony of humankind. We intend the

resumption of the cultural inheritance stolen from us under the guise of "intellectual property," as well as the medium of electromagnetic transportation.

Despite its pedigree, the term *bourgeoisie* seems misplaced since most of the referenced middle class (bourgeoisie) is probably considerably less well-off than the relatively elite group represented by free software developers from top-tier institutions; the real target is obviously overweening corporate power. The rhetoric seems excessive and reflects the kind of language that originally differentiated the Open Source Initiative from the FSF. Too bad, because many of the underlying grievances are legitimate. Also, though dotCommunist is a great take-off on the original Communist Manifesto, Eben Moglen – as we shall shortly see – seems much more effectively persuasive when he admixes with his advocacy some of his delightfully puckish sense of humor. In any case, the jeremiad against the consumer culture seems particularly well-placed. For example, the human right to the glory of the electromagnetic spectrum has a noble, even cosmic resonance.

The following demands, which are intended to identify what is needed to advance the class struggle for free software, are also directly quoted from Moglen (2003a, p. 7):

1. Abolition of all forms of private property in ideas.
2. Withdrawal of all exclusive licenses, privileges and rights to use of electromagnetic spectrum. Nullification of all conveyances of permanent title to electromagnetic frequencies.
3. Development of electromagnetic spectrum infrastructure that implements every person's equal right to communicate.
4. Common social development of computer programs and all other forms of software, including genetic information, as public goods.
5. Full respect for freedom of speech, including all forms of technical speech.
6. Protection for the integrity of creative works.
7. Free and equal access to all publicly-produced information and all educational material used in all branches of the public education system.

Prescinding from the merits of Moglen's position and the style of his advocacy, the ideological and rhetorical character of the presentation once again underscores the very different sensibilities that differentiate the open source movement in general from the FSF's expression of that movement in particular.

The tone of the FSF dialog is not always so provocative as in the dotCommunist manifesto. For example, we also hear Stallman expressing more measured and conventional sentiments: "The free software philosophy rejects a specific widespread business practice, but it is not against business. When businesses respect the users' freedom, we wish them success" (http://www.gnu.org/gnu/thegnuproject.html). Nonetheless, widespread concern about perceived antibusiness rhetoric (granted the Moglen quotations here are from 2003) was one of the issues that led to the formalization of the open source stream of the movement and its *open source* terminology.

Eben Moglen's tone is not always so provocative – in fact it is often downright entertaining. We referred in Chapter 6 to his legally astute but engaging description of how the FSF assures compliance with the GPL. The attitude is low-key, savvy, and pragmatic, with a delightful undercurrent of ironic, good-natured cajolery. Thus one of his descriptions of how he coaxes GPL violators into compliance is worth requoting because it illustrates how effective his style has been in practice. This is how he acts when he is speaking to license violators. "Look," I say, "at how many people all over the world are pressuring me to enforce the GPL in court, just to prove I can. I really need to make an example of someone. Would you like to volunteer?" (Moglen, 2001). Or, as he pithily states in Moglen (2003b, p. 9): "My client (the FSF) didn't want damages, my client wanted compliance. My client didn't want publicity, my client wanted compliance. We settled for compliance all the time. We got compliance all the time." That approach clearly converted the resistant as its perfect batting record demonstrates, and it did so with disarming good humor.

The presentation by Moglen (2003) reflects a balanced historical perspective of his philosophical views on free software. He describes the free software movement as neither novel nor idiosyncratic but merely a reflection of "the received understanding of our common culture with regard to the production of knowledge by collaborative effort. The free sharing of scientific information is the essence of Western science" (Moglen, 2003b, p. 2). He also marshals some fairly pragmatic economic arguments for its ascendancy. For example, with regard to software embedded in digital appliances like cell phones, he forecasts complete free software dominance by Linux in the near term for the simple reason that manufacturer's cannot afford to do otherwise. When the digital "box costs fifty bucks, there's no room left for paying $12.95 to Mister Gates" for an operating system license (Moglen, 2003b, p. 6). More boldly, he projects that in another generation, software development will focus around "project management, indemnification, distributional customization, and tailoring, piece by piece, to the individual needs of consumers" (Moglen, 2003b, p. 11).

The FSF's overall vision may sometimes be dramatically stated, but its objectives have been visionary and realized in historic, practical accomplishments, the most extraordinary being the increasingly widespread acceptance of the GPL. In addition to its continued support for the GNU project, some other more mundane activities include the major free software directory at http://directory.fsf.org/s that it manages and which extensively catalogs "free software programs that run on free operating systems." It also sponsors the GNU Savannah project that runs an open source development site for free projects. The Savannah hosting site (http://savannah.gnu.org/) strictly enforces policies that attempt to ensure that all of the hosted software is actually free and has no unnoticed or hidden nonfree, proprietary legal dependencies or other encumbrances or impediments. The site provides the usual software hosting services: bug-tracking, CVS, mailing lists, etc., in an ad-free environment. The hosting site at savannah.gnu.org is restricted solely to GNU projects. The complementary site at savannah.nongnu.org hosts non-GNU free software projects. Both Savannah sites differ from the Source-forge hosting service in that the latter hosts nonfree projects as well.

A final comment regarding the GNU Web site – it is, as they say, a fascinating read. As is typical of free developments, there is a multilingual cohort of volunteer supporters, with the result that many of the site pages are available in translations into many human languages. There are unexpected, informative, and provocative discussions on an array of topics, with interleaving political, technological, social, legal, scientific, and philosophical perspectives. For example, a glimpse at the *whatsnew* page on the site discloses a range of references, from EU actions on patents, a revised music score for the Free Software Song, Stallman on Patent Absurdity, even a sympathetic evangelical Christian perspective on the free software movement's philosophy (Parris, 2005). The tone in Parris's book is different from that evinced by Moglen, though no less filled with revolutionary fervor, with Parris concluding his forward with the quotation: "What the Messiah has freed us for is freedom! Therefore, stand firm, and don't let yourselves be tied up again to a yoke of slavery" – quoted from "The Complete Jewish Bible." The FSF's vision of the role of open software in society remains a passionate one.

References

Moglen, E. (1999). Anarchism Triumphant: Free Software and the Death of Copyright. First Monday, 4(8). http://www.firstmonday.org/issues/issue4_8/moglen/index.html. Accessed January 5, 2007.

Moglen, E. (2001). Enforcing the GNU GPL. http://www.gnu.org/philosophy/enforcing-gpl.html. Accessed December 20, 2006.

Moglen, E. (2003a). The dotCommunist Manifesto. http://emoglen.law.columbia.edu/publications/dcm.html. Accessed December 1, 2006.

Moglen, E. (2003b). Freeing the Mind: Free Software and the Death of Proprietary Culture. June 29, 15 pp. http://moglen.law.columbia.edu/publications/maine-speech.html. Accessed December 20, 2006.

Parris, D. C. (2005). Penguin in the Pew. Lulu.com, Morrisville, NC.

Stallman, R. (1997/2006). Why There Are No GIF Files on GNU Web Pages. http://www.gnu.org/philosophy/gif.html. Accessed January 5, 2007. Most recent copyright is 2006.

Stallman, R. (1985/2005). The GNU Manifesto. http://www.gnu.org/gnu/manifesto.html. Accessed January 5, 2007.

Stallman, R. and Moglen, E. (2005). GPL Version 3: Background to Adoption. http://www.fsf.org/news/gpl3.html. Accessed January 5, 2007.

9

Open Source in the Public Sector

The public sector is uniquely important to the success of open source for a number of reasons. It offers well-suited opportunities for open development, in domains ranging from technological infrastructure, science, and innovation to national security and education. Furthermore, not only do public agencies and society benefit from the use of open products, the public sector, through its role in policy formulation, also provides a vehicle for advocating the expanded use of open software in society. To appreciate the opportunities, consider some of the roles the public sector plays. It has a central position in supporting the maintenance and evolution of technological infrastructure for society, an area where open software has proven extremely successful. It has also historically played an extensive role in promoting innovation in science and technology. For example, the government was the leader in funding the development of the Internet with its myriad of underlying open software components. Thus, clearly, public investment in open development has paid dramatic dividends in the past and can be expected to continue to do so in the future. The public sector is also where decisions on national economic objectives and strategy are made. These decisions, whether of a legal, legislative, or policy-driven character, can significantly affect the expansion of open source use within the government or by the public at large. The public sector is broadly charged with responsibilities from education to national security, domains that are particularly compatible with the characteristics of open source. For example, free software offers cost advantages pertinent in education, though its low up-front cost is not necessarily a determinative factor in its adoption, and it also provides transparency advantages important in national security. This chapter considers various application domains for open source in government, on both the domestic scene and internationally, as well as the policy attitudes of different governments toward open source. We conclude the chapter by considering the use of open source in education, particularly its privileged role in computer science education.

9.1 Open Source in Government and Globally

We will first consider the use of open source in the U.S. government, subsequently addressing its use by and the attitudes of foreign governments. While open source products are used throughout the federal environment, two especially prominent consumers are the DoD (Department of Defense) and the NSA (National Security Agency). We consider these two first and then discuss the use of open source products by other agencies.

A study by the MITRE corporation, sponsored by the Defense Information Systems Agency (Bollinger, 2003), found extensive and diverse use of open software at the DoD, with over 100 open products being used in more than 250 applications. The study also offered reasons why the role of open source should be further expanded. Security applications were most prominent, such as those using the Unix-like OpenBSD operating system that explicitly focuses on system security. Widely used open security tools included Snort, a lightweight intrusion detection tool useful for plugging "network security holes when new attacks emerge," and SARA (the Security Auditor's Research Assistant), used for relatively straightforward network security risk analyses. Both these applications are licensed under the GPL, though SARA is done so indirectly (Bollinger, 2003). The MITRE report lists more than 100 open source products that have demonstrated superior records of security and reliability, as "measured by speed of closures of CERT reports in comparison to closed-source alternatives," that should be considered as "safe" for DoD use. Some of the applications involved only the use of the software, without exploiting the open character of its source code. However, other applications involved explicit modification of the code through development, in purely open or hybrid (proprietary/open) combinations. The MITRE study strongly encouraged the increased acquisition and use of open source products in defense applications. An important motivation was to promote product diversity. The idea is that product diversity reduces dependence on a more narrow set of proprietary products, thereby increasing the robustness of security and reliability for the DoD's overall software environment. This reduces the risk of catastrophic failure in the event of cyberattack. The report also advocated the use of proprietary products like Microsoft Windows Services for Unix that interface effectively with open source software.

The NSA is involved not only in using open source but also in developing *and* distributing secure open software. For example, the NSA announced in 2001 that it had developed a prototype of a secure Linux kernel named SELinux and would be publicly distributing the software (Benner, 2001). Development on the system continues to the present time. According to the NSA Web site for SELinux, the licenses used were under the same conditions as the original sources, with patches to the Linux kernel being released under the GPL as required and patches to some libraries released under the BSD. Notably, the licensing information on the site says that "some new libraries and new programs available here are released into the *public domain*" (NSA Web site, license for SELinux; italics added), rather than under a GPL or OSI-certified license. Of course, this is consistent with U.S. law which requires that intellectual property developed by the federal government be released, if it is released at all, as public domain, though in general this law does not also appear to require disclosure of the source code (Tyler, 2004). Also, as we have seen previously, in the federal environment new work creations are not copyrighted, so they are a priori ineligible for open source licensing. On the other hand, work that has been developed through outsourced collaboration with private organizations can be copyrighted and released under an open source license.

A key factor in the attractiveness of open software in security (and national security) applications is its *auditability*. It is obviously harder to conceal things in open source code, while, conversely, governments may have reason to be leery of what may lurk inside proprietary code. For example, the reader may refer to references under gnu.org/philosophy for an intriguing discussion of hidden NSA access keys embedded in proprietary Windows code as described in articles by Campbell (1999). In the U.S. context, the major proprietary vendor Microsoft is a domestic corporation, so at least the government can be expected to work out disclosure mechanisms with the vendor. However, this is a less likely scenario for foreign-held entities. For example, is Microsoft likely to disclose proprietary code to the government of Venezuela because that government wants to scrutinize Microsoft applications for security flaws or traps?

Governmental organizations with special responsibilities in security have a specific interest in the relative security performance of open systems. The issue of whether open source is intrinsically more or less secure than proprietary code is a disputed topic, where persuasive but inconclusive arguments have been marshaled on both sides (Payne, 2002). Earlier in the book, we described how the empirical study of Solaris, the Debian GNU/Linux distribution, and OpenBSD by Payne (2002) concluded that two factors the openness of the source together with specific development processes for reviewing security were the key ingredients for better security and in combination gave an overall advantage to the open model, at least in the systems considered. Strangely, the availability of open source can have odd side effects on proprietary code. For example, the process of open source review and open response to security attacks has sometimes had security implications for related proprietary systems. Hissam et al. (2002) describe the open community's response to the Teardrop Denial of Service attack around 1997. The community's solution of the underlying security flaw, which was in the Linux kernel IP stack, exposed a second vulnerability in the IP stack, which was resolved by the open community at the same time. However, ironically, the advertised Linux patch's revelation of the second flaw exposed Microsoft Windows' vulnerability to variations of the original Teardrop attack. Indeed variations successfully attacked Windows before Microsoft was able to correct this vulnerability, though Microsoft did fix it soon thereafter.

Open products are also used in many other U.S. federal agencies. As one illustration, consider the case of Perl. Perl is an open language, but it is also the implementation vehicle for a vast array of open Perl modules. These are available at the huge Perl module collection on the CPAN Web site. The use of Perl is a reasonable proxy for open source use. Perl can be embedded in closed applications that benefit from open Perl resources, on which they are at least partly built. Or, applications can be developed using Perl or Perl modules, where some of the new open components are donated back to the community, thereby expanding the open software commons. In either case, there's open development involved, either as consumed or as produced. A perusal of news stories on the application of Perl in government agencies (Perl Success Stories, 1999–2004) gives a sense of its widespread use. For example, economists at the U.S. Federal Reserve have long used Perl to glue different applications together, such as in converting the outputs from mathematical econometric models into the formats required for the simulation languages used at the Fed (Scoville, 1999). The extensive open Perl and CPAN resources have long made it attractive to the Census Bureau. The FedStats/IMF Web site, developed through the combined effort of many federal agencies including the Census Bureau, uses the Perl DBI and LWP modules to pull together statistical data from the Web sites of multiple federal agencies (Stephenson, 2001). NASA and Sandia Labs, agencies where scientific computing and simulation applications are prominent, have also developed open software released under the GPL (Bessen, 2002). An example is the SAP data analysis tool developed by NASA. It was intentionally implemented using as many open source components as possible, combined with a small number of COTS (Commercial-Off-The-Shelf) components. This might be called FOTS (Free-Off-the-Shelf) software development. A case study is described in Norris (2004), which documents not only the savings garnered, but also the high quality of the open components, their superior levels of documentation, and even the remarkable responsiveness of the open community, as opposed to the more costly closed source COTS suppliers.

These brief remarks are intended to illustrate the wide use of open software in the federal government. The government has also been an active promoter of open development, sponsoring the innovative R&D in computing that has been a major driving factor behind the creation of the open source paradigm, from the early Unix-like systems, servers, and browsers to the enormous volumes of scientific software produced in governmental research facilities. It will inevitably continue to play this role of supporting research that either enters into the public domain or is licensed under protocols that enable some form of transfer of the discovered technologies to the private sector.

The International Sector

We turn our attention next to the status of open software in countries and governments outside the United States. We first observe that the international market for open source products is increasingly substantial. For example, in 2004 alone, Russia and Poland bought almost $20 billion worth of Linux-related technologies according to Adelstein (2005). That's a lot of money for free software. These purchases do not all represent governmental spending but a significant part of it is. This gives some sense of the popularity of these products beyond the United States. The same growth in open source use is occurring in countries around the world as foreign governments have increasingly bought into the cost benefits of using open systems and the perception of greater national autonomy or independence it provides. Indeed, an increasing number of governments have created legislative policies that establish an active predisposition for the use of open source in their societies. The phenomenon is worldwide. For example, the government of Singapore offers "tax breaks to companies that use Linux instead of proprietary alternatives like Windows" (Hahn, 2002). The state provides governmental benefits to corporations that adhere to this policy. This kind of policy represents a macroeconomic decision by the government to foster the development of its own domestic industry in a certain, planned direction. It is also a strategic political decision related to a desire for political autonomy and issues of confidentiality and security. In Germany, an agreement between IBM and the German federal government involved discounted IBM machines that came equipped with Linux provided by the German Linux distributor SUSE. Once again, this policy simultaneously supported a domestic software vendor and promoted the use of open source in a governmental context. The European Union requires open products to be explicitly considered (though not mandated) when evaluating software for acquisition (Applewhite, 2003). In Italy, Brazil, and Peru, legislation actually mandates an open source software preference in government offices (Hahn, 2002).

An informed analysis of the issues involved was articulated in a letter to Microsoft from a Peruvian congressman (Gonzalez, 2002). The official demonstrates a remarkable grasp of the issues swirling around open versus proprietary code. Gonzalez critically and instructively dissects a range of problems, from the nature of intellectual property to the true cost of software use, offering a compelling argument for the open source case. In fact, there is increasing pressure for legislation both in the United States and worldwide that would require the open source option to be explicitly considered by state and federal agencies, though most of these proposals are not for a so-called hard preference for open source under which its use would be obligated. According to Applewhite (2003) over two dozen countries (in the year preceding his article) introduced legislation to at least encourage the use of open software. Predictably, Microsoft remains a useful boogeyman for political purposes even though its share of global revenue for packaged software is only about 10% (Evans, 2002, p. 37). Especially in Latin America, a combined animus toward the U.S. government and Microsoft appears to be a salient factor, as well as the perceived cost benefit from the software. In 2005, Venezuela mandated a move to open software by governmental agencies over a two-year period, including the software used in its extensive petroleum industry.

Factors that affect the global opportunities for deploying open software include price, legal and policy issues, national autonomy, and the size of the local market. We have already mentioned some of the legal, policy, and legislative dimensions. These interact with the other factors. For example, price is not always a significant barrier to the use of proprietary software in developing countries, particularly at the level of individual use. This is because software piracy is so widespread that the proprietary code may be free of charge, though not legally so. There are countermeasures at work against these practices. For example, globalization measures, like the World Trade Organization Agreement on Intellectual Property Rights, will require mandatory antipiracy enforcement by 2006, even by poor countries (Kshetri, 2004). The differing cultural, legal, and economic lenses through which nations interpret issues of intellectual property are overviewed in Marron and Steel (2000). At a corporate level, piracy is less of an option and this works much to the advantage of free software. For example, when proprietary software is bundled with PCs distributed in these markets, it significantly adds to the price of the final product. This presents a key opportunity to reduce price by using free software like Linux as the bundled environment. Another kind of opportunity is illustrated by the highly successful and inexpensive Indian-developed Simputer. This is a Linux-based, special-purpose, software appliance that provides affordable technology adapted to local needs (Kshetri, 2004). In addition to such hardware vendor applications, there are opportunities for cost savings in major software projects for government infrastructure functions like healthcare systems (Fitzgerald and Kenny, 2004). Free software also enables commercial software development with less capitalization. The availability of free-of-charge open source systems and tools dramatically reduces the cost of entry into the business of software development. Today, "even small programming shops with a couple of developers can use sophisticated tools that once only large and well funded development efforts could afford" (Spinellis and Szyperski, 2004, p. 31). Linux nationalism is also prevalent. National versions of Linux now exist in almost every Asian country, from India's enormous Indlinux.org project to the Chinese government-sponsored Yangfan Linux. This includes a Chinese-sponsored version of Wine, the open source API that lets "native Windows programs run on X Windows and Unix-like systems" (Lussier, 2004, p. 68). Another opportunity is represented by the older PCs that are widespread in developing markets due to factors like recycling and charitable distribution of computer hardware to poorer regions. This provides an important "window" of opportunity for free software like Linux, which works well on legacy hardware, at least versus newer versions of Windows. Localization effects vary with the size of the market. Although localization is addressed by proprietary systems like Windows for large Asian language groups such as Chinese, Japanese, and Korean, this adaptation is challenging for commercial vendors in markets that are too small to make a proprietary version viable. This represents an opportunity for open software, which can be modified to adapt it to the local languages.

References

Adelstein, T. (2005). Linux in Government: Outside the U.S., People Get It. July 18. http://www.linuxjournal.com/article/8449. Accessed December 1, 2006.

Applewhite, A. (2003). Should Government Go Open Source? IEEE Software, 20(4), 88–91.

Benner, J. (2001). NSA Takes the Open Source Route. http://www.wired.com/news/business/0,1367,42972,00.html. Accessed December 1, 2006.

Bessen, J. (2002). What Good Is Free Software? In: Government Policy toward Open Source Software, R. W. Hahn (editor). Brookings Institution Press, Washington, DC.

Bollinger, T. (2003). Use of Free (or Open Source) Software (FOSS) in the U.S. Department of Defense. Version 1.2.04. A Report by the MITRE Corporation.

Campbell, D. (1999). How NSA Access Was Built into Windows. http://echelononline.free.fr/documents/dc/nsa_access_windows.htm. Also: http://www.techweb.com/wire/story/TWB19990903S0014. Accessed December 1, 2006.

Evans, D. (2002). Politics and Programming: Government Preferences for Promoting Open Source Software. In: Government Policy toward Open Source Software, R. W. Hahn (editor). Brookings Institution Press, Washington, DC.

Fitzgerald, B. and Kenny, T. (2004). Developing an Information Systems Infrastructure with Open Source Software. IEEE Software, 21(1), 50–55.

Gonzalez, J. A. (2002). Letter to General Manager of Microsoft, Peru. April 8th. Letter copied in: MS in Peruvian Open Source Nightmare by T. Greene. http://www.

theregister.co.uk/2002/05/19/ms_in_peruvian_opensource_nightmare/.   Accessed December 1, 2006.

Hahn, R. (2002). Government Policy toward Open Source Software: An Overview. In: Government Policy toward Open Source Software, R. W. Hahn (editor). Brookings Institution Press, Washington, DC.

Hissam, S., Plakosh, D., and Weinstock, C. (2002). Trust and Vulnerability in Open Source Software. IEE Proceedings – Software, 149(1), 47–51.

Kshetri, N. (2004). Economics of Linux Adoption in Developing Countries. IEEE Software, 21(1), 74–81.

Lussier, S. (2004). New Tricks: How Open Source Changed the Way My Team Works. IEEE Software, 21(1), 68–72.

Marron, D. and Steel, D. (2000). Which Countries Protect Intellectual Property? The Case of Software Piracy. Economic Inquiry, 38(2), 59–174.

Norris, J. (2004). Mission-Critical Development with Open Source Software: Lessons Learned. IEEE Software, 21(1), 42–49.

Payne, P. (2002). On the Security of Open Source Software. Information Systems Journal, 12(1), 61–78.

Perl Success Stories. (1999–2004). http://www.oreillynet.com/pub/a/oreilly/perl/news/success_stories.html. Accessed December 1, 2006.

Scoville, T. (1999). Perl and the Crystal Ball Economic Forecasting at the Fed. http://www.oreillynet.com/pub/a/oreilly/perl/news'battenberg_0199.html. Accessed December 1, 2006.

Spinellis, D. and Szyperski, C. (2004). How Is Open Source Affecting Software Development? IEEE Software, 21(1), 28–33.

Stephenson, E. (2001). Learning to Count on Perl at the Census Bureau. January 2, 2001.   http://www.oreillynet.com/pub/a/oreilly/perl/news/census_0101.html. Accessed December 1, 2006.

Tyler, M. (2004). How Your Open Source Company Can Begin Government Contracting. June 08, 2004. http://www.itmanagersjournal.com/feature/341. Accessed December 1, 2006.

9.2 Open Source in Education

Open source software and open educational content can serve schools in a variety of ways in academic contexts from K-12 to university. There is a certain poetic justice to this because much of open software was originally created under federally supported programs in the first place. We have seen how open source provides the infrastructure for the Internet. It is now increasingly providing the infrastructure for the academic environment as well – and there are compelling reasons for dramatically expanding its use.

The use of open software in education offers many advantages of which the following are only a few:

1. It provides basic software platforms and tools for students and teachers.
2. It provides free-of-charge software for students and even their parents.

3. It exposes the inner workings of software code to IT and computing students facilitating apprenticeship in computing.
4. It supplies tools for learning specific academic subjects that are not themselves computing related.
5. Academic institutions can provide open courseware for distance learning education and open textbooks available free of charge.
6. Increasingly, open source is able to provide the underlying organizational tools needed to support academic administration, like student registration and library management systems.

These free solutions are low cost. Most open source programs are available for free even though the GPL does not require open products to be free in the sense of cost. Alternatively, for-charge copies may be purchased from a distributor in exchange for provision of premium service guarantees. The free-of-charge advantage of open source has direct and indirect cost benefits which are more compelling the more educational costs are constrained. For example, open software can play an irreplaceable role in underdeveloped nations or in poorer school districts in developed countries where cost may make the use of proprietary software prohibitive or encourage software piracy as an alternative. Of course, even wealthy communities are subject to budget constraints for which free software is attractive. Open licensing arrangements also reduce direct and indirect licensing costs. Open licenses are automatically scalable because they are free in the first place, in contrast to proprietary licenses where the cost is related to the number of copies used (Tong, 2004). Even after initial proprietary license costs are paid, subsequent costs for updates are incurred in proprietary environments that are free under open source. Schools are relieved of the burden of conducting software audits to verify that all their installed software is properly licensed, including software lurking on donated machines. There are even advantages for parents since they have the option of freely acquiring copies of open applications used at their children's schools, allowing students to use the same software at home without the major expense they could incur if the software were proprietary and had to be purchased separately. Even in situations where there is limited bandwidth available for downloading software, an initial disk copy of an application can be purchased for a nominal cost, and then copied repeatedly for free (Tong, 2004). There may also be security and reliability advantages to using open source. Especially in some countries, proprietary software may be suspect because the hidden, non-transparent nature of its code allows it to harbor spyware and other software threats (Hart, 2004). These cost benefits accrue without requiring one to settle for a second-rate product. Many open products are of top quality. We have previously mentioned empirical analyses like those by Reasoning (Reasoning

Inc., 2003) which documented, for example, that free MySQL has superior reliability, with six-times fewer defects than comparable proprietary databases (Tong, 2004).

A hypothetical scenario-of-use example can help underscore the deployment opportunities. Imagine if, instead of using the Microsoft Office Suite, one chooses an open source competitor like OpenOffice from OpenOffice.org. This software suite includes counterparts to Microsoft's word processing, presentation, and spreadsheet applications and works with files that interoperate with the proprietary Microsoft products Word and Excel (Hart, 2004). OpenOffice also comes with the ability to convert documents to PDF format. Migration to a more open inventory of applications can be done incrementally. For example, a tool like OpenOffice can be installed and tested first, and then other applications can be added as learning and familiarity progress. The initial learning curve for any new product including open ones may be a concern. However, it is worth noting that these products are often built to "follow the tail-lights" of proprietary products, imitating their interfaces and functionalities, so the learning involved in understanding how to use an open product with proprietary analogs may be minimal. Furthermore, open products even have an advantage over some proprietary ones, since they are often cross-platform, operating in Windows and Linux as well as Mac OS X. This kind of interoperability is commonplace in the open source environment and has the side effect of making learning how to use these applications portable. Costly applications like Adobe Photoshop can be served satisfactorily for basic educational purposes by alternatives like the open source GIMP image-editing-and-design application. Indeed, in some cases GIMP is arguably even more powerful than Photoshop. Apache is of course the classic open alternative to proprietary servers and is available in a variety of free forms, like the easy-to-use bundled package from Apachefriends.org that installs and configures Apache together with open source PHP and MySQL, providing everything you need for a three-tier Web architecture. *Content Management Systems* that enable users to develop and publish their own Web content are available through open products like PostNuke (postnuke.com), Joomla (Joomla.org), Plone (Plone.org), Zope (zope.org), and Bricolage (www.bricolage.cc). These packages represent a major opportunity for cost-cutting functionality in government and education.

Educational environments have a learning curve that is both steep and recurrent because there is a continual flow of new users as students flow into and through the system. Consequently, it is essential to have proper user support for the software products used in education. Open source has a variety of excellent mechanisms for support. First of all, just as with proprietary software, there are open source vendors who provide support services for a charge. Moreover and more basically, the open source community itself provides superb free service, over the Internet, delivered by means ranging from user forums and e-mail lists, to listservs and Web sites for user support. There may even be top-notch support provided by leaders in the field. For example, it is legendary how, in the course of developing Linux, Linus Torvalds would often fix bugs that had been brought to his attention by users and release an entire updated, patched version that corrected the bug within hours (Hart, 2004). Nowadays, specialized forum-based sites like JustLinux.com are dedicated to providing user support for the Linux environment. Because these are public forums, there are the proverbial open source "many eyes" looking at notices of problems or buggy occurrences, so it is often possible to get expert assistance and response in real time – a level of support that is unmatched by proprietary vendors.

The flagship operating system Linux has significant advantages as a free educational environment. It is highly cross-platform. In fact, it often works particularly well on older machines in contrast to the escalating hardware requirements of Windows. This ability is especially relevant to schools that rely on legacy equipment because they are unable to purchase newer machines for budgetary reasons. Contrast the situation for a proprietary platform like Windows, with newer versions of Windows frequently bringing with them the need to upgrade hardware requirements to more powerful but also more costly machines. Linux also has security advantages. For various reasons, it is arguably better than Windows at isolating a computer system from malware attacks such as in the famed Blaster worm episode that subverted Windows environments. Thus, free environments may be not only more reliable but more immune to security threats.

Open source resources and materials that support teaching standard academic subjects are widely available. The resources include programs for learning basic subjects such as geometry (Kig), chemistry (Ghemical), and physics (opensourcephysics.org) for K-12 applications. A variety of applications that are useful for children are offered by Tux4Kids.com as free and open software including mathematics and drawing programs. *Schoolforge.net* is a specialized site dedicated to the use of open source applications in education. The reader can refer to sites like *offset.org* for catalogs of open source educational software (Tong, 2003). The *K12 Open Source Now* Web site hosted by Red Hat is dedicated to precollege uses of open software and to promoting and supplying free downloads of OpenCourseWare for K-12 schools including curricular and learning materials licensed under the Creative Commons License (www.k12os.org). This site also serves as a forum where K-12 users from anywhere can pose questions to one another and receive guidance about the use of open software in their schools. The state of California has an initiative called the Open Source

Textbook Project (COSTP) to offer a wide array of K-12 open textbooks and related materials.

At the university and graduate level, Stanford University's online course management system *CourseWork* (see aboutcoursework.stanford.edu) is a useful open educational product which provides support for developing course Web sites, including tools for grading, discussion forums, scheduling, etc. Another such application is *Moodle* (available from moodle.org) which is a cross-platform system for distance learning and other educational uses (Tong, 2003). In addition to course development tools, the open availability of actual course content or courseware is becoming a major educational endeavor. For example, the MIT OpenCourseWare project provides open access to the course materials used in MIT courses for use by other educational institutions or by self-learners. The next generation version of Stanford's CourseWork product is the *Sakai Project*, a joint venture of Stanford, MIT, the University of Michigan, and Indiana University, the objective of which is to "integrate and synchronize their educational software into a preintegrated collection of open source tools" (www.sakai.org). Open textbook content is also available, especially on computing-related topics. A good example is the "How to Think Like a Computer Scientist" series (Downey, 2002) that uses Java as the programming language, with other versions in Python and C++. Printed copies of such texts are available for a charge from vendors such as www.GreenTeaPress.com.

It is natural to wonder what role open online encyclopedias can serve as a source of educational information for students. *Wikipedia* is an important example of such a vehicle which has significant utility for making factual content available, though less so for areas of controversy. Wikipedia was started in 2001. It was conceived as an alternative to traditional approaches to compiling factual information where articles by experts had to be reviewed prior to publication; in Wikipedia they are not. It has grown rapidly in a few years. According to its statistics page, Wikipedia has almost 1.5 million articles with over 5 million pages as of mid-2006. There has been an average of almost 15 edits per-page per-day since mid-2002. There are almost 2 million registered users and roughly 1,000 administrators. At this writing, almost 40 million people access Wikipedia everyday. About 60% of users access the English language site, with another 5–10% each for the German, Spanish, and Japanese versions. The Alexa.com traffic service ranked it in early 2007 as the 12th most commonly accessed site on the Web. Its information is distributed under the GNU Free Documentation license (GFDL). The key characteristic of Wikipedia is that anyone can edit the material. Intuitive expectations to the contrary do not seem to have been widespread disinformation disasters in its contributions. Users can edit pages without being logged in, but then their IP addresses are identified and maintained. However, users are encouraged to log in, which gives the user a Wikipedia identity, though this does not require a person to disclose his or her off-line identity. Edits that you make are credited to you under your login name or publicly to your IP address if you are not logged in. The logins of article authors do not appear at the bottom of the article as they would with a traditional encyclopedia, even though the logins of majority authors could be determined by backtracking through previous versions of articles (Ciffolilli, 2003). Registered users can be notified of any changes to any page for which they put themselves on a *watchlist*. *Administrators* are known, trusted members of Wikipedia who are given special privileges, like the ability to block other editors and to delete pages. Some of their responsibilities include keeping watch on new articles and removing "obvious vandalism." A general norm for community contributions is that they are supposed to be written from a *neutral* point of view. The site uses a change management approach that lets destructive changes be easily removed, like graffiti that can be easily erased. Each page is accompanied by a separate discussion page for editors. Graffiti or writing deemed nonneutral can be permanently removed by an administrator along with the entire history of the page. The IP addresses of offending individuals can even be banned.

Some obvious concerns regarding Wikipedia include the self-selecting nature of the participants on topics, including the administrators, and the question whether, on controversial topics, Wikipedia's "policy of neutrality" is really adhered to. In particular, sources that Wikipedia accepts as "reliable" may themselves be highly disputed. The content is intended to be encyclopedic and purely factual in nature, not original research or opinion, and is supposed to be verifiable in a reliable (published) source. The reliability of the articles on noncontroversial matters of straightforward fact seems generally to be quite reasonable. For example, if one looks up the article on the Poincare Conjecture, one will get a very useful statement of its meaning, history, and current standing, together with references and links. Certainly many of the articles on computing are extremely informative, like the excellent article on the X Window System or the intriguing article on Knuth's TeX system. However, on the many other matters that have cultural, political, religious, philosophical, or other personal dimensions or implications, or where factual analysis is problematic to determine, the representativeness and objectiveness of the content is significantly subject to the personal proclivities of the editing audience. The conclusion seems to be that for certain areas, Wikipedia serves a useful purpose for accessing information on a topic, but, just as in the case of even reviewed material, controversial topics provide coverage that must be carefully scrutinized, just like one would a magazine or newspaper article. Wikipedia articles can be quite helpful as quick preliminary sources of information about a topic.

This can then be scrutinized or elaborated on through subsequent research, like general Internet searches or article links, where a user can further develop the content presented and verify it from multiple sources.

Open source is a new paradigm for software development and an essential one that undergraduate computer science students must become familiar with. Aside from any putative cost benefits, undergraduates in computing-related fields should be exposed to free software in addition to proprietary products in order to broaden their exposure to its development model and creations. The availability of the open source code provides a unique educational benefit to computing students since it gives them an opportunity that is rare in the case of proprietary code. They can actually see professional code, written and tested by some of the best software experts in the world. The practice of learning by imitating the work of experts is universally applied in other fields. For example, a traditional method for improving one's writing is by imitating the work of master authors. This practice is equally important in professional software development, but it is underutilized in the undergraduate computing environment. It can also be thought of as a way to expose students early on to best practices in programming. Open source code allows students to study high-quality, tested, real-life applications code, written by groups of experts, usually under the leadership of a premier developer (Tong, 2004). Code availability also presents an opportunity for qualified students or teams of students to learn how open source development is actually done. Students can use open source development tools like CVS to participate in local open source development projects or existing real open projects initially as observers and possibly later as contributors.

Senior capstone projects in software development are a perfect opportunity to bring open venues into play. One possibility is to create an open version of a senior development project, with the team members following the open development model and using the standard development tools. Such projects can provide useful and marketable career-related training in open techniques. The likely programming languages to participate in actual projects are C, C++, or Java (which represent about 20% each of the languages used in OSS development projects), followed up by PHP and Perl (about 10% each – statistics from sourceforge.net). The very origins of open development were forged in an academic research context precisely as a reaction against closed, proprietary systems. The presence of a strong open source culture, even from the high school level and up, can act as an effective incentive for innovative software development where students experiment with transparent software products, incrementally tinkering and improving them, in the best spirit of inventive scientific development. This type of computing milieu will undoubtedly lead to major new technical developments in the future just as it has in the past, develop students' software talent, build career-related skills and prospects, maintain interest and enthusiasm, and encourage a sophisticated but pragmatic approach to computing education.

Granted the extraordinary advantages that can come from using open software in the budget-constrained area of education, one has to puzzle over the continuing widespread dominance of environments like Windows and Apple in academic settings. The phenomenon is partly a result of the high quality of these well-funded proprietary products, but it is compounded by inadequate public awareness of the benefits of open source as well as the inertia of lock-in to familiar systems. Therefore, increased public awareness of the quality of these products and their cost benefits is key to improving penetration of this sector. Studies like the BECTA (British Educational and Technology Association) study have helped publicize the cost benefits. BECTA conducted a study of about 60 primary and secondary schools in Britain that evaluated the cost advantages of nonproprietary solutions (see the overview in Wheeler (2005)). The study concluded that the secondary schools considered could reduce their total IT costs by 25% and primary schools could reduce total IT costs by 60% using an open source framework, versus proprietary software. One assumes that similar economies would apply in the United States. Public perception of the applicability of open source is also changing. The study in Abel (2005) surveyed awareness of various open source educational products in American institutions of higher education. The survey revealed a strong "cultural" predisposition for open products in these institutions. For some categories, like student information and financial systems, proprietary products were thought to be relatively immune to competition from open software. However, tools like course management systems (such as Sakai and Moodle), portal frameworks (like uPortal), and tools for facilitating "assessment" were perceived as seriously competitive with commercial software.

References

Abel, R. (2005). Preliminary Analysis of the Open Source in Higher Education Survey Conducted from April 15, 2005 to May 1, 2005 by the Alliance for Higher Education Competitiveness, published May 3, 2005. http://www.a-hec.org/media/files/A-HEC_os_survey_report_050305.pdf. Accessed November 29, 2006.

Ciffolilli, A. (June 24, 2003). Phantom Authority, Self-Selective Recruitment and Retention of Members in Virtual Communities: The Case of Wikipedia. First Monday, 8(12). http://www.firstmonday.dk/issues/issue8_12/ciffolilli/index.html. Accessed December 3, 2006.

Downey, A. (2002). How to Think Like a Computer Scientist. Java Version. http://www.greenteapress.com/thinkapjava/. Accessed November 29, 2006.

Hart, T. (2004). Open Source in Education. University of Maine. http://www.mbs. maine.edu/mitchell_james/OpenSource/Introduction.htm. Accessed November 29, 2006.

Reasoning Inc. (2003). How Open Source and Commercial Software Compare: MySQL White Paper MySQL 4.0.16. http://www.reasoning.com/downloads.html. Accessed November 29, 2006.

Tong, T. (2004). Free/Open Source Software in Education. United Nations Development Programme's Asia-Pacific Information Programme, Malaysia.

Wheeler, D. (2005). Why Open Source Software/Free Software (OSS/FS, FLOSS, or FOSS)? Look at the Numbers! http://www.dwheeler.com/oss_fs_why.html. Accessed November 29, 2006.

10

The Future of the Open Source Movement

This chapter attempts to present a balanced view of what the future seems likely to hold for the open source movement based on past and present trends and the underlying structural, social, political, scientific, and economic forces at work. We will first sketch what we believe are the likely dominant modes for software development and then we will elaborate on the rationales for our projections.

First of all, we believe the open source paradigm is moving inexorably toward worldwide domination of computer software infrastructure. Its areas of dominance seem likely to include not only the network and its associated utilities, but also operating systems, desktop environments, and the standard office utilities. Significantly, it seems that precisely the most familiar and routine applications will become commoditized and satisfied by open source implementations, facilitating pervasive public recognition of the movement. The software products whose current dominance seems likely to decline because of this transformation include significant components of the Microsoft environment from operating systems to office software.

However, despite a likely widespread increase in the recognition, acceptance, and use of open source, this does not imply that open software will dominate the entire universe of software applications. The magnitude of financial resources available to proprietary developers is enormous and increasing, giving such corporations a huge advantage in product development. One might note, for example, that expenditures on research and development by publicly traded software companies increased tenfold between 1986 and 2000, from 1 to 10% of industrial research expenditures (Evans, 2002). To put the relative sizes of the players in perspective, one might make the following, perhaps not quite apropos, comparison. Thus recall that, while Microsoft's share of global revenue from software packages may only be around 10% (Evans, 2002), its several

325

hundred billions of dollars in market capitalization compare rather favorably to the mere $2 million in assets of the Free Software Foundation that developed the GNU project (Moglen, 2003)! These David and Goliath differences hardly portend a minatory diminution in the resources that can be plowed back into improving the proprietary products that generate these immense revenues. Furthermore, the proprietary software industry is very healthy, competitively speaking. The Herfindahl-Hirschman Index, commonly used to measure concentration or competition in the industrial sector, rates the software industry as one-third *less* concentrated than average manufacturing firms. There are also frequent changes in the identity of the top firms (Evans, 2002); that is another indication of competitive robustness. This data indicates that at an objective econometric level the proprietary software sector is robust and highly dynamic. Thus it seems destined to continue to play a pervasive role in software development because it has the resources and dynamism needed to continue to produce highly attractive products.

The picture that emerges is one where the different modes of production that have already evolved seem likely to persist: open, proprietary, and hybrid combinations. Pure open source and proprietary modes will both grow, each dominant in certain market areas. Hybrid modes of cooperative development will continue to be increasingly widely used. While some existing proprietary systems will see their markets overtaken by open source replacements, other proprietary applications, as well as mixed modes of commercial development, can be expected to flourish. Specialized proprietary mega-applications serving large industries will continue to dominate their markets. The various distributed network services, built partly on open infrastructures that have been enhanced with sophisticated proprietary functionalities, will also continue to thrive. Another mixed mode that seems certain to significantly increase in scope is bilateral platforms that intermix Windows environments and applications with open platforms and applications, providing some of the advantages of both. The development of software for in-house purposes has historically represented the preponderance of software development. This kind of commercial development, in-house, nondistributed, and customized, will increasingly be built using open source components. It may remain proprietary by intention (for competitive purposes) or by default, but its software development process will be increasingly dependent on the software commons provided by open source. Existing symbiotic arrangements between the open community and proprietary developers, like the open sponsorship strategy promoted by IBM, will continue to strengthen. However, such arrangements will have to be handled gingerly and with appropriate deference to the underlying open community's native culture, *lest the entire dynamics of the model be undermined.*

In summary, the likely dominant modalities for software development seem to be as follows:

Open Infrastructure Commoditization

Open source in standard (commoditized) applications for business, personal, educational and government use, though complementary mixed approaches like WAMP and Wine will also be attractive.

Proprietary Mega-applications

Specialized complex proprietary mega-applications for major industries or applications sectors like entertainment, medical research, insurance, and manufacturing.

Vertical Synthesis of Distributed Services

Proprietary networked services for specialized or ubiquitous purposes, built on or integrated with non-distributed open source components and platforms.

Vertical Synthesis of In-house Applications

Special-purpose, in-house, vertical software development whose results are not distributed and are proprietary by default or intent, even though they employ open components.

Horizontal Synthesis with Complementary Open Software

Horizontal development and deployment of specialized proprietary software products or hardware which are supported or enhanced by complementary open source products.

The underlying factors that encourage these configurations appear to be cost effectiveness and risk reduction, geopolitical forces, professional/pedagogical, technological, and structural factors, as we will describe in the following.

Open Source Commoditized Infrastructure

Software is not an apolitical product. It is not just economic but geopolitical factors that will be decisive in the inexorable diffusion of open source in the global market. Independent nations cannot in the long term accept the dominance of their computer software infrastructure by foreign entities. This is a simple matter of national and regional identity and autonomy that will persist despite the interconnectedness of the "global village." In fact, this is simply a translation into the geopolitical realm of the kind of autonomy open source provides at the user/vendor level. For example, at the corporate or organizational level, open source provides sophisticated users with flexibility because they are potentially experienced enough to understand and adapt the code it discloses, reducing their dependence on proprietary vendors of code to help them modify it (Hahn, 2002). The same motivation is at least as compelling at the geopolitical level, especially in the case of economically powerful nations like China whose political policies and security concerns are likely to be increasingly divergent or at least independent of those of the United States. Consider that China started Red Flag Linux precisely to "reduce domination of the Chinese computer market by Microsoft's Windows operating systems" (Searls, 2002), quoting a Bloomberg News Report. The United States has an analogous perspective on its own national interests. For example, during the 1990s, the United States tried to restrict the export of cryptographic tools, though this only succeeded in precipitating the development of network security tools by overseas developers (Hohn and Herr, 2004).

The software profile of other nations seems likely to imitate the trajectory taken by the open source movement itself in developing commoditized software infrastructures. The first domains where free software should predominate are those where it has already established itself, in network infrastructures, platforms, and routine tools. This transformation will take longer to transpire in the United States because, since many of the dominant proprietary players are domestic, issues of political autonomy are less exigent. However, the United States ultimately has the same underlying concerns. As an example, consider the case of the open source security tool *Snort*. The United States blocked a deal for an Israeli company to acquire Snort in 2006 because it thought the foreign company might take the future development of the Snort code proprietary. This was deemed an unacceptable risk to the United States, given the widespread use of Snort by Federal agencies (Arnone, 2006). Hybrid complementary approaches to purely open systems, like *WAMP* (where Windows is used instead of Linux in the LAMP stack), are also likely to become more widespread. They offer intermediate venues that promise some of the savings of open source, combined with the learning curve and migration advantages of retaining Windows. The open source *Wine* project is also strategically significant because it implements the Windows API (Application Programming Interface), allowing native Windows programs to execute on Linux and Unix-like systems like FreeBSD. Wine opens the door to third-party proprietary applications on the basic free platforms, thereby significantly increasing the attractiveness of these systems vis-à-vis Windows (Lussier, 2004).

The nature of computer science education and the professional computing culture are also highly important driving factors in the propagation of open source. In a sense, open source and its creations now constitute a sort of lingua franca of global education in software engineering. Thus, even aside from geopolitical factors, the increasing prevalence of open source as a key operative paradigm to which computer science students are exposed will increasingly foster open source ubiquity. The dynamics will be similar to the way in which the Unix-culture of the 1980s and 1990s defined an educational nursery and environment for computer specialists. The consequences of that previous educational technological matrix are clear: Unix-like operating systems became increasingly widespread, at least partly because they were the ones computer scientists were weaned on. The point is that a combination of training, familiarity, and predisposition toward open source, combined with the natural influence of computer scientists in defining the future of the field, inevitably argues for a pervasive role for open source in the future. The GNU/Linux system (and other free Unix-like systems) will inevitably proliferate even more so over time. The same progression should be natural for other fundamental free software systems, such as the open KDE/GNOME desktops.

Proprietary Mega-applications

While certain geopolitical, cultural, and technological factors are promoting free software, other structural factors will continue to promote proprietary products. Though open applications will become familiar and routine, they will not prevail everywhere. To the contrary, vast opportunities will remain where the major applications continue to be proprietary and new ones will continually emerge. As an example, we will consider the case of Adobe Photoshop. Several forces conspire to drive its kind of secure market dominance and are likely to persist in the future. They are the following:

1. the existence of a major industrial base for the application;
2. the mission-criticality of the application;
3. the complexity of the application; and
4. the consequent return on development investment.

In the case of Adobe, the first driving element is that multimedia and graphics applications are prominent in massive industries, like entertainment, gaming, and advertising, that have enormous profits and capitalization as well as great growth potential. The second factor combines with the first. It concerns whether the industry-specific application software is *critical* to competitiveness and success in the industry, as is the case with Adobe. The third factor addresses whether the software is not merely mission-critical but serves an application area that is intrinsically *complex*, requiring software of substantial sophistication and effectiveness. Once again, this is the case with graphics software like Photoshop. The fourth factor is a consequence of the others and leads to self-perpetuating, feedback effects. These conditions jointly ensure that best-of-breed products will necessarily dominate such markets. A hypothetical decision by any serious commercial player in the industry to choose a lesser product as an essential software engine would be penny-wise and pound-foolish to say the least. The cost-savings of using similar open source tools are negligible compared to the advantage of using the top-of-the-line product. Even marginal advantages may be important under these circumstances, and in fact the advantages of the best such proprietary products are more than marginal. The sale of this kind of proprietary, effective, essential software in highly profitable industries invariably generates lucrative returns for the software provider. Two feedback effects help to bolster the proprietary product's competitive advantage against competing products. One is based on profit effects, the other on sunk costs in user learning. Firstly, profits from the product's sale can be recycled by the software producer back into R&D to further improve the product, making it difficult for potential competitors to ever close the performance gap with the leading product. Making the refinements necessary to produce a polished software product is detailed and costly work. Secondly, the complexity of the application makes acquiring a commanding understanding of how to use the product a major sunk cost in human capital. This same factor can also help to produce a vendor-product lock-in effect, making it costly for users to switch to alternatives. The advantages of this cycle of improvement can easily become self-perpetuating. Furthermore, there may exist a vast range of possible improvements for such applications, so a company that provides the market leader software is unlikely to be surpassed in the short term, and certainly less so by providers of open software with its far lower direct profit margins and its consequently limited financial resources for improving the product. The opportunities to create such proprietary mega-applications seem likely to continue and even expand.

There is one caveat regarding the preceding analysis. Again, we will continue the discussion by using the example of Adobe Photoshop. There may be a symbiotic or feedback relationship between proprietary products like Photoshop and open source competitors like GIMP. Features introduced in the proprietary tool can be reverse engineered or emulated (by following "taillights") after a delay in the open tool, leading to a mirrored tracking of the proprietary product by the open one. On the other hand, innovative developments in the open tool can be even more directly adopted by the proprietary tool by reimplementing the open functionality in the proprietary software without incurring a copyright or General Public License (GPL) violation, again after a delay. This combination of effects can tend to cause the development of the open product to track the evolution of the proprietary one over time, but with a time delay, perhaps a year or so. The advantage is still in favor of the proprietary product, due both to the greater financial resources of its corporate provider and the greater ease of reimplementing functionality based on an existing open source implementation, though the issue of software patents may also come into play. The consequence is that the special-purpose proprietary system will tend to represent the cutting edge of the tool's application category, with a continual positive differential advantage over any open source competitor. Thus, while the open tool may be always catching up, the proprietary tool can be always advancing as well and so maintains an incremental advantage. Therefore, for the reasons we have argued previously, the proprietary product should maintain its market leadership among major users for whom the cost of critical software is a relatively secondary factor. The only escape from this pattern occurs if the products eventually evolve to an asymptotic state where the potential functionality of this type of product has been saturated; that is, when (and if) the open and proprietary products sufficiently converge in functionality so that the product itself becomes commoditized. If that occurs in the long term, then at that point the two products become functionally equivalent for the purposes of most users. At that point, the open product can dominate the market since there would be no reason for users to pay a premium charge for a negligible advantage.

Vertical Synthesis of Distributed Services

Another domain where nondisclosed, proprietary applications are likely to dominate is in organizations that provide networked services built on infrastructures partly rooted in open source software, but which have been extended in a proprietary manner in order to provide specialized services. This is a form of vertical, in-house development of a platform that provides distributed services. The textbook example of this type of development model is Google. Google thrives by providing networked applications for search services that are constructed partly on top of open systems that have been enhanced by proprietary programs, algorithms, and data sources. Organizations using this model may merely use existing Linux or other free platforms via the normal operating system interface. However, they may also creatively leverage and adapt open-licensed applications to expedite the development of their proprietary systems. Some systems may be built on BSD-licensed open products for which enclosure in proprietary software distributions would be compatible with the license. But even the more restrictive GPL-licensed systems can be used in the nondistributed model because their mode of use obviates or bypasses the redistribution restrictions of the GPL. The software developed is not redistributed even though the services produced by these platforms may be distributed anywhere, anytime, to anyone. There is obviously an endless list of services of this type that can be created, but none of the proprietary enhancements that underlie them need ever be disclosed. Indeed, such systems arguably represent an even more secretive paradigm for software development than traditional distributed software since not even the binaries for the executables are distributed! Thus ironically, though the open source movement has been instrumental in enabling such providers, their level of software transparency has moved even further along the axis of proprietary secrecy and nondisclosure than traditional proprietary systems.

Vertical Synthesis of In-house Applications

Two-thirds of software is developed for in-house or customized use. There is no reason to expect this to change in the future. Thus though firms like Microsoft may be perceived as prototypical of software companies, in point of fact, historically "packaged software has never accounted for more than a third of software investment" (Bessen, 2002). In-house development can be based on internal software implementations which are essentially proprietary. However, it may also be based on originally open software which is modified, extended, or in some way customized for internal use, but which may not be distributed externally. Companies can also develop integrated compositions of proprietary and open source components. The availability of the open source code represents a significant advantage in such development, since it can make it easier for firms to customize the components because they have access to the entire code base (and the open community) and not just to an interface, as would be the case, for example, in Commercial-Off-The-Shelf software. This development model is increasingly widespread. In-house customization and integration is completely compatible with any open source license, including the GPL.

Horizontal Synthesis with Complementary Open Software

Horizontal synthesis is a proven successful business model that uses open source software as a complementary *adjunct* to a business' proprietary products. However, the open source products are not themselves the profit-making elements in the situation, though they indirectly benefit the proprietary product line by reducing costs. This differs from vertical approaches where, for example, systems are built whose services are distributed or used for in-house processing, but the system itself is not distributed.

A variety of horizontal strategies are possible. For example, a company may develop proprietary products some of whose components are open source. Of course, the use of the open components must be compatible with the terms of their free licenses. Or, the horizontal strategy may exploit the availability of free software platforms. For example, a company may develop proprietary product lines that run on platforms like Linux. This has the additional business advantage of undermining the dominance of competing proprietary platforms.

A company may take advantage of complementary open software that helps the company or its clients develop, maintain, or adapt its proprietary offerings. This strategy requires that the company reciprocate by supporting open projects that develop software that is useful in combination with the company's proprietary products. Support can come in the form of financial support or the use of regular corporate employees as full-time contributors to the open projects of interest. The company may also establish permanent relations with the communities of users and developers around the open projects of interest. Another widespread strategy is using free software on hardware platforms. The complementary free software product provides free or low-cost added value to the hardware product. In contrast, the use of proprietary software could make the cost of a functional hardware product prohibitive. Instances of this practice include the use of free software in digital devices that have sufficiently complicated interfaces that one needs a platform like a pared down Linux kernel to handle tasks like process scheduling. An example of this is the use of Linux versions in digital appliances like cell phones or PDAs. Another tactic, although it is not open source, is to adopt a half-open approach for proprietary products, emphasizing open standards and publicly defined interfaces for these products. This encourages third-party development of applications that can interoperate with the proprietary products, adding value and making them more attractive.

A classic example of the power of the horizontal model is illustrated by the strategic practices of IBM as described in Chapter 7. The company uses open source products to facilitate its own development and supports open communities whose products add value to its proprietary software (Capek et al., 2005). This sustains the open projects but also simultaneously lets IBM influence at least part of their evolution, a symbiotic relation which can benefit the open source community and the company. Corporations like IBM have been instrumental in increasing the credibility of the Linux platform worldwide, expanding its functionality and improving its performance. The corporation benefits from the expertise it gains in open products, as well as in open development methodology – expertise which can in turn be applied to its own product development and consulting. It is essential to the viability of such relationships that corporate sponsors handle them adroitly, in full compliance with the norms of the open source community whose passionate commitment is what makes the model possible in the first place.

Concluding Note

The GPL created by Richard Stallman of the Free Software Foundations has been decisive in "creating a large public commons of software that is freely available worldwide" (Rosen, 2005). This commons provides an inexorably expanding frame of reference for future software development. This principled, historic achievement has a counterpart in the accomplishments of the pragmatic Open Source Initiative and a long, ongoing history of industrial cooperation as reflected in the BSD and MIT licenses. Open Source Initiative cofounder Eric Raymond contends that a combination of economic forces and the scale of software development projects is compelling even large firms to spread development costs across a wider base that extensively utilizes open source development. This involves significant industrial cooperation and support for open projects like Linux and the Apache Software Foundation and "informal cooperative efforts regulated by open source licensing" (Raymond, 2004, p. 90). On the other hand, critical voices like IT expert David Messerschmitt believe that the open development model is seriously limited "in deeply understanding user needs" and is "incomplete as a software creation process" in contrast to commercial software (Messerschmitt, 2004, p. 89). Messerschmitt also underscores the necessity for realistic profit margins for software vendors, so they can fund research and risky, new product development, contending that were the industry dominated by open source, "products would be replaced by marginally profitable services, and research and risk-taking would be gravely damaged" (Messerschmitt, 2004, p. 91).

All these principles reflect highly informed, experientially based perspectives. Therefore, it seems prudent to assume that each of their perspectives contains a significant element of truth. As a consequence, it seems realistic to assume that the future software environment will be a syncretistic one. The industrial collaborative use of open source in certain areas of application, already historically established, will continue to grow, expanding for simple economic reasons and the quality of the results. Disparate economic, geopolitical, and technological forces will continue to strengthen the roles of free and open source development worldwide. A variety of free models, ranging from the essential GPL-based permanent software commons model to the more permissive licensing models, will continue to engage strong industrial, university, governmental, and global sponsorship, reflecting a spectrum of modes and relationship models, from purely open to hybrid. These will be counterbalanced by a variety of highly robust, proprietary modes of development.

References

Arnone, M. (2006). A New Direction for Open Source: Software Vendors Consider Switch to Fee-Based Model. http://www.fcw.com/article95251–07-17–06-Print. Accessed November 30, 2006.

Beesen, J. (2002). What Good Is Free Software? In: Government Policy toward Open Source Software, R. W. Hahn (editor). Brookings Institution Press, Washington, DC.

Capek, C., Frank, S., Gerdt, S., and Shields, D. (2005). A History of IBM's Open-Source Involvement and Strategy. IBM Systems Journal, 44(2), 249–257.

Evans, D. (2002). Politics and Programming: Government Preferences for Promoting Open Source Software. In: Government Policy toward Open Source Software, R. W. Hahn (editor). Brookings Institution Press, Washington, DC.

Hahn, R. (2002). Government Policy toward Open Source Software: An Overview. In: Government Policy toward Open Source Software, R. W. Hahn (editor). Brookings Institution Press, Washington, DC.

Hohn, S. and Herr, G. (2004). Open Source: Open for Business. A Report from Computer Science Corporation: Leading Edge Forum, September. http://www.csc.com/features/2004/uploads/LEF_OPENSOURCE.pdf. Accessed November 30, 2006.

Lussier, S. (2004). New Tricks: How Open Source Changed the Way My Team Works. IEEE Software, 21(1), 68–72.

Messerschmitt, D. (2004). Back to the User. IEEE Software, 21(1), 89–91.

Moglen, E. (2003). Freeing the Mind: Free Software and the Death of Proprietary Culture. June 29, 15 pp. http://moglen.law.columbia.edu/publications/maine-speech.html. Accessed December 20, 2006.

Raymond, E. (2004). Up from Alchemy. IEEE Software, 21(1), 88–90.

Rosen, L. (2005). Open Source Licensing: Software Freedom and Intellectual Property Law. Prentice Hall, Upper Saddle River, NJ.

Searls, D. (2002). Raising the Red Flag. 2002–01–30. http://www.linuxjournal.com/article/5784. Accessed November 30, 2006.

Glossary

Disclaimer: The legal terms defined in this glossary do not constitute legal advice and are for reference only. Any legal questions should be referred to an IP attorney.

Note: Most of the glossary terms are further discussed in the body of the text and referenced there as well.

Adware. This is free of charge software that displays advertisements. For example, the Opera browser is adware that lets the user eliminate the ads for a fee.

Apache license. This is a BSD-type license that allows modified versions of the source code to be redistributed in closed products. The license also protects the Apache trademark name from being applied to derivative works. The license is considered incompatible with the GPL because of a patent termination condition.

BIND. The open source Internet service that provides the APIs (Application Programming Interfaces) for translating symbolic domain names into numeric IP addresses. The acronym stands for Berkeley Internet Name Domain.

Black box reverse engineering. This refers to reverse engineering a software product on the basis of an inventory analysis of the system's scope and functionality. See also reverse engineering and white box reverse engineering. This may be legal if done for purposes of interoperability, but not to avoid a protection mechanism.

Branches in CV. Branches are alternate project evolutions that emerge form and diverge from earlier project releases, for example, because a bug is detected against that earlier release. Since the bug appeared in the context of the earlier release, a patch that fixes the bug should be applied against that release rather than a more current version of the project. A branch is split off from the trunk or main line of development at the old release, a working copy of that version is checked out and fixed, and the patch is committed to that branched version, not to the current development version which is unaltered. The current version can be similarly debugged and patched. If the same patch works for the earlier release that was branched and the current development version, the branch can be merged back to the trunk, with the history or record of all these changes still preserved in the repository (Fogel and Bar, 2003).

Brook's law. "Adding manpower to a late software project makes it later." Formulated by Fred Brooks in "The Mythical Man-Month." Contrast Eric Raymond in "The Cathedral and the Bazaar" (Raymond, 1998).

BSD (Berkeley Software Distribution) license. This is a very unrestrictive type of open source software license. BSD-licensed code or modifications can be incorporated in proprietary software whose source code is kept secret, which is completely unlike the General Public License (GPL). The license contains express warrantee and liability disclaimers, permits redistribution in either source or binary form, requires that the original copyright notice be included to allow proper attribution of modified works, and forbids using the names of the open source contributors for endorsement without their approval. The BSD license was first used for BSD UNIX in 1980 and is widely used in Linux distributions. The original version of the license included a so-called advertising requirement (that was later removed in the new or modified BSD license) which made the license GPL-compatible. See www.opensource.org for a copy of the license.

Build time. The object modules produced by, for example, a C compiler may contain unresolved references to other modules that were not available when the module was compiled. A linker program combines a set of such object modules into a single executable file called a build. The separation of responsibilities between the compiler and the linker is useful during development since the time to compile a set of object modules is typically much longer than the time to link them. Thus if changes are made to a single object module, then a new *build* can be created by just recompiling that single module and then quickly relinking the entire set of object modules. The build time for the rebuild is just the time for the single compilation plus the time for the entire linking operation. The operating system Loader runs the executable file, though there may still be dynamic linking to shared library modules like .dll files in Windows at run-time.

Closed software. Software distributed under a license that prevents it from being copied, modified, or redistributed. It may also be called proprietary software. To protect disclosure of the source code, the program is distributed only as binary.

Common Public License. This is an OSI-certified license but is considered incompatible with the GPL. IBM introduced this license for products such as Eclipse.

Compilation. This is a work formed by collecting together previously copyrighted works whose copyrights are still preserved in the compilation. In the case of software, this would include copyright permissions from the copyright owners of any components (Hollaar, 2002).

Concurrent Versions System (CVS). This is the most widely used version control system. It is a General Public Licensed client-server system under which software projects are stored in a so-called *repository* on a server, while client-side tools let multiple developers remotely and concurrently check out latest versions of a project from the repository, modify the source code on a client, and commit changes to the working copy back to the repository. This is the so-called copy-modify-merge development cycle. Conflicts caused by developers concurrently changing overlapping parts of the project are automatically detected at commit and must be resolved manually before the changes can be committed to the repository.

Contract. A legal agreement between two parties that identifies what each party promises to do as part of an exchange, such as an agreement for party A to pay for goods or services provided by party B. A contract can be enforced under the provisions of contract law.

Copyleft. Copyright limits the right of others to copy and redistribute a work. Copyleft has a somewhat contrary intent (whence the reversed name) in that it tries to guarantee that anyone who receives a copy of an original work (such as the source code for a program) also receives the right to copy, modify, and redistribute the original work and derived modifications of the work. This copyleft intent is asserted in a license that accompanies and is distributed along with the original work. This license requires that all redistributed copies of the original work and works derived from it must also include this same license, which is tantamount to a recursive propagation of the original copyleft license. Copyleft guarantees that every user in the redistribution supply chain preserves freedom with respect to the product. According to the GNU Web site: "Copyleft says that anyone who redistributes the software, with or without changes, *must pass along the freedom to further copy and change it*" (www.gnu.org). The owner of the original product, however, still preserves copyright ownership of the original work.

Copyright. Copyright gives the creator of a work the exclusive right to make a copy of the work, distribute copies of the work, disclose or display the work publicly, as well as to create so-called derivative works which are derived from the original product. The protection provided by copyright starts automatically as soon as the work is fixed in tangible form. Copyrights can be applied to software products like programs and image files. Copyright only protects the tangible implementation of an idea, not the idea itself. Thus it is not a violation of copyright to produce a similar product that is inspired by the overall look and contents of an original copyrighted product, subject to the criterion of substantial similarity.

Copyright infringement. The violation of a copyright condition is called a copyright infringement. One form of copyright infringement is redistributing multiple copies of a copyrighted software product, whether for free or for sale, which is called software piracy. Even making additional copies for personal use, unless as authorized by a software license agreement, is an infringement, since the copyright owner is the one who has the right to make copies. In the case of derivative works, a key legal test for the existence of a copyright infringement is based on so-called *substantial similarity* between an allegedly infringing work and the copyrighted work. Copyright infringement, whether intentional or not, is subject to civil and criminal liability.

Decompiling. This is an attempt to reverse the effects of compiling source code into object code by converting object code back to some high-level language that can be understood by a person. Decompilers, such as the Reflector tool for .NET, are generalizations of disassemblers that convert machine code back into assembly language. It is not always possible to decompile object code or create a humanly meaningful high-level version because of the intermixture of code and data in a program and the loss of symbol tables (containing the originally meaningful names) that are typically not still available in the executable code. Software tools called obfuscators make it harder to decompile object code and are used to protect intellectual property.

Derivative works. The U.S. Copyright Act defines a derivative work as one based on a previously copyrighted work, but does not address the case of software (Webbink, 2003). An ordinary copyright preserves to its owner the copyright for any derivative works based on the copyrighted work, but for software the definition of what constitutes a derivative work is sometimes tendentious. Simple translation of a copyrighted work into another (programming) language is prohibited by the Berne Convention without the permission of the original copyright owner. Generally, a software product is considered as derivative if it contains original, modified, or translated source code from an original program, but not so if it merely links to a preexisting copyrighted program library or plugs into a copyrighted program designed to accept plug-ins, absent indications of intent such as "whether the resulting program is being sold as an enhanced version of the original" (Rosen, 2003), though the legal issues do not appear to be settled. A key test is whether the work is substantially similar to the original.

diff. The Unix diff command shows the differences between a pair of files on a line-by-line basis. It indicates (depending on the format) whether different lines have been added (a), deleted (d), or changed (c), with shared lines not output. Conceptually, *diff* takes a pair of files A and B and creates a file C representing their "difference." The output file is also called a patch file because of its use in collaborative development where the difference represents a "software patch" to a current version of a program. The so-called *unified difference format* for the diff command is especially useful in open source development because it lets project maintainers more readily understand code changes. For example, the unified format includes surrounding lines that have not been changed as context, so it is easier to recognize what has been changed and where. The *diff* command works together with the *patch* command to enact the changes. The commands are key in open source development, either used explicitly or wrapped in a tool like CVS.

Dynamic linking. From a software development point of view, dynamic linking is the resolution by a linker of all the unresolved references an application's compiled (object) code makes to external library modules, but without combining the application and library objects into a single executable file; the executables remain separate.

End User License Agreement (EULA). The most common kind of software license, typically proposed to a user for acceptance during software installation as a precondition for use of the software. The licenses usually have extensive disclaimers about liability as well as restrictions on use and sharing of the software.

Fair use. This refers to the copying and use of limited parts of a copyrighted work for limited periods of time, with attribution, for such purposes as education and research, but without requiring the permission of the copyright holder. Such use does not constitute copyright infringement and is explicitly allowed by the U.S. Copyright Act. However, there are strict guidelines on how much of a work may be copied. Damage to any commercial value of the product is a key consideration. In the case of software, fair use in the traditional sense is immediately problematic, since the program's useful functionality requires copying the entire code, which is contrary to fair use restrictions, even in the case of educational use.

Fork. In an open source context, a fork occurs when a development team splits at some stage in the project development, with each team then independently pursuing a separate evolution of the product. If there was an original single leader of the open source project, the project of the group with that person preserves the project name and may get the lion's share of the associated reputation. A fork of the development team is different from a branch in a CVS-style development tree, since it involves a split in the development team, not merely an alternate line of development of a project.

Free Software Foundation. The foundation founded by Richards Stallman in the mid-1980s to financially support the GNU project's software development and serve as an advocacy organization for the free software movement.

Freeware. This is software provided *free of charge* by its developer or author but on which the developer retains the copyright. Distribution or redistribution remains under the control of the developer. The software license may permit limited copying and redistribution, but these copies cannot typically be sold by the user and commercial use may also be restricted. The software is usually provided without source code. Freeware is completely different from *free software* in the sense of the free software movement.

FUD. Dis-information marketing strategies directed against the products of other software or hardware companies are sometimes called FUD (Fear, Uncertainty, Doubt). Although first used in reference to IBM, it tends to be applied in an open source context to tactics attributed to Microsoft.

GNOME. An open source GUI environment for Linux and Unix-like operating systems, which emphasizes usability and is widely supported, for example, under the Red Hat Linux distribution. In addition to the desktop, the GNOME project includes the "GNOME development platform, an extensive framework for building applications that integrate into the desktop" (www.gnome.org). GNOME is written in C, unlike the C++-based KDE environment, but allows language bindings to other languages like C++ and Java. The GNOME libraries are licensed under the Lesser GPL while the GNOME project itself is licensed under the GPL.

GNOME Human Interface Guidelines. The GNOME project document that describes the design principles for the GNOME interface and provides highly specific advice for designers and developers on how to apply interface elements effectively. The guidelines are intended to help open source developers and interface designers create applications that "look right, behave properly, and fit into the GNOME user interface as a whole" (http://developer.gnome.org/projects/gup/hig/).

GNU. GNU (an acronym for "GNU is not UNIX") is a collection of free system programs and software development tools, including text editors and compilers (especially the widely used GNU GCC compiler for C), developed by the Free Software Foundation which are highly portable across operating system platforms. A fundamental goal of the GNU Project was to provide a nonproprietary, Unix-compatible operating system consisting of freely available source code which could be copied, modified, and redistributed under the terms of its GPL. The Linux kernel was integrated with the GNU system to form the GNU/Linux system.

GNU General Public License (GPL). This is the software license developed as part of Stallman's free software movement, which is intended to allow the downstream users of programs distributed under this license to preserve most of the freedoms and privileges of the original developer and copyright holder. These privileges include the *freedom* to run the programs without restriction on use, to see and learn from the source code of the program and modify it if desired, to redistribute the program or modifications of the program, though such redistribution must provide the modifications under the same conditions as the original GPL. The license explicitly precludes the inclusion of GPL-licensed software in *publicly* distributed proprietary programs, though this does not affect programs used only internally in an organization. The software does not have to be offered for free. The developer of the original program retains the copyright ownership of the program. GPL is the most popular form of license used for open source software (almost 70% of open source projects (Rosen, 2005)), with the Linux kernel being perhaps the most prominent example.

GPL. See GNU General Public License.

The Halloween documents. Internal Microsoft memos that expressed concerns about the competitive consequences of open source software and the implications of the GPL. The documents indicated that open source was too credible to be handled by simple FUD tactics. These memos are widely referred to in the open source literature.

Hunk. This refers to a situation when a pair of files A and B are diff'ed (see entry for diff above). The unified format patch shows all the contrasting new and old code segments and the changes they have undergone as well as their context. These contrasting segments of code are called hunks. Related hunks are displayed adjacent to each other for easy visual comparison. Using the diff and patch commands, and comparing hunks, is intrinsic to distributed software development.

Intermediate language (IL). The type of code that managed code compilers like Microsoft's .NET compilers for C# and VB.NET translate source code into, as opposed to, native assembly language code. IL code is intended to be cross-platform and cross-language, but it lends itself to reverse engineering, so Microsoft includes obfuscation tools to make harder to decompile.

KDE. The first open software GUI environment for Linux, similar in appearance to the desktop environments in Windows. Most major Linux distributions include the KDE desktop as well as GNOME. KDE runs on Unix-like systems. It is written in C++. See also GNOME.

Lesser GPL. This open source license is intended for open source software libraries and allows such libraries to be used or linked to by closed source, proprietary programs. In contrast to the Lesser GPL, if the library were instead licensed under the ordinary GPL, then any program that referenced the library would itself have to be licensed under the GPL and could not be proprietary.

License. A contract between the owner of a product and a prospective user that grants the user certain rights regarding the use of the product that would otherwise be illegal. The most common kinds of software licenses are proprietary licenses for commercial software and the various free or open licenses.

Linux. The widely used Unix-like open source operating system developed under the leadership of Linus Torvalds and licensed under the GPL.

Linux distributions. Software distributions that supplement the Linux kernel and core operating system components with a variety of components including installation software, configuration tools, software libraries, desktop environments like GNOME and KDE, applications, firewalls, etc. Red Hat is probably the most prominent Linux distribution. Distributions are usually organized into packages containing the different components which are managed using Package Management Systems that facilitate installation and update of packages.

Liteware. A shareware or other program that omits some of the functionality of the complete version, such as shareware that is not fully functional or is functional only for a limited time unless the software is purchased or registered.

Merging. In the context of version control systems, such as CVS, as used in distributed software development, merging refers to the process of integrating developer changes with the project master copy or repository. Disjoint changes that affect different files can be merged automatically, but overlapping changes cause conflicts which have to be resolved manually.

Microsoft shared source. This refers to an initiative that uses a range of software licenses for different products that lets selected customers and developers access some of Microsoft's source code, such as the Windows template Library, for their own use. Possible restrictions include nondisclosure agreements or restrictions on modifying code.

Mozilla Public License (MPL). This is the license that the Mozilla Web browser, the open source version of Netscape, was distributed under. As with the GPL, publicly distributed derived works that modify its existing MPL licensed files are required to remain under the conditions of the license. However, the license also allows proprietary files (provided they contain no original code or modifications of the original code) to be combined with the open source code, while remaining outside the terms of the MPL license. This is an OSI-certified license.

Nagware. Nagware is shareware that regularly reminds the user that the program is not free of charge and should be paid for.

Nondisclosure agreement. A *nondisclosure agreement* is a legal agreement according to which party A acknowledges receiving information from party B and is bound to protect its confidentiality.

Nonprotective open source licenses. This refers to open source licenses, such as the BSD and Apache licenses, that impose no restrictions on the distribution of derivative works, including the inclusion of such redistributions in proprietary code (Webbink, 2003).

Obfuscation. This refers to scrambling code and changing symbolic names so that the altered code's behavior remains equivalent but the code is confusing to human readers and harder to reverse engineer.

Open Source Initiative (OSI). The OSI established in 1998 is a nonprofit foundation whose objective is to promote the use of open source software. The foundation maintains a list of approved software licenses that it recognizes as consistent with the basic principles of open source development. Software distributed under any of these licenses can be labeled as "OSI-certified Open Source Software."

Open Standards Organizations. The World Wide Web Consortium (W3C) organization that develops standards for Internet technologies like HTML and the HTTP protocol, and the IETF (Internet Engineering Task Force) are examples of organizations that develop specifications and standards in an open manner.

OSI-certified Open Source License. A software license approved by the Open Source Initiative.

Paradigm shift. A phrase coined by Kuhn in 1962 to characterize how unprecedented breakthroughs affect scientific progress, fundamentally altering the theory of the subject and the interpretation of its facts (Kuhn, 1996), while also taking considerable time for their implications to be understood. In the field of computing, paradigm shifts arguably include commoditization of the standardized IBM PC architecture and the widespread use of open source development.

Patch. A Unix command that uses the textual differences between an original file A and a revised file B, as summarized in a *diff* file C, to update A to reflect the changes introduced in B. The complementary diff and patch commands allow source code changes (in the form of a relatively small patch file like C instead of the entire new version B) to be submitted by e-mail, after which the patch can be scrutinized by a project maintainer before being integrated into the development repository.

Patch files. Modifications to open source projects are typically submitted to the project developer's e-mail list, where interested developers evaluate the submitted code submitted by the contributor. The core developers decide whether a suggested patch is to be rejected or committed to the source repository, to which only developers have write access. The open source Apache Web server's name derives from its origin as "*a patchy*" server.

Patent. The U.S. Patent and Trademark Office defines a patent as "the grant of a property right to the inventor" by the government, for a novel, useful, and nonobvious invention, and which applies for 20 years "from the date on which the application for the patent is filed." A patent requires disclosure of the idea underlying the invention. It grants the owner the "right to exclude others from making, using, offering for sale, or selling" the patented invention. A patent covers the idea underlying an invention or the ideas embedded in software in the case of a software patent and not just a specific expression or implementation of the concept.

Product liability. If the use of a defective product causes harm, the developer or seller of the product may be legally liable for financial damages. Licenses for software products typically attempt to limit liability for damages to the purchase price, as a condition of use.

Proprietary software. This refers to private software, licensed by the owner typically under terms that restrict its use and redistribution, and usually distributed in binary form to protect the secrecy of the source code.

Protective open source licenses. This refers to open source licenses, such as the GPL and the Lesser GPL, that impose restrictions on the distribution of derivative works to ensure that the code and derivative works will remain open.

Public Domain Software. Software or other creative works which are not under copyright protection are said to be in the public domain. Anyone can copy, modify, redistribute, or sell such a work as if it were their own. Previously copyrighted works become public domain when the copyright expires. Works created by the government are automatically in the public domain.

Red Flag Linux. The Chinese language Linux distribution whose name puns the "Red Hat" distributor of Linux and the red flag of China. The distribution company was founded in 2000.

Red Hat Linux. Red Hat is one of the earliest purveyors of Linux distributions. Its current version is called Red Hat Enterprise Linux.

Release-early, release-often. Eric Raymond's catch phrase to describe the kind of release policy that Linus Torvalds followed in the development of Linux.

Repository. In the context of version control systems such as CVS as used in distributed software development, the repository is a shared database that embeds the revision history of a project and allows any earlier version of the project to be reconstructed.

Reverse engineering. This is basically the process of trying to figure out how something works. It refers to the analysis of a system for the purpose of identifying its internal components and their interrelations. This may be done to create a representation of the system in an alternative form or at a higher level of abstraction. Alternatively, it refers to the extraction of design information from a given system's behavior as identified by an inventory analysis of a system's scope and functionality. The latter is also called black box reverse engineering, as opposed to white box reengineering which involves a process like decompiling that exposes the implementation.

Revisions. In a distributed collaboration system like CVS, a revision is a modification to the project that has been committed to the repository. It differs from the version number of the project which is used for public identification of releases. Revisions can be accessed by revision number or date. When a working copy of the project is checked out, the latest revisions of all its files are provided.

Shareware. This is sometimes *try-before-you-buy* software or *trialware*. It is usually delivered digitally free of charge to the user, but the user is expected (on the basis of an honor system) to pay some small amount for the product after a trial usage period, if the user retains the product. After payment, the user's copy is typically registered with the shareware's distributor. Upon purchase, a more complete version of the product may be supplied, as well as access to future product updates and possibly some level of technical assistance or support. The shareware product is copyrighted, so the users cannot redistribute it as their own.

Software commoditization. This occurs when software products in a particular application area become so standardized or routine or similar that the differences between products are perceived as marginal. The products then exhibit the behavior of typical commodities.

Software piracy. A form of copyright infringement where multiple copies of a copyrighted software product are redistributed for sale, rented, or given away.

Static linking. From a software development point of view, static linking is the resolution by a linker of all the unresolved references an application's compiled (object) code makes to external library modules, until the separate modules are all knitted together into a single executable file. From a copyright point of view, the resulting unified object code seems likely to constitute a derivative work of a General Public Licensed open source library because the application code and library parts are now inseparable (Asay, 2003).

Statutory damages. A law may allow a plaintiff a monetary damage even in the absence of a demonstration of actual loss. Such damages can even apply for what might appear to be minor copyright infringements.

Tarball. Tar files collect a set of files into a single archive file in such a way that the separate file information is preserved. They are commonly used for software distribution. Tar files compressed with zip programs are called tarballs. Tarballs are often used to distribute new releases of projects such as those released by CVS-based open development projects.

Trade secret. This refers to information that provides a commercial advantage to its owner and which is kept secret by using mechanisms such as confidentiality and nondisclosure agreements that employees are required to sign in order to be able to work for the owner of the product. Violation of such agreements entails significant monetary damages. The owner is expected to exert considerable caution in protecting the secret. Unlike patents, trade secrets have the advantage of not requiring disclosure of the hidden information, but conversely they are also not protected by reverse engineering, though this may possibly be prohibited by a software license (but see Samuelson (2002)).

Trademarks. Trademarks are names or symbols that are used to brand the name of a product for such purposes as protecting the reputation of the product or differentiating the product from competitors. They are especially useful in environments like open source (where it is easy to enter derivative products into the market) because established names can use trademark to promote customer loyalty and attention. For the same reason, trademarks also tend to limit forking in open code. Trademarks can be registered with the U.S. Patent and Trademark Office, but only marketing for public awareness and use of the trademark on products can make a trademark valuable. Red Hat Linux is an example of a valuable trademark that indicates a premium organization is behind the software and so connotes a superior product (Rosen, 2001).

Trialware. See shareware.

Usenet. The collective name for Internet newsgroups. This distributed set of bulletin boards was instrumental in popularizing public adoption of the Internet. It was used for e-mail and software (as well as many other forms of) collaboration and was a key technological enabler of open source collaboration.

Wiki. A Web site consisting of the ongoing work of many authors where anyone can modify content that has been placed on the site.

White box reverse engineering. This refers to reverse engineering a software product by attempting to decompile its object code. This may be legal if done for the purposes of interoperability, but not to avoid a protection mechanism (Jones, 2005).

References

Asay, M. (2003). Open Source's General Public License: Why Microsoft Is So Scared. Wasatch Digital IQ, 3(1), www.wasatchdigitaliq.com. Accessed January 20, 2007.

Fogel, K. and Bar, M. (2003). Open Source Development with CVS, 3rd edition. Paraglyph Press. http://cvsbook.red-bean.com/. Accessed January 20, 2007.

Hollaar, L. (2002). Legal Protection of Digital Information. BNA Books. http://digital-law-online.info/. Accessed January 20, 2007.

Jones, P. (2005). Software, Reverse Engineering, and the Law. http://lwn.net/Articles/134642/. Accessed December 1, 2006.

Kuhn, T. (1996). The Structure of Scientific Revolutions, 3rd edition. University of Chicago Press, Chicago, IL.

Raymond, E. S. (1998). The Cathedral and the Bazaar. First Monday, 3(3). http://www.firstmonday.dk/issues/issue3_3/raymond/index.html. Accessed December 3, 2006.

Rosen, L. (2001). Naming Your Open Source Software. http://www.rosenlaw.com/html/GL6.pdf. Accessed January 20, 2007.

Rosen, L. (2003). Derivative Works. January 1. http://www.linuxjournal.com/article/6366?from=50&comments_per_page=50. Accessed January 20, 2007.

Rosen, L. (2005). Open Source Licensing: Software Freedom and Intellectual Property Law. Prentice Hall, Upper Saddle River, NJ.

Samuelson, P. (2002). Reverse Engineering Under Siege. Communications of the ACM, 45(10), 15–20.

Webbink, M. (2003). Understanding Open Source Software. Computers and Law Journal, March http://www.nswscl.org.au/journal/51/. Accessed January 20, 2007.

Subject Index

351

Author Index

Lerner, J., 248, 272, 286, 289
Lessig, L., 30
Levy, S., 171
Lohr, S., 41
Lussier, S., 315, 328

Machlis, S., 74
Macmillan, J., 187, 188, 189
Magid, L., 236
Margolis, E., 269
Markoff, J., 38
Marron, D., 314
McCool, R., 21, 25, 26, 27, 28, 29, 30, 141,
    170, 200
McGrath, J.E., 192, 197, 202, 209, 210, 214
McHugh, J., 43
McKusick, M., 15, 84, 86, 245
McLuhan, M., 159
McMillan, A., 7
McMillan, R., 148, 149, 150, 248
Meeker, H., 256, 257
Messerschmitt, D., 219, 334
Mintzberg, H., 218
Mockus, A., 28, 29, 30, 31, 32, 33, 34, 35,
    104
Moczar, L., 62, 272
Moglen, E., 7, 164, 234, 255, 257, 260, 286,
    297, 302, 303, 304, 305, 306, 307,
    326
Monk, A., 215
Moody, G., 29, 184
Mook, N., 44
Moon, J.Y., 92, 94, 95, 96, 97, 98, 163, 168
Morgan, B.B., 197
Myers, J., 99

Nichols, D., 110
Norris, J., 312
Nosek, J., 188
Nunamaker, J.F., 199, 200, 203, 204, 205,
    207

O'Conaill, B., 213, 215, 216
O'Reilly, T., 39, 48, 77, 79, 151, 270, 283, 284
Olson, G., 184, 185, 197, 207, 208, 209, 210,
    211, 212
Olson, J., 184, 185, 197, 207, 208, 209, 210,
    211, 212
Olson, M., 69, 289
Osterlie, T., 27
Ou, S., 165

Park, J., 285
Parker, I., 7
Parris, D.C., 307
Payne, C., 59, 60, 240, 311
Perens, B., 15, 231, 244, 245, 297
Peters, D., 257, 258
Pirolli, P., 187
Poole, M.S., 192

Raggett, D., 39, 41
Raymond, E., 4, 5, 15, 22, 42, 50, 51, 52, 53,
    54, 55, 56, 57, 58, 63, 71, 82, 86, 164, 171,
    174, 182, 187, 244, 260, 289, 297,
    334, 337
Raynor, M., 284
Reagle, J., 163, 164, 173
Reid, R.H., 40
Reimer, J., 99, 101
Richardson, M., 75
Ritchie, D., 82, 83, 86
Robillard, M.P., 187
Robillard, P.N., 187
Robles, G., 162
Rooney, G., 145, 201
Rosen, L., 224, 226, 228, 233, 234, 235, 236,
    237, 243, 244, 247, 249, 251, 252, 253, 254,
    259, 260, 334, 340, 342, 348
Rosenberg, D.K., 244
Ross, B., 44, 45, 46, 108, 170
Russell, A., 29, 30

Sacks, H., 215
Salamon, A., 78
Samuels, E., 227
Samuelson, P., 239, 348
Scacchi, W., 58
Schach, S., 93
Schaeffer, E., 215
Schecter, S., 225
Schegloff, E.A., 215
Schneider, G., 104
Schneider, J., 71, 72, 276
Schumpeter, J.A., 285
Schwartz, M., 240
Scott, G., 82, 85
Scoville, T., 312
Searls, D., 328
Serrano, N., 275
Shah, R., 24
Shankland, S., 277
Shapiro, C., 231